Birth of the Bill of Rights

Birth of the Bill of Rights

Encyclopedia of the Antifederalists

VOLUME ONE: BIOGRAPHIES

Jon L. Wakelyn

GREENWOOD PRESS

Westport, Connecticut • London

Library of Congress Cataloging-in-Publication Data

Wakelyn, Jon L.
    Birth of the Bill of Rights : encyclopedia of the Antifederalists / Jon L. Wakelyn.
      p. cm.
    Includes bibliographical references and index.
    ISBN 0–313–31739–9 (set : alk. paper) — ISBN 0–313–33194–4 (v. 1 : alk. paper) —
    ISBN 0–313–33195–2 (v. 2 : alk. paper)
    1. Statesmen—United States—Biography. 2. Politicians—United States—Biography.
  3. Revolutionaries—United States—Biography. 4. United States—Politics and government—To
1775—Sources. 5. United States—Politics and government—1775–1783—Sources. 6. United
States—Politics and government—1783–1809—Sources. 7. Constitutional history—United
States—Sources. 8. Political science—United States—History—18th century—Sources.
  9. Political science—United States—History—19th century—Sources. 10. Federal
government—United States—History—Sources. I. Title.
    E302.5.W35   2004
    973.4'092'2—dc22   2004047546
    [B]

British Library Cataloguing in Publication Data is available

Library of Congress Catalog Card Number: 2004047546
ISBN: 0–313–31739–9 (set)
     0–313–33194–4 (vol. 1)
     0–313–33195–2 (vol. 2)

First published in 2004

Greenwood Press, 88 Post Road West, Westport, CT 06881
An imprint of Greenwood Publishing Group, Inc.
www.greenwood.com

Printed in the United States of America

∞™

The paper used in this book complies with the
Permanent Paper Standard issued by the National
Information Standards Organization (Z39.48–1984).

10 9 8 7 6 5 4 3 2 1

Contents

List of Entries

Preface and Acknowledgments

Few events have been more important to this country's history than the debates over the ratification of the Federal Constitution in 1787–1788. The Constitution, even more than the Declaration of Independence, remains the defining political statement of this country. The Federalists who supported ratification, and their seminal book *The Federalist Papers*, have received much attention. Those who opposed ratification in each state, though they wrote and spoke eloquently against the Constitution, have received less attention than the Federalists, perhaps because they lost their struggle. Antifederalists did not agree among themselves, either on issues, merits, or how to either rewrite or amend the Constitution. Nevertheless, they offered dissent in the form of a dialogue on the nature of governance that has influenced this country's political system down to the present. This biographical dictionary of those who opposed ratification, the Antifederalists, seeks to recreate their importance to this country through a review of their careers, their political values, and their arguments against the Constitution.

One hundred and forty Antifederalists have been selected for inclusion in this volume. The number is to some extent arbitrary, because there were no doubt many more in their own time who were important to the cause. This selection process is based on my judgement of who contributed the most to the cause, both writers and actors. I have been drawn to those leaders deemed most important in the best histories of the ratification controversy. (Those authors are discussed in the essay on sources.) A few Antifederalists were not seen as major leaders during the controversy but were later selected for higher office, thus making them important. In addition, major works of printed Antifederalist speeches and pamphlets have been used to discern the most important writers, orators, and debaters among the Antifederalists; these works include Bernard Bailyn's *Debate on the Constitution*; Jonathan Elliot's *The Debates in the Several State Conventions on the Adoption of the Federal Constitution*; Herbert J. Storing's *The Complete Antifederalist*; and Merrill Jensen and John Kaminski's *Documentary History of the Ratification of the Federal Constitution* (The value of these works to this study is also discussed in the essay on sources.) From those many volumes of analysis and documents, the one hundred and forty leaders have been selected to profile.

In order to be comprehensive, representative leaders from all thirteen states and the territories of Maine, Tennessee, and Kentucky have been included. Though Delaware, New Jersey, and Georgia unanimously voted for ratification, there was some dissent in each of those states, so at least one from each of them has been included. As one might expect, since North Carolina had two conventions and held out until 1790 before it joined the Union, a large number of leaders, though little known today, have been included from that state. New York, Massachusetts, and Virginia were Antifederalist bulwark states and thus necessitate a large number from each of them. Although Maryland, South Carolina, and Pennsylvania produced only a few Antifederalists, all three had a number of leaders who were important to their friends in other states and were of value for their activities in opposition to the Constitution.

Criteria for selection is based on actions and individuals involved in the states' ratification process, which include major publications, important speeches and debates at the conventions, those who made publications possible, and non-convention leaders who worked in behalf of the opposition. All of the Antifederalists whose writings are of such great importance to history, whether members of the conventions or not—such as Mercy Otis Warren— have been included. Although the majority of Antifederalist leaders selected for this volume served in their state ratification conventions, nondelegates like Elbridge Gerry were included because of their activities against ratifcation outside of the convention. Some delegates, like Melancton Smith and Samuel Adams, temporarily deserted the cause to vote for ratification. Their roles in adumbrating their reasons for opposition and then reversing themselves make them too important to exclude. Besides, all of them believed they continued to support the Antifederalist cause. Other important antiratification activists included are the newspaper owners who published and disseminated Antifederalist writings and speeches. Leaders too young to have been convention members, such as DeWitt Clinton, assisted in the politics of opposition with other valuable non-delegates within their states and require inclusion. Thus, the many and various ways the most important Antifederalists served the cause constitute the major reason why each was selected for this volume.

Much attention has been given to what to include about the life of each. Later historical controversy about the Antifederalists' reasons for opposing the Constitution, including age, allegiance to the past, career activities, both public and private experience, and location within their states, has influenced the choice of what to include in each of the entries. Family life and education begin each entry, followed by a study of the individual's early career in business and rise in public life. Role in the American Revolution, a key factor in national and localist allegiance, is discussed, and activities, including national and state service, are considered to assess political values and attitudes and political experience on the national and state scene in the immediate period before the ratification controversy. Also included is post-Revolution business activity. Most importantly, each of the Antifederalists' arguments for opposition to ratification are looked at in depth. That many of them have been included for their arguments in print and at the convention, in short for their opposition to the new governmental system, calls for allowing them to speak for themselves. Short extracts and quotes from their publications and speeches are thus included. That Antifederalists repeated one another's objections adds weight to their arguments against ratification. Lastly, though some were old and retired and others were deprived of future office by the Federalist majority in their states, a number went on to have important post-ratification careers in national and state government, and those careers are discussed. Their continued loyalty to the Antifederalist cause during the Federalist era and after influenced their opposition to the new federal government. After all, without those leaders active in public life, it is doubtful that their most important cause, the Bill of Rights, as well as the rise of Jeffersonian Republicanism, would ever have been adopted and would ever have thrived.

Through this book, the largest and most comprehensive collection of data on the Antifederalists known to date, those leaders often lost to history will have their views aired and actions analyzed. The debate over ratification in each state tells us so much about the early republic and the making of this country's government. The Antifederalists offered in their often chaotic and even divisive fashion major dissent to the way this country was constructed politically. That they went along with the new government meant that the experiment in republicanism has had a chance to succeed. For this reason, we owe these Antifederalist leaders a close look at their lives, to connect their political values and their activities.

A work such as this could never have seen daylight without the assistance, the inspiration, and the support of many others. Once again I owe to Dave Kelly of the Library of Congress a debt unrepayable. Now that the fantastic F section has been closed to scholars, the search for some obscure Antifederalists in old state records has been made nigh unto impossible. But Dave and his colleagues in the Reference Room and the Genealogical Room managed to help me to reconstruct bibliography from the data files, thus shedding light on those old lives. It is sometimes daunting to know that the staff of the Genealogical Room know more than you do about that distant past and its leaders. Alan Kraut and Bill Freehling, while wondering if I would ever come back to the southern Unionists, have seen merit in understanding the grandparents of some of my antebellum activists. Randall Miller, too, while impatient with my pause in work on the South, understands my commitment to those other founders of this democracy. Although she had little to do with this volume and thus cannot be blamed for any of the selections, Rosemarie Zagarri's study of Mercy Otis Warren helped me to see the value in Antifederalist political theory. To my partner in the pursuit of knowledge, Joyce Walker, I owe much patience and forbearance.

Introduction:
Profile of Antifederalists

Much may be learned about the founding of this nation by looking at the lives and accomplishments of the Antifederalists. In their opposition to ratification of the Constitution of 1787, the Antifederalists contributed to a dialogue about the political structure of this country. Their worries about the shape of the proposed government resonate throughout this country's history. By looking at their activities from their pre-Constitution experience, the many ways they opposed the Constitution, and even their actions during the Federalist era, we should get a view of just what so many leaders found wrong with the new government. What follows are some thoughts, based on the Antifederalists' life stories, on why they opposed ratification of the Constitution. These tentative conclusions about their motivations merely offer suggestions and by no means criticize the fine historians who have been concerned with explaining Antifederalist opposition.[1]

What in their early lives assists us to understand why these leaders opposed the Constitution? Scholars have suggested that many of the Antifederalists were yesterday's men, or that they believed in the earlier times of limited government in a small republic, or even separate governments based on the state model in a society of small farmers.[2] Remember that those leaders selected for this study represent a subjective sample in which biographical information is uneven. For some, a full early life is easily reconstructed; for others, information is scant. Their age is thus important as a cohort to identify their political values.

Those born between the late 1720s and 1750s were likely to have been involved in the American Revolution in some capacity and were connected to the generation that feared large, oppressive government like that of Great Britain. Of the known birth dates of 130 of the 140 Antifederalists, 117 were of an age to have participated in the American Revolution. Two were born in the 1710s, and thus unlikely to have been active in the war. Eleven were born after 1760, though three of them served in the War. One born in 1768, and another born in 1770, were almost too young to have participated in their state conventions, let alone be veterans. With fifty-three born between 1720 and 1740, a sizeable percent were close to their fifties—considered old for their time—and yet were to some extent active in the war effort. (At least two of them earned reputations of supporting the British, though they denied it, and obviously were not penalized by their constituents.) Seventy-eight were under the age of fifty in 1787 and thus could be considered new men, those made by the Revolution, similar in age to the delegates of the Constitutional convention, the majority of whom were Federalists. A number may be considered old republicans, but they were by no means the only leaders of the Antifederalists.

Next to age cohort and identity, much has been made of the educational attainments of the two sides in the confrontation over the Constitution. Fully thirty-five of the delegates to the Constitutional convention in Philadelphia in 1787 had been to college. The Federalists there and in the later state conventions have been regarded as better educated and thus more familiar with political structures and theory and more urbane than the Antifederalists. James Madison is always singled out as a brilliant student of political theory, and he had gone to the College of New Jersey (soon to be renamed Princeton). (Of course, neither Benjamin Franklin nor George Washington had been to college.) But some of the best-trained delegates to that convention refused to vote for the Constitution and left Philadelphia, often out of protest. Such future Antifederalists as George Mason, though without college training, did have an excellent preparatory education. College-educated Luther Martin and William Paca from Maryland, among others who voted against the Constitution, became leading Antifederalists.

Just how many Antifederalist leaders had college training, and what is its significance to understanding their behavior? In a country where less than 2 percent of the male population went to college, 45 of the 140 Antifederalists had been to college. The Federalists depicted them as unlearned, but the evidence reveals the opposite. Also, higher education in those years usually meant that the students had come from privilege. Many of the Antifederalists attended colleges such as William and Mary in Virginia, Yale, Harvard, and the College of New Jersey. A few received education abroad, having attended medical school in Edinburgh, studied at the Inns of Court, and matriculated at Eton and later Oxford. As one might expect, Antifederalist Virginia planters born to privilege attended William and Mary. James Warren, Samuel Adams, James Winthrop, Elbridge Gerry, to mention only the most famous Massachusetts Antifederalists, attended their home college, Harvard. Since James Madison the Federalist attended Princeton and probably learned his science of politics there, it is also noticeable that two Antifederalists attended that bastion of conservatism. Some of the most outspoken, eloquent, and even thoughtful Antifederalists, such as Patrick Henry, Willie Jones, and George Mason, did not attend college. Mercy Otis Warren, unable to go to college because of her gender, received a private training second to none and certainly produced one of the most important Antifederalist treatises. What education does reveal, as well as status and perhaps occupation tendencies as lawyers and preachers, is the erudition of the Antifederalists. Their writings and speeches are the equivalent of the Federalists'. Understanding the past and political philosophy made the brilliance of the Antifederalists' arguments equal to that of their opponents.[3]

Pre-Constitution occupation patterns of the Antifederalists have been fraught with contention among historians. Many historians have claimed that the Antifederalists largely represented the farmer interests from the interior of their states. Indeed, a number of the southern or slave state leaders belonged to the category of small farmer. But many, like Richard Henry Lee, George Mason, John Tyler, Benjamin Harrison, North Carolina's Willie Jones, and the wealthiest of them all, South Carolina's Wade Hampton, belonged to the exporting planter class. In fact, most of the Virginia Antifederalists were wealthy planters. Few of the southern Antifederalists were small farmers. As for Maryland, Pennsylvania, New York, and Massachusetts, their leaders who farmed were hardly poor. Some northern New Englanders were ambitious large farmers from the territory of Maine. Only twenty of the Antifederalists may be considered middling farmers. Fully thirty-three of all of the Antifederalists were planters. Though recent work has created a third cohort of small western farmer Antifederalists, most of these leaders in agriculture were successful, and some wildly successful.[4]

It is in the coastal or maritime trades where historians have claimed the largest imbalance between Federalists and Antifederalists. Federalists with large overseas investments naturally desired a large national government to protect their interests. Yet, of the 140 Antifederalists studied here, it is known that sixteen were large merchants in the overseas trade, including Elbridge Gerry. It is true that most of the merchant Antifederalists resided along the coast in New England, but a few came from the urban trade centers of New York City, Philadelphia, New Haven, and Baltimore, which are usually regarded as bastions of Federalism. The center of New York Antifederalism, Albany, was the trading and merchant port for farmers along the Hudson River. Many of the planters also exported and dealt with an international market. As one might expect of leaders versed in politics, a number of Antifederalists at one time practiced law. Forty-one of them were lawyers, a number of whom planted and did business in the merchant trades. None of them were mere country lawyers. What is clear from this cursory survey of Antifederalist business careers is that a number of them, like their Federalist opponents, had connections to merchant trade.

Antifederalist leaders held other business and professional positions, and that made them part of the economic elite of the country. Ten practiced medicine. One of the ten, Arthur Lee, studied both medicine and the law. But, aside from a tour of public diplomatic service, Lee in reality was a man of leisure. Then there were careers of social prestige if not of wealth. James Winthrop, deprived of a classroom career, was Harvard's librarian. Four were ordained preachers of some note. Five ran newspapers, hardly a lucrative position but certainly of much importance to the Antifederalist cause. Samuel Bryan, son of the radical Philadelphia merchant, made his living in government service. Three were teachers, hardly profitable but not without prestige in those days. There were a smattering of careers that began in the lesser trades, such as innkeeper, store owner, and salesman. None of the Antifederalists remained in those young career positions, as all seemed ambitious to rise in business. Six of them began their careers as surveyors. All of those surveyors eventually became well-to-do farmers or planters, including Thomas Sumter and Wade Hampton.

If some of the Antifederalist leaders began life on the so-called frontier, and thus were perhaps part of the east-west division in their states, no discernible pattern exists to link many of them to western interests. Many indeed desired to trade in western land and believed agriculture expansion important to their interests. But even such western-identified men as Wade Hampton and Patrick Henry exported goods and had ties to the eastern parts of their states. A number of Pennsylvania Antifederalists, it is true, made up an anti-Philadelphia, western farmer cohort. Mainers who served in the Massachusetts Antifederalist cause certainly had frontier agrarian ties and wanted a separate state. But most of them also had coastal economic links. The Kentucky and Tennessee Antifederalists from Virginia and North Carolina no doubt looked to the west, yet only a handful of them took active part in Antifederalist activities. The upstate New York Albany-centered, anti-New York City Antifederalists were a stronghold of commercial agricultural interests. Thus, the western man as Antifederalist, as seen by many historians, at least as represented by this group of 140, hardly seemed motivated by geographical division. The largest number of these Antifederalists looked eastward, or had strong ties to the eastern seaboard.

Another career test for future Antifederalist actions is political experience, for two reasons. James Madison labeled the Antifederalists as selfish statists, mediocre leaders determined to dominate and gain in a small political pond.[5] Did they come from parochial politics and thus have little experience and interest in the national scene? Madison's accusation of Antifederalist ignorance of the functioning of government outside of provincial experience is false. If Antifederalists had little experience in national politics, they could not have had any interest in or understanding of the national structure of governance. Their experience was not so local that they could not imagine a large national government.

Forty-eight of the Antifederalists considered in this study held their highest office in their state legislature, thus suggesting a parochial political vision. Twenty rose in office only as far as their state senate, also a position perhaps of state defensiveness. Many of those state legislative leaders also served in the American Revolution, possibly giving them knowledge of the functioning of other state governments. Four held office as governors, with such leaders as

George Clinton of New York having participated in a number of border confrontations that taught him much about other states. Governors Thomas Nelson and Benjamin Harrison of Virginia had national connections, and both also served in the Continental Congress. Five were judges, three of whom were state justices and heard cases dealing with interstate affairs. Most important for the controversy over the Constitution, twenty-nine of the leading Antifederalists served in the Continental Congress. They knew intimately the workings of federal government, mostly believed the Articles of Confederation needed amending, and had reason to distrust leaders from other parts of the country who had competing interests. Those men included Elbridge Gerry, five of the seven Maryland Antifederalists, Samuel Osgood, Richard Henry Lee, William Grayson, John Lansing, Melancton Smith, and Abraham Yates, all of whom delivered sophisticated and brilliant critiques of the federal governmental structure. In all, over 120 of the 140 Antifederalists in this study had pre–state debate political experience. They had learned the functioning of government first hand and had displayed loyalty to their states and regions.

These Antifederalist political leaders also knew and cherished colleagues from other states, had studied and participated in governance together, and exchanged ideas in print and in person during the crucial days of ratification. The cohort from Massachusetts organized political discussion groups in which they aired concerns about the powers of the proposed federal government over themselves, their state, and their region.[6] Clearly, the Antifederalist career patterns, public and private, reveal anything but a parochial, isolated, and disinterested group. They distrusted central power because they had experienced it firsthand; they distrusted other states and regions because they had competed with outsiders for their own version of power. To understand more of how their career patterns influenced their opposition to the Constitution, we must turn to the state convention debates, the written efforts of the Antifederalists, and their political activities in opposition.

At least 95 of the 140 served in their state conventions. In varying degrees all ninety-five spoke out against the Constitution. Some, like Patrick Henry, dominated discussion, perhaps to the detriment of the cause. Others spoke little, and when they did, claimed to be inarticulate and ineffective. In that they were wrong, as they wisely used self-effacement as a political weapon. Some, like Henry, George Mason, Lansing, Abraham Yates, Melancton Smith, Martin, and Samuel Chase, actually drafted and introduced into debate reform measures that eventually made up the Bill of Rights. To those leaders much is owed. Forty-four wrote major works on the proposed federal powers. Writers such as Mercy Otis Warren, Melancton Smith, Abraham Yates, and George Clinton have left printed works on the nature of governance that some will ponder as long as this country exists. A few were the editors who printed the works of the Antifederalists. Posterity and those times owe those publishers a great debt. Their defense of a free press, and their dissemination of the arguments, were invaluable to the cause. A few were ei-

ther too young to serve in the conventions, deprived of election because of
where they lived, or dissatisfied with the proceedings; Federalist Boston
would not elect Elbridge Gerry, and Richard H. Lee refused to serve; nevertheless all assisted the cause. Young men like DeWitt Clinton served their
relatives at the conventions as organizers of the opposition, spreading information, and writing up the issues. Most important to understanding their
reasons for opposition, however, are the speeches and writings of the Antifederalists.

In the entries, I have included some of the actual words of these extraordinary people, for the reader to judge the quality and importance of their views.
(For details of their arguments the reader is referred to the individual entries.
Refer to volume two for specific documents.) Often they repeated themselves,
and they duplicated the efforts of others. Occasionally they had flashes of brilliance. They used the past for present understanding. They revealed a grasp of
political theory.[7] Their central focus in criticizing the Constitution was over the
structure and the functioning of government. Powers given to various parts of
government concerned them. The nature of leadership interested them. The
people as participants in such a large country influenced their views of power.
Above all, individual rights guaranteed by a functioning government obsessed
them. (Books have been written on their political thoughts, and the reader may
turn to the bibliography for further guidance.)

Some Antifederalist speakers and writers worried about the structure of the
proposed federal government. They wondered whether a large federal government would usurp the privileges of the states. The House of Representatives, which the Federalists claimed to represent the people, some
Antifederalists worried would have little power. Others feared that a House
based on population allowed the larger states to dominate the smaller. That
money bills came from the House some found a dangerous usurpation of
states' rights to tax. The Senate, because of its six-year terms, would be, they
said, a fortress of aristocracy unconcerned with the needs of ordinary people.
Bills to regulate commerce and trade emanating from the Senate meant to
southerners that the northern states could run roughshod over southern trade
in exports; conversely, northerners believed that including slaves in the over-
all count for representation meant that the South would dominate the free
states. Powers given to both houses would lead, said others, to excessively corrupt government. Others thought the proposed presidency as either too weak
or recreating a monarchy. Antifederalists feared the president would serve for
life and that there were few ways to remove a despot from office. They said
federal judges could not in any way be sensitive to local legal rights of the
people.

Other Antifederalists showed great concern over just what powers the ordinary people would have in such a federal structure. State powers and local
government, those political bodies closest to the people, were to them over-
whelmed by the federal. Elections, the date and place set by the federal con-

gress, effectively disenfranchised many of the people. Why not, Antifederalists said, allow the state legislatures to set the dates and place of elections. The major question raised from the Antifederalist camp on popular power centered on the size of the country itself. No republic, said these students of republican politics, ever had been made from such a large landmass. Not only would large interests gang up on smaller, but the size of the country meant ungovernability and thus absence of accountability. Antifederalists also believed that a large number of locally elected officials best represented the views of the voters. Votes of individuals would be lost in such a large, impersonal, and potentially corrupt system. A few Antifederalists preferred separate republics, thus making certain that the United States could never exist. For them, to protect voter interests many nations had to be created, which would reflect the separate interests of separate sets of people. Identity of interest, even ethnic type, meant such a diverse people in a vast territory could not function as a government.

Perhaps most important to the Antifederalists was the proposed government's lack of protection of individual rights. Antifederalists believed the Federalists were vague on rights, and they claimed the Constitution itself had purposely been written so that its real powers could not be defined. What did applied powers mean? asked some. What did reserved power mean? asked others. Why in this land of litigants were the courts so vague about who had jurisdiction? Historically, the common law reserved the right to a trial by a jury of one's peers. Why was this sacred right left out of the Constitution? Even worse, the national courts could try people from different states with different values and views of the law. It would be impossible, in this view, to get a fair trial.

Next to the law, freedom of the press most concerned the Antifederalists. They had already watched as Federalists burned their presses and kept the Antifederalists from disseminating information to the people. The very newspapers that gave the people information were threatened. Then there was the muddled issue of freedom of religion. Some Antifederalists believed churches would be victims of the Constitution, and others believed religious freedom and the right to many different churches in the country were under fire. Lastly, northerners fulminated against the continued slave trade, claiming it immoral. Southerners worried that the rights to slave property were jeopardized by northerners who did not believe in the sanctity of private property.

Indeed, if one follows the suggestions of David C. Hendrickson, the issue that concerned the Antifederalists the most was distrust of people outside of their respective regions or states.[8] The Antifederalists' political experiences and theoretical arguments did seem to center on that distrust. Different people, north versus south, could never form a country, said some presciently. Slave state and free had conflicting political and economic objectives. Large land mass worked against unity. Unity could never exist, yet the Constitution proposed to force unity. This led Antifederalists to debate the meaning of power and to call for better representation. Their fear of lack of clarity on individual or state rights led the Antifederalists to demand a written bill of rights. Though they lost their struggle over ratification, the Antifederalist legacy of defense of individual rights and suspicion of power and outsiders is central to American political values.

The Antifederalist opposition to the federal government persisted into the Federalist era and beyond. If they had capitulated to the Federalist victors, or been deprived of future public office, their contributions to this country may have been lost.[9] Affirmation of their motivations for opposition to the proposed new government and to the victorious Federalists was sometimes tested in their post-Constitution career. Of the 140 Antifederalists studied, eighty-nine served in post-ratification public life. Since Antifederalist opinion had been in the majority in a number of states, when some of these leaders voted for the Constitution because of Federalist promises of a bill of rights, their constituents refused them further political office. Governor George Clinton withheld support for some of those turncoats, but political needs allowed a few of them back into his good graces. Most Antifederalists found ways to reunite because they needed one another. Some became permanent Federalists, that is, if they died before their friends eventually delivered Jeffersonian Democracy. Many of them were too old to participate in the post-Constitution period.

What of those eighty-nine who did participate? What did they do, and what can we learn from their later public lives? A few continued the so-called parochial pattern of service in state government. Thirteen held office in the state legislatures, and eleven served in the state senates. Four became governors of their states. Governor John Mercer was symbolized as the father of Maryland democracy. Thirteen also became either local or state judges, fiercely loyal to local rights. Seven either held local clerkships or confirmed Madison's old fear of lustful parochialism by becoming quite successful collectors of their local ports. But the majority went into national politics where they continued the Antifederalist cause. One, James Monroe, became president of the United States. Two, Gerry and Clinton, served as vice president. DeWitt Clinton ran for president as a Federalist, but rejoined the Republicans in New York politics. One each served as treasurer of the United States, postmaster general, and justice of the Supreme Court. Thirty-eight served in the United States House of Representatives, and eight became U.S. Senators. Altogether fifty-two served the Antifederalist cause in federal office, and thirty-seven held state office. In post-ratification public life, former Antifederalists supported the spread of suffrage, helped to pass a bill of rights, and created the Jeffersonian Republican Party dedicated to the rights of states and individuals. Those who lived to 1812 supported that national and eventually divisive war with England. Though they served in national office, it is clear that most of the old Antifederalists remained devout supporters of state and region, and defenders of individual liberties. Thus they were true to the Antifederalist heritage.

NOTES

1. The best, recent bibliographical essay on historiographical arguments over the identity and motivation of the Antifederalists is Patrick T. Conley and John P. Kaminski (eds.), *The Constitution and the States* (Madison, Wisc.: Madison House, 1988), 316–324.

2. Drew McCoy, *The Republic in Peril* (Chapel Hill: University of North Carolina Press, 1976), 121–132. See also Pauline Maier, *The Old Revolutionaries* (New York: Alfred Knopf, 1969).

3. Herbert J. Storing (ed.), *The Complete Anti-Federalists* (Chicago: University of Chicago, 1981), vol. 1.

4. Conley and Kaminski (eds.), 316–318; Saul Cornell, *The Other Founders* (Chapel Hill: University of North Carolina Press, 1999), chaps. 1–3.

5. McCoy, *The Republic in Peril*, 121–132.

6. Maier, *The Old Revolutionaries*; Jean Fritz, *Cast for a Revolution* (Boston: Houghton Mifflin, 1972).

7. Michael Lienesch, *New Order for the Ages* (Princeton: Princeton University Press, 1988).

8. David C. Hendrickson, *Peace Pact: The Lost World of the American Founding* (University Press of Kansas, 2003), 252, 254, and all of chap. 28.

9. David Siemers, *Ratifying the Republic* (Stanford: Stanford University Press, 2002). See his appendix on Antifederalists in the Federal Congress.

Abbreviations of Frequently Cited Works

Bailyn, *Debate*. Bernard Bailyn (ed.), *The Debate on the Constitution*, 2 vols. (New York: Library of America, 1993).

Elliot, *Debates*. Jonathan Elliot (ed.), *The Debates in the Several State Conventions on the Adoption of the Federal Constitution*, 5 vols. (New York: Burt Franklin Reprints, 1968).

Jensen and Kaminski, *Documentary History*. Merrill Jensen and John P. Kaminski (eds.), *The Documentary History of the Ratification of the Constitution*, 19 vols. (Madison: State Historical Society of Wisconsin, 1976–).

Storing, *Complete*. Herbert J. Storing (ed.), *The Complete Anti-Federalists*, 7 vols. (Chicago: University of Chicago Press, 1981).

Birth of the Bill of Rights

A

SAMUEL ADAMS *(September 27, 1722–October 2, 1803)* was born in Boston to Samuel and Mary (Fifield) Adams. The elder Adams was a successful businessman and later brewer in Boston, and his wife came from a prominent family. In all, the Adams had social status and financial position in that small but bustling seaport town of Puritan divines, worldly merchants, and a growing legal class. Educated at Boston Grammer School, young Adams entered Harvard College in nearby Cambridge in 1736 at the age of fourteen and graduated somewhere in the middle of the class in 1740. In 1743 Adams received the M.A. from Harvard. In evaluating Adams's formative early years, Ralph Harlow stated, "the intellectual and emotional environment of his early youth therefore furnished him with a hard, unyielding, even uncompromising atttitude toward all questions, an attitude imperially noticeable in politics" (3).

Following the customary soul searching of thinking about the ministry—some say he never stopped being a Puritan—young Adams joined many other young men from Harvard who chose to study the law. Apparently he had no interest in practicing but was intrigued by legal reasoning, the history of freedom, and the potential for business gain that the law seemed to offer. Adams then entered into business with Thomas Cushing and later helped to run his father's brewery. But in reality, Adams cared little for business or any other kind of work. He loved the exchange of ideas with his cronies, hung out in local coffee houses, and generally received a reputation as a clever, argumentative wastrel. Even his marriages to Elizabeth Checkley, from a prominent family, in 1747 and, upon her death, to Elizabeth Wells in 1764 seemed to have little effect on his leisurely ways.

In 1747 Adams established the Whipping Post Club, an organization of his peers committed to reform politics. He also developed a keen writing style, filled with historical analogies and prone to didacticism. Adams contributed to the *Independent Advertiser*, a paper that opposed the policies of Lieutenant Governor Thomas Hutchinson. It hardly paid in those days to fight with such a powerful conservative as Hutchinson, a wealthy Bostonian as well as loyal Englishman, and Adams made a lifetime enemy of the leader. In 1763 Adams joined the Caucus Club and used that position to support issues concerning Boston workingmen and skilled mechanics.

Years of political discussions with leading dissenters, as well as his many writings, made Adams famous among those who had grown to resent British domination of Massachusetts political and economic affairs. His opportunity to fight against oppression came during the Stamp Act crisis of 1765. Elected to the Massachusetts House in 1765, he served until 1774, rising to become clerk of the House. He wrote the "Resolutions of the House," a guide to anti-British activities. For that act of arrogance, Hutchinson attempted to have Adams censored but failed. In 1768 Adams organized the Non-Importation Association to oppose the Townsend Acts of economic coercion. He drafted a "Circular Letter" of opposition to the acts and wrote scathing articles for the local press about how England was bent on destroying Boston trade. In 1770 Adams helped to form the Boston Committee of Correspondence, a political action organization, and in 1772 he wrote the Boston Declaration of Rights. A founder of the Sons of Liberty in 1773, Adams planned the Boston Tea Party, in which his followers, dressed as Indians, pitched tea over the side of boats in the Boston harbor. In 1774 he took the lead in resistance to the Quebec Acts, or so-called Coercive Acts, claiming that they prohibited Massachusetts farmers from moving west and thus constituted an act of war. In 1774, with the publication of the Suffolk Resolves, Adams called for resistance to Great Britain's oppressive policies.

Most importantly, Adams was not only a fomenter of dissent and rebellion but an advocate of a separate nation dedicated to undermining oppressive central authority. He joined with those who created the Continental Congress and became a member of the first Congress in 1774. Elected to the Second Continental Congress, Adams became a leading advocate of independence and signed the Declaration of Independence. He served ably in Congress until 1781. Adams was instrumental in drafting the Articles of Confederation, the first United States Constitution. As an author of that document, Adams wanted to make certain that political power was dispersed and that the new states held sovereignty in the new nation. Also, busy back in Massachusetts, he became a delegate to the convention that drew up the Massachusetts Constitution of 1780. He drafted the famous "Address of the Convention," a blueprint for republican representative government. In all, Samuel Adams became one of the great founders of the American republic through his political activities in behalf of liberty.

In postwar political events Adams participated with gusto. Many students of his life have said that if Adams had died after American independence was achieved but before the controversy over the Constitution in 1787, his reputation would never have been brought into question. As Harlow says: "his mind was so lacking in the qualities of imagination and flexibility that he could not adjust himself to the new era" (302). Perhaps that is true. But Adams's role in the postwar period as a leading Antifederalist, defender of the rights of Massachusetts, and, to some, a turncoat who finally supported the federal Constitution of 1787–1788, is of utmost importance. Perhaps the real story is that Adams and his friends, as Paulene Maier so aptly stated, were the old revolutionaries who felt that the new proposed Constitution violated the small government values of those who had forced the American Revolution. Also, Adams seems to have enjoyed being an opponent rather than one who goes along with the needs of peace. Perhaps more than anything, Adams had lived to foment rebellion, and the new nation required settled leaders.

Still, the role of Adams as an Antifederalist leader remains important for anyone who wants to understand how that post-Revolutionary dialogue over the place of government and governance in this country's future affected the young nation's development. Adams at first thought his duties had ended after the war and with the creation of the Massachusetts state constitution, or at least that is what he told his close friend, the Antifederalist James Warren (q.v.). Adams had for years belonged to a group of Harvard graduates and friends who debated government and discussed the future of this country's politics. He had been shocked by the Shays's uprising of western Massachusetts farmers, because he feared internal unrest. Adams's political faction sympathized with the farmers' economic plight but rejected their activities of resistance and wanted them suppressed. In this reaction to the Shays's Rebellion, he was joined by other old Massachusetts revolutionaries. When the opportunity to meet with those who were sent to the Philadelphia convention to revise and strengthen the Articles of Confederation presented itself, Adams decided to decline the invitation fearing that revision of the Articles could go too far.

From his perspective, the new proposed Constitution eroded state sovereignty and lacked specifics on protection of the precious individual rights gained from the Revolution, and Adams joined and at first led the opposition in his state's ratifying convention. In 1785 he had worked with his friend and fellow former revolutionary Elbridge Gerry (q.v.) to reject changes to the Articles of Confederation. Adams, however, wanted to amend the proposed Constitution with rights for the states spelled out. He met with Gerry, Warren, and others with hopes of radically amending the proposed Constitution. Adams wrote to Virginia Antifederalist leader Richard Henry Lee (q.v.) on December 3, 1787, that he feared "seeds" of aristocratic takeover of the country had been sown in the Constitution. "The few haughty Families, think *They* must govern," he claimed. And most dangerous to Adams was the question of whether "this National Legislature [can] be competent to make laws for the *free* internal Government of one People, living in climates so remote and whose habits and particular Interests are and probably always will be different." His principal concern, Adams told Lee, was the proposed erosion of state sovereignty (Bailyn, 446–447). Adams also used the writings of George Mason (q.v.) of Virginia on the need for a bill of rights in his speeches and writings during the days building up to and later in the Massachusetts Convention.

Thanks to his descendent William Wells and the excellent detective work of Herbert Storing, it is possible to see just why Adams attempted to force the state convention to require that a bill of rights be added to the Constitution as a stipulation for Massachusetts' acquiescence. He submitted a bill of rights to "to remove doubts" that the Constitutionalists cared little about individual rights. He expected Massachusetts to have an influence on other states' conventions as they also struggled with popular rights such as trial by jury and freedom of expression (Wells, 262). It is possible that Adams either wrote or coauthored with Benjamin Austin (q.v.) the influential "Candidus" essays printed in the Boston *Independent Chronicle* from December 1787 to January 1788. In them the author stressed fears over surrendering state powers to a new central government and its impact on Massachusetts commerce (Storing, 125). He also rejected the taxing privileges of the new proposed government, preferring that Congress merely provide for the defense of the country and promote commerce. Likewise, Adams worked with James Warren in drafts of *Letters of a Republican Federalist*, a diatribe on the possibilities of corruption in the excessive powers of central government.

Yet, not long into the state's debates, the old and tired Adams became suddenly quiet and almost, for him, introspective. Perhaps the sudden death of his son, Dr. Samuel Adams, on January 17, 1788, affected his actions. In addition, his loyal allies, the Boston mechanics, had asked him to support the Constitution. Maybe the old revolutionary knew that his friends could not stop history, and that the pro-Constitution forces, though in the minority in Massachusetts, had the momentum to achieve success. After his old ally and political competitor John Hancock shifted to become a Federalist leader, Adams knew that the Antifederalists could only hope for major compromises in the Constitution, such as the addition of a bill of rights to specifically clarify the rights of citizens. Adams ended up voting for the Constitution and angered his Antifederalist friends. In his finest moment after that vote, despite his real reservations about the powers in the Constitution, Adams warned, "let us then be cautious how we disturb the general harmony" (Storing, vol. 4, 135). Obviously, though Adams praised John Hancock for his moderation and accepted the state's verdict on ratification, he continued to worry about its results (Elliot, 123–124).

In 1788 Adams lost an election for the first United States Congress to the arch-Federalist Fisher Ames. Instead, He became lieutenant governor of Massachusetts in 1789, a position he held until 1793, and he served feebly as governor from 1794 until 1797. Adams died in Boston on October 2, 1803, his career in eclipse and his reputation in tatters. His true feelings about the United States Constitution have aroused controversy ever since. From having been the great revolutionary, he became the seemingly failed statesman of the new republic. Later supporters of the Constitution in a conservative Massachusetts found only good things to say about his vote for the Constitution. James Hosmer said that "his contemporaries indeed declared that his influence *saved* the Constitution in Massachusetts" (360). Even the democratic historian George Bancroft, in his monumental history of the formation of the Constitution, claimed that Adams only recommended amendments and did not, as those localist Massachusettsans believed, vote for the Constitution only after being promised that the states would demand a bill of rights. William Wells insisted that the old revolutionary's fear of federal government could not have anticipated the horrors of a later civil war in which the Antifederalists became the allies of the Confederates. In comparing him to other old revolutionaries, some of whom decried in conservative terms what their revolution had unleashed in mob and material rule, Pauline Maier claimed that Adams's actions as an Antifederalist showed that he "never lost faith in the people or their Revolution" (49). Adams himself deserves the last word on his courageous defense of liberty and the rights of local government in the nation. In a letter to the disappointed Richard Henry Lee in July 1789, Adams declared, "I am an Anti-Federalist."

REFERENCES

Bailyn, *Debate*, vol. 1; George Bancroft, *History of the Formation of the Constitution of the United States* (New York: D. Appleton, 1882); Henry A. Cushing (ed.), *Writings of Samuel Adams* (New York: Octagon Press, 1968), vol. 6, 1778–1802; Elliott, *Debates*, vol. 2; John R. Gabin, *Three Men of Boston* (New York: Thomas Y. Crowell, 1976); Ralph V. Harlow, *Samuel Adams, Promoter of the American Revolution: A Study in Psychology and Politics* (New York: Farrar, Straus, and Giroux, 1975); James K. Hosmer, *Samuel Adams* (1898; repr., New York: Chelsea House, 1980); Pauline Maier, *The Old Revolutionaries* (New York: Alfred Knopf, 1968); John C. Miller, *Samuel Adams: Pioneer in Propaganda* (Stanford: Stanford University Press, 1936); Storing, *Complete*, 4; William V. Wells, *Life and Public Service of Samuel Adams*, vols. 2, 3 (Boston: Little, Brown, and Co., 1865).

SAMUEL ASHE *(?, 1725–February 3, 1813)* was born near Beaufort, North Carolina. The exact date of his birth is unknown. He was the son of John Baptista Ashe, a powerful Beaufort District political leader in the colonial North Carolina General Assembly. John Baptista also owned large property in that part of the colony, and young Samuel was raised in luxury on the rich Cape Fear River section of the colony. Samuel's mother, a Swan, died when he was quite young, and his father followed in 1734, leaving him orphaned. As was usual in those days, Samuel was raised by his uncle and guardian Samuel Swan. The able lawyer and planter Swan also led North Carolina colonial politics, having served as speaker of the North Carolina Assembly. Swan, unlike some of his fellow wealthy leaders, had no love for the British government and instilled in his ward principles of republican ideology. He sent young Ashe north for an education, supported his study of the law, and assisted him in setting up a practice in the Wilmington District.

Rising in the legal profession, Ashe became a crown attorney, though he had many a dispute with the royal governors of North Carolina. He married into the Cape Fear aristocracy, first Mary Porter with whom he had three sons and, upon her death, Elizabeth Merrick, and solidified his place among the most important leaders of that region. Ashe rose in political life to become an important pre-Revolutionary judge. He also acquired considerable amounts of plantation land along the Cape Fear. In all, Ashe followed the pattern of young, rich public figures in their rise to positions of power in late colonial North Carolina.

Although never a radical republican or an ultra-democrat, he became a leader of North Carolina's revolutionary activist party and helped to organize the colony for resistance to England. In 1774 he wrote often against British policies, sided with recalcitrant Massachusetts rebels, and entered the first North Carolina State Legislature. His peers elected him president of the North Carolina Council of Safety, a position in which he assisted the war effort. Ashe also served as captain in the Revolutionary army, although he was overshadowed by his brother General John Ashe, a military hero and later radical leader and political power in North Carolina. In 1776 Samuel helped to write North Carolina's first state constitution. He took credit for most of the Republican ideas contained in that governing document. Ashe rose to become speaker of the state senate and later served as a judge of the state's first supreme court.

After the Revolution, along with his brother, he broke with other Cape Fear aristocratic leaders and defended the Articles of Confederation. Ashe insisted that the state constitution which he had largely drafted, had been of some influence on the construction of the Articles, and he resisted amending either document. His biographer, Samuel A. Ashe, described him as "one who early became a Republican; and later he stood for state's rights and for the rejection of the Federal Constitution; and he was an earnest adherent of Jefferson's policies" (8, 22). Though he did not take part in the state's Constitutional ratification convention, Ashe's importance in state public life and his contribution to the law made him a leader of the Antifederalists. As a result of his close ties to Judge Samuel Spencer (q.v.), one of the state's leading Antifederalists, Ashe decided to write for and politick among those who rejected the federal Constitution and called another state ratifying convention. He became reconciled to the Constitution only after the new nation's government had begun to function and because he desired that North Carolina become a part of the nation.

Large, strong, quite intelligent, and with a dominant presence, Ashe soon assumed a major role in state politics. He assisted in the formation of the new state government under the Constitution. From 1790 to 1795, Ashe served as chief justice of the state supreme court, where he decided many important cases, especially a number on property rights in the state's western region and on the right of judicial review for the state higher court. He became a leader of the Jeffersonian party in North Carolina and served as governor from 1795 to 1798. During the 1790s crisis with France, Ashe feared for coastal Carolina trade and temporarily broke with the Jeffersonians, as he tried to unite

Carolinians around support for the policies of the federal government. Later he turned on President John Adams and supported Thomas Jefferson in the election of 1800. In 1804 Ashe served as a presidential elector on the Republican ticket. Disappointed when his war hero son, Samuel, Jr., deserted the family politics to become a Federalist, the governor took some delight when most of his family remained loyal to republicanism.

Upon leaving the governorship, Ashe retired from public life and spent winters at his Rocky Point plantation and summers in the Piedmont at Hawfield. He served as president of the Board of Trustees of the University of North Carolina and helped to build a fine university. Other honorary duties followed, and in retirement Ashe became one of North Carolina's grand old revolutionaries. He died at Rocky Point on February 3, 1813, just shy of his eighty-eighth year. Although later southern scholars and family historians have attempted to see Ashe's vehement state's rights position as strongly in favor of southern rights, he remained until his death a nationalist and defender of representative rights who feared excessive and intrusive central government's dominance over local interests. Only when the Constitution was amended to protect individual rights, and when the Jeffersonians came into power to deemphasize central powers, did he make his peace with that document. Later generations of Ashes served their state and their country as southern progressives in the Jeffersonian mold.

REFERENCES

Samuel A. Ashe (ed.), *Cyclopedia of Eminent and Successful Men of the Carolinas in the Nineteenth Century*, 2 vols. (Spartanburg, S.C.: The Reprint Company, 1973); Samuel A. Ashe, et al., *Biographical History of North Carolina* (Greensboro, N.C.: Charles L. Van Nappen, 1917), vol. 8; R.W.D. Conner, *History of North Carolina* (Chapel Hill: University of North Carolina Press, 1955); James Sprunt, *Chronicles of the Cape Fear River* (Raleigh, N.C.: Edwards and Broughton, 1918); John H. Wheeler, *Historical Sketches of North Carolina*, 2 vols. (1851; repr., Baltimore: Regional Publishing Co., 1964).

JOSHUA ATHERTON *(June 20, 1737–April 13, 1809)* was born in Worcester County, Massachusetts to Peter and Experience (Wright) Atherton of Andover. Peter practiced the lucrative trade of blacksmithing and served as a local magistrate. He also became a colonel in the Massachusetts colonial militia, then seen as a political position, and gained election to the colony's General Court. Young Joshua attended local common schools, and local clergy tutored him. Brought up to become a farmer and enter his father's blacksmith business, Joshua was a sickly boy so the family deemed him unable to take on heavy labor. Instead, he went to college, along with his older brother Isaac. Joshua tutored local children and conducted a school to earn the funds necessary for college tuition. He entered Harvard College in 1758 at twenty-one, an older age for a student, and graduated with the class of 1762. Joshua studied law under the well-known James Putnam of Worcester, King's Attorney General of Provincial Massachusetts. He also clerked with the excellent lawyer Abel Willard of Lancaster.

Beginning his law practice in nearby Petersham, Massachusetts in 1765, Atherton also continued to conduct a school. While a teacher, he met Abigail Goss of Boston, the daughter of a Congregational minister, and married her in 1765. Realizing that Massachusetts had a plethora of young struggling lawyers, Atherton decided to seek better legal opportunities in rural and provincial New Hampshire. An ambitious young man, he settled in Litchfield, and then Merriman, and developed a successful practice during the years 1765 to 1773. In 1773 he moved to Amherst on the Merrimac River, where he spent the rest of his life.

Also a successful farmer, Atherton became register of probate of the county of Hillsborough in the summer of 1773. But the winds of revolt were blowing over his small community, and the rising young politician at first joined the opponents to Great Britian. However, he refused to join the local Sons of Liberty, favored the British cause, and attempted to remain neutral in the Revolution. Atherton simply believed the colonials could not prevail in war with England. His neighbors took umbrage over his actions and in 1777 had him arrested and placed in jail in Exeter. He was fired as Register of Probate and as a justice of the peace, and reduced to farming.

In 1779 Atherton took the oath of allegiance to the new state of New Hampshire and was allowed to practice law again. He soon restored his lost income, and the local citizenry again required his services in public life. After the war came to an end, his law practice grew, and he soon gained readmittance into local society. In 1782 Atherton became the Amherst leader of the committee to write a state constitution. In 1783, as a member of the state constitutional convention, he assisted in drafting a revised set of state laws. He especially advocated a bill of rights for the citizens of New Hampshire. Atherton also actively sought to settle former loyalist land claims and made a few enemies in doing so.

Due to his reputation as a local lawyer, Atherton's friends wanted him to assume an active role in the debate concerning New Hampshire and the proposed federal Constitution of 1787. A delegate from New Ipswich at the state ratification convention, he supported his community and became a leader of the Antifederalist majority. The Federalists accused him of having been a Tory in the Revolution, but Atherton nevertheless won election to the state convention in a tight race. His friend, Charles Barrett (q.v.), gave him the public support necessary for victory. He opposed the Constitution with the claim that it was poorly written, demanded a bill of rights to protect private beliefs and actions, and defended the rights of town and state government against a too-strong central government. In fact, Atherton's skills at debate and legal procedures helped to delay the state's ratification of the Constitution until

June 21, 1788. Though he well knew that Massachusetts's ratification of the Constitution must eventually force New Hamsphire's acquiescence, he remained faithful to the wishes of his Amherst constituents that he vote in the negative. Even though political enemies held old grudges over his support for the loyalists of the Revolution and his stubborn opposition to the Constitution, Atherton continued his fidelity to local interests. He maintained, as Joseph Walker, a historian of the New Hampshire convention, stated, that "ratification was tyranny in the extreme and despotism with a vengeance" (29). Atherton's demand for amendments resonated with those delegates who finally ratified the Constitution, and many of them later called for a revised Constitution. Walker says, "[O]f the opponents of the Constitution, Joshua Atherton was undoubtedly and early the chief. . . . Without him the Antifederalists would have been weak indeed" (53).

Atherton's most important contribution to the Antifederalist cause at the convention was a major speech during February 1788, in which he eloquently laid out his reasons for rejecting the Constitution. He focused on the evils of slavery and declared that the southern states had made him a "partaker in the sin and guilt of this abominable" traffic in buying and selling slaves. The Federalists in the state had claimed that the compromise over the slave trade effectively had ended slavery, and Atherton responded that the clause "[had] not secured its abolition. . . . We will," he swore, "not lend the aid of our ratification to this cruel and inhumane merchandise, not even for a day." Atherton went on to describe what it was like to be stolen and shipped as a slave. He believed that humans were dragged away from everything they held dear: "A parent is sold to one, a son to another, and a daughter to a third . . . never to behold the faces of one another again! The scene is too affecting" (Elliott, 2, 203–204). Thus, this northern New Englander had fixed on the sectional divide over slavery that for him made the Constitution a violation of the laws of God. In his memoir of those times, as recorded by Daniel Secomb, Atherton predicted baneful consequences for the proposed federal union if slavery were allowed to continue (27–28).

Although the state's Federalists had capitalized on ratification to gain power and deprive Atherton of election to the first United States Congress, the Amherst lawyer managed to rise again in state politics. He was made a justice of the peace again in 1791 and elected to the August 1791 Concord convention that drafted the new state constitution to revise the previous of 1783. It is said that he was the principal author of the state constitution of 1792. In 1791, true to his earlier interest in education, Atherton helped to found the Aurean Academy in Amherst. From 1792 until 1793, he served in the state senate, but resigned because he wanted stronger state courts than the legislature would permit. In 1793 he was elected state attorney general. Meanwhile, Atherton became a supporter of the United States government and an admirer of Alexander Hamilton. He said that he had always feared changes in government, from the revolution to the Constitutional revisions of 1787–1788, and thus worried about those who would throw out the Federalists.

In 1798 Atherton became commissioner of the county of Hillsborough. But the people turned on him because he had supported the collection of taxes, and ironically, because he had been such a strong Antifederalist. In 1803 he retired from public life because of an heart ailment. Still, in his last years he continued in public service becoming a founding member of the Franklin Society, a library for the youth of Amherst designed to remind all of the recent historical events that had so changed his state and its role in society. A man of heavy brow, prominent nose, broad shoulders, and old-school manners, Atherton looked every bit the part of the English country gentleman to which he had aspired. He died of heart disease at his farm in Amherst, New Hampshire on April 3, 1809.

REFERENCES

Charles H. Atherton, *Memoir of Joshua Atherton* (Boston: Crosby and Nichols, 1852); Charles Henry Bell, *Bench and Bar of New Hampshire* (Boston: Houghton Mifflin, 1894); Jere R. Daniell, *Experiment in Republicanism: New Hampshire Politics and the American Revolution, 1741–1791* (Cambridge: Harvard University Press, 1970); Elliot, *Debates,* vol. 2; Robert Rutland, *Ordeal of the Constitution: The Antifederalists and the Ratification Struggle, 1787–1788* (Norman: University of Oklahoma Press, 1955); Daniel F. Secomb, *History of the Town of Amherst, Hillsborough County, New Hampshire* (Concord, N.H.: Printed by Evans, Sleeper, and Woorbury, 1883); Joseph B. Walker, *A History of the New Hampshire Ratification Convention* (Boston: Supples and Hurd, 1888).

BENJAMIN AUSTIN *(November 18, 1752–May 4, 1820)* was born in Boston, Massachusetts. His father, also Benjamin, was a merchant, an important local political leader, and a member of the colonial Council of Massachusetts. His mother, Elizabeth Waldo, came from a rich loyalist family. In his capacity as a merchant, the senior Austin became a close friend of Samuel Adams (q.v.), and young Benjamin grew up surrounded by the world of radical Boston politics. He had private tutors and attended local schools. Benjamin entered his father's merchant business, traveled abroad, and eventually owned his own factory.

Too young to take leadership responsibility during the Revolution, Austin nevertheless became a member of Boston radical groups and worked closely with Samuel Adams. He made patriotic speeches and published inflammatory articles in the Boston press. In 1783 he toured Europe, visited prerevolutionary France, and attempted to establish new trade opportunities for Boston merchants. Austin had a strong dislike for the English and especially abhorred that country's postwar trade policies with New England. He blamed local lawyers for colluding with British agents, though he could not prove it, and some friends believed this damaged his reputation. In 1785, expecting to settle down to business, he married Jane Ivers, daughter of a prominent Boston merchant.

The Shays's Rebellion brought him back into public life, as Austin secretly sympathized with the indebted western farmers but worried over the effect of civil unrest on eastern commerce. In 1786 Austin wrote the influential *Observations on the Pernicious Practice of the Law* under the pseudonym "Honestus." In that work, he called for reform of the state's legal code. He even accused lawyers of fomenting the Shays's Rebellion. Going too far in his criticism, the quirky Austin demanded that the state abolish the legal profession, or at least exclude the English common law from American legal practice. He feared that the common law justified strong government, something he believed contrary to the republican revolutionary heritage. In this judgement, the now-rising local political leader agreed with a circle of former revolutionaries centering around the intellectual family of Joseph Warren (q.v.). Austin grew close to Joseph and Mercy Otis Warren (q.v.).

Elected to the Massachusetts State Senate in 1787, Austin became an active Antifederalist in opposition to the new central government proposed in the federal Constitution. In support of the anti-Constitutionalists in the Massachusetts ratification convention, he wrote articles under the pseudonym "Candidas," published in the Boston *Independent Chronicle* on December 6 and 20, 1787. In them, Austin discussed at length his fears of loss of freedoms gained from the Revolution. He had taken the position that opponents of the Constitution should not call themselves Antifederalists. They were Republicans and should be so called. The American Revolution, Austin and his Warren allies said, had resulted in an old republic of small local governments, based on the simplicity, honesty, and integrity of the leaders. The new federal Constitution, he maintained, protected corrupt government and a material society bent on rejecting the ideals of the Revolution. Indeed, for Austin the Constitution destroyed republican values. (Samuel Adams may have contributed to those articles, and Austin may have collaborated in writing Adams's early remarks in the Massachusetts convention debates.)

Although he had failed to gain election to the state ratifying convention and Boston had become a center of Federalist power, Austin's writings in behalf of republicanism certainly influenced the Massachusetts Antifederalist cause. This well-to-do merchant also linked commerce with republican values. The Federalists, said Austin, had tried to frighten the people of Massachusetts with fear tactics into believing that without a Constitution commerce would fail. Austin countered with his mixed verdict on commerce. Herbert J. Storing called him a classic old republican, supportive of the rise of commerce but furious at a commercial republic living beyond its means. Austin also advised his friends in the convention that to deliberate on and to amend the Constitution before passage would do no harm to New Englanders. Why did the Federalists want to adopt with such haste? he asked. Austin advised the convention members to press for a bill of rights to protect individual liberty. He called the state's power to tax of great value and did not want to give over that right to a federal government. No government, contrary to the Federalists' claim, could "save a people from financial ruin," he declared (Storing, 125). Astutely, Austin suggested that first the states must learn to cooperate; those that specialized in agriculture and those in manufacturing could aid the other's interests. Another commercial problem for the Antifederalists, he insisted, concerned payment of domestic debt. Austin offered revenue from the sale of western land as the solution to the national debt (Storing, 125–133). Of course, all of his efforts to defeat ratification came to naught.

Because of his courageous stand against the Federalists, Austin rose in Massachusetts radical political circles. He served in the state senate from 1789 to 1794, and again in 1796. This highly influential merchant became the Republican political boss of Boston. He opposed the national policies of George Washington's administration. In retaliation, Boston Federalists viciously satirized Austin's republicanism and referred to him as a demagogue. In 1797 Austin wrote the book *Constitutional Republicanism,* in which he once again described his opposition to the Federalists. In 1803 he served on the Massachusetts Committee on Loans. As a public servant, Austin also became an overseer of the poor, and he managed the Harvard College lotteries. He also led the Republican Boston Constitutional Club. Considered the leader of the Boston radicals, Austin even accused Elbridge Gerry (q.v.) of betraying the Republican party by refusing to give political patronage to its radical members. Gerry had been one of Austin's heroes, and this break among former allies caused much harm to the republican cause.

The tragedy of Austin's life was the death of his son in 1806. Thomas Selfridge, a Federalist lawyer and party hack, had shot and killed Charles Austin on the streets of Boston, claiming to have resisted an attack on his person. Austin wrote the poignant *Memorial* to his fallen son, describing the shattering of his hopes for a continued radical future in Boston. Soon thereafter, Austin retired from public life, old and worn out before his time. He died, many thought a broken man, in Boston on May 4, 1820.

REFERENCES

Benjamin Austin, *Constitutional Republicanism, in Opposition to Fallacious Federalism* (Boston: Adams and Rhoades, 1803); Benjamin Austin, *Memorial* (Boston: Adams and Rhoades, 1806); Van Beck Hall, *Politics Without Parties: Massachusetts, 1780–1791* (Pittsburgh: University of Pittsburgh Press, 1972); Ansor Ely Moore, *The Federalist Party in Massachusetts* (Princeton: Princeton University Press, 1909); Storing, *Complete*, vol. 4.

$\mathcal{B}$

JOHN BACON *(April 9, 1738–October 25, 1820)* was born in Canterbury, Connecticut, to John and Ruth (Spaulding) Bacon. The young Bacon first studied at home and later attended a local school. He graduated from the Presbyterian College of New Jersey (later Princeton) in 1765. Licensed to preach in the Presbyterian Church in 1765, he went to Lewes, Delaware, and later to Maryland, where he preached at two small, poor churches. He married Gertrude Henry in 1767 and she died in 1769. In 1771 Bacon became the pastor of the prestigious Old South Church in Boston, Massachusetts. That same year he married Elizabeth Goldthwaite.

A staunch Presbyterian and brilliant preacher, Bacon was ill-suited to the Congregational Old South Church. He soon ran afoul of the church members because he appeared to support British Royal Governor Thomas Hutchinson. Certainly the revolutionaries among them engineered his dismissal in 1775. But Bacon did not oppose the war when it came. He did, however, resist the first Massachusetts State Constitution because it did not abolish slavery.

In 1781 Bacon moved to Stockbridge, Massachusetts, to farm and begin a political career. From 1781 until 1807, he served as associate judge of the Court of Common Pleas of Berkshire County and as presiding judge from 1807 until 1811. Bacon also served on the General Court for a number of years. He served twelve times in the Massachusetts House and ten times in the state senate, with one term as president of the Massachusetts Senate. As such, he became a power in western state politics.

During the debates over the ratification of the federal Constitution in the state house in 1787, and during the state ratifying convention, Bacon opposed ratification. Although he was not elected to the ratifying convention, perhaps because of the old Tory accusation, he rallied opposition to the Constitution. Bacon became a champion of the small farmers, a staunch antislavery advocate, and a supporter of small government. Bacon wrote an article in the January 12, 1788, issue of the *Massachusetts Centinel* that summed up his opposition to a powerful national government. In it, he claimed that the proposed Constitution undermined popular rights and, as such, was too burdensome for the people to bear. After the state had ratified the Constitution, the thoughtful Bacon decided to go along with the decision. Perhaps he had come under the influence of the arch-Federalist political leader, Theodore Sedgewick. More likely, Bacon had the good sense to understand further opposition in Massachusetts was fruitless.

During the 1790s, Bacon emerged as a strong Republican. Elected to the United States House of Representatives as a Jeffersonian Republican he served from 1801 until 1803. In 1804 he was a presidential elector on the Jefferson ticket. Bacon's son, Ezekial, served in Congress as a Jeffersonian Republican and became a judge in Utica, New York. John Bacon died in Stockbridge, Berkshire County, on October 25, 1820. Though never a famous or doctrinaire author of Antifederalist works, Bacon's career shows the importance of local opposition to the Constitution and the rewards of elevation to national office. He is one of the forgotten men of the Antifederalist cause, yet in his time Bacon led the state's western small government forces.

REFERENCES

Samuel B. Harding, *The Contest over the Ratification of the Federal Constitution in the State of Massachusetts* (Cambridge: Harvard University Press, 1896); Electa Fidelia Jones, *Stockbridge, Past and Present* (Springfield, Mass.: Samuel Bowles and Co., 1854); Thomas H. O'Connor and Alan Rogers, *Massachusetts and the Ratification of the Constitution* (Boston: Harvard University Press, 1987); *New England Historical and Genealogical Register, January 1890*; David J. Siemers, *Ratifying the Republic: Antifederalists and Federalists in Constitutional Time* (Stanford: Stanford University Press, 2002).

JOSEPH BADGER *(October 23, 1746–January 15, 1809)* was born in Bradford, Massachusetts. He was the son of Captain Joseph Badger, who resettled in Gilmartin, New Hampshire, when Joseph was a youth. Before the Revolution the younger Badger became a successful farmer. It is also known that he served as an officer for some thirty years in the New Hampshire militia and that he was an ardent patriot. He assisted in the capture of the British general John Burgoyne. During the war, he rose from captain to brigadier general in the state militia. Badger became a state councillor in 1784. He also was a judge of probate. Badger rose in state politics to serve in the state legislature in 1784, again from 1790 until 1792, and during the terms of 1795 and 1796.

As a local leader, Badger became a major advocate of the Antifederalist forces in the state of New Hampshire. In the state's convention, Badger opposed ratification of the Constitution on grounds that the small states and the ordinary people would be ignored in the new federal government. This leader who voted against ratification led the committee authorized to bring amendments to the New Hampshire convention.

Like many another Antifederalist, Badger knew he had little choice but to go along with the new Constitution. This did not keep nationalist opponents from attempting to destroy his career. Pro-Federalists later removed him as a judge, insisting he was ignorant of the law. Nevertheless, he continued to participate in the life of his community. Badger founded the Gilmartin Academy during the 1790s. His son, William, soon rose to represent the state as a Jeffersonian Republican in federal Congress and as governor. Badger died in Gilmartin, New Hampshire, on January 15, 1809.

REFERENCES

Jere F. Daniell, *Experiment in Republicanism* (Cambridge: Harvard University Press, 1970); Nathaniel J. Eisenman, "Ratification of the Federal Constitution by the State of New Hampshire" (PhD dissertation, Columbia University, 1937); Lynn Warren Turner, *The Ninth State* (Chapel Hill: University of North Carolina Press, 1983); Joseph B. Walker, *A History of the New Hampshire Convention for the Investigation, Discussion, and Decision of the Federal Constitution* (Boston: Supples and Hurd, 1888).

NATHANIEL BARRELL *(?, 1732–April 13, 1831)* was born in Boston, Massachusetts, to John and Ruth (Greene) Barrell. His father was a wealthy Boston merchant and shipowner. It is said that Barrell was descended from Abraham Barrell, a judge in the treason trial of Charles I of England. Educated for the mercantile business, young Barrell had an adventurous spirit. In 1755 he entered the army as a recruiting officer. He served in the Quebec expedition against the French and was made a captain in 1759. In 1760 he went to England to attempt to take advantage of the new trade rights connected to the British control of the St. Lawrence River.

Sometime during the 1750s, Barrell had removed to Portsmouth, New Hampshire, to set up an export business. He served in the New Hampshire provincial council from 1763 until 1765, and joined the governor's council. Because of his close ties to England, some of the local opponents of British control of trade accused him of being a Tory. A follower of the Scots immigrant preacher Reverend Robert Sandeman, Barrell had assisted in organizing his church in New Hampshire. Sandeman believed in loyalty to the king of England and persuaded Barrell to refuse to fight against England. In 1765, feeling no longer welcome in New Hampshire, Barrell closed his business and moved to York, Maine, to live on the estate of his father-in-law. There he became a successful farmer. Supposedly, he took little part in the Revolution. While some called him a Tory, others knew that he remained neutral.

On the onset of debate over ratification of the Constitution in the territory of Maine, Barrell spoke often in York against the proposed document. A delegate to the town meeting, he was elected to serve in the Massachusetts ratifying convention. There he took part in debate, and in a lively fashion spoke against ratification. Samuel Harding, the most cogent analyst of Massachusetts's role in ratification, regarded him as a "flaming Antifederalist. . . . He would sooner lose his arm than put his assent to the new proposed Constitution" (92). Yet, by the convention's end, it has been supposed that it was his brother Joseph who persuaded Barrell to vote for the Constitution. Jackson Turner Main suggested that a series of exchanges with his father-in-law led this wealthy man to forsake the cause (203–204). Others have said that Governor John Hancock persuaded him to change his vote. Actually, Barrell did so reluctantly, believing further opposition was hopeless. Thus, he joined the active Antifederalists who at the last changed their votes.

Despite his vote in favor of the Constitution, at the convention and in letters to friends Barrell had enunciated reasons to worry about the new government and its leaders. In a letter to the Federalist George Thatcher, he laid out his opposition to the Constitution. Harding cites this letter as evidence that Barrell never really deserted his Antifederalism, and it is worth quoting from. In the letter, Barrell wrote that the Constitution encouraged corrupt and undemocratic officeholders by making it difficult to remove them from office. He said, "I see it pregnant with the fate of our liberties. . . . I see it entails wretchedness on my posterity—slavery on my children—for as it now stands congress will be vested with much more extensive power than even Great Britain exercised over us" (92–93). He opposed the six-year term for senators, and he found pay for public officials impertinent. He added, "I think such a government impractical among men with such notions of liberty as we Americans" (Peirce, 50). Speaking as a plain farmer in the Massachusetts convention, he proclaimed that the Constitution was "pregnant with baneful effects." He feared that the Constitution gave public officials too much power and believed they would infringe upon popular rights. The government, he said, would cost too much, and the ordinary people would have to pay their own oppressors. Finally, he believed the new laws too complex, and he proposed amendments to protect what he called his "zeal for liberty" (Peirce, 264–265).

This former so-called Tory had invoked the image of excessive British power. On January 15, 1788, he stood firm in his opposition. By February 6, 1788, he had joined the Constitutionalists. Barrell had actually wanted to adjourn the convention and go home to Maine to talk to his constituents about his change of heart. He desired to inform his constituents that the convention was determined to vote in favor of the Constitution, and that to save parts of the best of the deficient Articles of Confederation he had to go along with the Constitutional forces. But his political friends called him a hypocrite who had gotten elected on a staunch Antifederalist platform and then turned coat. Evidently they soon forgave him. Barrell represented York in the Massachusetts General Court in 1794. But his health soon failed, and he retired to the life of a gentleman farmer. Barrell died in York (now Maine) on April 3, 1831. He belongs among those who found much fault with the Constitution but knew they could not stop its ratification.

REFERENCES

Bailyn, *Debate*, vol. 2; Samuel B. Harding, *The Contest over the Ratification of the Federal Constitution in the State of Massachusetts* (Cambridge: Harvard University Press, 1896); Bradford K. Peirce (ed.), *Debates and Proceedings in the Convention of the Commonwealth of Massachusetts* (Boston: William White, Printer to the Commonwealth, 1856); Jackson Turner Main, *The Antifederalists* (Chapel Hill: University of North Carolina Press, 1955); George Thatcher Papers (Boston: Massachusetts Historical Society).

CHARLES BARRETT *(?, 1740–September 21, 1808)* was born in Concord, Massachusetts. His family had first settled to farm in Concord around 1640. He had little education, and almost nothing is known about his family or youth. Barrett did build along with a brother a grist and sawmill in Macon Village, Massachusetts. But in 1764 he moved to New Ipswich, New Hampshire, where he bought the farm Knight's Hill. Barrett, a Unitarian, married Rebecca Minot of Concord that same year. They would have six children.

By the Revolution Barrett had become a prominent and well-to-do farmer, and also he owned a house in Concord. He became a close political ally of New Hampshire's most powerful leader, James Atherton. Barrett served as a captain in the Revolutionary War, although some of his neighbors thought that, like Atherton, he had Tory sympathies. In 1781 he sold his New Hampshire farm and participated actively in public life. He did, however, buy land in Maine, which he farmed. But he also retained property in New Hampshire. His friends forgave his supposed Toryism and elected him to public office. Barrett became a member of the state legislature and held office for more than fourteen years.

This prominent farmer and officeholder won a close election over the important Federalist Timothy Farrer to the state's Constitution ratification convention and ably represented the people of New Ipswich, New Hampshire as an Antifederalist. There he joined the Antifederalist Joshua Atherton (q.v.) as a leader of the opposition. A wealthy opponent of the Constitution, Barrett claimed that the Constitution supported the return to British-style monarchy. He feared if the president served in office for four years it could lead to claims on the office for life. Robert Rutland wrote that "Atherton and Barrett were symbols of the resentment that Hillsborough County felt against a state government that had spurned their pleas for economic relief" (75). They led the debtor farmers in opposition to the Constitution. Barrett served on the important convention committee of fifteen that offered amendments to the Constitution. Unable to achieve a breakthrough on amendments, he voted against ratification of the Constitution. Barrett seldom spoke at the convention, but his aid to Atherton and others certainly helped the Antifederalist cause.

This Antifederalist continued in state politics for a short time. Although he farmed near Camden, Maine, in 1790, Barrett held office in the New Hampshire State Senate in 1791, 1793, and 1794. He erected a mill and soon built a series of locks to funnel energy to it. Barrett later started a cotton mill in New Hampshire. A public servant, he also assisted in founding a male school, the New Ipswich Academy, in Maine. On September 21, 1808, he died near Camden, Maine. Joseph Walker said of him that Barrett "was an impulsive man, possessed of great energy" (16).

REFERENCES

Charles H. Chandler, *The History of New Ipswich from its First Grant in MDC-CXXXVI* (Boston: Gould and Lincoln, 1852); Robert Rutland, *Ordeal of the Constitution* (Norman: University of Oklahoma Press, 1955); Edwin D. Sanborn, *History of New Hampshire, from its Discovery to 1830* (Manchester: J. B. Clarke, 1875); Lynn Warren Turner, *The Ninth State* (Chapel Hill: University of North Carolina Press, 1983); Joseph B. Walker, *A History of the New Hampshire Convention* (Boston: Supples and Hurd, 1888).

ELISHA BATTLE *(January 9, 1723–March 6, 1799)* was born in Nansemond County, Virginia. He was the son of William and Sarah (Hunter) Battle, emigrants from England. Battle's family and descendants in North Carolina were famous in that state as military, politicial, and educational leaders for generations to come. Although he had little formal education, the young man became a great reader and developed his mind. Battle served as a prominant lay leader in the Baptist church. In 1742 he married Elizabeth Sumner, and they had eight children. In 1747 he moved to Tar River in Edgecombe County, North Carolina, where he farmed 400 acres. In 1748 he removed to Rocky Mount and again farmed successfully.

This ambitious young man soon rose in public life in his region of North Carolina. Battle first entered politics as a justice of the peace in Edgecombe County in 1756, a position he held until 1759. In 1759 he became justice of the Edgecombe County Court. In 1760 Battle joined the committee to found the town of Tarboro, North Carolina. He joined the Tar River Baptist Church as deacon and clerk in 1764, and he assisted in forming the Kehukee Baptist Association, becoming its clerk in 1769. He served as a member of the colonial legislature in 1771. Battle became close to Thomas Person (q.v.), during the time that both men served as members of the Edgecombe County Committee of Safety in 1774 and 1775. An ardent patriot, he actively supported the coming of the American Revolution. In 1776 he served in the provincial congress at Halifax. Battle helped to draft the first North Carolina State Constitution, a document of which he was proud. Battle served in the state senate from Edgecombe County from 1777 until 1781, in 1783, and again in the crucial years of 1785 to 1787.

As a leader of the state senate, Battle chaired important committees. He helped to call the state ratifying convention for the federal Constitution, and in the legislature began to air the grievances of the Antifederalists. Battle became a major figure in the Antifederalist cause, as he helped to rally Baptists in the state against the Constitution. He spoke often in the convention against ratification. At the Hillsborough convention of 1788, Battle chaired the powerful committee of the whole from which he launched the movement to amend the Constitution to adopt a bill of rights. Battle especially worried over the lack of specific prerogatives for state government in the Constitution, which led him to vote against ratification of the Constitution in 1788.

This Anitfederalist leader never really came to support the Constitution. He retired to his plantation and refrained from public service after 1790. Battle died in Edgecombe County on March 6, 1799. He is buried on the family plantation.

REFERENCES

Samuel P. Ashe, et al., *Biographical History of North Carolina* (Greensboro, N.C.: Charles L. Van Nappen, 1917), vol. 2; Herbert B. Battle, *The Battle Book, A Geneaology of the Battle Family in America* (Montgomery, Ala.: Paragon Press, 1930); Lemuel Burkitt and Jesse Read, *History of the Kekuhee Baptist Association* (Philadelphia: Lippincott, 1850); *North Carolina Manual* (Raleigh: North Carolina Historical Commission, 1918); William S. Powell (ed.), *Dictionary of North Carolina Biography* (Chapel Hill: University of North Carolina Press, 1979), vol. 1; Louise Irby Trenholme, *The Ratification of the Federal Constitution in North Carolina* (New York: Columbia University Press, 1932); J. Kelly Turner and John L. Bridgers, *History of Edgecombe County* (Raleigh, N.C.: Edwards and Broughton Printing Co., 1920); John H. Wheeler, *Historical Sketches of North Carolina*, 2 vols. (1851; repr., Baltimore: Regional Publishing Co., 1964).

PHANEUL BISHOP *(September 3, 1739–January 6, 1812)* was born at Rehoboth in Bristol County, Massachusetts. Little is known about his early life save that he received a public school education. He was an innkeeper, and although he was often called the "Captain," there seems to be little reason for this title. If he served in the Revolutionary War, there is no record of it.

The Captain appears to have been pro-Shays in that 1786 rebellion in western Massachusetts. Because of his radical politics, Bishop incurred the animosity of the Federalist Jeremy Belknap. He gained much state political experience during the ratification crisis. Bishop served ably in the state legislature from 1783 until 1786, befriended other Maine leaders, and became a skilled politician. Political opponents at first refused to seat him in the legislature, as they claimed he deceived the solons by mispelling his name. Eventually, with the assistance of radical friends, he gained his seat. Bishop also served in the state senate from 1787 until 1791, where he supported the debtor cause. He again was in the state senate in 1792, 1793, 1797, and 1798.

As a member of the state ratifying convention from Bristol County, Bishop spoke out against the federal Constitution and voted against ratification. In the convention, he argued against the powers given to the federal Congress to control election dates. He feared that the liberties of his yeoman farmer allies would be lost if Congress could make an election date in conflict with their usual time of voting. Bishop also worried about excessive federal power over state governments. Specifically, he said, "In an uncontrolled representation . . . lies the security of freedom." The Federalists, he claimed, "sported" with popular freedoms (Elliot, 2, 23–24). Bishop also refused to accept Governor John Hancock's belated promise of support for a bill of rights. He wanted proposed amendments ratified by the Massachusetts convention. Van Beck Hall, a keen student of early Massachusetts politics, believed that Bishop and his fellow radical leaders rose in power because "men like Gerry, Sullivan, Winthrop, and Warren lived in commercial towns and were seldom chosen as delegates to the convention." Thus, the "most articulate or establishment Antifederalists were shut out of the Antifederalist arguments" and the shrewd political leaders like Bishop and Amos Singletary (q.v), or Maine separatists like William Widgery (q.v), had to lead the cause (275). In fact, all of those leaders in many ways made their presence felt in the cause of Antifederalism.

Remaining true to his oppositional position after the convention, Bishop opposed Federalist post-ratification economic changes while a member of the legislature. Through this action he incurred the hatred of Fisher Ames. Samuel Harding quotes Bishop as responding to hopes for amendments in the new federal Congress just after the Massachusetts convention had come to an end. Bishop wrote, "If the amendments proposed with the ratification of the late convention had been made a condition of ratification they would have gone some way tho not fully to a conciliation of our minds to the System—but your excellency [John Hancock] will permit us to say that as they now stand they neither comport with the dignity or safety of this Commonwealth" (200).

This ardent popular leader rose in Federal era politics, despite the hatred of Federalists for his obstructionism. Voters from his part of the state elected Bishop to the federal House of Representatives in 1799. He served as an ardent Jeffersonian Republican until 1807, always supporting the rights of the states. Bishop died in Rehoboth, Massachusetts, on January 6, 1812. He is buried in Providence, Rhode Island.

REFERENCES

Kenneth R. Bolling, "Politics in the First Congress" (PhD diss., University of Wisconsin, 1968); Elliot, *Debates*, vols. 2, 4; Van Beck Hall, *Politics Without Parties: Massachusetts, 1780–1791* (Pittsburgh: University of Pittsburgh Press, 1972); Samuel B. Harding, *The Contest over the Ratification of the Federal Constitution in the State of*

Massachusetts (Cambridge: Harvard University Press, 1896); Bradford K. Peirce (ed.), *Debates and Proceedings in the Convention of the Commonwealth of Massachusetts* (Boston: William White, Printer to the Commonwealth, 1856).

THEODORICK BLAND *(March 21, 1742–June 1, 1790)* was born in Prince George County, Virginia. His father, also Theodorick, was a wealthy planter, local county clerk, and leading layman in the Episcopal church. Frances Bolling, his mother, was the daughter of the wealthy planter Drury Bolling. Young Theodorick was also the nephew of Richard Bland, one of Virginia's leading revolutionaries. An only son, Theodorick's parents doted on him. They sent the delicate child to school in Wakefield, England, from 1753 to 1758. A classmate, Richard Henry Lee (q.v.), a future Virginia revolutionary leader and Antifederalist theoretician, became, along with his brother Arthur Lee (q.v.), a lifelong friend. Bland went on to Liverpool in 1759 to study medicine, and then to the prestigious medical school at the University of Edinburgh from 1761 to 1763, from which he received the M.D.

In 1764 Bland returned to Prince George County to practice medicine. He married the wealthy Martha Dangerfield. In 1771 he retired to his plantation, perhaps contemplating a life of leisure and study. But it was not to be. Throughout 1770 Bland had kept up a correspondence with Arthur Lee, who was back in England, from whom he learned much about British hostilities toward and aggravation with the colonies. In support of the patriotic cause, Bland wrote letters to the *Virginia Gazette* in which he attacked the Royal Governor of Virginia. In 1775, Bland was part of a band that removed weapons from the Governor's Palace in Williamsburg, fomenting rebellion in Virginia. In 1776, Bland became a captain of the Virginia cavalry, and in 1779 colonel of the First Continental Dragoons. He fought beside General George Washington in New Jersey and Pennsylvania, and at the battle of Brandywine in 1777. In 1779, Washington placed Bland in charge of the command post at Charlottesville, Virginia. He was present at the deciding battle of Yorktown in 1781.

Bland also had an active career in Virginia state politics. Elected to the Continental Congress in 1780, he served until 1783. Bland then returned to his plantation, Farmingdale, in Prince George County. All the time he kept up a correspondence on governmental problems with Arthur Lee. An ally of the radical Patrick Henry (q.v.), Bland kept his hand in local politics as director of the county militia. Bland entered the Virginia House of Delegates in 1786 and served until 1788. As a Henry ally, he ran unsuccessfully for governor against Edmund Randolph in 1788.

Meanwhile, Bland became a leading Virginia Antifederalist in the state legislature and served in the state ratification convention. Although he rarely spoke at the convention, Bland assisted Henry in keeping the Antifederalists united, and he sent much correspondence on Virginia's resistance to the Constitution to allies in New York and Massachusetts. He also worked closely with Antifederalist leader Joseph Jones (q.v.), and he kept Richard Henry Lee apprised of events at the convention. In a June 1788 letter to Arthur Lee, Bland claimed that the Virginia convention delegates were divided enough to ensure that amendments were forced on the proposed Constitution. In this view, events proved him incorrect. Bland's own position was that of a staunch Republican revolutionary who believed that the central government's powers as outlined in the Constitution meant the formation of a semimonarchical state. As Charles Campbell, the editor of his papers, wrote, Bland "was in the minority that voted against ratification . . . believing it to be repugnant to the interests of the country" (I, xxxi).

After Virginians had accepted the Constitution with promises of a forthcoming bill of rights, Bland acquiesced to his state's verdict. Aware of the power of the Antifederalist forces, Bland believed it was only a matter of time before his followers controlled state politics. Though he had lost in his contest for governor in 1788, his constituents sent him as an Antifederalist to the first United States House of Representatives. There, he actively opposed the assumption of state debt policies of the Federalists. Patrick Henry also enlisted Bland in a scheme to call for a second Constitutional Convention, but it came to naught. Bland, in addition, joined William Grayson (q.v.) in Congress to politick for a bill of rights. A tall but corpulent, aristocratic looking leader, he had about him the dignified manner befitting a great planter of old Virginia. Bland died while in Congress, in New York City, on June 1, 1790. He was buried at Farmingdale.

REFERENCES

Charles Campbell (ed.), *The Bland Papers: Being a Selection from the Manuscripts of Colonel Theodorick Bland* (Petersburg, Va.: S. and J. Ruffin, 1840–1843); Woody Holton, *Forced Founders* (Chapel Hill: University of North Carolina Press, 1999); Richard Henry Lee, *Life of Richard Henry Lee* (Philadelphia: H. C. Carey and J. Lee, 1829), vol. 2; Robert Rutland, *Ordeal of the Constitution* (Norman: University of Oklahoma Press, 1955).

TIMOTHY BLOODWORTH *(?, 1736–August 24, 1814)* was born in New Hanover, North Carolina in 1736. Little is known of his family background save that his father farmed, had almost no education, and lived on the lower and poorer section of the Cape Fear River. Timothy did have an older brother who looked after him and preceded his entry into late colonial politics. Bloodworth for a time was apprenticed to a cobbler, learned wheelwrighting, taught school, and declared himself a Baptist minister. It appears that he had no tolerance working for others. Even though he had little formal schooling, he educated himself and became a successful teacher.

Never much of a success as a farmer, Bloodworth's true calling was in radical populist politics. He became a leader among the radical forces in the Revolutionary War era, played a major role in the crucial debates in opposition to the federal Constitution, and served in national politics during the Federalist era. First elected to the colonial legislature in 1758, he represented Hanover County on and off for over thirty years. In 1775 he served as a justice of the peace. He was said by his biographer in the *Cyclopedia of North Carolina* to have been "a man of broad views and charitable instincts" (592). That translates into a colonial political career forged in local affairs, solicitous of his constituents' needs, and a reputation as an able organizer of voters and politicians.

In 1775 this ardent patriot chaired the New Hanover County Committee of Public Safety. As such, he came to know many of North Carolina's leading revolutionaries. For a time he had contracts to make weapons for the Continental Army. From 1779 to 1784, he served in the new state legislature. Hostile to North Carolina's Tories, he gained local fame in 1783 as commissioner of confiscated property. Bloodworth made certain his poor constituents acquired some of that land. He also served in the Continental Congress from 1784 until he resigned in 1787, in opposition to congressional support for the new Constitution. In the Congress, he opposed all federal treaty-making powers, out of fear that North Carolina's claims to western lands would be lost.

After he resigned from Congress, Bloodworth was elected to the North Carolina State Senate, a position in which he continued his opposition to the federal Constitution. His biographer in the *Cyclopedia* said that Bloodworth "held very radical views upon the subject of statesmanship and morals which carried him quite to the verge of eccentricity" (593). As a member of the state ratification convention, he became an active participant in debate, known to use personal attacks on his opponents' integrity. Not above using fear tactics, Bloodworth warned in dire terms of the fate of local government at the hands of a powerful federal entity. He also knew how to maneuver in politics, and he worked closely with Samuel Spencer (q.v.) to defeat ratification in the first state convention. He again voted against ratification in the state's second convention, despite full knowledge that his cause was lost.

Why was Bloodworth such a staunch Antifederalist? He had always been a localist, believing representative government functioned best in small areas where the voters knew their leaders. No clear and thoughtful student of political theory, he nevertheless had been an ardent revolutionary trained in hostility to oppressive government. Louise Irby Trenholme, a close student of North Carolina Antifederalist behavior, said that Bloodworth represented the poorer farmers who feared that strong central government would support trade over agrarian interests. But Trenholme also grasped a central Antifederalist tendency among some slave state leaders. She points out that Bloodworth worried that "northern states being more populous might pass laws harmful to the South" (176). In short, though he owned few slaves, Bloodworth stood with the proslavery forces of his state and region of the country. Before he died, through shrewd use of his political connections, this once poor farmer managed to accumulate 4,000 acres of land.

Bloodworth also recorded in the state debates his views of the Constitution. He spoke often of the dangers of government consolidation. He said that the state government did not have the power to secure the rights of and to protect the people. Because he knew "there was a corruption in human nature," Bloodworth looked to the free man "under no control" as the best way to secure personal freedom (Elliot, 167–168). He lashed out at the proposed court system, alleging that the federal government opposed trial by jury. Then Bloodworth revealed what really bothered him about a consolidated government. The Confederation had given up control of the Mississippi River, and North Carolinians, he maintained, had no way to expand. All measures seemed designed, he complained, to give power to the northern states and they had no interest in the welfare of the southern states. Control of the power to print money and of regulation of trade meant to him that the federal government had designs to handicap southern trade. That explains why Bloodworth and many other Antifederalists from North Carolina did not worry if the state remained out of the Union for some time. Bloodworth was taken with Thomas Jefferson's view that staying out of the Union was the only way to force amendments to the Constitution favorable to southern interests (Elliot, 179–185, 235–236).

This popular Antifederalist regional leader parlayed his leadership of local and state resistance to a northern-dominated federal government into his own national career during the Federalist and Jeffersonian eras. As lieutenant colonel of the militia, he was able to organize many Antifederalist voters in the greater Wilmington district. He was elected to the first United States House in 1790 but left national politics to serve in the state legislature in 1793 and 1794. Still, while a member of the Congress, Bloodworth worked with the New York Antifederalist John Lamb (q.v.) to try to amend the Constitution. Back in North Carolina, he helped to place the state capitol in Raleigh, and the state legislature rewarded him with elevation to the United States Senate in 1795. Bloodworth ably served there until 1801. A staunch Jeffersonian, Bloodworth became a strong sectionalist. After his term in the Senate, he took the lucrative position of collector of customs at the port of Wilmington. Bloodworth died in Washington, North Carolina, on August 24, 1814. As his *Cyclopedia* biographer said, "the public records have done but partial justice" to the life of this important North Carolina poor people's leader (12).

REFERENCES

Samuel A. Ashe, et al., *Cyclopedia of Eminent and Successful Men of the Carolinas* (Raleigh, N.C.: Edwards and Broughton Printing Co., 1925), vol. 2; Bailyn, *Debate*, vol. 2; *Cyclopedia of Eminent and Representative Men of the Carolinas of the Nineteenth Century* (Spartanburg, S.C.: Reprint House, 1918), vol. 2; Elliot, *Debates*, vol. 4; James Sprunt, *Chronicles of the Cape Fear River* (Spartanburg, S.C.: Reprint House,

1973); Louise Irby Trenholme, *The Ratification of the Federal Constitution in North Carolina* (New York: Columbia University Press, 1932); A. M. Wadsworth, *History of New Hanover County, North Carolina* (pub. unknown); John H. Wheeler, *Historical Sketches of North Carolina*, 2 vols. (1851; repr., Baltimore: Regional Publishing Co., 1964).

GEORGE BRYAN *(August 11, 1731–January 27, 1791)* was born in Dublin, Ireland, to Samuel Bryan, a Dublin merchant, and Sarah Dennis. Of Scotch-Irish Presbyterian stock, George Bryan came to Philadelphia in 1752 to operate his father's importing and exporting business. He later set up as a merchant on his own and became quite well off. In 1757 he married Elizabeth Smith, daughter of the prominent Pennsylvanian Samuel Smith. Bryan's son, Samuel Bryan (q.v.), would follow in his father's radical political footsteps.

Charming, controversial, and reckless, Bryan had a disfigured face and was ill much of his later life. Nevertheless, this successful merchant became the leader of Philadelphia's Scotch-Irish immigrants, active in his church and in political life. In his *Tit for Tat* articles of 1755, Bryan attacked Benjamin Franklin's political forces, which endeared him to the city's recent settlers. In 1758 he gained election to the Congregational Committee, the governing organization of the First Presbyterian Church. During the years 1764 to 1775, he had personal and political problems. A church separatist movement, the Sprout-Alison controversy, weakened Bryan's leadership of the Scotch-Irish. He went bankrupt in 1771, had severe health problems from 1773 to the end of his life, and he stood by helplessly as a number of his children died.

Still, Bryan became a force in Pennsylvania colonial, revolutionary, and new national politics. In 1762 he joined the prestigious commission to improve the Philadelphia harbor. In 1764 the Conservative Party elected him to the colonial assembly, where he temporarily joined the elite Proprietary Party. Named a judge of the Orphan's Court and the Court of Common Pleas in 1764, Bryan began his movement toward radical politics. Elected to the Stamp Act Congress in 1765, as a merchant he joined with others who refused to accept imports from Great Britain. In 1768, along with other radical merchants, Bryan published the *Centinel* papers. In them, he attacked those who wanted to bring Church of England bishops to the colonies because he feared the dissenting faiths would come under pressure to conform to the established church. Bryan also wrote in *Centinel* of his hostility to Parliament's restrictions on trade. Having lost much of his wealth, Bryan retired in 1772 from his merchant business to devote himself fully to insurrection against Great Britain.

When the Revolutionary War broke out, Bryan became a naval officer at the port of Philadelphia. More a political than a military position, nevertheless, in making major improvements on the port and harbor, Bryan assisted in the city's defense. He also contributed to statehood politics. Bryan became a leader of the Constitutional Party and helped to draft the radical first state constitution for Pennsylvania. As a leader of the radical Constitutionalist Party, his constitutents elected him an assemblyman and a judge of the wartime state supreme court. In that capacity, Bryan prosecuted Pennsylvania Tories and helped to confiscate their lands. He served as vice president of the State Supreme Executive Council from 1777 to 1779, a most powerful political position. That political ofice led to Bryan's becoming a member of the committee to settle the boundary dispute with Virginia. In addition, as chairman of an assembly committee on slavery, in 1779 the radical Bryan moved for the gradual abolition of slavery in Pennsylvania.

During the postwar Confederation period, the increasingly agitated leader of the Constitutional Party took on additional political duties. He also became a trustee of the young University of Pennsylvania. In 1784 Bryan was elected to the Council of Censors, where he became quite defensive about the accomplishments democratic government had made in drafting the first state Constitution. As such, he opposed the nationalizing tendencies of those who wanted to revise the state constitution. Bryan also opposed any attempt to set up a banking system designed to control the flow of the state's finances, as he believed such proposals favored the city's wealthy. He supported the powers given to the state under the Articles of Confederation and believed that the Confederation government best suited the interests of the individual states.

Bryan opposed the calling of a Constitutional Convention in the summer of 1787, and as a state Constitutional Party radical leader, he became one of eastern Pennsylvania's most ardent Antifederalists. A member of the Harrisburg convention, along with his son Samuel and western allies, Bryan took leadership in the opposition to ratification of the federal Constitution. He met with John Nicholson (q.v.) and others to serve as, in the words of his biographer John Foster, "a clearinghouse for Antifederalist information" from other states (148). Bryan believed that Pennsylvania, led by rich eastern business leaders, ratified the Constitution too quickly, and he called for a second state convention to meet in late 1788. In this he failed.

Even though the radical Antifederalist leader had been unable to forestall ratification, along with his son he left a legacy of letters called "Centinel" published in the *Independent Gazetteer* between October 1787 and November 1788. Although scholars now believe that Samuel Bryan wrote most of those letters, in their radicalism those writings ably revealed the elder Bryan's reasons for opposing the Constitution. In them, he attacked the state's wealthy leaders, because he believed their political power only led to corruption in government. For him "the consolidation of authority in any form was a mistake." Byran especially feared the power of government to tax because it would destroy the "sovereignty of state governments." Alexander Graydon, Bryan's contemporary, said, "it was . . . his passion or his policy, to identify himself with the *people*, in opposition to those, who were termed the *well-born*, a designation conceived in the genuine spirit of democracy, and which . . . he did yeoman's service to his cause" (Storing, 287).

Modern scholars of the Antifederalist period also believe that Bryan wrote the Antifederalist manifesto of 1788, *Old Whig*. Both Bernard Bailyn and Herbert Storing regard that pamphlet as an important contribution to anti-Constitution thinking. It is a document pessimistic in its content. To begin with, the author wrote, the Constitution offered no defense of a free press, and thus protection for free speech was lost. He wrote that he feared that "no amendments will ever be made without violent convulsions or civil war." For this radical Philadelphian, the major requirement for a republican government was an informed public, which was impossible if the Antifederalist opposition was unable to change the Constitution to allow for freedom of expression. The important potential political contributions of a free press had been lost (Bailyn, 122–126).

Having lost in his bid for a second Constitutional Convention to force a bill of personal rights and to provide for a free press, Bryan felt defeated. He wrote his ally, Governor George Clinton of New York (q.v.), that he had tired of public life. Still, the enfeebled and discouraged radical continued to oppose the powerful Robert Morris head of the Bank of North America located in Pennsylvania, attempted to be vigilant in protection of the state constitution, and reentered the public scene to resist calls for the state Constitutional Convention of October 1789. In 1790 his son Samuel hoped to build on his father's antislavery reputation to get that elder statesman elected governor. Broken in health, perhaps even senile, the senior Bryan died in Philadelphia on January 27, 1791, before the election. His biographer, Joseph Foster, believed him a most important Antifederalist, who had given his life to the cause (160). Joseph Reed, a contemporary, said of Bryan that he was "an ardent Constitutionalist, and a man of great integrity and independence of character." Reed stated of Bryan and his allies, "There never was a braver or truer set of men" (197).

REFERENCES

Bailyn, *Debate*, vol. 1; Joseph S. Foster, *In Pursuit of Equal Liberty: George Bryan and the Revolution in Pennsylvania* (University Park: Pennsylvania State University Press, 1994); Alexander Graydon, *Memoirs of a Life, Chiefly Passed in Pennsylvania* (Harrisburg, Pa.: Printed by John Wyeth, 1811); Burton Alva Konkle, *George Bryan and the Constitution* (Philadelphia: W. J. Campbell, 1922); William B. Reed, *Life and Correspondence of Joseph Reed* (Philadelphia: Lindsay and Blakiston, 1847); Storing, *Complete*, vol. 2.
Bryan's letters are in the Historical Society of Pennsylvania, and his diary is at the Library of Congress.

SAMUEL BRYAN *(September 30, 1759–October 6, 1821)* was born in Philadelphia, Pennsylvania. He was the eldest son of the merchant, political activist, and Antifederalist leader, George Bryan (q.v.). His mother, Elizabeth Smith, was the daughter of an important Philadephia merchant. He gained an education in local schools, and as a youth, he worked in his father's company. When the merchant business went bankrupt, Samuel took a number of odd jobs and joined his father in politics. Too young to participate in the American Revolution, he nevertheless supported the patriot cause.

During the immediate postwar period, Bryan served as secretary to the powerful state Council of Censors in 1784. Bryan had supported the first Pennsylvania State Constitution, and he was allied with his father in the Constitution Party, an organization opposed to the wealthy merchants and bankers of Philadelphia. He believed those eastern business leaders were bent on rewriting the state constitution to favor their interests, and Bryan helped to forge a political bond with western Pennsylvania farmer interests who supported both the state constitution and the Articles of Confederation as beneficial to their values and interests. In a close vote, thirty-three to thirty, he was elected clerk of the state assembly in 1785, a position he held until 1786. Altogether he had worked long and hard in learning the politics of state governance. If he had held no major elective office as yet, Bryan had trained ably for the impending political and intellectual struggles over ratification of the United States Constitution.

In 1787 Bryan became an ardent Antifederalist. He served as the principal author of the famous "Centinel" essays, published in the Philadelphia *Independent Gazette*, and became a major political leader of Antifederalist politics. Bryan immediately attacked the integrity of the Federalists' position on government powers. He held little faith in the Federalist view that separation of political and governmental powers checked strong government, the principal threat to individual liberty. Bryan claimed that the intricate government structured in Federalist #10 only confused people so that they would not see the tyranny of the rulers. Too much of an idealistic English emphasis on aristocratic public servants existed in the proposed Constitution, he said. Instead of balance between competing interests, Bryan envisioned a government under the control of the aristocrats. The proposed federal lower house he regarded as having too few members to adequately represent the people, and the Senate he believed to be totally unequal in powers to its small numbers. Bryan also worried about the size of the new country, and he suggested that it was inimical to democratic principles. Bryan wrote, "From this investigation into the organization of this government, it appears that it is devoid of all responsibility or accountability to the great body of the people, and that so far from being a regular balanced government, it would be in practice a permanent ARISTOCRACY" (Bailyn, 61). Bryan called for a bill of rights to ensure freedom of expression and the press, to protect property, to give rights to a person to confront accusers and bear arms, and to allow for a militia instead of a standing army. He proclaimed that the new Constitution would abuse the rights of Pennsylvanians. It was "a conspiracy against the liberties of a free people" (Bailyn, 690). As such, he applied his pen along with his political activities to lead the Pennsylvania minority who opposed ratification.

The Antifederalists lost the struggle to defeat ratification in Pennsylvania, but Bryan became famous as a radical polemicist. Along with Robert White-hill (q.v.), he wrote the "Dissent of the Pennsylvania Minority," a ringing charge of corruption and secrecy in the Philadelphia Constitutional Convention. The work circulated among Antifederalists throughout the nation. As Saul Cornell pointes out, "Centinel" was also widely circulated among and thus influenced the debates in a number of states. Parts of that document continue to be reprinted in anthologies today. Bryan not only appealed to western farmers, but he also influenced the emerging Philadelphia middle classes, especially on the matter of democratic principles. That he believed the state government served as the best guardian of popular liberty made him a force in state politics. It was in the marketplace of ideas, according to Cornell, that Bryan shined (99–105).

As his father grew ever weaker, Bryan continued the family tradition of political opposition. During the post-Constitution period, he spoke out often on issues of local rights. He opposed the movement to revise the state constitution and opposed calls for a state convention in October 1789. Bryan also published ten more "Centinel" articles, these being in opposition to state constitution revisions. In doing so, he made an enemy of the powerful Federalist banker Robert Morris, and in 1790 lost his bid for election as clerk of the state senate. But he still had friends in high places, and in 1795 Governor Thomas Mifflin appointed him state register general, a position he held until 1801. In 1799, realizing he had no future in Philadelphia politics, Bryan moved to Lancaster, the state capital. There he continued to receive appointments to petty offices. 1801 found him in the elevated position of state comptroller general. Bryan had become a supporter and personal friend of Governor Thomas McKean, but the governor soon removed him from office, ostensibly for refusing to follow state laws. In 1807 Bryan lost an election for state treasurer. In 1809 he went back to Philadelphia, where he served as register of wills until 1821. He had lost his campaign for the lucrative post of collector of the port of Philadelphia. Always loyal to the emergent Republican Party, even when a number of his allies joined with the radical state's rights Quids, Bryan remained a Jeffersonian. Bryan died in Chester County, Pennsylvania, on October 6, 1821.

REFERENCES

Douglas M. Arnold, *A Republican Revolution: Ideology and Politics in Pennsylvania, 1776–1790* (New York: Garland Publications, Inc., 1989); Bailyn, *Debate*, vol. 1; Robert Brunhouse, "Counter-Revolution in Pennsylvania, 1776–1790" (PhD diss., University of Pennsylvania, 1940); Saul Cornell, " 'Reflections on the Late Remarkable Revolution in Government': Aedanus Burke and Samuel Bryan's Unpublished History of the Ratification of the Constitution," *Pennsylvania Magazine of History and Biography* 112 (1988): 103–130; Russell Jennings Ferguson, *Early Western Pennsylvania Politics* (Pittsburgh: University of Pittsburgh Press, 1938); Joseph S. Foster, *In Pursuit of Equal Liberty: George Bryan and the Revolution in Pennsylvania* (University

Park: Pennsylvania State University Press, 1994); Sanford W. Higginbotham, *The Keystone of the Democratic Arch, 1800–1816* (Harrisburg, Pa.: Pennsylvania Historical and Museum Commission, 1952); Glenn W. Jacobson, "Pennsylvania and the Federal Constitution of 1787: Radicalism Versus Conservatism in a Democratic State" (master's thesis, Kent State University, 1957); Storing, *Complete*, vol. 2.

AEDANUS BURKE *(June 16, 1743–March 30, 1802)* was born in
Galway, Ireland. Little is known about his early life save that he came from a prosperous farming family. He studied for the Roman Catholic priesthood at the College of St. Omer in France but soon dropped out, but not before he received an excellent classical education. In 1769 he emigrated to North America where he studied law in Stafford County, Virginia. In 1775 Burke settled in wealthy Charleston, South Carolina to practice law.

Antagonistic to Great Britain and an early supporter of Charleston's Sons of Liberty, Burke welcomed the coming of the American Revolution. He joined the Continental Army and served as a lieutenant of the Second South Carolina Continental Regiment until 1778. In that year, this excellent lawyer resigned from the army to become associate justice of the South Carolina Court of Common Pleas. He remained an active judge until December 1779. In that capacity, Burke assisted in establishing republican government in the new state. Like his fellow patriots, he fought to defend Charleston from British invasion. He served as a militia captain from 1780 until 1782, though British occupation forced him to flee Charleston. Present at the battle of Yorktown, the staunch republican expressed glee at the surrender of the hated British.

A strong supporter of the government under the Articles of Confederation, especially the policies sustaining small federal government and strong state authority, Burke had an active political and writing career in his adopted city during the Confederation period. In 1781 he gained election to the state legislature as a representative of St. Philip and St. Michael parish, and served in that capacity again in 1782 and in the years 1784–1789. In 1782 Burke joined the committee to revise and write a digest of state laws. He published his own edition of the state laws in 1789. Burke also believed that the Charleston Tories who had remained in South Carolina should be forgiven and reintegrated into society. Writing as "Cassius" in 1783, Burke published *An Address to the Freemen of South Carolina* in which he urged "no scars to divide this group from that" and desired "one harmonious democratic-republican society" (Rogers, 78). He even hid to avoid having to prosecute men who had once been his friends.

A keen student of social relations, Burke took umbrage at what he believed was a conservative post-Revolutionary trend in his state. In 1783 he published *Considerations on the Order of the Cincinnati*. Burke opposed founding that society made up of ex-fellow officers, believing the organization meant to establish an American aristocracy. He also was well aware that British merchants had come to South Carolina after the war with the intention of competing with local merchants for trade. The British demanded the right to sue the merchant community for restitution of lost Tory property, and Burke defied them. He turned once again to his facile and learned pen to protest the harm to native businessmen. The historian George Rogers has established that Burke wrote and published in 1786 *A Few Salutary Hints, Pointing Out the Policy and Consequences of Admitting British Subjects to Engross Our Trade and Become Our Citizens.* General Nathanael Greene assisted him in gathering facts for that important pamphlet, as local businessmen rallied around Burke's leadership. Louise Bailey and Elizabeth Cooper maintain that "Burke's real fear was that the state would become embroiled in a power play among special interest groups and that the common man would be deprived of his rights" (106).

Because of those cares, Burke soon found himself at odds with some of his friends over the proposed ratification of the Constitution in South Carolina. He used ties to the Bryan family in Philadelphia, Abraham Yates (q.v.) in New York, and Elbridge Gerry (q.v.) in Massachusetts to gather information against the Constitution. Burke both wrote and politicked to defeat the proposed Constitution. At the South Carolina ratifying convention, he assumed leadership, along with Thomas Sumter (q.v.), of the backcountry farmers' opposition to the Constitution. Burke wrote openly of his fears of a conservative conspiracy to take over the entire country, as he regarded the eligibility of the president to serve successive terms as a means of perpetuating aristocratic power and perhaps even leading to a monarchical government. He represented the district between the Broad and Saluda Rivers, and he served on the convention's committee of elections and rules and orders. In June 1788, Burke wrote a long letter to John Lamb (q.v.) explaining why he believed New York ought to oppose the Constitution. To Lamb he also lamented the South Carolina minority's weakness, and he held out little hope to stop the Federalist majority. Still, he voted against ratification. George Rogers said of Burke that he led the Antifederalist forces in the State ratifying convention (83).

After the debates and South Carolina's ratification, Burke reconciled himself to the new Constitution and ran for the first federal Congress. He gained election even though the Federalists opposed him. Burke then joined in the opposition to Alexander Hamilton's plans for a new national economy. The old Antifederalist opposed the excise tax and the formation of the Bank of the United States. But Burke did want the government to assume the cost of state debts, and he favored a strong state militia. A supporter of the proposed Bill of Rights, Burke rejected the final version of the first ten amendments to the Constitution in the belief that they did not adequately protect individual freedoms.

As an opponent of the new government, Burke decided to write a history of the Antifederalist movement to point out the dangers of that government. He gathered all of his speeches and letters from the state conventon in preparation for his book. Burke wrote Samuel Bryan of Pennsylvania and Elbridge

Gerry of Massachusetts asking a series of questions about Federalist activities in their states. Principal to his concern was fear that the Federalists in government attempted to block freedom of the press. He worried that Federalist propagandists would use their power to persuade the citizenry that they meant to share power with the states, when of course he believed they did not. Burke's attempts at historical reconstructionism were designed to prove to the people that the Federalists had deceived them over their true intent. Saul Cornell points out that through his history of those events Burke also wanted to "further the cause of republicanism" (104). He "saw the movement for the Constitution as the outcome of a deliberate plot against liberty by a secret cabal" (105). Unfortunately, Burke never found the time to write his history, perhaps because he was too busy in politics opposing the Federalists. Nevertheless, as Cornell points out, Burke's questions put to Bryan and Gerry reveal that he had the wherewithal to have written "the most complex historical inquiry undertaken by anyone involved in the ratification struggle" (103).

Indeed, this loyal Carolinian continued to voice his worries even as Federalist dominance began to fade. Burke, having become an ardent defender of southern slavery, opposed the Jay Treaty of 1795, believing it stifled the growth and expansion of slaveholding society. As his national career waned, Burke rekindled his interests in local affairs. His previous work on the state's statute law had influenced the revised version of the South Carolina Constitution, which he helped to write in 1790. Burke had remained on the local courts, and in 1799 he was named chancellor of the Court of Equity. In 1799 he also served as a second for an Aaron Burr duel. Burke died in Charleston on March 30, 1802, leaving in his will a brace of pistols to Burr.

Burke had never married. He lived the life of a prominent bachelor about town. His friends in the local Hibernian Society regarded him as a man of integrity and sincerity. His Burr relationship also showed him as an independent and eccentric republican. Others in Charleston felt the sting of his bitter denunciations of conservatives and called him a vulgar immigrant with a loud Irish brogue. To the regret of history, Burke had his correspondence and unpublished manuscripts burned after his death.

REFERENCES

N. Louise Bailey and Elizabeth Ivey Cooper (eds.), *Biographical Directory of the South Carolina House of Representatives* (Columbia: University of South Carolina Press, 1981), vol. 2; Aedanus Burke, *A Few Salutory Hints* (Charleston: Burch and Haswell, 1786); Saul Cornell, " 'Reflections on the Late Remarkable Revolution in Government': Aedanus Burke and Samuel Bryan's Unpublished History of the Ratification of the Constitution," *Pennsylvania Magazine of History and Biography* 112 (1988): 103–130; John C. Meleney, *The Public Life of Aedanus Burke* (Columbia: University of South Carolina Press, 1989); John Belton O'Neal, *Bench and Bar of South Carolina*

(Charleston: S.J. Bryan, 1851); Benjamin F. Perry, *Biographical Sketches of Eminent American Statesmen* (Greenville, S.C.: no pub., 1860); George C. Rogers, Jr., "Aedanus Burke, Nathanael Greene, Anthony Wayne, and British Merchants of Charleston," *South Carolina Historical Magazine* 67 (1968): 75–83; Storing, *Complete*, vol. 5.

LEMUEL BURKITT *(April 26, 1750–November 5, 1807)* was

born on Yeopin Baptist Church land, near Edenton, Chowan County, North Carolina. He was the son of Thomas and Mary (Evans) Burkitt. Burkitt received a local education and became active in his church. In 1771 he was baptized and ordained a Baptist minister. Burkitt preached in eastern North Carolina and southeastern Virginia, but mainly had churches in Bertie County, North Carolina. In 1773 he founded the Kehukee Baptist Association, and became its historian. In 1775 Burkitt led the split in the Church over support for the American Revolution. He also farmed and owned 935 acres and eleven slaves. In 1778 he married Hannah Ball, daughter of a Baptist minister. They had seven children. In 1807 the widower married Prudence Watson.

After the Revolution and during the crisis over ratification of the Constitution, Burkitt allied with the prominent Baptist political leader Elisha Battle (q.v.). As an elder in his church, he met with other leaders and spoke out against ratification. His principal concern was over the size of land given to and the location proposed for the federal government. He regarded the potential site as a "walled fortress . . . to enslave the people, who will be gradually disarmed" (Bailyn, 1155). He also spoke out about his fears for the rights of states and personal liberties. Burkitt's efforts to incite religious opposition to the Constitution make him an important figure in the movement. The state's Federalists attempted to besmirch his reputation, but the local voters sent him to the convention anyway. Burkitt gained election to the first state ratification convention at Hillsborough in 1788, representing Hertford County. He also was instrumental in getting the effective politician Elisha Battle elected chair of the convention. Burkitt was furthermore allied with the important Antifederalist Willie Jones (q.v.).

Burkitt probably returned to the pulpit soon after ratification. It is known that he worked on a history of the Baptist Church in North Carolina, and he continued to farm his land. He also wrote an *Abridgement of the English Grammar* in 1793 and the *Concise History of the Kehukee Baptists* in 1803. He died at his plantation in Hertford County, on November 5, 1807.

REFERENCES

Samuel A. Ashe, *Biographical History of North Carolina* (Greensboro, N.C.: Charles L. Van Nappen, 1925), vol. 2; Bailyn, *Debate*, vol. 2; Lemuel Burkitt and Jesse Read, *History of the Kehukee Baptist Association* (Philadelphia: Lippincott, 1850); *North Carolina Manual* (Raleigh: North Carolina Historical Commission, 1917); George Washington Paschal, *History of the North Carolina Baptists* (Raleigh: The General Board, North Carolina Baptist State Convention, 1930), vol. 1; William S. Powell (ed.), *Dictionary of North Carolina Biography* (Chapel Hill: University of North Carolina Press, 1979), vol. 1; Louise Irby Trenholme, *The Ratification of the Federal Constitution in North Carolina* (New York: Columbia University Press, 1932).

WILLIAM BUTLER *(December 17, 1759–November 15, 1821)*

was born in Prince William County, Virginia to James and Elizabeth (Simpson) Butler. Young Butler received an education in local schools. In 1772 his father moved the family to the Ninety-six District of South Carolina. An ardent western patriot, Butler served in the early Indian campaigns of the American Revolution, including the 1776 expedition against the Cherokee. In 1779 he held the rank of lieutenant in Pulaski's Legion under General Benjamin Lincoln. In 1780 he served with General Andrew Pickens at the siege of Augusta, and he became a captain of Pickens's mounted rangers in 1782. Butler's major contribution to the war effort was to help rid the South Carolina backcountry of loyalists.

In the fluid land-acquisition days after the Revolution, Butler received a grant of 635 acres in 1785 in the lush land of the Ninety-six District. In addition, he owned much land near Edgefield. Butler owned forty-five slaves and rose to become a successful planter. In 1784 he married Behethland Foote Moore, from a planter family. They had eight children, including the later South Carolina leaders Andrew Pickens Butler and Pierce M. Butler. His grandson, Matthew Calbraith Butler, would become a Confederate general.

As a rising planter, Butler entered the South Carolina state legislature in 1787 and served continuously until 1795. He became sheriff of the Ninety-six District in 1791. Representing the western part of the state in the Constitution ratifying convention, Butler led the antiratification forces there. In the convention, he spoke out against federal encroachment on state and local prerogatives. An ally of the radical James Lincoln (q.v.), together they argued against the idea of the federal government's right to set impost duties. In fact, even before the days when cotton became king, Butler understood that South Carolina, an agricultural exporting state, would be immeasurably hurt by high impost duties. Accordingly, Butler joined the minority that voted against ratification.

Continuing in public life after the convention, Butler rose steadily in popular recognition. He was a member of the state constitutional convention of 1790 and helped to revise that document. He again served as sheriff of the district in 1794, 1798, and 1800. A rising Jeffersonian Republican, Butler ran for the federal Congress in 1796, only to lose to the Federalist Robert Goodloe Harper. Elected to Congress in 1800, he served through 1813 and retired from public life in 1815. While in Congress, Butler supported the movement to recall judges and United States Senators, believing that to serve was a privilege not to be abused. In 1810 he chaired the committee that brought charges of treason against General James Wilkinson. An ardent supporter of slavery, Butler opposed all antislavery measures in the federal Congress. He also revived his military skills for the war of 1812. He became a general in command of the upstate militia, and became major general in command of all troops in defense of South Carolina during that war. When offered an appointment in the United States Army, Butler declined, maintaining his preference was to serve his state first.

After his retirement from public life, Butler returned to his plantation in Ninety-six, and he supported the spread of the Methodist Church into the upcountry. Butler died at his plantation, Mount Willing, in Edgefield County, South Carolina, on November 15, 1821. He is buried in the family cemetery there.

REFERENCES

N. Louise Bailey and Elizabeth Ivey Cooper (eds.), *Biographical Dictionary of the South Carolina House of Representatives* (Columbia: University of South Carolina Press, 1981), vol. 4; Elliot, *Debates*, vol. 4; Emma Plunkett Ivey, *As I Find It: Butler* (Atlanta: E. P. Ivey, 1968); *Journal of the South Carolina Convention of 1788* (Charleston: State Printer, 1801); George C. Rogers, *Evolution of a Federalist: William Loughton Smith* (New York: Columbia University Press, 1955); Thomas P. Slider, *Memoirs of General William Butler* (Atlanta: J. P. Harrison and Co., 1885).

C

SAMUEL JORDAN CABELL *(December 15, 1756–August 4, 1818)* was born in Albemarle County, Virginia. He was the son of William Cabell (q.v.) and Margaret (Jordan) Cabell. His father belonged to an old and important Virginia family. William had been a member of the state conventions of 1776 and 1777. He also became a leading Antifederalist. Young Samuel entered the privileged classes, as he prepared for college at the prestigious school of the Reverend Peter Fontaine. He joined a number of relatives who attended the College of William and Mary in Williamsburg, Virginia. There, during the years 1772 to 1775, he studied with the great jurist George Wythe. Like many a young planter, Cabell joined the Revolutionary army. He served as a captain with the Amherst County volunteers in 1776, as a major of the Sixth Virginia Regiment in 1777, became an aide to General George Washington from 1778 to 1779, and rose to the rank of lieutenant colonel. Cabell served heroically at the battle of Trenton, New Jersey, in 1777. He fought in the defense of Charleston in 1780, was made a prisoner of war, and was repatriated in 1781.

After the war, Cabell turned to planting and in 1785 lived at "Soldier's Joy" in Nelson County. In 1781 he married Sarah Syme, whose father was the half-brother of Patrick Henry (q.v.). Cabell also took his accustomed place in political life. Elected to the Virginia House of Delegates in 1785, he served continuously until 1792. Cabell served on the important Committee of Claims in 1785, 1787, and 1788. Along with his father William, he gained election to the Virginia Constitutional ratifying convention in 1788. James Madison identified him as a strong Antifederalist. A friend of the localist defender of the Articles of Confederation Benjamin Harrison (q.v.), Cabell joined the Antifederalist cause representing Amherst County and spoke out against ratification. Like many others in Virginia, he worried about how his large and wealthy state fit into a new nation with a strong central government. Cabell supported Patrick Henry in his demand for amendments to the Constitution. At the convention, he voted against the ratification of the Constitution.

Continuing in the House of Delegates in the new nation, Cabell opposed the growing Federalist central government. He ran for the federal Congress in 1795 in the Albemarle District against the Federalist Francis Walker, and, with the assistance and support of former Antifederalists John Dawson (q.v.) and James Monroe (q.v), gained election. Cabell served the Republican cause continuously until 1803. A follower of Thomas Jefferson, Cabell distrusted a strong national government. In 1797 the Federalists in Congress accused Cabell of being pro-French because he had written that President George Washington had tried to provoke war with France. The Antifederalist retaliated with the accusation that Federalist judges interfered with the policies of Congress. Jefferson came to Cabell's defense and the Virginia Republican gained from the confrontation. Richard Beeman wrote that "Cabell, a popular Virginia congressman, was speaking out courageously against the policies aimed at increasing United States dependence on Great Britain at the expense of republican France and agrarian Virginia" (172). In 1803 Cabell lost his bid for re-election to Thomas Mann Randolph, President Jefferson's son-in-law.

After retirement from Congress, Cabell returned to his plantation of some 5,000 acres in Nelson County. He also served as a local justice of the peace. Cabell died there at Soldier's Joy near New Market, Virginia, on August 4, 1818. He is buried in the family cemetery.

REFERENCES

Sara B. Bearss, et al., *Dictionary of Virginia Biography* (Richmond: Library of Virginia, 2001), vol. 2; Richard Beeman, *The Old Dominion and the New Nation* (Lexington: University Press of Kentucky, 1972); Alexander Brown, *The Cabels and Their Kin* (Boston: Houghton Mifflin, 1895); Hugh Blair Grigsby, *The History of the Virginia Federal Convention of 1788* (1828; repr., New York: Da Capo Press, 1961), vols. 1 and 2; Jensen and Kaminski, *Documentary History*, vols. 9 and 13; Samuel P. Jordan, *Political Leadership in Jefferson's Virginia* (Charlottesville: University Press of Virginia, 1983); Jackson Turner Main, *The Antifederalists* (Chapel Hill: University of North Carolina Press, 1961); Norman K. Risjord, *Chesapeake Politics* (New York: Columbia University Press, 1978).

WILLIAM CABELL *(March 13, 1730–March 23, 1798)* was born

at Licking Hole Creek, Goochland County, Virginia. He was the son of William Cabell and Elizabeth Burke. The elder Cabell had been born in England and trained as a physician. He came to Virginia in 1726 and quickly rose in provincial public life. An Indian fighter and a surveyor, he also practiced medicine, planted, and became sheriff and justice of the peace. The family moved probably during the 1740s to Union Hill in Albermarle County, later Amherst County, where the elder Cabell planted. He took his place on the local Church of England vestry, his due as the most successful planter in the county of Amherst.

Accorded the privileges of wealth, young Cabell had private tutors at home and later attended the prestigious College of William and Mary. Also elected to the Episcopal Church vestry, at the young age of twenty-one, he used his family's prominence to enter politics. In colonial Virginia, leading families rose in local politics through church polity and volunteering for public service. Cabell next became county sheriff. Both positions were regarded as stepping-stones to provincial political power. Cabell married Margaret Jordan in 1756, also from a wealthy planter family, and they had a number of children. In 1761 Cabell served as presiding magistrate of Amherst County. He variously held posts as a surveyor (also seen as land speculators) and county coroner, and became a stockholder in the Hardware River Iron Company and the James River Canal Company. Cabell's father arranged the deed of a 2,700-acre grant for him from crown lands. Thus, this privileged young man entered the ranks of Virginia's wealthiest tobacco planters.

As he rose in public service, Cabell's local farmer constituents elevated him to the House of Burgesses as early as 1756. In the Burgesses, he hoped to achieve reconciliation with England and to avoid the growing clashes over trade, the church, and local government authority. But in 1769 Cabell turned revolutionary. A delegate to the Virginia revolutionary convention of 1775, he also served on the Committee of Safety. In 1776, Cabell became a member of the committee that drafted the Virginia Declaration of Rights. Throughout the Revolution, he served in the state senate from his district. He declined to become a member of the Council of State in 1781. In 1782 he chaired the legislative committee on religion and favored a statute of religious freedom. At the close of war, Cabell hoped to retire from public life.

During the Confederation period, Cabell, who had become a close ally of Patrick Henry (q.v.), returned to the state legislature. He held office in 1781–1783, and again in 1787–1788. Along with other wealthy planters from his region of the state, he came to oppose the new proposed federal Constitution. Elected to the state ratification convention of 1788, Cabell spoke out against the Constitution. He attempted to persuade Governor Edmund Randolph to support the Antifederalists, but failed. Cabell also kept the tally of supporters for Patrick Henry, served as a behind-the-scenes organizer of Antifederalist forces, and became a powerful member of the Committee on Privileges and Elections. Federalists regarded him as one of the Constitution's fiercest opponents. Cabell spoke infrequently, but when he did, he made his views tell. He opposed the powers of Congress to tax, because he regarded the control of the purse as detrimental to local needs. Cabell also joined with others to demand prior amendments to the Constitution before the delegates could defend ratification. Along with his son, Samuel Jordan Cabell (q.v.), Cabell voted against ratification.

After the debates had ended and seeking to reconcile the state's opposing forces, as a Virginia presidential elector Cabell voted for George Washington in 1788. But he also attempted to keep James Madison from being elected to Congress. Worried over divisions in the state and tired from local strife, Cabell retired from public office to lead the life of a gentleman planter. He became a director of the James River Company. He had served in 1783 as a trustee of the newly created Hampden-Sidney College, and he continued in that capacity. He died at his plantation in Amherst County, on March 23, 1798. Cabell is buried in the family cemetery. Six feet tall, of imposing style and manner, Cabell had much energy and powerful intelligence. He was one of the conservative planters who believed fervently in the importance of local rights.

REFERENCES

Sarah B. Bearss, et al., *Dictionary of Virginia Biography* (Richmond: Library of Virginia, 2001), vol. 2; Alexander Brown, *The Cabels and Their Kin* (Boston: Houghton Mifflin, 1895); Thomas E. Buckly, *Church and State in Revolutionary Virginia, 1776–1787* (New Haven: Yale University Press, 1977); Randolph B. Campbell and L. Moody Simms, Jr., "Revolutionary Virginia: The Life and Times of Colonel William Cabell," *Virginia Phoenix* 7 (1974): 53–61; Hugh Blair Grigsby, *The History of the Virginia Federal Convention of 1788* (1828; repr., New York: Da Capo Press, 1961), vols. 1 and 2; Jensen and Kaminski, *Documentary History*, vols. 9 and 13.

DAVID CALDWELL *(March 22, 1725–August 25, 1824)* was born in Lancaster County, Pennsylvania. He was the son of Scotland-born Andrew Caldwell, who had emigrated to a farm in Pennsylvania, and Ann Stewart. The elder Caldwell also was a successful carpenter. Young Caldwell, a bright student, studied at local schools, practiced carpentry with his father, and later attended the Presbyterian College of New Jersey (Princeton), from which he graduated at the age of thirty-six. Caldwell then studied for the Presbyterian ministry. The church received his credentials in 1763 and ordained him in 1765.

That same year he took up missionary work in North Carolina, and in 1767 opened a school in Guilford County. Caldwell settled in Alamance in 1768, farmed, practiced medicine, and preached. In 1766 he had married Rachael Craighead, daughter of Dr. Alexander Craighead of Muhlenburg County, North Carolina. They had many children, some of whom went on to prominence as preachers and educators. Caldwell's school became famous, and many wealthy North Carolina planters sent their sons to it. Caldwell also took an active part in colonial political affairs, which was then thought outside the purview of clergy, especially dissenting clergy.

In 1771 he supported the Regulation cause, the western farmers' demands for equal representation in the North Carolina colonial legislature. He acted as peacemaker, warning the competing forces against violence. In 1776 Caldwell was made state clerk of the Orange Presbytery, a position of some local importance. At first he sought to avoid revolution, believing the patriot side would suffer much harm in insurrection. Still, he became a revolutionary when the war broke out. He served as a member of the state constitutional convention of 1776, and helped to write the first North Carolina Constitution.

Active in public life throughout the war, he traveled far and wide preaching rebellion. The English burned Caldwell's house and school in reprisal at the battle of Guilford Courthouse.

After the war had ended, Caldwell worried that religious skepticism was on the rise, and that the social chaos resulting from warfare had created an immoral society. Named a member of the Presbyterian synod of North Carolina of 1788, he chaired its organizational committee. Although he worried about the weakness of the Confederation Congress and wondered whether a stable government could be created in the United States, Caldwell mostly was devoted to the rights of local communities. Caldwell became an important force in Antifederalist circles. As a member of the state ratifying convention of 1788, he voted with the majority in opposition to the Constitution as it was written. Seldom speaking in debate, he worked behind the scenes with Baptist leader Elisha Battle (q.v.) to organize religious opposition to the Constitution. Caldwell's major objection to the Constitution was the absence of a religious test for holding office. He continued to worry about the place of religion in the new country, and on July 30, 1788, he went beyond tolerance to suggest that pagans stood to gain from the proposed Constitution. "Moreover," he said, "even those who do not regard religion, acknowledge that the Christian religion is best calculated to make good members of society, on account of its morality" (Bailyn, 908). Thus, he opposed inviting immigrants to these shores, and especially spoke out against Jewish people.

Caldwell's biographer, E.W. Carruthers, suggested that this preacher who represented Guilford County knew that a more organized government had to be formed, but he worried over distant central authority. Caldwell, said Carruthers, knew only a little about governmental practice, but, "being an advocate of state rights, and afraid of putting too much power in the hands of the President," he joined the opposition (247). Caldwell also revealed in his arguments a sensitivity to the opinion of his followers, a people he knew who feared the sound of marching armies and believed that too much executive patronage meant a hereditary monarchy backed with military might. Even Congress had the powers, he claimed, to remain in control of legislation for years with the support of the military (Bailyn, 861). Perhaps because of his and his friends' wartime experience with marauding British and Tory soldiers, he spoke in nearly conspiratorial terms of his fears of the army.

After the state of North Carolina finally ratified the Constitution in 1790, Caldwell returned to full-time ministry. He reopened his school, became a famous teacher, and, it is said, taught five future state leaders. He also became a landowner, with over 800 acres and 8 slaves. A staunch Jeffersonian, also active in public affairs, he supported the second war with England in 1812. At one time this preacher-teacher had been offered the presidency of the University of North Carolina. He declined, insisting he was too old for such an important office. Caldwell died in Alamance, North Carolina, on August 25, 1824, in his ninety-ninth year. A cautious but eloquent man, he had successfully bridged the gap between private devotion and public service to his adopted state.

REFERENCES

Samuel A. Ashe, et al., *History of North Carolina* (2 vols., Greensboro, North Carolina: Charles L. Van Nappen, 1908–1925), vol. 1; Bailyn, *Debate*, vol. 2; E.W. Carruthers, *A Sketch of the Life and Character of Reverend David Caldwell* (Greensborough, N.C.: Swain and Sherwood, 1842); William H. Foote, *Sketches of North Carolina: Historical and Biographical* (New York: R. Carter, 1846); Alexander Harris, *Biographical History of Lancaster County* (Lancaster, Pa.: E. Barr, 1872).

JOSEPH CALHOUN *(October 22, 1750–April 14, 1817)* was born in Augusta County, Virginia. He was one of four sons born to William and Agnes (Long) Calhoun. In 1756 the elder Calhoun moved his family to the South Carolina Ninety-six District. Young Joseph grew up surrounded by cousins and settled in the Abbeville District. Around 1779 he married his cousin Catherine Calhoun. He planted there, ran a sawmill, and eventually owned eleven slaves. During the American Revolution, he was a lieutenant and then captain of the South Carolina militia in the years 1779 to 1783.

For politicial purposes, Calhoun continued in the militia after the war, as a lieutenant colonel, and by 1809 as brigadier general. He entered the state house from the Ninety-six District and also gained election to the Constitutional ratification convention of South Carolina in 1788. Calhoun became a leader of the upcountry Antifederalists along with his friend James Lincoln (q.v) and joined the minority in opposing the Constitution.

Elected also to the state constitutional convention of 1790, Calhoun wanted to see more equitable representation in the state legislature for western farmers. He then served in the state legislature from Abbeville in 1791, 1792, 1794, and in 1795. Calhoun was elected to the state senate in 1796 and served continuously until 1808. He was colonel of state militia in 1807, largely a political position. In 1807 this former Antifederalist gained election to the federal Congress and served there until 1811. His famous nephew, John C. Calhoun, succeeded him in Congress. Joseph Calhoun staunchly supported the Jeffersonian Republicans and became an early proponent of the second war with Great Britain, like many of South Carolina's backcountry leaders who favored war as a means of gaining the expansion of the southern states.

After his retirement from politics, Calhoun returned to Abbeville to plant. After the death of his wife Catherine, Calhoun married Martha Moseley in 1802. Calhoun died at his plantation near Abbeville, South Carolina, on April 14, 1817. He is buried in the family cemetery.

REFERENCES

N. Louise Bailey and Elizabeth Ivey Cooper (eds.), *Biographical Dictionary of the South Carolina House of Representatives* (Columbia: University of South Carolina

Press, 1981), vol. 3; *Journal of the South Carolina Convention of 1788* (Charleston: State Printer, 1801); A. S. Salley, Jr., *The Calhoun Family of South Carolina* (Atlanta, Ga.: self-published, 1906).

JEREMIAH TOWNLEY CHASE *(May 23, 1748–May 11, 1828)*

was born in Baltimore, Maryland. He was the son of Richard Chase, who died young. His uncle, the Episcopal minister Reverend Thomas Chase, raised Jeremiah. Chase was the second cousin of Maryland's powerful political leader Samuel Chase (q.v.) and forever linked to the politics of that state and national leader. He studied law with his cousin Samuel in Annapolis, and Chase spent most of his life in Annapolis as a lawyer and land speculator. In 1779 he married Hester Baldwin.

An ardent patriot, he became a member of the prorevolutionary Maryland Committee of Correspondence in 1774. This supporter of independence rose in state politics during and after the Revolution. He served in the convention of 1776 in Baltimore City, having moved temporarily to that town, that made the state constitution of Maryland. Chase gained election to the state of Maryland's lower house of representatives from Baltimore from 1775 to 1777. He was on the state executive council from 1779 until 1783, and again from 1785 until 1788. In 1779 Chase had moved permanently to Annapolis. In 1783 and 1784 he served as mayor of Annapolis. During those years, he also served in the Continental Congress where he became a friend of David Howell (q.v.) of Rhode Island. He was on the committee to draft the Northwest Ordinance of 1784. Chase also held the office of tax commissioner of Anne Arundel County in 1788. In that capacity, he joined Charles Ridgely (q.v.) and his cousin Samuel in speculating in ex-Tory lands in Annapolis and the port of Baltimore. It is said that state party alignments date back to membership in the state constitutional convention of 1776 and to land speculators in the postwar period. Cerainly that was true of the political friendships Chase made and kept.

Those connections surfaced anew in the politics and ideology surrounding Maryland's position on ratification of the federal Constitution in 1788. Old state ties and commitments to local governance made a number of leaders wary of federal encroachment. Connections among the land speculators also made a number of shady leaders worry that the federal government would interfere with their schemes. At any rate, Chase joined his cousin, John Francis Mercer (q.v.), and Ridgely to oppose vigorously the ratification of the federal Constitution. Chase gained election to the state convention and soon became a leader of the Antifederalist forces. In remarks on his opposition, Chase spoke of his fears that the Federalists planned to abolish the state laws that protected personal rights. Chase called for a federal bill of rights at the convention. Although he had once owned eleven slaves, by the mid 1780s Chase wanted to free Maryland's slaves. At the state ratification convention of 1788, he spoke out against a federal Constitution that supported slavery. Chase joined the eleven other prominent leaders who voted against ratification of the federal Constitution.

After the constitutional crisis, Chase returned to state politics. He was elected to the state General Court in 1789 and served until 1805. Chase also held office in the Maryland State Senate in 1796. He became a strong Republican in a state that supported the Federalists. But his early stand on principle, his reputation as a lawyer, and his experience on the courts allowed Chase to rise despite his party loyalties. From 1806 until 1826, he was chief justice of the court of appeals. He retired from the bench in 1826. Chase died in Annapolis on May 11, 1828, and he is buried in the city cemetery. He left much land to his family, some of it confiscated from the state's Tories. Chase also left a legacy of distrust of strong federal government and fear of that government's neglect of civil liberties.

REFERENCES

Steven R. Boyd, *The Politics of Opposition* (Millwood, N.Y.: KTO Press, 1979); Edward C. Papenfuse, et al., *A Biographical Dictionary of the Maryland Legislature* (Baltimore: The Johns Hopkins University Press, 1979), vol. 1; Norman K. Risjord, *Chesapeake Politics* (New York: Columbia University Press, 1978); Robert Rutland, *Birth of the Bill of Rights* (Chapel Hill: University of North Carolina Press, 1955); Robert Rutland, *Ordeal of the Constitution* (Norman: University of Oklahoma Press, 1965); John T. Scharf, *History of Maryland* (Hartboro, Pa.: Tradition Press, 1967), vol. 2; John T. Scharf, *The Chronicle of Baltimore* (Port Washington, N.Y.: Kennikat Press, 1972); David Curtis Skaggs, *Roots of Maryland Democracy* (Westport, Conn.: Greenwood Press, 1973).

SAMUEL CHASE *(April 17, 1741–June 19, 1811)* was born in Somerset County, Maryland. His father was the Reverend Thomas Chase, born in England and rector of St. Paul's in Baltimore, of the Church of England. His mother, Martha (Walker), was from a farming family. Samuel's father tutored him, and he later studied law in Annapolis. Chase set up his practice in 1761 in Annapolis and moved to Baltimore in 1786. He married Anne Baldwin in 1762, and Hanna K. Giles in 1782 after Baldwin's death. Both marriages into families with landed wealth added prestige and personal power for Chase. The ambitious and intelligent Chase soon rose to prominence in Maryland legal and political circles.

Fiercely political, Chase served in the Maryland colonial assembly from 1764 to 1775, where he opposed the growing powers of the royal governor and the loyal Court Party. He supported the Maryland Sons of Liberty and early advocated separation from England. In 1774 Chase joined the Maryland Committee of Correspondence, in which he supported the Baltimore riots of 1774. In 1775 he was elected to the Maryland Convention of the Council of Safety, where he led in the opposition against British imports to Maryland. A delegate to the First Continental Congress, Chase supported the Confederation government, even though Maryland delayed in ratifying the Articles of

Confederation. He signed the Declaration of Independence, and backed the selection of George Washington to command the Continental Army. He also played a major role in drafting the first Maryland State Constitution. Chase would remain devoted to that document for years to come. In 1776, perhaps in a headstrong act, Chase led a failed expedition to gain support for the Revolution from patriotic Canadians. But this revolutionary also looked out for his own interests. Chase speculated in foodstuffs to sell to the Continental Army. In 1778 he attempted to corner the flour market so as to set his own price for bread to the army. When this action was discovered, Chase resigned from Congress in disgrace.

After the war ended, Chase soon redeemed himself, at least in the eyes of Marylanders. In 1783 he travelled to England as an emissary of Maryland businessmen and large farmers who wanted to collect debts owed to them by British merchants. He also contested what he believed was Britain's growing interest in new American banking practices. Chase's removal to Baltimore in 1786 soon added to his growing interests in trade. He also joined business associates in speculating in confiscated Tory property in the harbor of Baltimore with hopes to control that port and make himself a power in overseas trade. Yet, he also represented those citizens who wanted leniency for Tories and to allow them to return to Maryland. Chase used his land profits to speculate in western coal and iron land. When that venture failed, Chase went broke.

But Chase continued to influence political life in Maryland. His land speculations and attempts to control banking activities led him to take the lead among the paper money advocates in the young state. Those people believed that paper rather than hard currency was easier to borrow, and thus available to a large number of business and agrarian adventurers. Thus, Chase had joined the radical merchant and other small businessmen debtors, and had restored himself to political power in the young state.

In addition to his position among the state's debtor businessmen, Chase became a staunch advocate of the powers of the states as opposed to those of national government. Still, in 1785 Chase supported the trade convention between Maryland and Virginia that proposed shared control and responsibility for maintenance of the Potomac River. But he opposed the calling of the Constitutional Convention in 1787. Elected to that convention, Chase feared to leave Maryland politics and declined to attend. He remained a supporter of the Confederation government.

As a member of the Constitutional ratification convention in Maryland, Chase took on leadership of the Antifederalists. He wrote the famous "Caution" articles, later printed as a pamphlet and circulated throughout the states. His central argument in the articles was that all legal rights emanated from local civil society. Local civil society was, for him, the best way to represent the governed. Small government devoted to local interests, local investments protection, and divided powers between the local and the larger government together made up Chase's political values, so he said. The new Constitution, he maintained, planned to destroy local interests, and he could not allow that to happen. At the time, the politically circumspect Chase refused to acknowledge authorship of "Caution." Knowing that Maryland Federalists were in the majority at the state convention, the Antifederalist leader made the decision to join his close ally in the paper money cause, the lawyer Luther Martin (q.v.), and propose amending the Constitution to protect local rights. Martin had written the influential article "Genuine Information," and Chase had helped him develop the ideas for it. Chase failed in his efforts to obtain amendments before passage, and then voted against ratification of the Constitution.

If Chase refused to acknowledge "Caution," he did deliver a speech to the convention and then publish it in April 1788 as "Notes of Speeches Delivered to the Maryland Ratifying Convention." In the "Notes," he first spoke of the Philadelphia convention's having exceeded its authority. Realizing that it was too late to stop the juggernaut of Federalist power, Chase once again put his ideas on the powers of central government into perspective, perhaps to use in opposition at a future date. He stated that the new federal government swallowed up state governments and state legislatures. Drawing from the writings of the French political philosopher the Baron de Montesquieu, he suggested the new government could not function in such a large nation. Besides, government on the state and local level much better served human rights than did a large, impersonal federal government. Chase concluded his argument in the "Notes" with this statement: "I object because the representatives will not be the representatives of the people at large; but really of a few rich men in each state" (Storing, 79–91).

Maryland's most careful student of the Constitutional debates in the state write that Chase's radical Antifederalism may well have been because of his personal indebtedness. Certainly, Chase's heavy speculation and worries about the opportunities to rebuild the port of Baltimore had upset his political equilibrium. He did go broke from speculation and he did fear that a strong central government would make matters worse financially for local investors. As Philip Crowl said, "two years of bitter political dispute with the leading members of the Federalist party over paper money had aroused personal antagonisms which were inevitably reflected in the division of votes in the Constitution" (143). Nevertheless, Chase stands out as a powerful force in defense of state and local government.

Support for radical Antifederalism did not destroy Chase's public career. His reputation as an able lawyer gained him in 1788 the chief judgeship of the Baltimore criminal court, despite the city's heavy Federalist majority. In 1791 he became chief judge of the General Court of Maryland, even though not a few lawyers believed him crooked. Chase at that time also managed to get out of debt in ways that, to say the least, appeared questionable to some of his opponents. In 1793 the ambitious judge turned Federalist. For his apostasy, said former friends, President George Washington nominated him to the

United States Supreme Court in 1796. As a member of the highest court in the land, Chase became an advocate of an independent judiciary, a position he had opposed in the Antifederalist cause. On the Supreme Court, Chase became much too political, as he helped to craft many decisions favorable to Federalist interests.

Out of revenge and for the safety of his own party, President Thomas Jefferson wanted Chase removed from office. Chase's dubious activities to try to get John Fries off in his treason trial, his overbearing personality, and his candid partisanship gave the Republican Congress an excuse to impeach him in 1804. Luther Martin, the brilliant lawyer and old Antifederalist ally, represented Chase in his removal trial, and he was able to get Chase acquitted in 1806. It appears that Chase's blatant Federalism abated in later years, and that perhaps he remembered why once he had opposed a powerful federal judiciary. At any rate, he again became a respected justice. Chase died in Washington, D.C., on June 19, 1811.

REFERENCES

Paul S. Clarkson and R. Samuel Jett, *Luther Martin* (Baltimore: The Johns Hopkins University Press, 1970); Philip A. Crowl, *Maryland During and After the Revolution* (Baltimore: The Johns Hopkins University Press, 1943); James Haw, *Stormy Patriot: A Life of Samuel Chase* (Baltimore: Maryland Historical Society, 1980); Norman K. Risjord, *Chesapeake Politics* (New York: Columbia University Press, 1978); James T. Scharf, *History of Maryland* (Hartsboro, Pa.: Tradition Press, 1967), vol. 2; Gregory A. Stiverson and Phoebe R. Jacobson, *William Paca* (Baltimore: Maryland Historical Society, 1976); Storing, *Complete*, vol. 5; Melvin Yazawa (ed.), *Representative Government and the Revolution: The Maryland Constitutional Crisis of 1787* (Baltimore: The Johns Hopkins University Press, 1975).

ABRAHAM CLARK *(February 15, 1726–September 15, 1794)* was

born near Elizabethtown, New Jersey. His father was the successful farmer Thomas Clark, who became town alderman and later a judge. His mother was the daughter of Samuel Winans, an Elizabethtown businessman. An only child, Abraham worked with his father on the farm but was sickly, and the farm life became unsuitable for him. Clark had little schooling, but he apprenticed as a surveyor and learned to trade in land and to deal with land disputes. Although never a lawyer, Clark's expertise on land claims brought him success as a legal advisor. Clearly, this quick, alert young man gained his education through personal experience. Clark also was a Presbyterian lay leader. In 1749 he married Sarah Hatfield, daughter of a well-to-do farmer, and they had a number of children.

Legal expertise led Clark into politics. He served as clerk of the New Jersey colonial assembly from 1752 until 1756. In 1764 the New Jersey assembly appointed Clark to a committee to survey and divide the town of Bergen. Clark also became part of a team that surveyed and constructed the road from Newark to Trenton. In 1766 the citizens elected him sheriff of Elizabeth and

Essex County, a plum political office. Thus, on the eve of the American Revolution he had achieved some local prominence, especially through his work in laying out towns and road construction.

Clark joined a number of local leaders in 1774 to prepare for resistance to Great Britain. That year he became secretary of the County Committee of Safety. Stepping into a larger political venue in 1775, the citizens of Essex County elected him to the provisional state congress. He assisted in drafting the first state constitution. Elected to the Second Continental Congress in Philadelphia in 1776, Clark signed the Declaration of Independence. Active in the Third Continental Congress, he supported funding the war effort in both Congress and the New Jersey legislature. In 1779 he spoke out about his fear that the government and the military leadership were not giving enough assistance to the ordinary soldier. Clark then took a leadership role in raising funds for and supplying General George Washington's army. During the war, he coined what became "Clark's Law," a reference to his opposition to special privilege for lawyers and to inflationary paper money. He had become a radical leader of the young state's ordinary people, whom he believed to be victims of lawyers and bankers.

During the Confederation period after the war, Clark remained in the Continental Congress. He took a leadership role in advocating release of prisoners of war, believing they could be productive members of society. In 1786 he wrote *The True Policy of New Jersey Defined*, in which he laid out his grievances against excessive fees to lawyers. That document turned former army officers and lawyers into his bitter enemies. Clark also advocated defining the western limits of states, in the belief that small states like New Jersey would be lost in the sweepstakes to settle western land. He also worried that a commercial treaty with England favored New York over New Jersey. He led negotiations for New Jersey with Governor George Clinton (q.v.) of New York over issues of commercial trade. Clark feared that New York control of Hudson River ports had damaged New Jersey trade, and he wanted some sort of accommodation. New Jersey lost in its request, and Clark became a bitter enemy of Governor Clinton. Accordingly, Clark became an advocate of closer support among the states, and he favored the Annapolis convention of 1786.

Elected to the Philadelphia Constitutional Convention of 1787, due to illness, or worry about the potential of too much central power for the new government, Clark declined to attend. Also, his old concerns about a national elite made up of former army officers and lawyers may also have influenced his reasons for opposing a convention that might attempt to strengthen the federal government and thus empower the country's elite. As a member of the Continental Congress, he had agreed to send the new proposed Constitution to the individual states for ratification, but he had severe reservations that the document had no provision for a bill of rights for the people.

Clark refused an active part in New Jersey's deliberations over the Constitution, perhaps because he knew the state's leaders overwhelmingly supported ratification. Richard P. McCormick, an excellent historian of the Constitutional struggle in New Jersey, said: "no leader came forth to rally the opposition. Abraham Clark might have essayed such a role . . . as he spoke of his fears of consolidated government, the expenses of government, and the excessive power of the judiciary" (276–277). But Clark did speak out in favor of amendments. He wrote, "strong fears remained on my mind until I found the Custom of Recommending amendments with the adoptions began to prevail" (277). Certainly he acknowledged often in those days his fears for the liberties of the people, yet later he denied he had been an Antifederalist.

Clark lost in his bid for election to the first federal Congress, as the Federalists accused him of supporting the Antifederalists. But his talents were too much in demand, and as a member of the state legislature, he became a leader on the committee appointed to settle financial accounts with the federal government. Clark gained election to the second Congress and served continuously thereafter until 1794. He was quite active in Congress. In 1794 he supported James Madison's resolution to retaliate against England's restrictions on American trade. An opponent of the discriminatory British trade policy, Clark submitted his own bill to cut off trade until England compensated American businessmen for destroying their ships and retaining western forts. He opposed John Jay's trip to England to negotiate over western territory. Later that year, in the summer of 1794, Clark suffered a sunstroke in Rahway, New Jersey and died there on September 15. He was buried on the grounds of the Rahway Presbyterian Church.

Mary R. Murrin said of Clark's life: "Clark loathed privileges, distrusted lawyers, and had few kind words for merchants" (70). Ann Clark Hart claimed he was a "rigid economist and sterling advocate of popular measures. During the whole period of his public service he proved himself an incorruptible patriot, a faithful and prudent legislator, a judicious counsellor, and a true friend of the people" (11). It can not be said for a fact that Clark was an active Antifederalist, and most of his biographers have tried to place him on the side, even with restrictions, of ratification. But his demand for a bill of rights, his defense of debtors, and his worries about government powers and lawyer corruption identify him as a leader of those few politicians in New Jersey who had reservations about the Constitution.

REFERENCES

Ruth Bogin, *Abraham Clark: Signer of the Declaration of Independence* (Madison, N.J.: Fairleigh Dickinson University Press, 1982); Ruth Bogin, "New Jersey's True Policy: The Radical Republican Vision of Abraham Clark," *William and Mary Quarterly* 35 (January 1978): 100–109; Ann Clark Hart (ed.), *Abraham Clark: Signer of the Declaration of Independence* (San Francisco: The Pioneer Press, 1923); Richard P. McCormick, *Experiment in Independence: New Jersey in the Critical Period, 1781–1789* (New Brunswick N.J.: Rutgers University Press, 1950); Mary R. Murrin, "New Jersey and the Two Constitutions," in Patrick J. Conley and John P. Kaminski (eds.), *The Constitution and the States* (Madison, Wisc.: Madison House, 1988); Carl E. Prince, *New Jersey's Jeffersonian Republicans* (Chapel Hill: University of North Carolina Press, 1964); Storing, *Complete*, vol. 2.

DeWITT CLINTON *(March 2, 1769–February 11, 1828)* was born

in Little Britain, Orange County, New York, to James and Mary (DeWitt) Clinton. His father was a Revolutionary War hero, and his mother descended from the Old Dutch of colonial New York. His uncle, whom he well served in the ratification crisis in New York, was the famed Governor George Clinton (q.v.). Young DeWitt received an excellent education, first at the school of the Reverend John Moffat, then at Kingston Academy, and at the young Episcopal Columbia College, from which he graduated first in his class in 1786. Clinton studied law with the Antifederalist Samuel Jones (q.v.), and began a successful practice in New York City. In 1796 he married Maria Franklin and later married Catherine Jones in 1819.

Clinton theoretically was too young to participate in New York ratification politics—he could neither hold office nor vote—but he actually played an important role among the Antifederalist forces. While a law student, he supported his uncle's cause by writing the influential letter "A Countryman," published in the *New York Journal* in December 1787, in which he opposed the Constitution. "A Countryman" received wide circulation in the city and the state. In that letter, he summed up Antifederalist worries about excessive central government, the problems of an unguided and uncontrolled elite, and the concerns about the lack of Constitutional safeguard for individual rights and liberties. Young Clinton also wrote a major report in behalf of the Antifederalist cause for the Poughkeepsie convention. He became private secretary to his uncle, the Governor, and assisted in the plots to reject the proposed federal Constitution. Although he would remain a supporter of small and local government the remainder of his life, this young Antifederalist well understood that the Federalist forces had prevailed and that they controlled New York City. Because Clinton planned to become involved in business activities and in political life in that city, he had to find a means to get along with its Federalist majority.

Still, "A Countryman" appeared especially to criticize "Publius," New York City's powerful Federalist, Alexander Hamilton. Though written by a young man with little experience in public life, "A Countryman" is well worth looking at as a major Antifederalist document. Clinton viewed the proposed Constitution and the Federalist defense of it as faulty on the central issue of the unity of the country. Contrary to uniting the states, the Constitution as written hopelessly divided them, said the young Antifederalist. He insisted that "Publius" had attacked the right of private conscience, and that its argument required a response. On other issues, Clinton spoke out with feeling. Slavery especially concerned him. Clinton declared that the Constitution "trifled with the Great God" who had made everyone free. With political malice, Clinton also suggested that the Federalists were determined to keep more Irish from emigrating to New York just when so many of their family members already lived there (Storing, 78). Perhaps he was preparing for his future political allegiances among the growing number of Irish voters.

In addition to his theme of unity, Clinton insisted that the Federalists had lied about the implied powers of state governments and deceived the people on the exact duties of the federal government. In fact, said Clinton, citing the Italian political thinker Beccaria, the excessive powers of the federal government kept down the common people. After all, he stated, the Federalists had met in secret and seemed in no way interested in what the people thought of the Constitution's large and dominant federal government. Publius insisted that the best and the brightest leaders made the Constitution and thus should lead the new nation, and Clinton worried about how those men would control the people under them. For Clinton, the state governments produced quality leaders closer to the interests of the people and thus less interested in personal power than the Federalists (Storing, 85–87). The youth displayed his erudition by lacing his essay with comments on the functions of the British government and referencing European political theoretical works. In particular, Clinton had seized upon the fears of many citizens that the hastily constructed document supported by worrisome conservatives like Hamilton threatened civil liberties while placing too much emphasis on the powers of a central government.

The remainder of Clinton's life is a fabled one, both in public life and in the world of business. When the Republicans fell from favor in 1795, he lost his political job with his uncle. Clinton then studied natural science in the hopes of improving his finances as an inventor useful to the young republic. In 1797 he gained election to the New York Assembly. In 1799 the Republicans regained control of the state legislature and named the young man to the United States Senate, where he became a political assistant to President Thomas Jefferson in 1801. He resigned from national office in 1803 to pursue a life of public and private service to both city and state.

From 1803 until 1815, except for the years 1807–1808, 1810, and 1811, Clinton served as mayor of New York City. In that office, he organized the Public School Society in 1806 and fortified Governor's Island. Clinton also worked on city sanitation reform, debtor relief, moved to abolish slavery, and became involved in steam navigation. Indeed, he controlled the Jeffersonian party in New York. But in 1807, former New York allies feared his power and threw him out of the party. Despite his grievances, Clinton never broke with the national policies of President Jefferson. In 1812 the Federalists nominated him for president, even though he attempted to work for both parties.

After another ill-fated venture into national political waters, with hopes to regain the favor of the people of New York Clinton took charge of the movement to build the Erie Canal to link New York with the Great Lakes. As governor of the state in 1817, he began the work to build the canal, as he expected it to enhance the trading and financial power of New York State. He retired as governor in 1823 and turned against the Albany Regency of Republican Governor Martin Van Buren. In 1824 Clinton supported the Republican cause of Andrew Jackson for president. Always a friend of state rights, always true to his Antifederalist heritage, he ended life a Jackson supporter. Clinton died at his home in Albany, New York, on February 11, 1828. He is buried on Wall Street on the grounds of the famous Trinity Episcopal Church. Though certainly the youngest of New York Antifederalists, he was by no means the least. A mercurial and brilliant man, at times his reach exceeded his grasp.

REFERENCES

Jensen and Kaminski, *Documentary History*, vol. 13; Howard McBain, *DeWitt Clinton and the Origins of the Spoils System* (New York: AMS Press, 1967); Clarence E. Miner, *The Ratification of the Federal Constitution by the State of New York* (New York: Columbia University Press, 1921); Mary R. Murrin, "New Jersey and the Two Constitutions," in Patrick T. Conley and John P. Kaminski (eds.), *The Constitution and the States* (Madison, Wisc.: Madison House, 1988); Robert R. Rutland, *Ordeal of the Constitution* (Norman: University of Oklahoma Press, 1965); David J. Siemers, *Ratifying the Republic* (Stanford: Stanford University Press, 2002); Steven Edwin Siry, "DeWitt Clinton and American Political Economy" (PhD diss., University of Cincinnati, 1986); Storing, *Complete*, vol. 6.

GEORGE CLINTON *(July 26, 1739–April 12, 1812)* was born in
Little Britain, Ulster County, New York. His father Charles was born in County Longford, Ireland, and came to the colonies in 1731 to farm in Ulster County. Ambitious and restless, young Clinton worked for a while on his father's farm before shipping out to sea in 1758 on the *Defiance*, a British privateer. He fought on Lake Ontario in the French and Indian War. During the 1760s Clinton read law in the New York City offices of William Smith, a prominent lawyer. He practiced law in Ulster County, entered politics, and in 1768 was elected to the New York colonial legislature. There he joined the political faction opposed to the loyalist Philip Schuyler. Clinton also defended the radical Alexander McDougal's right to free speech. In 1770 Clinton married Cornelia Tappan, daughter of a powerful Anglo-Dutch political leader, and thus united with the Wynkoop political faction. He had risen from the ranks of the yeomanry to take an important place in New York radical politics, and he spent the remainder of his life as a political activist.

Also radical in his support for freedom, in the colonial legislature Clinton opposed British control of New York commerce and politics. He resented excessive taxes as well as Britain's opposition to New York's expansion into the Vermont territory. Clinton was elected to the Second Continental Congress, where he voted for separation from Great Britain. In 1775 he became brigadier general of militia and took charge of the defenses of the Hudson River. Realizing he had few talents for military leadership, Clinton resigned his commission in 1777 to run for governor of the new state of New York. Thus began a career in executive leadership that would elevate him as the dominant figure of his state for nearly the next thirty years. As governor, he took charge of the wartime state finances and managed New York's considerable financial and military contributions to the patriot cause. He also helped to remove the remaining Indian forces in western New York, thus ingratiating himself with the upstate farming population.

As the war came to an end, this once staunch nationalist became a state particularist and defended upstate New York's interests against what he perceived as an aggressive Continental Congress and a New York City determined to control the entire state. In 1781 he attempted to persuade New York's delegates in Congress to reject the payment of import duties and worked with allies in the state legislature to veto any such duties. Strong on state sovereignty, Clinton boldly stated that New York had not gained from the new federal union. Again thwarted in his desire to acquire Vermont for New York, this time by the United States government, he became an ardent leader of an antifederal government party and political organization.

In the crisis over ratification of the Philadelphia Constitution of 1787, Clinton assumed leadership of New York's Antifederalists. His political allies, Abraham Yates (q.v.) and John Lansing (q.v.), with his blessing had resigned from the Constitutional Convention and thus prevented New York from recording a vote on that document. As president of the New York ratifying convention in Albany, he wrote and politicked to defeat his state's ratification of the proposed Constitution.

Although there is no absolute proof, Clinton probably wrote the seven "Cato" letters, published in Thomas Greenleaf's (q.v.) *New York Journal* from September 1787 to January 1788. Those letters were some of the most powerful and thoughtful Antifederalist arguments against the new central government created by the Constitutionalists. Herbert F. Storing, perhaps the closest student of the Antifederalist writings, believes Clinton wrote "Cato." He cites Clinton's attention to the dangers of consolidation as his major contribution to the arguments over ratification. Storing regards "Cato" as having "sufficient claim to the attention of not only the student of historical movements and personalities but also the student of Antifederalist thought" (vol. 2, 101).

Even if the letters were not his, at the least they conveyed Clinton's long-held sentiments. In those letters, the author opposed the New York City Federalist forces of John Jay and Alexander Hamilton, who would write the *Federalist Papers*, in part to respond to "Cato." The letters' central theme was the preservation of personal liberty, and the author believed only local and state government properly and adequately protected the interests of the people. Small republics and unicameral legislatures made the best government,

"Cato" stated. "Cato" also expressed fears about the vague federal powers put forth in the Constitution, believing the Federalists actually were bent on making a powerful central government instead of the mixed government they professed to support. In addition, if Congress regulated elections, the letters said, then it could decide who could run for office and who could vote for the candidates. Lastly among his many worries about the power of central government, "Cato" demanded specific rights be adumbrated with a bill of rights before any new government could be set up.

In addition to "Cato," Clinton, in his speeches at and his notes on the convention, gives many other cogent reasons for his opposition to the Constitution. Clinton's own experience led him to insist that small government best countered the office of a president, which he compared to the hated English monarchy. In addition, Clinton's notes from the state convention have proved invaluable to later scholars attempting to understand the debate's meaning. His notes are similar in tone and in ideas to "Cato." Storing also finds that Clinton's notes on the state convention relate important Antifederalist views (vol. 6, 177–191).

Both as governor and as president of the convention, Clinton attempted to maintain the appearance of neutrality. But Alexander Hamilton forced his hand, and Clinton openly took the side of the Constitution's opponents. Clinton kept in touch with his New York allies and with his close friend from Virginia, Richard Henry Lee (q.v.), and wanted to print the major arguments from around the country in opposition to ratification. But, for all his efforts, Clinton's opposition was doomed to disappointment. Despite the large majority of New York Antifederalists, when Virginia and New Hampshire announced ratification, some New Yorkers changed sides and voted for the Constitution. A close Clinton ally, Melancton Smith (q.v.) of New York City, decided to vote for the Constitution if the Federalists promised support for a bill of rights. Clinton dropped Smith and the others who had turned to the Constitution from his political organization. He later reunited with them over state rights, but the governor never again would trust them. After failure to defeat the Constitution, Clinton recommended that his Antifederalist followers accept the new government but cautioned them to adopt a stance of eternal vigilance about the powers of the new central government.

New Yorkers had become bitterly divided during the debates. Greenleaf's press had been destroyed and the Governor's house looted. Nevertheless, Clinton returned to active political life, even hoping to be named George Washington's vice president in 1792. In 1789 Robert Yates (q.v.), once and soon again to be an ally, ran against him for governor on the Federalist ticket, and Clinton barely won the election. He named Aaron Burr as New York attorney general, launching that brilliant and angry leader onto the national stage. In 1792 the Federalist-dominated state legislature took away many of the governor's powers, and in 1795 he declined to run again for office. Much too popular to retire long to his upstate farm, the citizens of New York called

Clinton back to office again in 1800. Thomas Jefferson, acknowledging his national fame, selected Clinton for vice president in 1804. Clinton wanted to run for president in 1808, but he had to again take second place as vice president under James Madison. He worked with Madison on antifederal issues and assisted in killing the bill to recharter the Bank of the United States in 1811. A War Hawk and expansionist, Clinton helped lead the forces for war with Great Britain in 1812. Clinton died in office in Washington, D.C., on April 12, 1812.

A simple and unassuming demeanor hid the brilliance and ambitions of this professed leader of the people. Throughout his life, Clinton was able to rally the ordinary people around his beliefs and ambitions. A man of integrity, he never personally profited from public office. A keen student of finances, his adroit appeal to fiscal responsibility and opposition to taxation kept him faithful to the idea of a small government with little economic power. He was one of the country's greatest reformers from the Revolution through the Federalist age and one of the most important and consistent Antifederalist leaders during the Constitutional crisis and after. His principles were reflected in the "Cato" letters, and that document remains a major statement about the dangers excessive central authority in a democratic republic posed to liberty. Elbert Herring, an old friend, wrote an oration on Clinton's death in which he captured elements of the man's character and beliefs. Herring called him a strict legal constructionist, loyal to his country, but who mostly believed in "state sovereignties in a union of interests, of objectivity and power, beholding a commonwealth of free states and of free citizens" (13).

REFERENCES

Thomas C. Cochran, *New York in the Confederation* (Philadelphia: University of Pennsylvania Press, 1932); Elbert Herring, *An Oration on the Death of Clinton* (New York: Pelsue and Gould, 1812); Major B. Jenks, "George Clinton and New York State Politics" (PhD diss., Cornell University, 1936); John P. Kaminski, *George Clinton: Yeoman Politician* (Madison, Wisc.: Madison House Publishers, Inc., 1993); M.A. Kamm, *Famous Families of New York* (New York: G. P. Putnam's Sons, 1902), vol. 1; Cynthia A. Kiener, *Trader and Gentlefolk: The Livingstons of New York, 1675–1790* (Ithaca: Cornell University Press, 1992); Clarence E. Miner, *The Ratification of the Federal Constitution by the State of New York* (New York: AMS Press, 1968); Stephen L. Schecter (ed.), *Reluctant Pillar: New York and the Adoption of the Federal Constitution* (Troy, N.Y.: Russell Sage College, 1985); Ernest W. Spaulding, *His Excellency, George Clinton, Critic of the Constitution* (New York: Macmillan Co., 1938); Storing, *Complete*, vols. 2 and 6; Papers in New York Historical Society, reprinted in 10 vols (New York: AMS Press, 1973).

ISAAC COLES (*March 2, 1747–June 3, 1813*) was born in Richmond, Virginia. His father was the planter John Coles. The younger Coles, as did many other upper-class planters' sons, attended the College of William and Mary. He owned a considerable amount of land on Church Hill in Hal-

ifax County, Virginia. Coles married an Englishwoman, at that time considered somewhat dangerous. Although suspected of being pro-England, Coles served in the Virginia militia during the American Revolution. He rose to the rank of colonel.

Like others of his status in the new state, Coles also held office in the state House of Delegates. He had previously served in the House of Burgesses from 1772 until 1774. As a representative from Halifax County, he served in office in 1780 and 1781, and from 1783 to 1788. In the assembly, Coles helped to open navigation on the Roanoke River. Also a follower of his cousin Patrick Henry (q.v.) in the Antifederalist cause, Coles served in the Virginia ratification convention of 1788. He spoke rarely but was an able ally of Henry, and helped to organize votes from delegates in the rich and conservative southside of Virginia. Coles voted against ratification of the Constitution.

Returning to his large plantation in Halifax County, Virginia, after the struggle, Coles hoped to retire to private pursuits. But Virginia Antifederalist leaders nominated him for the first federal Congress. He was one of three Virginia Antifederalists elected to that first Congress. While there, Coles helped to persuade James Madison to support the Bill of Rights. Coles voted against all procedures to limit the strength of the Bill of Rights. He served again in the United States House of Representatives from the Sixth District during the years 1793 to 1797. In 1798 Coles moved to a family plantation in Pittsylvania County, Virginia. He retired from public life and became a full-time planter. Coles died at his plantation, "Coles Hill," in Pittsylvania County, on June 3, 1813. He is buried in the family cemetery. He passed his commitment to public service onto his son, Walter, who would become a Democratic United States Congressman.

REFERENCES

Richard Beeman, *The Old Dominion and the New Nation* (Lexington: University Press of Kentucky, 1972); Steven R. Boyd, *The Politics of Opposition* (Millwood, N.Y.: KTO Press, 1979); Hugh Blair Grigsby, *The History of the Virginia Federal Convention of 1788* (1828; repr., New York: Da Capo Press, 1961), vol. 2; Cynthia Miller Leonard (comp.), *The General Assembly of Virginia, July 30, 1619–January 11, 1978* (Richmond: Virginia State Library, 1978); Albert J. Morrison, *Halifax County, Virginia* (Richmond: Everett Waddy Co., 1907); David J. Siemers, *Ratifying the Republic* (Stanford: Stanford University Press, 2002).

JOHN COLLINS *(June 8–18, 1717–March 4, 1795)* was born in Newport, Rhode Island to Samuel and Elizabeth Collins. Collins received a private education, entered the merchant trade business and became successful, and married Mary Avery.

The businessman soon became interested in public life and rose rapidly in colonial and later Rhode Island state politics. He served in the general assembly from 1774 until 1777. In 1776 the state government sent him to meet with General George Washington to plead for assistance to shore up the weak Rhode Island defenses. In 1778 Collins entered the Continental Congress, where he voted to ratify the Articles of Confederation. As an ally and close personal friend of the New Jersey localist leader, David Howell (q.v.), Coles served in the Continental Congress from 1778 until 1783. He made a name for himself as an opponent of any centralizing measures in the Congress, and especially did he resist those who opposed allowing members to send information to their home constituents. In 1786 Collins was elected governor of Rhode Island. He held that office as a leader of the "Paper Money" or antimercantile party from 1786 until 1790. While governor, he supported agrarian interests against those who wanted a stronger state government. He also led the state forces in opposition to impost duties on imports. As governor, Collins also supported the movement for legal tender laws, favored public relief, and wanted to pay off the state debt. Collins supported all radical, antimercantile power initiatives in the state.

With that record, it seems Governor Collins was destined to become an Antifederalist leader. But Keith Polishook, the historian of the Constitutional crisis in Rhode Island, said that, "[l]ong before January 16, 1790, John Collins had become a resolute Federalist" (213). As governor, he did support calling the Philadelphia Constitutional Convention. But Robert Rutland said that Collins made little effort to send delegates to Philadelphia because he believed the convention a threat to the existing Articles of Confederation (125). Collins also supported calling the state ratification convention, with the full knowledge that most of the delegates planned to oppose ratification. He had a number of New York Antifederalist friends, and many farmers in the state of Rhode Island believed he opposed ratification. On September 15, 1787 he stated that the Constitution violated the existing laws of the land (Jensen and Kaminski 227). In a letter to members of the Continental Congress on April 5, 1788, Collins explained that the popular vote in Rhode Island was against calling a convention. He stated that the people of Rhode Island opposed the Constitution as written, yet they knew some changes had to be made in the Articles of Confederation. But he also knew that the Constitution eventually had to be ratified, so in 1790 he called on Rhode Islanders to join the federal union. Yet, all his life he remained devoted to republican principles.

Those practical political activities in support of the politically inevitable led former radical allies to turn on their former leader. After Collins called on the state to go along with the Constitution, many of his old allies turned against him, and in 1790 he was dropped as their candidate for governor. Yet, there is some evidence that a few old friends supported sending him to federal Congress. Collins rejected any further political overtures, however. He left politics and became a farmer. He died on March 4, 1795, in Newport, Rhode Island. A man of ability and courage, Collins also had a vicious temper and fought back when riled. Perhaps Polishook and others misunderstood his reconciliation with ratification in Rhode Island. But his own actions and words reveal that Collins died believing himself the supporter of Rhode Island's poor Republican farmers.

REFERENCES

Bailyn, *Debate*, vol. 2; Thomas W. Bicknell, *History of the State of Rhode Island and Providence Plantation*, 5 vols. (New York: American Historical Society, 1920); *Biographical Cyclopedia of Representative Men of Rhode Island* (Providence: National Biographical Publishing Co., 1881); Steven R. Boyd, *The Politics of Opposition* (New York: KTO Press, 1979); Jensen and Kaminski, *Documentary History*, vol. 1; Jackson Turner Main, *The Antifederalists* (Chapel Hill: University of North Carolina Press, 1961); Irwin W. Polishook, *Rhode Island and the Union* (Evanston, Ill.: Northwestern University Press, 1969); Robert Rutland, *Ordeal of the Constitution* (Norman: University of Oklahoma Press, 1965); William R. Staples, *Annals of the Town of Providence: From Its First Settlement to the Organization of the City Government* (Providence: Printed by Knowles and Vose, 1843).

D

NATHAN DANE *(December 29, 1752–February 15, 1835)* was born in Ipswich, Massachusetts. His family had settled in Ipswich in 1638. He was the son of the farmer Daniel Dane and Abigail Burnham. Educated at various common schools, he excelled at mathematics. Dane worked on his father's farm until he was twenty. In a burst of energy, he prepared for entrance examinations to Harvard College in eight months, mastering Latin and Greek, and then entered in 1774. Dane graduated in 1778 with high honors. He taught school in Beverly, Massachusetts, for a time. Then Dane read law with Judge William Wetmore of Salem, and he set up practice in Beverly in 1782. Meanwhile, in 1779 he had married the widow Mary Brown. They had no children.

The Dane family had been ardent patriots but did not participate in the Revolutionary War. Young Dane, however, soon rose in state politics. He became a member of the General Court of Massachusetts and served there from 1782 until 1785. His brilliance caught the attention of local leaders, and in 1785 he was elected a delegate to the Continental Congress. He was re-elected in 1786 and 1787. Thomas Jefferson enlisted him to assist in drafting the Northwest Ordinance, in which he drew up the clause forbidding slavery in the new west. It is said that he had mediocre writing skills and lacked the art of oratory or debate, but that he had an excellent mind that enabled him to influence others. As a member of the Continental Congress, he voted to send the Philadelphia Constitution of 1787 to the states for ratification. He had opposed the Annapolis convention of 1786. By September 1787, Dane accepted the need for amendments to the Articles of Confederation but opposed discarding the Articles entirely. His vote in October 1787 remitting the proposed Constitution to the states for action appears to be consistent with the need for amendments and the right of the states to decide on those amendments.

A cautious and conservative man, Dane actually opposed the Constitution. Privately, he encouraged friends in Massachusetts and New York to join the Antifederalist cause and defeat or force amendments to the Constitution. Dane did not gain election to the state ratification convention, but he worked with opponents of ratification. In a most important letter of July 3, 1788, to the New York Antifederalist Melancton Smith (q.v.), who at that time was leaning toward shifting to support ratification, Dane set out his views on ratification and his many problems with the Constitution. That leader of strong convictions told Smith that he feared violence and social upheaval if the Constitution was not ratified. So he supported ratification, only with many amendments. Most of Dane's New York allies believed he opposed the Constitution. After all, Dane had said to them that he expected the first federal Congress to amend the Constitution.

As a Massachusetts moderate, Dane sought election to the first Congress. But his reputation as an Antifederalist led to his defeat. Instead, he gained election to the Massachusetts state Senate in 1790, and again from 1793 to 1798. In the senate, he served on a number of important committees. In 1793 he became judge of common pleas in Essex County but resigned in 1794. Dane's legal expertise led his fellow senators to name him to a committee to revise the laws of Massachusetts, to make them more democratic. He was named again to revise the Massachusetts Colonial and Provisional Law from 1811 to 1812. Dane worked closely with the celebrated jurist Joseph Story to achieve reform in those laws.

Although Dane grew increasingly deaf, he continued to practice law. He also became more and more a localist, or regionalist, in his politics. During the trade crisis before the War of 1812, he attacked the federal government's embargo of British goods. Dane gave of his own stores to feed citizens of coastal Massachusetts put out of work by the embargo. In 1814 he attended the Hartford convention but did not advocate secession from the Union. Dane gained election to the state constitutional convention of 1820 but declined to attend. During the Nullification controversy of 1828 to 1832, Dane wrote against South Carolina's resistance to federal laws and threat of secession. Between 1823 and 1829, Dane published a nine-volume *General Abridgement and Digest of American Law*. He left in manuscript form, never published, his life's work in defense of state government and regional cultural values, the Antifederalist *Moral and Political Survey of America*. An admirer of that work, Edwin M. Stone, wrote that the object of the survey was to "view the moral and political principles of the various parts of America, . . . to form a just idea of the moral and political condition and character of men here" (140). Much like an autobiography, the *Moral and Political Survey* captured the values and beliefs of that man, perhaps on the periphery of Antifederalist political action but certainly at the center of its values. Dane died in Beverly, Massachusetts, on February 15, 1835.

REFERENCES

Joy A. Barrett, *Evolution of the Ordinance of 1787* (1891; repr., New York: Arno Press, 1971); Patrick T. Conley and John P. Kaminsky (eds.), *The Constitution and the States* (Madison, Wisc.: Madison House, 1988); John Dane, *A Declaration of Remarkable Providences* (Boston: S. G. Drake, 1894); Jensen and Kaminski, *Documentary History*, vol. 1; Edwin M. Stone, *History of Beverly, Civil and Ecclesiastical* (Boston: J. Monroe, 1843).

JOHN DAWSON *(?, 1762–March 30, 1814)* was born at St. Mary's Parish, Caroline County, Virginia. He was the son of the Church of England minister Musgrove Dawson, who had come to Virginia during the 1750s. Musgrove served parishes in the counties of Amelia, Essex, and Caroline. He married Mary Waugh, from a Caroline County planter family. The young Dawson also was the nephew of the Reverends Thomas and William Dawson, presidents of the College of William and Mary. Dawson graduated from Harvard College in 1782. Dawson had acquired a reputation as a bit of a dandy in his manners. He never married.

Exactly what Dawson did for a living in those early years after the American Revolution isn't known. Some evidence points to a law practice and that he ran a plantation at the time he entered Virginia state politics. He became an ally of the fast-rising young politician James Monroe (q.v.). Dawson represented Spotsylvania County, where he owned a home in the town of Fredericksburg, in the House of Delegates from 1786 to 1789. As a member of the state house, he opposed paying the state's debt to England. Dawson also served in the Continental Congress in 1788. He had hoped to attend the Philadelphia Convention of 1787 along with his friend James Madison, but had been denied election.

Dawson was elected as an Antifederalist to the Virginia ratification convention. Well aware of his youth and of the number of famous Virginians who supported the Constitution, the young politician planned to act with care. Still, in the ratification convention, that follower of Patrick Henry (q.v.) and George Mason (q.v.) delivered one major and memorable speech. In a somewhat self-effacing manner, Dawson said that he spoke only out of deference to his constituents' feelings. In that speech, printed as "Fears for the Future," he claimed that the Constitution hurt American liberties. He believed consolidated government threatened individual liberties, that the executive office had been given the powers to dominate the legislature, and he feared the power of a standing army. Dawson lamented the "confederation of independent states (being) turned into a consolidated government . . . incompatible with republican liberty" (742). Like other educated Antifederalists, he invoked Montesquieu's dictum on the problems of maintaining a republic over such a large amount of land as existed in the new nation. In addition, Dawson also questioned the president's powers to make treaties, fearing damage to the southern states if forced to cede their western regions to the federal union. He finished his speech with a plea that his fellow convention delegates demand a declaration of rights be appended to the Constitution (Bailyn, 742–750).

After the Virginia convention ratified the Constitution, Dawson temporarily retired from public life. He did accept service on the privy council in 1789. Dawson soon made friends with the powerful Washington camp and became a presidential elector in 1792. He appeased the progovernment forces when he said that he believed the Virginia Federalists supported amendments to the Constitution. From 1797 to 1814, Dawson served in the United States House of Representatives. He became active as a Jeffersonian Republican, obviously now free to take sides in his home state. He chaired the committee on the District of Columbia. Dawson also spoke out against the Alien and Sedition acts. Dawson soon gained the reputation as an active and influential congressman. In January 1801, President John Adams, despite Dawson's opposition to Federalist policies, sent that talented Antifederalist to negotiate with the French government over trading rights. During the War of 1812, he served as an aide to General Jacob Browne and later to General Andrew Jackson. But during that war, Dawson contracted tuberculosis. After he retired from Congress in 1814 due to illness, Dawson became a member of the Executive Council of Virginia. He died in Washington, D.C., on March 30, 1814. Dawson is buried there in the Congressional cemetery.

REFERENCES

Bailyn, *Debate*, vol. 2; Richard R. Beeman, *The Old Dominion and the New Nation* (Lexington: University Press of Kentucky, 1972); Charles C. Dawson (comp.), *A Collection of Family Records, with Biographical Sketches* (Albany, N.Y.: Joel Munsell, 1874); Elliot, *Debates*, vol. 3; Sylvanus J. Quinn, *History of the City of Fredericksburg, Virginia* (Richmond: Hermitage Press, 1908).

PATRICK DOLLARD *(c. 1746–February 28, 1800)* was born in Ireland and came to South Carolina in 1770, where he became an innkeeper in Prince Frederick Parish. Dollard eventually owned the successful Red House Inn there. Like so many immigrants, the complete story of his past appears lost, as some ambitious young men perhaps even liked that situation of anonymity. During the Revolution, Dollard became a strong patriot. He supplied the new state militia with food and clothing, and made a good profit. Dollard's tavern became an important site for trade and supply of goods to the army. He served in the war under Francis Marion. After the war ended, Dollard bought land, became a planter, and owned eighteen slaves. Dollard's wife was named Anne.

This newly successful land owner and planter also entered state politics. Dollard served in the general assembly in 1789 and 1790. He gained election to the South Carolina ratification convention where he became an Antifederalist and opposed the Constitution. At the convention, he said to his fellow delegates that "the general voice of the people, to whom I am responsible, is against it. I shall never betray the trust reposed in me by them: therefore, shall give my hearty dissent" (Elliot, 380). Nevertheless, this shrewd student of politics told Aedanus Burke (q.v.), a fellow Antifederalist, how difficult the political and social powers in Charleston made it for their opponents. Nevertheless, Dollard spoke out. He claimed that the Constitutional issue was the most important political dilemma the people of South Carolina had ever faced.

He was especially concerned for the people of Prince Frederick, who had lost much during the American Revolution. All of those brave people, he said, opposed the Constitution due to its lack of a bill of rights, and the absence of a guarantee of personal rights compromised their many sacrifices made to win the war.

Reported in the Charleston *Daily Advertiser*, of May 29, 1788, Dollard's printed speech reveals much about his Antifederalist views. South Carolina's prime dilemma if it supported the needed change in government was its effect on the people. Dollard admitted that the Articles of Confederation were flawed and needed changing, but he believed that the proposed Constitution went too far to take away personal liberty. In that speech, this self-effacing man with little education declared that he lacked the talent to oppose the Constitution, but he would speak anyway. Dollard indeed spoke eloquently in behalf of the "unalienable rights of men," and said, "without a full, free, and secure enjoyment of which there can be no liberty" (330). Further, he proposed that the Constitution violated the Magna Carta. A student of the English Civil War, Dollard compared the Federalists to the followers of Archbishop William Laud, insisting that they believed the Antifederalists would not resist change. He said that his constituents would resist. As to the Constitution, its despotic and depraved drafters created aristocratic control of the government. He called on the state's leaders to resist the standing army, fearing that under men like the English monarchists, the army would be used to enforce a flawed Constitution. Dollard concluded that "the voice of the people was the voice of principle," and he would support it as he supported "the voice of God" (Elliot, 330–338).

After casting his negative vote in the state ratifying convention, Dollard returned to state political office. He became court justice in the Georgetown District in 1790. Later he served as commissioner to open navigation of the Black Mingo Creek. That action allowed interior trade to flow to the coast. Dollard also resumed planting. He died at Villebon Plantation, Prince Frederick Parish, on February 28, 1800. George Rogers said of Dollard that he was true to his constituents: "In his mind, Dollard was still engaged in the age-old fight for liberty. . . . In the new constitution he saw something of the old tyranny, and he meant to warn the men of the convention" (170). History remains the poorer for knowing so little about immigrants such as Dollard who contributed so much to the dialogue over the new nation.

REFERENCES

N. Louise Bailey and Elizabeth Ivey Cooper (eds.), *Biographical Dictionary of the South Carolina House of Representatives* (Columbia: University of South Carolina Press, 1981), vol. 3; Elliot, *Debates*, vol. 4; Jackson Turner Main, *The Antifederalists* (Chapel Hill: University of North Carolina Press, 1961); George C. Rogers, *Evolution of a Federalist: William L. Smith of Charleston* (Columbia: University of South Carolina Press, 1962); George C. Rogers, *Georgetown County* (Spartanburg, S.C.: Georgetown Historical Society, 1990); Robert Rutland, *Ordeal of the Constitution* (Norman: University of Oklahoma Press, 1965).

F

PETER FAYSSOUX *(?, 1745–February 1, 1795)* was born in Charleston, South Carolina to Daniel and Frances Fayssoux, who had come to South Carolina in 1737. The family was Presbyterian. Daniel, a struggling baker in the town, died in 1747. Fortunately, the bright and gifted young Peter's talents were recognized early. His stepfather, James Hunter, apprenticed him to the famous physician Alexander Garden. Dr. Garden later enabled him to go to Edinburgh to study medicine, from 1766 until 1769, where he then received his medical degree. Fayssoux practiced medicine in Charleston. In 1772 he married Sarah Wilson, and they had one child. As a widower in 1777, Fayssoux married the widow Ann Smith Johnston, and they had six children.

This successful young doctor soon rose in society and public life. In 1770 he joined the prestigious Charleston Library Society. In 1773 he helped found the museum of natural history. Fayssoux also belonged to the St. Cecilia Society, Charleston's most prestigious gentleman's club. Through his successful medical practice and fortunate marriage, Fayssoux acquired a plantation on the Cooper River and another one in Ninety-six District. He eventually owned nine slaves. During the Revolution Fayssoux served as a senior physician to the Continental Army. He helped the wounded at the battle of Fort Moultrie in 1776 and the siege of Savannah in 1779, and at the fall of Charleston in 1780, he was arrested by the British authorities. Later released, Fayssoux saw duty at the siege of Ninety-six and the battle of Eutaw Springs, both in 1781. He lent money to the state government to finance the defenses of Charleston during the war. Fayssoux also wrote a treatise on the treatment of American prisoners by the British during the war.

From 1786 until 1790, he represented St. John's Berkeley Parish in the South Carolina House. He declined reelection in 1790. Fayssoux served on the privy council from 1784 until 1786. He also was warden of Charleston's Sixth District in 1786 and 1787. Representing St. John's Berkeley in the house, Fayssoux spoke out against vagrancy laws. He also wanted to allow aliens to settle in the state. In this action, he stood with Rawlins Lowndes (q.v.). In the house, Fayssoux became an expert on finances.

As a member of the state house, he voted in January 1788 to hold the state ratifying convention for the Constitution. The citizens of St. John Berkeley elected this man of political moderation to the state convention. His friend Aedanus Burke (q.v) worried that moderates such as Fayssoux would support ratification after Maryland had done so. He need not have worried. Fayssoux remained steadfast in his concerns about excessive central control. At the state convention, he spoke out about "the abuses and misconstructions of which the Constitution was susceptible" (Elliot, 342). Fayssoux argued against the suspension of individual rights he discerned in the Constitution, even though he said he feared that many Carolinians appeared unaware of the dangers to their personal freedoms (Elliot, 342). He also debated with Dr. David Ramsay over whether the convention should address parts of the Constitution rather than consider the entire document. In the end, Fayssoux voted against ratification of the Constitution.

In 1790 Fayssoux continued his faithfulness to the idea of small but representative government. However, he had lost the will to resist. Fayssoux believed that continuing to fight the Federalists only would lead to further divisions within South Carolina. The Federalists, recognizing his talents and needing to bring some of the old enemies into politics, chose him as chairman of the house of representatives. As a member of the state constitutional convention of 1790, he supported removal of the state capital to Columbia, believing the population of the state had shifted to its center and that was where government belonged. Fayssoux also returned to his interests in medicine, as he was instrumental in establishing the Medical Society of South Carolina. He became its president and served from 1788 until 1793. On February 1, 1795, while treating the sick poor of the city, he contracted disease and died in Charleston. His biographer, Chalmers Davidson said of him, "as an advocate of a lost cause, Peter Fayssoux the statesman received scant attention from the historians" (101).

REFERENCES

N. Louise Bailey and Elizabeth Ivey Cooper (eds.), *Biographical Dictionary of the South Carolina House of Representatives* (Columbia: University of South Carolina Press, 1981), vol. 3; Chalmers G. Davidson, *Friend of the People, the Life of Dr. Peter Fayssoux of Charleston* (Columbia: University of South Carolina Press, 1950); Elliot, *Debates*, vol. 4; Jackson Turner Main, *The Antifederalists* (Chapel Hill: University of North Carolina Press, 1961); Alexander S. Salley (ed.), *Journal of the Convention of South Carolina which Ratified the Constitution of the United States* (Atlanta: Foote and Davis Co., 1928).

WILLIAM FINDLEY *(1741/1742–April 15, 1821)* was born in

northern Ireland in 1741 or 1742. His family had originally come from Scotland to Ireland, and he was said to have been descended from a signer of the Presbyterian Solemn League and Convenant. Findley received little education, save that he read avidly in his father's library on church history and theology. Findley had planned to emigrate to South Carolina, but his antipathy to slavery deterred him. He first settled in Philadelphia in 1762, and came to western Pennsylvania in 1763 as a member of the Octorara settlement. Findley joined the Scotch-Irish settlers near Waynesboro, in Franklin County. For a time he taught school, then was apprenticed as a weaver, in which trade he made his living. He also farmed. Findley married another Scotch-Irish immigrant, Mary Cochran, in 1769.

Loyal to his adopted land, this man of humble origins served in the revolutionary state militia and rose to the rank of captain. In 1780 he moved to Westmoreland County and farmed in Latrobe. From 1783 to 1790, he was on the state council of censors. Devoted to Pennsylvania's first state constitution of 1776, Findley opposed all revisions to that document. As such, he clashed with western conservatives who wanted a new constitution. He entered the Pennsylvania State Assembly and served there from 1784 to 1788. A member of the Scotch-Irish "white hut" political faction, he clashed politically with fellow westerner Hugh H. Brackenridge, who later lampooned him in that lusty first American novel *Modern Chivalry*. Findley became a leader of the debtor, paper money forces, and in 1786 debated Robert Morris, the powerful Philadelphia leader, over those issues and the formation of the state bank. Although he could sway voters to his side and could persuade ordinary farmers of his cause, Findley did not regard himself as a great debater. Often he appeared ill at ease in the presence of such practiced politicos as Morris and Brackenridge.

Nevertheless, fellow westerners supported the legislature's election of Findley to the convention in Philadelphia in the summer of 1787 to discuss revisions to the Articles of Confederation, perhaps revealing how well this newcomer was regarded in the state. However, he declined appointment to the convention, because, he said, he refused to attend without receiving traveling expenses, but in reality he did not trust the other Pennsylvania conventioneers.

Findley took a prominent part in the 1787 ratification convention in Pennsylvania as a leader of the moderate western farm faction of Antifederalists. As a delegate to the November 20–December 13, 1787, state ratification convention, he spoke out against ratification, was politically intrigued with other Antifederalists, published important writtings on the subject, and voted against the Constitution. He signed the "Address and Reasons of the Dissent of the Minority of the Convention" and lobbied for a second state convention. Under attack from the Federalist majority, Findley nevertheless managed to convey to others the resentments of the beleagured minority. An ally of the westerner John Smilie (q.v.), Findley had spoken of the sovereignty of the people against oppressive government. It is possible Findley also wrote the rather crude but effective Antifederalist "Letter by an Officer of the Late Continental Army," in which he outlined more fully why he opposed the Constitution. Herbert Storing regards Findley as, along with George Bryan (q.v.), the two most able Antifederalists in Pennsylvania (5).

Indeed, "An Officer of the Late Continental Army" deserves careful consideration. Findley had written that work to try to influence elections to the state ratifying convention. He wanted to give pointers to the delegates. First, Findley wrote against how the Constitution proposed election to office. Without rotation in office, he wondered whether the Constitution really desired conservative leaders in office for a lifetime, rather than give others a chance to serve. He suggested the secretly written Constitution really had been the work of "an aristocratic majority." In an attempt to persuade moderates to his cause, Findley stated that Benjamin Franklin had reservations about the Constitution. A major worry of this small-farm supporter was the bargain struck over the slave trade, which could have led to the revival of slavery in Pennsylvania (Bailyn, 99–104). With eloquence he declared: "if the sacred flame of liberty has not extinguished in your breasts, if you have any regard for the happiness of yourselves, and your posterity, let me entreat you, earnestly entreat you by all that is dear and sacred to freemen, to consider well before you take the awful step which may involve in its consequences the ruin of millions unborn." Do not, he concluded, combining his feelings for the African Americans and his own people, let these despots make us slaves (Storing, 97).

After the Antifederalists lost state power, Findley left the board of censors. However, he gained election to the Supreme Executive Council and served as a delegate to the state constitutional revision convention of 1789–1790. Findley assisted in writing the new state constitution and supported the inclusion of a bill of rights in it. He was elected to the Pennsylvania State House of Representatives in 1790 and 1791, and held office in the state senate from 1799 to 1803. In that body, he supported democratic values, the rights of individual states, and advocated the abolition of slavery in Pennsylvania. (Ironically, Findley held a bond servant until 1812.)

The citizens of western Pennsylvania chose him over Brackenridge to serve in the federal Congress, and he did so ably from 1791 to 1799, and again from 1803 until 1817. Findley remained loyal to the Antifederalist cause and values and actively opposed Alexander Hamilton's national financial schemes. In 1794 he wrote a *Review of the Revenue System Adopted by the First Congress*, a polemic against Hamilton's policies. In 1794 Findley also championed the cause of the Whiskey Rebels, believing they were unfairly taxed. He rejected President George Washington's call for troops to put down the rebels. But Findley soon turned moderate, and in 1796 published a book, *History of the Insurrection*, in which he condemned the rebels' violent actions. In his service in the federal Congress, Findley also helped to formulate the duties and policies of the first House Ways and Means Committee, destined to become the most important committee in the House of Representatives. Between terms in the federal House, Findley served in the state senate from 1799 until 1803. Back in Congress, from 1803 until 1817, he chaired the important

Committee on Elections. In that committee, he assisted the growth to power of the Jeffersonian Republicans. In 1812, this staunch Presbyterian wrote a vindication of support of the separation of church and state, a manifesto on religious freedom.

Findley retired from Congress in 1817, returned to his farm, and died in Unity Township, near Greensburg, in Westmoreland County, Pennsylvania, on April 5, 1821. Beloved by the western farmers, he remained loyal to Antifederalist principles throughout his active political career. George W. Albert, in evaluating Findley's life and personality, said, "He had a large personal acquaintance, and his manners were such as to make him a favorite in a democracy. Besides this, he had the sympathy and the influence of the strongest church organization in the country at that day" (209). He remained true to the needs of the ordinary people, and was a staunch Presbyterian in his faith and a Republican in politics. That combination, along with his ability to appeal to westerners, made him one of early Pennsylvania's great men of the people, and an Antifederalist.

REFERENCES

George W. Albert, *History of the County of Westmoreland, Pennsylvania* (Philadelphia: L. H. Everts, 1882); Bailyn, *Debate*, vol. 2; William H. Engle, *An Illustrated History of the Commonwealth of Pennsylvania* (Philadelphia: E. M. Gardner, 1880); Russell J. Ferguson, *Early Western Pennsylvania Politics* (Pittsburgh: University of Pittsburgh Press, 1938); Storing, *Complete*, vol. 3; Findley's papers are in the Western Pennsylvania Historical Society, in Pittsburgh.

ELISHA FITCH was from Salisbury, Connecticut. Little is known about his early life. He did practice law. In May 1787, as a member of the state house of representatives, he spoke against appointing delegates to the Philadelphia convention: "The privilege of the people he was afraid would be exposed; . . . he would not see them abridged, but would ever support them to the last degree" (Jensen and Kaminski, 109). Fitch served as one of the few Antifederalist leaders in the state of Connecticut.

REFERENCES

Steven R. Boyd, *The Politics of Opposition* (Millwood, N.Y.: KTO Press, 1979); Jensen and Kaminski, *Documentary History*, vol. 13.

G

BENJAMIN GALE *(December 14, 1715–May 6, 1790)* was born in Jamaica, Long Island, New York to John and Mary Gale. In 1721 his family moved to Goshen in Orange County, New York. Gale attended the common schools of Goshen and graduated from Yale College in 1733 with an M.A. He then studied medicine under the famous Dr. Jared Eliot, a senior trustee of Yale. In 1739 Gale married Eliot's daughter Hannah. He settled in Killingworth, Connecticut, and soon took over Eliot's lucrative medical practice.

But medicine was only part of this brilliant and opinionated man's life. Before the Revolution, Gale entered public life and became a controversial spokesman for a number of reform movements. In 1755 he attacked the Yale Corporation and President Thomas Clapp after the colonial Connecticut government reduced its expenses by cutting the annual annuity to the college. Gale was a deeply religious man and an excellent Bible scholar, and he insisted the changes in Yale over the New Light religious reforms had ruined the college. Gale's 1755 pamphlet, *The Present State of the Colony of Connecticut Considered*, contained his attacks on Yale. In 1759 he published *A Few Brief Remarks*, on the laws of governance at Yale. Seen as controversial, sarcastic, and bitter, in his pamphlet Gale revealed his personality in his excessive fault-finding with Yale's system of student fines and what he believed was too-high tuition. Also, he became controversial in the field of medicine with the publication of *Historical Memoirs, Relating to the Practice of Inoculation for Small Pox* in 1765. He favored a radical departure in the vaccine. For his work in medical reform, Gale was named in 1765 a corresponding member of the Society of Arts in London.

Aside from his public criticism and advances in medical research, Gale was an inventor. He kept up a large correspondence with other physicians and scientists in the colonies and abroad. His 1769 letter to J. W. Esquire sought to advance scientific study in the colonies by calling for science instruction in college. Gale invented a drill plough to support agricultural advancement in Connecticut. In 1775 he invented a bomb, a kind of torpedo, which the revolutionary navy used against the British naval fleet. In 1783 Gale published

Observations on the Culture of Smyrna Wheat. This also was a major contribution to agricultural developments in the state.

In his entry on Gale in a book on Yale Graduates, Franklin Dexter quoted Yale president Ezra Stiles on Gale's activities in politics. Stiles said, "He was always against the American Revolution, highly displeased with the new Constitution, and the whole government by Congress, greatly against the French alliance, and wished and believed the breaking up of the states and their reunion to Great Britain" (478). Gale's political career was thus in its own way quite consistent. He served in the colonial assembly from 1747 to 1767, compiling a controversial antiestablishment but deeply conservative record. Gale opposed the Stamp Act, but he declined to support Connecticut's radical Sons of Liberty. Though he assisted scientifically in the revolutionary cause, he lamented the actions that caused separation from England. Still, Gale supported the war.

In the crisis in Connecticut over the Philadelphia Convention and the proposed new federal Constitution, Gale attempted to defeat ratification. In 1787 he wrote "Objections to the New Plan of Government," a work never published but available in manuscript form at Yale. In that work, he denied the majority opinion in Connecticut in believing that his state would become subservient to the larger dominant states surrounding it. Gale regarded himself as the voice of the ordinary people, so he spoke often in town meetings against the Constitution. In his remarks made in Killingworth on November 12, 1787, Gale called for the election of Antifederalists to the state ratifying convention. Christopher Collier identifies Gale and James Wadsworth (q.v.), along with Erastus Wolcott (q.v.), as the most important Antifederalists in the state (222). Gale's opposition reflected his fears of the strong aristocratic Federalist faction and its control of state and national affairs. Suspicion of authority, though he was himself conservative, often surfaced in Gale's opinions. Collier points out that ratification was inevitable in Connecticut, and that opponents like Gale were never able to arouse the debtors and bondholders of the state to the perils the central powers of the Constitution held for them (234). Still, Gale continued to oppose the Constitution even after ratification in Connecticut.

Gale died in Killingworth on May 6, 1790. In his last years, he befriended the poor of his community, giving to libraries and reading the Bible to the unlettered. He kept up his interest in science, continued to study biblical history, and became a Greek scholar. James Thacher, in his *American Medical Biographies,* compared Gale's career favorably to the career of his father-in-law, Jared Eliot. Medicine, science, and religion were their passions. "But he was unlike his predecessor in his attention to the politics of the day, as he took great interest in the events . . . that passed during the formation of the federal Constitution, and employed much of the latter part of his life in writing political essays for the newspapers of the time" (268–269). A true eighteenth-century man of ideas, Gale's reasons for opposing the Constitution contained

similar fears of other Antifederalists who favored a small republic led by socially responsible, intelligent, and conservative leaders. Ezra Stiles perhaps best
captured Gale's personality and character. Stiles said, "he always meant to be
a friend to civil religious liberty and to his country. He was of an acrimonious
temper" (Dexter, 479). Gale was a staunch if conservative Antifederalist.

REFERENCES

Richard Buel, *Dear Liberty: Connecticut's Mobilization for the Revolutionary War*
(Middletown, Conn.: Wesleyan University Press, 1980); Christopher Collier, *Roger
Sherman's Connecticut: Yankee Politics and the American Revolution* (Middletown,
Conn.: Wesleyan University Press, 1971); Franklin Bowditch Dexter, *Biographies of
the Graduates of Yale College* (New York: Henry Holt, 1885–1912), vol. 2; George
Gale, *The Gale Family Records in England and the United States* (Galesville, Wisc.:
Leith and Gale, 1866); Christopher Grasso, *A Speaking Aristocracy* (Chapel Hill: Uni-
versity of North Carolina Press, 1998); Bernard Steiner, "Connecticut's Ratification
of the Federal Constitution," *Proceedings* of the American Antiquarian Society, new
series, 25 (October 1915): pt. 2; James Thacher, *American Medical Biographies*
(Boston: Richardson and Lord, 1828).

JAMES (GALLAWAY) GALLOWAY *(?–1798)* was born in Scotland

and probably moved to Guilford County, North Carolina, sometime before
the American Revolution. He became a large landowner in the river valley,
planted, and owned twelve slaves. Around 1778, Galloway worked in the mercantile business with his uncle Charles Galloway. In 1784 he became a trustee
to improve navigation on the Dan and Roanoke rivers. Galloway also owned
a canal company. He married Elizabeth Sproggins, and they had two sons.

He served in the North Carolina General Assembly from Guilford County
in the years 1783 and 1784. Galloway held office in the state senate in 1784
and 1785, and again in the state house from Rockingham County from 1786
until 1789. He was active against state taxing policies, served on committees
on Indian affairs, wanted to change rules concerning criminal incarceration,
sponsored educational bills, and even took a progressive position on limited
slave emancipation. In 1784, Galloway opposed giving lands in western North
Carolina to the federal government. In the legislature, Galloway resisted calls
for the state ratification convention. As a delegate to the state ratification convention, this ally of Willie Jones (q.v.) spoke often in support of the Antifederalist cause. Considered a political leader in the south-central part of the state,
Galloway served in both North Carolina conventions and, with his uncle
Charles, voted against ratification both times.

What were his objections to the Constitution? True to his adopted state,
Galloway feared a northern-controlled government would end slavery. He had
little use for slavery, but he worried about the number of freed slaves who
would live in his part of the state. "It is impossible for us to be happy," he
said, "if after manumission, they are to stay among us" (Elliot, 101). Galloway also disliked the federal Congress's control of the electoral process, and

believed that power would adversely affect the growing democracy in the state and give too much authority to the Federalist eastern part of the state. He also resented what he believed was excessive foreign policy power of the new government. Galloway advocated population growth in North Carolina to build the state's white base and to expand economic opportunities, and he accused the Federalists of wanting to keep immigrants out of the new nation. The Constitution as written, he said, undermined North Carolina's fiscal integrity, because it did not allow the state to redeem its own securities. Galloway insisted: "this country never will leave it to the hands of the general government to redeem securities which they have already given" (Elliot, 190). Even in the second state convention, when he knew North Carolinians had to enter the new federal union, Galloway continued to hope for amendments to what he believed was a flawed document. He also served with his friends Timothy Bloodworth (q.v.) and Samuel Spencer (q.v.) on a committee to prepare amendments for the leaders elected to the federal Congress. In the second state convention, he took over Antifederalist leadership and chaired the rules committeee, when Willie Jones refused to serve in that body.

After the convention, Galloway left politics. He became a partner in Charles Galloway and Company, and planted. Galloway died in Rockingham County sometime in 1798.

REFERENCES

Samuel A. Ashe, et al., *Biographical History of North Carolina* (Greensboro, N.C.: Charles L. Van Nappen, 1908, 1928), vol. 2; Bailyn, *Debate*, vol. 2; William A. Candler, *Bishop Charles B. Galloway* (Nashville, Tenn.: Cokesbury Press, 1927); John L. Cheney, Jr. (ed.), *North Carolina Government, 1585–1974* (Raleigh, N.C.: North Carolina Department of the Secretary of State, 1975); Elliot, *Debates*, vol. 4; William S. Powell (ed.), *Dictionary of North Carolina Biography* (Chapel Hill: University of North Carolina Press, 1979), vol. 2; Louise Irby Trenholme, *The Ratification of the Federal Constitution in North Carolina* (New York: Columbia University Press, 1932).

ELBRIDGE GERRY *(July 17, 1744–November 23, 1814)* was born

in Marblehead, Massachusetts. His father, Thomas, had come to Marblehead from Devonshire, England, and become a successful merchant and shipper. Gerry's mother was Elizabeth (Greenleaf). Gerry attended local schools and graduated with the class of 1762 from Harvard College. He entered business with his father, became himself a successful merchant, and a leader of the Congregational Church.

Conservative in his business and personal activities, Gerry had a radical political streak to him, especially toward England, which he believed was oppressing the people of Massachusetts by putting unneeded pressure on merchant trade. He entered the Massachusetts General Court (legislature) in 1772, where he came under the influence of Samuel Adams (q.v.). Gerry assisted the local Committee of Correspondence in 1773, and in 1774 he was elected to the Essex County convention that drew up the resolves in protest to British taxation of merchant trade. In October 1774, Gerry gained election to the first provisional congress, and worked on the Committee of Safety. He wrote a draft remonstrance against the British attacks at Lexington and Concord. His close friend and fellow rebel, Joseph Warren, was killed at the battle of Bunker Hill, and Gerry joined with James Warren (q.v.) and Mercy Otis Warren (q.v.) to grieve and to plot revenge. In 1776 he served as a delegate to the Second Continental Congress, then gained appointment to the Treasury Board and left Philadelphia before signing the Declaration of Independence, only adding his name to that document in September 1776.

Throughout the Revolutionary War, Gerry worked untiringly in behalf of the patriot cause, both in Massachusetts and in the young national government. He used his merchant talents to assist in supplying the Continental Army. Gerry also was a delegate to the New Haven price fixing convention of 1778, where he supported a uniform price for wartime sales to the United States government. He opposed the alliance with France, fearing that country would dominate American trade policies. In 1780, in a spat over the powers of states in the new government, Gerry left the Continental Congress. Throughout his term in national office, he had been a staunch advocate of the central government's power to prosecute the war. But, like his friends the Warrens, Gerry was an ardent republican defender of state rights. He supported the Articles of Confederation's designation of each state having only one vote, and believed in state veto power over national legislation. Before the war ended, Gerry became a privateer, preying on British merchant shipping off the coast of Massachusetts. He also belonged to the anti–John Hancock faction in Massachusetts politics.

Rejoining Congress after peace, Gerry continued his support of local interests. A leader on foreign affairs in that body, he was especially interested in and worried about the impact of foreign trade on Boston merchants. Gerry forged an alliance with members from Maryland and became especially close to the Lees of Virginia, Richard Henry (q.v.) and his brother Arthur Lee (q.v.). Gerry feared a reemergent aristocracy in the young country, desired a reduction in the standing federal army, and advocated abolishing the newly formed Society of Cincinnati, made of up ex-military officers. He also had an interest, personal and for the young nation, in the eastern states acquiring land in the new northwest territory. In 1786 he became a member of the Massachusetts legislature where George Billias, his most thorough biographer, says his sectionalist support for Massachusetts and New England merged fully (94). Gerry staunchly defended New England rights to offshore fishing. In 1786 he married Ann Thompson, daughter of a New York merchant, which gave him a link to those leaders in New York who sought to defend the rights of states. In 1787 Gerry moved to Cambridge, Massachusetts. His worries over the excesses of Shays's rebels linked Gerry to conservative republican politics.

When nationalists met in Annapolis in 1786, Gerry refused to attend. He did become a delegate to the federal convention in Philadelphia in the summer of 1787 and at first aligned with the Constitutional reformers. But during the debates, this shrewd man of both conservative and radical politics joined the opposition, declaring his aversion to democracy and his jealousy of national power. He argued that the republican values, which had produced the Revolution, would be lost to strong central government. Gerry refused to sign the Constitution.

Returning home a hero of the localist forces, Gerry joined Samuel Adams and the Warrens as Antifederalist leaders. But the citizens of Cambridge favored the new Constitution, and Gerry was not elected to the state ratifying convention. Invited to attend the convention anyway, Gerry soon walked out because he was not allowed to speak. Still, he wrote and politicked against ratification, and probably gave Mercy Otis Warren much of the information for her important *Observations on the New Constitution*. At one time he was thought to have been the author of that work, but Billias accurately claims he was not (344). Gerry corresponded with Richard Henry Lee and with the New York Antifederalists and certainly influenced their positions against the Constitution. He knew that the states were bent on ratification, and he hoped for major reforms in that document before it was accepted. But Gerry also knew that he had to acquiesce in its passage.

Why did this conservative republican stand with the Massachusetts Antifederalists? Gerry, Adams, and the Warrens believed that the new nation had been founded on the principles of a small republic hostile to overbearing national authority like that of England. Ambitious, too, Gerry wanted to leave a legacy to his people, and thus aligned himself with famous revolutionary leaders who had opposed the Constitution. Impetuous also, Billias says, "he tended to meet what he viewed as extreme dangers with extreme measures" (152). His views of the purpose of government and fears of federal power, however, were the main reasons why he opposed the Constitution. At the Philadelphia convention, Gerry had spoken against the Three-fifths Clause as too favorable to slave state interests, and he was devoted to stable government adequately divided between small and large state powers, the wealthy and the ordinary people. Gerry said he rejected the Constitution because it made government too strong, threatened liberties, and subverted state independence.

In a letter to the Massachusetts General Court of November 3, 1787, Gerry laid out in detail his objections to the Constitution. Published in the Massachusetts *Sentinel*, the letter no doubt influenced the arguments of his fellow Antifederalists. Gerry wrote: "my principal objections to the plan, are, that there is no adequate provision for a representation of the people" (Storing, 4). He also believed that the authors of the Constitution had purposefully written a vague set of laws in hopes that they could persuade people to support their actions without looking at the work in detail. The new system of government, he said, lacked a Bill of Rights and therefore afforded little protection for popular rights. Gerry argued that the powers of the judiciary had not been spelled out, and he feared such loose powers. Still, "the welfare of the union requires a better Constitution than the confederation" (Storing, 6), and "I shall think it my duty as a citizen of Massachusetts, to support that which shall be finally adopted" (Storing, 8). And he did.

This fearful leader understood that by his outspokenness he had lost a number of Federalist friends, and he attempted to repair his reputation by supporting the new national government once the Constitution had been ratified. He became the Antifederalist candidate for governor in 1788 but lost to John Hancock. But in 1789 Gerry gained election to the federal Congress, and he insisted he desired to work with the new government. At first he rejected the Antifederalist call for a bill of rights. Sensitive to changing public opinion, especially back home, Gerry supported Alexander Hamilton's funding programs, joined the bank charter advocates, and sided with the merchant speculators. Seemingly, his business interests had won over his fears. But he also opposed slavery, and again he spoke of too much southern state power.

In 1793 he retired from Congress. In 1796 Gerry attempted to bring the arch enemies Thomas Jefferson and John Adams together, and he supported Adams for president. He believed that Adams had prevented war with France. But the talk of a renewed military posture for national defense turned him back to the Republicans, and he supported Jefferson for president in 1800. Calling himself now a moderate Republican, he again ran for governor of Massachusetts in 1800 and again lost. In 1807 Gerry attempted to renew his relations with Adams but failed. In 1810 he was finally elected governor, and his name has gone down in history with the bill of 1812 to realign election districts in Massachusetts. (Unfortunately for him, the term "gerrymander" has become one of opprobrium.) In 1812 James Madison chose Gerry for his vice president, as the New Englander became a strong advocate of the conquest of Canada. In 1813 he had a stroke, and he died in Washington, D.C., on November 23, 1814.

History has picked over this able republican's legacy. James T. Austin, his first biographer, said that Gerry attacked Federalists merely because of his acerbic personality, and sought to resurrect him as a moderate who really favored the Constitution (vol. 2, 24, 45). But Austin also captured the man's values thusly: "all the objectors suggested Mr. Gerry regarded the tendency of the constitution to impair the liberties of the people and the sovereignty of the states, and that it was on this precise ground that all the opposition it experienced throughout the United States was founded" (vol. 2, 84). Billias concluded most thoughtfully that Gerry belonged to a special group of eastern Massachusetts Harvard-centered leaders who went to war to make a conservative republic (330). No man of the rank and file, Gerry and his allies were Antifederalist elitists who well understood the powers of government in a republic and sought to harness that power to the best interests of the locality from whence they came.

REFERENCES

James T. Austin, *The Life of Elbridge Gerry*, 2 vols. (Boston: Wells and Lilly, 1829); Bailyn, *Debate*, vols. 1 and 2; George Athan Billias, *Elbridge Gerry: Founding Father and Republican Statesman* (New York: McGraw-Hill, 1976); C. Harvey Gardiner (ed.), *A Study in Dissent: The Warren-Gerry Correspondence, 1776–1792* (Carbondale, Ill.: Southern Illinois University Press, 1968); Van Beck Hall, *Politics Without Parties: Massachusetts, 1780–1791* (Pittsburgh: University of Pittsburgh Press, 1972); Eugene F. Kramer, "The Public Career of Elbridge Gerry" (PhD diss., Ohio State University, 1955); Clifford K. Shipton, *Biographical Sketches of Those Who Attended Harvard* (Cambridge: Harvard University Press, 1933–1975), vol. 6; Storing, *Complete*, vol. 2. Gerry's papers are in the Manuscript Division of the Library of Congress.

JAMES GILLESPIE *(?, 1747–January 11, 1805)* was born in 1747 in County Monaghan, Ireland, the son of David Gillespie. Gillespie received a classical education in Dublin, Ireland. His Scots Presbyterian father emigrated with his family to New Bern, North Carolina. The younger Gillespie acquired land in Kenansville, Duplin County, North Carolina. By 1790 he owned over two thousand acres of land and thirty slaves. Gillespie married Dorcas Munford, and they had seven children.

Held in good regard by his peers, Gillespie was elected to the 1776 convention that drafted the first state constitution. He was devoted to that document. Gillespie also participated in the American Revolution as a militia officer. Gillespie became captain of the first battalion of North Carolina volunteers in 1776. The state's Tories burned this patriot's farm. He also served in the state house of representatives from 1779 until 1783 and became secretary to the Governor. Gillespie also was a member of the state senate from 1784 until 1786 and a trustee of the academy in Duplin in 1785.

Considered a leader in the first North Carolina ratifying convention in 1788, he voted against the Constitution. Gillespie also served in the second state convention in 1790, and again voted against ratification of the Constitution. Though he said little in debate, he ably represented the localist values of his constituents. Gillespie was one of those leaders who rejected any worries that North Carolina stood to lose by remaining outside of the new government until it was ready to join and participate.

After the controversy over the Constitution had ended, this Antifederalist rose in state and national politics. He served in the United States House of Representatives from 1793 until 1799. He was again elected to the federal Congress and served as a Jeffersonian Republican from 1803 until 1805. Gillespie died in Washington, D.C., on January 11, 1805, and was originally buried in the Presbyterian cemetery in Georgetown, but is now interred in the Congressional cemetery.

REFERENCES

John L. Cheney, Jr. (ed.)., *North Carolina Government, 1585–1974* (Raleigh: North Carolina Department of the Secretary of State, 1975); William S. Powell (ed.), *Dictionary of North Carolina Biography* (Chapel Hill: University of North Carolina Press, 1979) vol. 2; David J. Siemers, *Ratifying the Republic: Antifederalists and Federalists in Constitutional Time* (Stanford: Stanford University Press, 2002); Louise Irby Trenholme, *The Ratification of the Federal Constitution in North Carolina* (New York: Columbia University Press, 1932); John H. Wheeler, *Historical Sketches of North Carolina* (1851; repr., Baltimore: Regional Publishing Company, 1964).

WILLIAM (GOWDY) GOUDY *(1745–1791)* was born about 1745 in Guilford County, North Carolina. He received a local education, studied law, and became a lawyer and farmer. He married Jean Paisly White of Guilford. Before the Revolution, he served as a justice of the peace in his home county. He served five terms in the state house, including the years 1780 to 1782, 1787, and 1788. Goudy also was in the state senate in 1786 and 1789.

At the North Carolina federal Constitutional ratification convention of 1788, Goudy steadfastly opposed ratification. A strong Antifederalist, he spoke often of his worries about the proposed federal Constitution. Goudy said that he was "jealous and suspicious of the liberties of mankind. . . . That the Constitution has a tendency to destroy state governments, must be clear to every man of understanding" (Elliot, 93). Goudy, as a westerner, opposed federal control of local funds. He feared that the new federal government resisted western growth and refused loans for development and expansion in those parts of the states. Therefore, he rejected giving any federal body the power over the purse. "I ask," he said, "when we give them the power of the purse in one hand, and the sword in another, what power have we left?"(Elliot, 93). Posing as a man of the ordinary, unlearned people, he claimed that he could not follow all of the arguments of the state's Federalists. But this so-called simple man well understood the relationship between leaders and those led. Goudy insisted that the clause about elections that the Federalists so fervently supported as in the people's interests indeed endangered the people's right to choose their own leaders. If the federal government had the power to plan both the time and the place for all elections, it could make it inconvenient for the ordinary people to vote for their leaders (Elliot, 170). Jackson T. Main said that Goudy believed power belonged to the people, but if they were not vigilant, they would lose it to those who would run the new federal government. Goudy said "we are freemen, and we ought to have the privileges as such" (Main, 151). Needless to say, the delegate from Guilford County voted against ratification at both state conventions.

After the battle over ratification, Goudy returned to his plantation of 1,200 acres. In 1791, Goudy was elected to the council of state. He died that year at his home in Guilford County, North Carolina.

REFERENCES

Bailyn, *Debate*, vol. 2; Elliot, *Debates*, vol. 4; Jackson Turner Main, *The Antifederalists* (Chapel Hill: University of North Carolina Press, 1961); Sallie Walker Stockard, *The History of Guilford County, North Carolina* (Knoxville, Tenn.: Gaut-Ogden Co., 1902); Louise Irby Trenholme, *The Ratification of the Federal Constitution in North Carolina* (New York: Columbia University Press, 1932).

AMOS (ABRAHAM) GRANGER was born in Suffield, Hartford County, Connecticut. He may have been the son of Robert and Anne (Seymour) Granger. He was a member of the Connecticut lower house before the debate over ratification of the Constitution. As a member of the state legislature, he opposed sending delegates to the Constitutional convention in Philadelphia. Granger said that the original royal charter of Connecticut and the Articles of Confederation guided his views of the structure of government. He became, along with his political ally James Wadsworth (q.v.), one of the few outspoken Antifederalists in Connecticut.

As a member of the state legislature in 1787 from Suffield, during the debates over calling the ratification convention in Connecticut, Granger spoke out against a proposed Constitution he believed would encourage monarchy in the United States. Besides, he said, the Articles of Confederation gave sufficient power to the federal government. Granger also believed that the Connecticut Constitution would be undermined by a federal Constitution (Jensen and Kaminski, 108). No more evidence for his opposition was needed, said Granger. Although a leader of the agrarian party, Granger did not get elected to the state Constitutional ratification convention.

REFERENCES

Steven R. Boyd, *The Politics of Opposition* (Millwood, N.Y.: KTO Press, 1979); Jensen and Kaminski, *Documentary History*, vol. 13; Robert R. Rutland, *Ordeal of the Constitution* (Norman: University of Oklahoma Press, 1965).

WILLIAM GRAYSON *(?, 1736–March 12, 1790)* was born in Prince William County, Virginia. His father was the wealthy planter Benjamin Grayson, and his mother was Susanna (Monroe), aunt of James Monroe (q.v.). Young Grayson received an education from private tutors, attended the College of Philadelphia, did the customary grand tour of Europe, and went to school in Oxford, England. He then read law at the Inns of Court in London. Grayson practiced some law but mainly planted in Dumfries, Virginia. He married Eleanor Smallwood, sister of the planter and politician William Smallwood.

An early patriot, Grayson opposed Virginia's colonial governor and allied himself with the radical Patrick Henry (q.v.). In 1774, he led the Prince William County Committee of Safety. In 1776 he became a lieutenant colonel in the Continental Army, having supplied arms to his troops, and served as aide to General George Washington. Promoted to colonel in 1777, Grayson fought at the battles of Long Island, White Plains, Brandywine, and Germantown. He was at Valley Forge in that horrible winter of 1777–1778. Grayson retired from the army in 1779 to become Virginia's commissioner of the Board of War. When it was evident that the war had been won, he resigned that position.

After the war, Grayson resumed planting and practicing law. Public service drew him into the Virginia House of Delegates in 1784, and he held office there again in 1785 and 1788. From 1785 to 1787, Grayson served in the Continental Congress. There he became a friend and ally of Massachusetts's Elbridge Gerry (q.v.), who helped shape his views of state and local authority. Like many a Virginia landowner, Grayson held interests in western land and wanted to develop his holdings. Grayson joined the debates with other states over Virginia's western boundaries, and he helped to write the Northwest Ordinance of 1787. He supported the prohibition on slavery in the northwest. But Grayson also believed that the northern states had decided to give Spain control of the Mississippi River, thus prohibiting the expansion of the southern states. Yet, for Grayson, the Articles of Confederation, by giving each state power over federal legislation, best protected local interests. These concerns over local issues and western lands would influence his behavior concerning the proposed federal Constitution of 1787, which is why he opposed calling the convention in Philadelphia in 1787.

As a member of the Virginia ratifying convention in 1788, Grayson allied with Patrick Henry, Richard Henry Lee (q.v.), and young James Monroe, his relative. During the convention, Grayson spoke often and carefully in opposition to the Constitution. He well knew that important leaders in Virginia had designed the Constitution, so Grayson wanted to avoid accusing any of them of betraying local interests. He acknowledged that the present Confederation constitution was defective, but certainly, he said, the problems of Virginia in the nation did not stem from that document. Grayson attempted to show that the Articles had worked effectively for all of the disparate interests in the country. He claimed that the people "have been told of phantoms and ideal dangers to lead us into measures which will, in my opinion, be the ruin of the country" (Elliot, 274). Though Virginia leaders were blameless, he claimed, other Federalists had used fears of the so-called failed Confederation to attempt to persuade the citizenry to support the proposed Constitution.

The next step for the thoughtful Grayson in his series of speeches at the convention was to turn to the flaws in the proposed Constitution. First he claimed that the consolidation of power was out of step with the interests of the people. When Federalists in Virginia insisted that if the state did not join the new government it would be left behind, Grayson countered with reasons why Virginians should hesitate. Experiments in government, unproven and untested, he insisted were what Federalists asked the people to support.

Grayson made comparisons between the new Constitution and the hated English monarchy, in an attempt to appeal to patriotism among the people. The people controlled the right of taxation, and, like England, the Federalists wanted to abolish the people's rights and put the power to tax into the hands of a national elite. In England, one supreme power, he said, took away local rights. To follow the Federalists, said Grayson, was to believe in the benefits of divided power. For him, only state power was good for the people of a state. Therefore, strict state rights was the only sure form of governance (Elliot, 278–282).

Ominously, Grayson also placed his argument strictly in a southern interest mode. "I mean not to give offense to any part of America," he said, "but mankind are governed by interests." This new government, he railed, planned to operate as a faction of seven northern states to control all of the rest. The interior, and the southern states' interests in the west, would give way to eastern state interests in the Atlantic carrying trades. Thus, the northeast planned to give up any claims to the Mississippi River. "I look upon this as a contest for empire," he said about the struggle over the Constitution (Elliot, 418). When corrupt central government controlled finances and, worse, the army, Grayson warned, the southern states would be held in captivity. Grayson expected the new government to be despotic. The seven eastern states would control the presidency, and therefore also dictate all treaty-making power. The power to admit new states, for Grayson, meant the northern states would never again allow another southern state. Thus, Virginia and the other slave states would lose power under the new Constitution. The final proof of southern state losses for Grayson centered on the "vague and indefinite" social compact proposed (433). He concluded that the only reason Virginians supported the Constitution was because their own George Washington would be the first president. He questioned what would happen to the southern states once Washington left office (Elliot, 582, 565, 583, 615–616).

No radical but merely a localist with regional fears, Grayson even appeared to Virginia slaveholding Federalists as a moderate. He and Richard Henry Lee were elected from Virginia to the first United States Senate. In the senate, he led the forces against the first federal tariff of 1789. But that was the last public action of this committed and prescient sectionalist. Grayson died at his home in Dumfries on March 12, 1790.

REFERENCES

Elliot, *Debates*, vol. 3; Worthington Chaucey Ford (coll.), *The Federal Constitution in Virginia, 1787–1788* (Cambridge: John Wilson and Son, 1903); Hugh Blair Grigsby, *The History of the Virginia Federal Convention of 1788* (Virginia Historical Society Collections, 1890–1891), vols. 9–10; Storing *Complete*, vols. 1 and 4.

THOMAS GREENLEAF *(?, 1755–September 14, 1798)* was born in Abingdon, Massachusetts. His father was Joseph Greenleaf, justice of the peace of Plymouth County, and a strong patriot who wrote for the *Massachusetts Spy*. His mother was Abigail Payne. Young Greenleaf took up the printing trade in the Boston print shop of Isaiah Thomas. During the American Revolution, Greenleaf printed many prorevolutionary pamphlets.

In 1785 this ambitious young man moved to New York City. He joined Eleazor Oswald (q.v.) to manage the *New York Journal*, also called the *Weekly Register*. By January 1787 he owned the newspaper. In November 1787, he renamed the paper the *New York Journal and Daily Patriotic Register*. Although Greenleaf had some success with his paper, competition over circulation in that growing city required him to change names of his paper and to be constantly in tune with public opinion.

As his paper grew in circulation, Greenleaf became more and more involved in the city's political differences. He served as the most important printer to the financially strapped Antifederalists of New York. As a close henchman of the powerful New York Antifederalist leader John Lamb (q.v.), Greenleaf received the contract to print most of the pamphlets and broadsides, and he opened the paper's editorial pages to the efforts of the Antifederalists. He had been the first New York editor to print "Cato," "Brutus," and "A Country Man." Greenleaf also printed the Marylander Luther Martin's (q.v.) "Genuine Information." In that way, he ably served the Antifederalists in New York who used those major pamphlets in their arguments against ratification. Athough he had been a moderate on political and governmental reform before the Constitutional convention, because he printed Antifederalist works Greenleaf incurred the wrath of the city's powerful Federalist leaders. Seeking to silence him, a mob of Federalist "toughs" attempted to set fire to his office and burn his printing press. Greenleaf lost his office in the fire, but he resisted the mob and drove it off before his press and printing stock were destroyed.

After the Constitutional crisis in New York had ended, Greenleaf, who had lost a number of Federalist customers and advertisers, attempted to restore his business. He turned the paper into a weekly, and he managed to publish it until 1793. In 1791 Greenleaf had married Anna Quackenbos, a niece of Governor George Clinton (q.v.), and the governor gave the Antifederalist printer a bit of state government printing business. In 1795 he was able to establish *Argus and Greenleaf's New Daily Advertiser*, as a Republican Party political organ. Greenleaf became an ally of Aarron Burr. But in the summer of 1798, a yellow fever epidemic swept the city, and on September 14, 1798, Greenleaf died of that illness. Only forty-three, he had been the Antifederalists' most important printer and publisher, crucial to the cause of presenting that party's case to the public.

REFERENCES

Jeremy Belknap, *The History of New Hampshire* (Boston: for the author, 1791–1792); Saul Cornell, *The Other Founders* (Chapel Hill: University of North Carolina Press,

1999); Linda Grant DePauw, *The Eleventh Pillar* (Ithaca, N.Y.: Cornell University Press, 1966); Jonathan E. Greenleaf, *Genealogy of the Greenleaf Family* (New York: E. O. Jenkins, 1854); Thomas Greenleaf, *Geographical Gazeteer of the Towns in the Commonwealth of Massachusetts* (Boston: Greenleaf and Freeman, 1785); Storing, *Complete*, vol. 2; Isaiah Thomas, *History of Printing in America* (Albany: J. Munsell, 1874).

JONATHAN GROUT *(July 23, 1737–September 8, 1807)* was born in Lunenburg, Worcester County, Massachusetts. He studied law and began his practice in Petersham, Massachusetts. Grout took part in the Canadian expedition against France in 1757–1760, and he fought in the American Revolution. Also in politics, Grout served in the Massachusetts lower house in 1781, 1784, and 1787. He also developed a successful law practice and became the most influential lawyer in Worcester County. Grout served as a popular justice of the peace in his part of the county. He entered the Massachusetts State Senate in 1788. Considered radical in his politics, Grout supported the western farmer cause in Shays's Rebellion of 1786.

After having been elected to the Massachusetts ratifying convention, Federalists denied Grout his place in the state senate. But Antifederalist allies demanded he be seated. His ally, Phaneul Bishop (q.v.), had also been denied his seat. That action made both Grout and Bishop, along with their friend Levi Lincoln, staunch opponents of the Federalists and of ratification of the Constitution. His allies regarded Grout as a supporter of the small farmers who were suspicious of strong central government. Certainly that radical lawyer acted in their behalf at the convention. Grout spoke little in the convention, yet gained a reputation as an organizer of Antifederalist supporters. He voted against ratification.

After the convention, the western farmers elected Grout to the first federal congress. There he became an ally of Elbridge Gerry (q.v.), though he did not enjoy Gerry's popularity in that body. He took strong Antifederalist positions and supported Gerry's call for strict construction of the Constitution. Grout supported the federal government's assumption scheme for state debts. But he opposed an excise tax on distilled liquor. In 1790 his archenemy, Artemus Ward, defeated him for election to the second Congress. Grout may have then left Massachusetts for New Hampshire, perhaps to try to appeal to that state's Antifederalists. After his resettlement, Grout seems to have left public life. He was back in Lunenberg, Massachusetts by 1803. Grout died in Dover, New Hampshire, on September 8, 1807.

REFERENCES

Paul Goodman, *The Democratic Republicans of Massachusetts* (Cambridge: Harvard Universty Press, 1964); Van Beck Hall, *Politics Without Parties* (Pittsburgh: University of Pittsburgh Press, 1972); Albert Bushnell Hart (ed.), *Commonwealth History of Massachusetts* (New York: Russell and Russell, 1966), vol. 3; William Lincoln, *History of Worcester, Massachusetts from its Earliest Settlement* (Worcester: Charles Hersey, 1862).

H

WADE HAMPTON *(May 3, 1754–February 4, 1835)* was born in Halifax County, Virginia, to Anthony and Elizabeth (Preston) Hampton. The family moved to Surry County, North Carolina, and later to South Carolina near the present town of Spartanburg sometime thereafter. Around 1773 the father moved his family to the Ninety-six District of South Carolina. Anthony Hampton was killed by Indians in 1776. Young Wade had hardly any education and was left in charge of his family. In 1776 he joined the South Carolina Sixth Regiment to fight in western Carolina under Thomas Sumter (q.v.). In 1780, Hampton took the oath of allegiance to the British government, but he repudiated his oath that same year and again joined Sumter. He became a colonel, and a hero at the battle of Eutaw Springs.

During the Revolution, Hampton also supplied the Continental Army with food and weapons and made enough profit to buy land. In 1785 he owned nearly 3,000 acres, and by 1786 he had enlarged his holdings to own land in Alabama near the Mobile River. At one time in his life, Hampton owned some 238,000 acres of farmland. Hampton parlayed his great wealth into a political career. He became the justice of the peace in Richland County, South Carolina. From 1784 until 1794, he served as a member of the state legislature. Hampton also was involved in politics in the Camden District.

Wealthy and well-respected in his community, Hampton gained election from Saxe-Gotha District to the South Carolina state ratification convention of 1788. There he joined his fellow western Antifederalists to oppose ratification of the Constitution. Though he spoke rarely at the convention, he used his standing as a planter, and his political skills to build a following among Antifederalists. Hampton voted against ratification.

After the convention, Hampton reentered the state legislature in 1791 and was elected sheriff of the Camden District that same year. His allies elected him as a Republican to the United States Congress from the Orangeburg District in 1797, and again in 1803. He lost his bid for reelection in 1804. He had been a Jefferson presidential elector in 1800. Jefferson offered him the Postmaster Generalship of the United States in 1801, but Hampton declined the appointment. Hampton also served as a general in the army in 1808 and commanded at New Orleans in 1809. In 1812 and 1813, he built fortifications at Norfolk, Virginia. In 1813 he was a major-general and commanded troops on Lake Champlain. After he failed in battles around Montreal, Hampton resigned from the army.

As a cotton planter in upcountry Camden District, he built a cotton gin and soon became the wealthiest man in that part of South Carolina. He acquired more land in the west, in the Yazoo area, and around New Orleans where he grew sugarcane and owned a sugar refinery. Hampton and his sons became the most important family in upcountry South Carolina. He also rose in social status throughout the state, even belonging to the prestigious South Carolina Jockey Club in Charleston. Hampton married three times: first to Martha Epps Howell, then to Harriet Flud, and last to Mary Cantey. He had numerous children, including a son, Wade, and a grandson, Wade, who was a general in the Civil War. Hampton belonged to the Episcopal Church, and he built Trinity Church in Columbia, South Carolina. Hampton died in Columbia on February 4, 1835. He is buried at Trinity Church there.

REFERENCES

N. Louise Bailey and Elizabeth Ivey Cooper (eds.), *Biographical Dictionary of the South Carolina House of Representatives* (Columbia: University of South Carolina Press, 1981), vol. 3; Roland Edward Birdwell, "The South's Wealthiest Planter: Wade Hampton I of South Carolina" (PhD diss., University of South Carolina, 1980); Charles Edward Cauthen (ed.), *Family Letters of Three Wade Hamptons* (Columbia: University of South Carolina Press, 1953); Edward McCrady, *History of South Carolina in the Revolution* (New York: Macmillan Co., 1901).

JOHN ANDRE HANNA *(1761/1762–July 13/23, 1805)* was born

in Flemington, Hunterdon County, New Jersey, the son of Reverend John Hanna and Mary (McCrea). He received a classical education from his father, a Presbyterian minister, and graduated from the College of New Jersey (later Princeton) in 1782. Hanna studied law with Stephen Chambers of Lancaster, Pennsylvania. As a youth, he had served under Chambers in the Revolution. Hanna began the practice of law in Lancaster County, in 1783. He moved to Harrisburg, Dauphin County, Pennsylvania in 1785. Hanna made an advantageous marriage to the daughter of John Harris, the founder of Harrisburg, which took him to that growing western town.

Evidently Hanna had received early political recognition, and the citizens of Dauphin County sent him as a delegate to the Pennsylvania Constitutional ratification convention in 1787. On December 18, 1787, Hanna signed a petitition stating that the Constitutional Convention had violated the Thirteenth Article of the Articles of Confederation. He also signed the *Address and Reasons of the Dissent of the Minority of the Convention of Pennsylvania to Their Constituents* of December 18, 1787. Hanna became secretary of the Antifederalist conference in 1788. Active among those Antifederalists who desired a second Constitutional Convention to revise the proposed Constitution, he spoke often. When he lost in that debate, Hanna voted against ratification of the Constitution.

Returning to Harrisburg, Hanna took part in deliberations to call a second state convention, but soon left the group to enter active political life. He was elected to the Pennsylvania State House in 1791. Hanna became lieutenant colonel of the Dauphin County militia in 1792 and brigadier general of the county brigade in 1793. He commanded the county's troops during the Whiskey Rebellion of 1794, although he sympathized with the rebels. Hanna served as major-general of the Third Division of the state militia in 1800. Hanna gained election as a Republican in the United States House of Representatives from 1797 to 1805. There he opposed the Alien and Sedition bills, and generally sided with the Jeffersonian Republicans. Hanna enthusiastically supported the purchase of Louisiana in 1803. He died while still in national office at his home in Harrisburg, Pennsylvania, on July 13 or 23, 1805. This talented leader thus had his career cut short.

REFERENCES

Steven R. Boyd, *The Politics of Opposition* (Millwood, N.Y.: KTO Press, 1979); Jensen and Kaminski, *Documentary History*, vol. 15; Luther Reily Kelker, *History of Dauphin County, Pennsylvania* (Chicago: Lewis Publishing Co., 1907), vol. 2; John Bach McMaster (ed.), *Pennsylvania and the Federal Convention of 1788* (Philadelphia: Historical Society of Pennsylvania, 1888); David J. Siemers, *Ratifying the Republic* (Stanford: Stanford University Press, 2002); Storing, *Complete*, vol. 3.

BENJAMIN HARRISON *(?, 1726–April 24, 1791)* was born at his family's home, Berkeley, in Charles City County, Virginia. He was the son of Benjamin and Anne (Carter) Harrison, the daughter of the wealthy Virginia tobacco planter Robert "King" Carter. Young Harrison received an excellent classical education at home and attended the College of William and Mary. Like many other young planters, he left college without taking a degree. In 1745 Harrison inherited land from his wealthy father to start his own plantation. He married the wealthy Elizabeth Bassett.

Also like others of his class, Harrison soon took his place in Virginia colonial politics. He was first elected to the Virginia House of Burgesses in 1749 and served continuously until 1775. He often was speaker of that body. In 1764 Harrison joined the legislative committee to protest the Stamp Act. In 1774 this patriot worked with the Virginia Committee of Correspondence to organize the people of Virginia to support the rebels. In 1774 he joined others in the call for a colony-wide congress, and he was elected a delegate. From 1774 until 1778, he was a member of the Continental Congress. He presided over the debates that produced the Declaration of Independence and was a signer. Harrison also served in the Virginia convention that wrote the first state constitution in 1776. Elected to the Virginia House of Delegates, he served from 1776 until 1781, and from 1778 until 1781 as its speaker. In 1781 he became governor of Virginia and held that office until 1784. While governor, he helped to persuade Virginians to give up their claims to western lands. In 1784 Harrsion was again in the House of Delegates. He was one of the major leaders in Virginia revolutionary politics.

During the postwar era, Harrison continued his role in Virginia politics. Because of his opposition to change and his state rights position, Harrison had to establish residence in a county more favorable to his views to get re-elected to the house in 1785. James Madison regarded him as a supporter of state and local politics over federal policies. Indeed he was, as Harrison sided with those localists who refused to pay debts owed to Britain until that country paid for the slaves stolen during the Revolution. Harrison also denounced the actions northern delegates took against slavery in the Continental Congress. He feared the slave states would have to bow before the power of the newly freed northern states, and he did not like it.

When Harrison was elected to the state ratification convention for the new Constitution, he became a leader of the localist or Antifederalist forces. Although he did not speak often, Harrison chaired the Committee on Privileges and Elections, a most powerful committee, which he used to promote the Antifederalist cause. Harrison did speak against the unlimited federal power to levy taxes and the right of a central government to regulate trade. He feared that the need for a new Constitution had made many forget that they had fought a Revolution to free themselves from central authority. Harrison also worried about the power of the smaller states to compete with the larger, wealthier states. He expected little cooperation in the new nation from New England or other northern states, since those states had given no support to the beleaguered southern states during the Revolution (Elliot, 627–628). Harrsion joined those Antifederalists who wanted to amend the Constitution before the state ratified it. When that movement failed, Harrison voted against ratification. But after the Antifederalists had failed to stop ratification, he acquiesced in the new government.

This aristocrat had fallen afoul of George Mason (q.v.), the state's most important Antifederalist, when he accepted the Constitution. Of course, Harrison had supported Mason on the call for a bill of rights. He also had fought with his fellow Antifederalist John Tyler (q.v.) over state political issues. So, when the state house refused to elect him speaker at the end of 1788, Harrison retired from public life. He had given major service to his state and nation during the Revolution, and had taken a decidedly southern stand on the Constitution. Harrison left a legacy of state rights to his sons, who would also rise in public life. On April 24, 1791, Harrison died at his estate, Berkeley, in Charles City County, Virginia.

REFERENCES

Richard Beeman, *The Old Dominion and the New Nation* (Lexington: University Press of Kentucky, 1972); Elliot, *Debates*, vol. 3; Hugh Blair Grigsby, *The History of the Vir-*

ginia Federal Convention of 1788 (1890; repr., New York: Da Capo, 1969); Norman K. Risjord, *Chesapeake Politics* (New York: Columbia University Press, 1978); Robert A. Rutland, *Ordeal of the Constitution* (Norman: University of Oklahoma Press, 1965); Storing, *Complete*, vol. 4; Lyon G. Tyler, *The Letters and Times of the Tylers* (1884; repr., New York: Da Capo Press, 1970), vol. 1.

JOHN HATHORN *(January 9, 1749–February 19, 1825)* was

born in Wilmington, Delaware, and attended a local preparatory school. After schooling, he began his career as a teacher, one path for a young man to gain recognition in late colonial America. He managed to study for and then become a surveyor in Orange County, New York. Hathorn joined the colonial militia and rose to the rank of captain. Active as a radical revolutionary, he served the patriot cause throughout the American Revolution. Hathorn's peers elected him colonel of the Fourth Orange County Regiment in 1776. By 1786 Hathorn was brigadier general of the New York state militia, and by 1793 he had been promoted to major general.

Military prestige led Hathorn into New York state politics. He served in the state assembly as a George Clinton (q.v.) ally in 1778, 1780, from 1782 to 1785, in 1795, and in 1805. He was speaker of the state house in 1783 and 1784. Hathorn also held office in the state senate from 1786 until 1790, and again from 1799 until 1803. Elected to the Continental Congress in 1788, he strongly supported the existing Articles of Confederation.

As a leader in defense of local issues and rights, Hathorn became a power among the state Antifederalists in the state legislature of 1788. Although he was not elected to the state ratifying convention for the federal Constitution, he advocated amendments to the proposed document and opposed its ratification. Hathorn's fellow Antifederalists put him up for election for the first federal Congress from the state's Fourth District and he won. But the Federalist power in that part of the state organized to defeat him in 1790. Hathorn again was elected to the federal Congress in 1795 and served a term before being defeated in 1797. He supported Antifederalist causes while in Congress and became a Jeffersonian Republican. This staunch Republican then reentered state politics and ably served the cause of state rights. He also was a merchant in his county. Hathorn died at his home in Warwick, Orange County, New York, on February 19, 1825.

REFERENCES

Steven R. Boyd, *The Politics of Opposition* (Millwood, N.Y.: KTO Press, 1979); Russell Headley, *The History of Orange County, New York* (Middletown, N.Y.: Van Deusen and Elms, 1908); David J. Siemers, *Ratifying the Republic* (Stanford: Stanford University Press, 2002).

JONATHAN J. HAZARD *(1744–c. 1824)* was born in Narrangansett,

Rhode Island. His father was Jonathan Hazard, a descendent of the founder of Newport, Rhode Island, and his mother was Abigail (MacCoon). The family was prominent in Washington County society and public life. Hazard received a public school education. He practiced law in his home county and rose in the legal profession. For this courtly, well-dressed, eloquent speaker, public service became the vocation of his life. Hazard married three times; first to his cousin Pretence Hazard, then Hannah Brown, and last Marian Gage.

Elected in 1776 to the Rhode Island House of Representatives from Charleston, Hazard became an ardent patriot. This staunch revolutionary led his constituents in support of the Declaration of Independence. Hazard then became paymaster of the Rhode Island Continental Battalion in 1777. He fought in the battles in New Jersey during that year. In 1778, as a member of the state General Assembly, he led the Council of War. At the war's end, Hazard made efforts to restore the estate of his Tory brother Thomas, but Thomas left for England never to return.

After the war, Hazard rose to become the political boss of Rhode Island republican politics. He belonged to the antimercantile party. In 1786 he defeated the "Hard Money," or mercantile party by force of his political powers and what some called his demagogic speeches. William Updike, the historian of the Episcopal church in Rhode Island, said Hazard "argued that the state currency based on real estate was safer than the obligation of any bank" (302). In the general assembly in 1786, he took the side of the farmers and forced through the Paper Money Act. In 1787 the legislature sent Hazard as a delegate to the Continental Congress where he became a strong supporter of the Articles of Confederation.

The people of Rhode Island opposed the federal Constitution of 1787, and Hazard became the leader of the Antifederalist forces in the state, a "fiery opponent of the adoption of the Federal Constitution," in Updike's words (73). Indeed, it was Hazard who convinced the voters of Rhode Island that they had little to fear for their economy by refusing to ratify the Constitution, even though other states had ratified it. Hazard and his friend Thomas Joslyn (q.v.) sponsored the resolution to send the Constitution to the people for their appraisal. At a town meeting in March 1788, Hazard explained his opposition to the Constitution. Fears for personal liberties were high on his list. But above all Hazard believed that state agricultural interests would be hurt by a neomercantilist large central government. As a delegate to the South Kingston convention of March 1790, he remained consistent in voting against ratification. Hazard continued to write and to politick against the Constitution until the state finally moved to ratify.

Though he had defended Rhode Island's decision to remain out of the Union, the adroit political radical knew that the state's Federalist Party had made gains when it pointed out that the state had been hurt by not having delegates at the national Congress. Federalists had also helped to liquidate the state's debts. Accordingly, he finally supported ratification after Rhode Island had been left out of the new federal government, though he continued to demand that popular opinion be heard. Elected to the state assembly in 1790, Hazard began to lose his influence as leader of the opposition. As Updike pointed out, Hazard "shook the confidence of the public and his party, and he fell in popular estimation, and never regained his former elevated position" (74).

As an older man and no longer the state's political leader, Hazard decided to leave Rhode Island and settle near Rome, Oneida County, New York. He purchased an estate and lived until at least 1824, enjoying the life of a much respected country squire. To a friend he wrote bitterly that his former allies had deserted him. "I have been a principal actor in three state revolutions, and . . . I have been thrice sacrificed, once in the year 1790, and twice since" (Robinson, 308).

REFERENCES

Bailyn, *Debate*, vol. 2; Frank G. Bates, *Rhode Island and the Formation of the Union* (New York: Columbia University Press, 1908); *Biographical Encyclopedia of Representative Men of Rhode Island* (Providence: National Biographical Publishing Co., 1881); Patrick T. Conley, *Democracy in Decline: Rhode Island's Constitutional Development, 1776–1841* (Providence: Brown University Press, 1977); Irwin W. Polishook, *Rhode Island and the Union* (Evanston, Ill.: Northwestern University Press, 1969); Caroline F. Robinson, *The Hazard Family of Rhode Island* (Providence: Published for Author, 1895); William Updike, *History of the Episcopal Church in Narragansett*, 2 vols. (Boston: D. B. Updike, Merrymount Press, 1907); William B. Weeden, *Early Rhode Island* (New York: Grafton Press, 1910).

PATRICK HENRY *(May 29, 1736–June 6, 1799)* was born in Hanover County, Virginia. His father, John Henry, had been born in Aberdeen, Scotland. His mother was Sarah (Winston), daughter of an immigrant from Yorkshire, England. Young Patrick was raised in the Church of England and lived as a faithful communicant throughout his life. Educated largely at home, he also attended the famous school of Samuel Davies. Henry then clerked in a store, and by the age of sixteen owned his own mercantile establishment. At the young age of eighteen, he married Sarah Shelton, and they had a number of children. Upon her death, in 1776 Henry married a wealthy planter's daughter, Dorthea Dandridge. They also had a number of children. With some success as a merchant, Henry managed to purchase land and join the planter class, but soon failed in that business. Later in life he would own as much as 22,000 acres gained in land speculation in Kentucky, North Carolina, and western Virginia. He would own sixty-six slaves.

A man of engaging personality, keen wit, and quick understanding of an issue, and able splendidly to control the pitch and projection of his voice, Henry decided on the law as a means to his success. He was licensed in 1760. In 1763, Henry achieved his first fame in arguing the Parson's Cause case for religious freedom for dissenters, despite his personal support for the Episcopal Church. He bought land in then rural Louisa County in the west and again planted. In 1764 Henry gained election from the west to the Virginia House of Burgesses. With his talent for debate and politics, and the support of western farmers, he rose rapidly in that body.

In opposition to the British Stamp Act, Henry spoke eloquently against mercantile oppression. In 1774 he supported calling the Continental Congress and became a delegate to that first Congress. It was in 1775 in Richmond, in beautiful St. John's Episcopal Church, that the great orator placed his name among the legends of this country. His "give me liberty, or give me death" speech became a clarion call of revolutionary resistance. Henry also led the Virginia militia of Hanover County on a march to the capital. In 1776 he resigned his military position to devote himself to the politics of resistance, and he assisted in drafting Virginia's first state constitution. Elected governor of the new state, he defended fellow Virginian George Washington's then much maligned military policies of 1778 and 1779. Henry retired as governor in 1779. He then reentered the state assembly in 1781, where he rose to become the state's most powerful legislator, and became a bitter lifelong enemy of Thomas Jefferson, then the governor.

After the Revolution, Henry continued as the major political force from the west in the House of Burgesses. He advocated reopening trade with Britain to help the depressed tobacco planters and the poorer upcountry farmers. Henry also wanted Virginia's Tories to return, some said because of his ties to the English Church, but also because he believed that they could make valuable contributions to the restoration of trade and agricultural practices. He developed an interest in popular education, in part because he had a number of sons to educate, and he became a trustee of nearby newly founded Hampden-Sidney College. In 1784 Henry attempted to reinvigorate the fallen Episcopal Church by providing tax relief for it. Although he did not advocate reestablishment, he now took a different position than he had in the Parson's Cause case. In 1784 Henry once again gained the governorship, but that office made it difficult for him to continue to dictate the legislative agenda. As governor, he supported the Alexandria conference of 1785 called to mediate the boundary and water disputes between Virginia and Maryland. He also favored the Annapolis convention of 1786, again in hopes of reinvigorating trade. But Henry did not like the results of that convention, finding the proposed second convention in Philadelphia unnecessary. As governor, he also voiced Virginia's problems with the northern states giving away trade on the Mississippi, fearing it would hurt investors who wanted to encourage settlement in Kentucky.

Retiring from the governorship once again in 1786, after two terms, Henry settled in Prince Edward County to plant, practice law, and to restore his empty coffers. But in 1787 this consummate political man reentered the House of Burgesses. When nominated to attend the Philadelphia convention in 1787, he declined because he feared that convention was bent on altering the Articles of Confederation. He would become Virginia's most important opponent of the proposed federal Constitution, and perhaps the country's most famous or infamous Antifederalist.

Before the Virginia convention met, Henry read the *Letters of an American Farmer*, then thought to have been written by his ally, Richard Henry Lee (q.v.). That work influenced his views toward the Constitution. Henry then met with the Philadelphia Antifederalist editor Eleazor Oswald (q.v.), who gave him important letters and pamphlets from General John Lamb (q.v.), one of New York's leading Antifederalists. He had begun to gather the information necessary for his elaborate defense against the nationalist forces. So, why did this former revolutionary, conservative church leader, and heretofore nationalist governor become such an important outspoken Antifederalist? Perhaps he had too long represented the interests of small western farmers, or perhaps he lived too long in the west, isolated from the pressures of national integration.

A look at Henry's pithy arguments and raw political actions against ratification of the Constitution at the Virginia convention allows some understanding of this difficult man's motivation. Henry plotted politically with the brilliant Lee and George Mason (q.v.) as to the best way to keep Virginia's Antifederalist majority united. He said again and again, as did they, that excessive federal powers damaged the rights of states and the liberties of the people. Not really a republican, and certainly no democrat, that leader of the people based his main arguments on the rights of states in a federal government. When he realized the Constitution would be ratified, Henry sought to force support for amendments from the state convention, and he called for another federal convention to revise the proposed Constitution.

The state ratifying convention met in June 1788 in Richmond, not far from St. John's Church where Henry had made his Revolutionary War speech in behalf of national liberty. Throughout the convention of 1788, he spoke often and for long, tedious periods of the threats the new Constitution held for those very liberties for which he would die. Henry and his allies' strategy was to alarm the many conflicting interests in the state, raising their particular fears about the proposed Constitution in order to build a majority coalition. First he instructed the small farmers about how their rights to trial by jury had been lost. Next he tried to frighten planters by telling them that the rights of the slave states and the very future of slavery was at stake because the free states desired to control the new federal government and use central power against slavery. To all those southerners who had interests in Kentucky, he warned that the territory was in great danger because Federalist nationalists opposed the rights to navigate the Mississippi River. "The seven Northern States are determined to give up the Mississippi," he claimed (Bailyn, 683). In these efforts Henry received much assistance from William Grayson (q.v.) and from James Monroe (q.v.). Henry then challenged the legal authority of the Philadelphia convention, insisting it had gone beyond its mandate. In this he enlisted the support of George Mason.

Failing to convince his fellow delegates at Richmond to send the Constitution back to the Continental Congress for revision, Henry turned to what he claimed was the Constitution's greatest danger to personal and states' rights: "You are going to join with men who will pay no respect even to this state" (Bailyn, 629). Executive power was much too great, said the orator, and the federal authority to organize a national army harmed local militias and made the president something akin to a dictator or monarch. "It squints toward monarchy," he said (Meade, 213). This was Henry's personal fear for Virginia, as he concluded that his large and powerful state would have little representation in the proposed federal House of Representatives.

But Henry and his allies were unable to build a majority coalition to stop state ratification. They turned to their last tactic, as Mason and Henry drew up a bill of some forty rights they insisted were not protected in the Constitution. Although none of their requests gained passage in the state convention in June of 1788, the state's Antifederalists succeeded in forcing the Federalists to promise support for a bill of rights. Henry then asked the Virginia state legislature to pass a resolution favoring amendments. "My mind will not be quieted," said he, "till I see something substantial come forth in the shape of a Bill of Rights" (Meade, 251). These checks on government's structure from the states and through a bill of rights were for Henry motivated by his "dread [of] the depravity of Human nature" (Bailyn, 687). In October 1788, using information from Governor George Clinton of New York (q.v.), Henry persuaded the Burgesses to instruct the state's first federal congressmen to introduce a bill of rights. To assure his own allies would lead that cause, the nimble Henry managed to defeat the Federalist James Madison and have William Grayson and Richard Henry Lee elected to the first U.S. Senate. Theodorick Bland (q.v.), another ally, introduced in the first Congress in 1789 a call for a second Constitutional Convention, but the vote failed. Then, Henry's Virginia allies proposed a bill of rights. Although Henry's large number of amendments were not passed, the bill of rights certainly incorporated his and Mason's thoughts on freedom and liberty, and perhaps stands as their finest achievement in defense of personal rights.

Feeling his tasks accomplished and growing weary, Henry nevertheless took one last stand against the Federalists and persuaded the Virginia Burgesses to protest Alexander Hamilton's scheme to assume state debts. He left public life for good in 1791, but continued to intrigue with Monroe to resist Federalist nationalist measures. Henry resumed the practice of law, tried many successful cases, and bought large tracts of land in North Carolina and Kentucky. In 1795 he retired to his Red Hill plantation in Charlotte County. But he was continuously called upon to consult, and friends asked him to return to public office. In a series of complicated and still unexplained political moves, the great orator joined with the Federalists and made amends with President George Washington. He turned against the hated Jefferson and his new ally James Madison. Washington offered Henry a Supreme Court seat, and President John Adams later asked him to become ambassador to France. Still, if Henry had come to believe the Federalists had created an effective government, he never accepted public office from them. He died at peace with himself on June 6, 1799, at Red Hill.

If he spoke too often—and he had—or appeared more eloquent and wordy than thoughtful—and he had done that, too—Henry nevertheless left a great gift to his country. It is the image of a leader determined to protect individual liberties at all costs. That he also is linked as a father of the rights of states has left his legacy mixed and perhaps muddy.

REFERENCES

Bailyn, *Debate*, vol. 2; Richard Beeman, "The Democratic Faith of Patrick Henry," *Virginia Magazine of History and Biography* 95 (1987): 301–316; ———. *The Old Dominion and the New Nation* (Lexington: University Press of Kentucky, 1972); John Daly Burk, *History of Virginia From the First Settlement* (Petersburg, Va.: n.p., 1804–1816), vol. 3; Hugh Blair Grigsby, *The Virginia Convention of 1788*, 2 vols. (Richmond: Virginia Historical Society, 1890); William Wirt Henry, *Patrick Henry: Life and Speeches*, 3 vols. (New York: Charles Scribner's Sons, 1891); Michael Lienesch, *New Order of the Ages* (Princeton: Princeton University Press, 1988); David A. McCants, *Patrick Henry the Orator* (Westport, Conn.: Greenwood Press, 1990); William Henry Meade, *History of the Episcopal Church in Virginia* (Philadelphia: J. B. Lippincott, 1861), 2 vols.; Norman K. Risjord, *Chesapeake Politics* (New York: Columbia University Press, 1978); Robert Rutland, *Ordeal of the Constitution* (Norman: University of Oklahoma Press, 1965); Moses Coit Tyler, *Patrick Henry* (New York: F. Ungar, 1966).
Henry's papers are at the Library of Congress.

SAMUEL HOPKINS *(April 19, 1753–September 16, 1819)* was born in Albemarle County, Virginia, and he received an education from private tutors. During the American Revolution, he served on the staff of General George Washington. A successful officer, Hopkins rose in rank to lieutenant colonel and then colonel of the Tenth Virginia Regiment.

During the state controversy over ratification of the federal Constitution, Hopkins sided with George Mason (q.v.) and Patrick Henry (q.v.), and joined the Antifederalist cause. He had been an outspoken local rights advocate in the state legislature, but, as a member of the state ratification convention, Hopkins felt overshadowed by the great old leaders and rarely spoke. However, he did speak in favor of funding the travels of the delegates in hopes of enticing Antifederalist delegates from the state's west to attend the convention. He also wanted to have the convention pay the costs of Antifederalists traveling to other states to consult with their allies. Hopkins voted against ratification of the Constitution.

Perhaps because his side had been defeated in the convention, or perhaps because he foresaw opportunity, Hopkins moved in 1796 to Kentucky. He settled at Red Banks, near the Ohio River. Hopkins soon became a respected lawyer in Kentucky and rose in that new state's political hierarchy. He served as chief justice of Kentucky's first court of criminal law, and chancery from 1799 until 1801. Hopkins also held office in the Kentucky state legislature in 1800, 1801, and from 1803 until 1806. He was in the state senate from 1809 until 1813, where he espoused the Republican cause. Hopkins commanded as a major general the state's western frontier in 1812. From 1813 until 1815, he was a War Hawk in the federal House of Representatives.

Always faithful to the cause of Antifederalism, Hopkins's service in Kentucky's legislature and in the federal Congress reflected his radical localist western views. After his federal government service, Hopkins retired to his country estate, Spring Garden, in Henderson County, Kentucky. He stopped practicing law and led the life of a gentleman farmer. Hopkins died there on September 16, 1819.

REFERENCES

Richard J. Beeman, *The Old Dominion and the New Nation* (Lexington: University Press of Kentucky, 1972); Steven R. Boyd, *The Politics of Opposition* (Millwood, N.Y.: KTO Press, 1979); Elliot, *Debates*, vol. 3; Hugh Blair Grigsby, *The Virginia Convention of 1788* (Richmond: Virginia Historical Society, 1890), vol. 2; David Siemers, *Ratifying the Republic* (Stanford: Stanford University Press, 2002).

DAVID HOWELL *(January 1, 1747–July 30, 1824)* was born in Morristown, New Jersey. His father was the business leader Aaron Howell, and his mother was named Sarah. From a staunch Baptist family, he received a religious education at Reverend Isaac Eaton's Hopewell Academy in New Jersey. Howell graduated from the College of New Jersey (later Princeton) in 1766. A close friend of the educator and Baptist leader James Manning, Howell was recruited to teach at the recently founded College of Rhode Island in Providence (later Brown University). In 1769 Brown awarded him the M.A., and Howell became professor of natural philosophy and mathematics there. In 1768 he had begun the practice of law in Providence. He was married in 1770 to Mary Brown, daughter of a Baptist minister, and they had five children.

Howell rose in academic and political life in his adopted state of Rhode Island. From 1773 until his death in 1824, he served on the Board of Fellows at Brown. He gave up the natural sciences to teach Latin, Greek, and law there. Howell resigned his professorship in 1779 to become a fulltime lawyer and political leader. During the American Revolution, he spoke actively in support of the patriot cause. In 1780, now highly regarded in local circles as a leader, Howell returned to Brown University to become its secretary and chief financial officer. Howell traveled to Europe in 1784 to raise funds for the college.

After the Revolution, Howell became associate justice of the state supreme court, and served in that office in 1786 and 1787. From 1781 until 1785, the state legislature sent him to the Continental Congress. Witty and a brilliant speaker, Howell often caused trouble for himself there because of his outspokenness. In 1782 he bragged in Congress that the northern states, especially those of New England, were strongly democratic, but the slave states were autocratic. As a member of the Confederation Congress, he voted against the impost or tariff resolutions, which some felt hindered the young country's revenue-raising opportunities. Because one state alone could defeat a money bill in Congress, other states' delegates heaped approbrium on Howell for his vote and wanted him impeached. Still, he had made some allies because he served on the prestigious committee to draft the western ordinances in 1784 and, with his good friend Elbridge Gerry of Massachusetts (q.v.), helped to write the ordinance of 1785. In a letter to the governor of Rhode Island in 1782, Howell said he had begun to fear strong governnment, and he wondered why government needed so many officials. He also opposed amending the Articles of Confederation, as he believed the Articles supported small government.

Because of his defense of the north from what he called excessive southern power and his strong support for local rights, Howell became an Antifederalist. Federalists in Rhode Island kept him from being reappointed to his judgeship because of his political stand on the Paper Money Act. This political blow, plus his worries about threats to small government, led Howell to oppose the ratification of the Constitution of 1787. He joined many of Rhode Island's Baptists in rejecting that document. Howell called himself a moderate, and as "Solon Junior" in an article printed in the *Providence Gazette*, on August 9, 1788, said that he wanted any new government to display a "reformation of manners." By that he alluded to flaws in the Constitution, but also stated that the proposed Constitution "will soon be made such as the good sense and virtue of the people choose to have it" (Bailyn, 534–535). Despite his belief that the people themselves made good government, Howell's "Extracts and Affairs; or, Farmer's Letters" revealed his unease about putting his faith in people from all sections of the young nation. His work was a stirring antislave manifesto, directed against those who wanted a nation with slave states. Over issues of taxation, state powers, and slavery, Howell, the so-called moderate, helped to persuade Rhode Islanders to reject the Constitution until 1790.

Like many other Antifederalists, Howell realized that the state must join the federal Union, and he eventually acquiesced in its ratification. But he wanted revisions and never really trusted the Federalists. In 1789 he became attorney general of Rhode Island. In 1789 Howell also founded the Providence Antislave Society. In 1790 once again he was named a professor at Brown, this time of law. After his mentor, Manning, died, Howell served as Brown's president. Despite his distaste for the Federalists, Howell was a longtime friend of President George Washington, and at the president's request, he served on the Boundary Committee, which accepted the Jay Treaty of 1794. In 1812 President James Madison appointed this Republican United

States District Judge for Rhode Island, a position he held until 1824. His son Jeremiah became a Republican United States Senator. On July 30, 1824, this longtime educator, able judge, and staunch defender of democratic society died in Providence, Rhode Island.

REFERENCES

Bailyn, *Debate*, vol. 2; Walter C. Bronson, *The History of Brown University, 1764–1914* (New York: Arno Press, 1971); *Biographical Cyclopedia of Representative Men of Rhode Island* (Providence: National Biographical Publishing Co., 1881); Gertrude S. Kimball, *Providence in Colonial Times* (Boston: Houghton, Mifflin, 1912); Irwin H. Polishook, *Rhode Island and the Union* (Evanston, Ill.: Northwestern University Press, 1967).
The Howell papers are at Brown University.

HUGH HUGHES *(1727–1802)* was born in Dutchess County, New York. Although little of his early activities are known save through the comments of his son James Miles Hughes, a New York City lawyer and Dutchess County landowner, it is obvious that he had a fine education. Hugh Hughes had associations with John Lamb (q.v.), later a powerful leader in Dutchess County, where Hughes owned a farm. During the American Revolution, he served in the Continental Army as a quartermaster. His assistant was the later Antifederalist Charles Tillinghast (q.v.). It is said that Hughes also tutored the sons of John Lamb. Mostly, before and during the Revolution, Hughes made a living as what we now call a publicist, writing for newspapers, assisting others in composing speeches, and generally supporting the careers of leading political figures.

An outspoken Antifederalist, Hughes contributed mightily to that cause both in print and in political organization. He assisted Abraham Yates (q.v.) in writing "The Federal Farmer." He also worked on Yates's "Brutus" essays that attacked "Publius" the Federalist. He wrote a private letter to "Publius" called the "Interogation," which circulated among his friends. Hughes also wrote a series of six letters in the New York *Journal* from November 21, 1787, to February 14, 1788. Called "A Countryman" (not to be confused with DeWitt Clinton's work of the same title), the letters received praise from Thomas Greenleaf (q.v.), the newspaper's editor. Hughes, an ally and sometimes speechwriter for Governor George Clinton (q.v.), fulminated in those essays against the Federalist attempts to create a strong federal government. Most particularily, Hughes attacked Philadelpha's Robert Morris's banking policies. He believed Morris was determined to control the finances of the United States.

Perhaps Hughes's most famous work was in a letter of March 7, 1788, to Charles Tillinghast. The letter that Tillinghast released to the public captures the Antifederalist fears of the Federalists' proposed central government. Quoted by Jackson Turner Main, the letter deserves reprinting. In one part of it, Hughes said: "From the conduct of our Church and Senate, we see how absolutely requisite it is, to continually guard against Power; for, when once Bodies of Men, in authority, get Possession of, or become invested with, Property or Prerogatives, whether it is by Intrigue, Mistake or Chance, they scarcely ever relinquish their Claim, even if found in Inequity itself" (10).

Although little is known about Hughes's postratification activities, it is assumed that he returned to his farm in Dutchess County, New York. Presumably he died there sometime in 1802. His son, James Miles Hughes, became a prominent New York lawyer.

REFERENCES

Steven R. Boyd, *The Politics of Opposition* (Millwood, N.Y.: KTO Publishers, 1979); Jensen and Kaminski, *Documentary History*, vols. 1, 2, and 13; Jackson Turner Main, *The Antifederalists* (Chapel Hill: University of North Carolina Press, 1961). Hughes papers, Library of Congress.

JAMES HUTCHINSON *(January 29, 1752–September 5, 1793)*

was born in Wakefield Township, Bucks County, Pennsylvania, the son of the farmer and Quaker Randal Hutchinson. Precocious, the younger Hutchinson was sent early to study with Paul Preston at a school in Virginia. Hutchinson attended the College of Pennsylvania (later the University of Pennsylvania), from which he graduated number one in his class. He studied medicine at the Medical College of Pennsylvania in 1774. Hutchinson then went to England to study medicine with the celebrated Dr. Edward Fothergill.

When Hutchinson attempted to return to the United States in 1777, the ardent patriot had a harrowing experience, as he had to sneak through France to leave Europe, and the British regarded him as a spy and tried to imprison him. Back home he served in the United States Army as surgeon general of Pennsylvania. He also was on the Committee of Safety when the English army left Philadelphia. The Quakers considered expelling him for his military activity, but thought better of it. Famous already for his heroics, Hutchinson was made a trustee of the new University of Pennsylvania in 1779. After the Revolution he married Lydia Biddle from a distinguished Philadelphia mercantile family. Upon her death he married Sydney Howell.

On the faculty of the university medical school, and a physician to the port of Philadelphia, Hutchinson also became active in local politics. He was a committed localist. Hutchinson served in the Continental Congress in 1787, and he became a close friend of the Antifederalist Richard Henry Lee (q.v.) of Virginia.

Although he was not elected to the Pennsylvania state ratifying convention, Hutchinson took part in the opposition to the Constitution. He had been a strong defender of the state constitution and wanted to protect it against outside interference. Hutchinson was the friend of other Philadelphia Antifederalists William Shippen and John Nicholson (q.v.), and assisted Nicholson in developing anti-Constitutional arguments for the convention. He met with Richard Henry Lee in Philadelphia in November 1787, and the two leaders worked to unite Virginia and Pennsylvania Antifederalists. Hutchinson also sent copies of his writings to Elbridge Gerry (q.v.) in Boston. He may also have been one of the authors of the celebrated "Centinel" essays. His ties to the Antifederalist editor Eleazor Oswald (q.v.) gave Hutchinson and his friends access to a leading local newspaper. He also purchased and circulated widely a number of Antifederalist pamphlets. With George Bryan (q.v.) and John Smilie (q.v.) he wrote "The Old Whig," a major Antifederalist document. In that diatribe against ratification, Hutchinson helped to keep Antifederalism alive in the state. In it the authors called for another general convention to amend the Constitution before the states ratified it. Hutchinson wanted amendments for a bill of personal rights agreed to in advance of any discussion of ratification. In this, he along with his fellow Antifederalists failed.

After the convention, Hutchinson returned to his teaching and to the practice of medicine. He became chair of the department of chemistry of the University of Pennsylvania and continued as physician to the port of Philadelphia. His fame soon led to a high honor—election to the American Philosophical Society. Hutchinson also resumed his position in local politics, as he continued to speak in favor of small government and to oppose changes in the state constitution. As a physician at the Pennsylvania Hospital, at great personal risk he helped in the effort to stem the outbreak of a yellow fever epidemic. He died in Philadelphia on September 5, 1793, a victim of that epidemic. He died committed to medicine and to the cause of Antifederalism.

REFERENCES

Douglas M. Arnold, *A Republican Revolution: Ideology and Politics in Pennsylvania, 1776–1790* (New York: Columbia University Press, 1989); Steven R. Boyd, *The Politics of Opposition* (Millwood, N.Y.: KTO Press, 1979); Saul Cornell, *The Other Founders* (Chapel Hill: University of North Carolina Press, 1999); Howard M. Jenkins (ed.), *Pennsylvania Colonial and Federal* (Philadelphia: Pennsylvania Historical Publication Association, 1903), vol. 3; Jensen and Kaminski, *Documentary History*, vols. 2 and 14; Henry Simpson, *The Lives of Eminent Philadelphians* (Philadelphia: William Brotherhead, 1859).

I

DANIEL ILSELY *(May 30, 1740–May 10, 1813)* was born in Falmouth, Cumberland County, Massachusetts (Maine territory). He received a classical education. Ilsely became a successful shipper and a distiller. During the Revolution, he belonged to the Massachusetts committees of correspondence and safety. He served in the Revolution as a major from Falmouth, Maine. Possibly, he practiced law in Falmouth.

Active in provincial politics, Ilsely was an Antifederalist delegate to the Massachusetts state Constitutional ratifying convention of 1788, where he spoke little but attended all sessions and worked to oppose ratification. He was one of two delegates from Falmouth who voted against ratification. After the convention, Ilsely continued to be active in Massachusetts state politics, serving in the state legislature in 1793 and 1794. He also became a Republican in the federal Congress for the 1807–1809 term, but failed in his bid for reelection. Unlike many others from his state, Ilsely supported President Thomas Jefferson's embargo on British imports, which perhaps explains his defeat for reelection. Ilsely died in Portland, Maine, territory on May 10, 1813. He had always hoped to represent Maine in Congress, but died before it became a state.

REFERENCES

Samuel B. Harding, *The Contest over the Ratification of the Federal Constitution in the State of Massachusetts* (Cambridge: Harvard University Press, 1896); Jensen and Kaminski, *Documentary History*, vol. 5; David J. Siemers, *Ratifying the Republic* (Stanford: Stanford University Press, 2002).

J

JOSEPH JONES *(?, 1727–October 26, 1805)* was born in King George County, Virginia, part of the northern neck. His father, James, ran a country store and a tavern. His mother was named Hester. James Jones later became quite successful as a merchant and had many ties back in England. Joseph received a local education, and then went to the Inner Temple in London in 1749, the Middle Temple in 1751, and became a British barrister. He later returned to Virginia and became a successful lawyer in the thriving up-country town of Fredericksburg. In 1754 Jones became King's attorney for Fredericksburg. In 1758 he married Mary Taliaferro, daughther of Colonel John of Spotsylvania County. In 1772 Jones entered the colonial Virginia House of Burgesses.

A cautious patriot, in 1774 Jones chaired the Committee of Correspondence of King George County. As a member of Virginia's second state committee of safety in 1776, he supported the Revolution. In 1776 he also gained election to the state convention that framed the Virginia Declaration of Rights and where he assisted in drafting the first state constitution. Jones held office in the Continental Congress in 1777 and 1778, became a judge of the General Court from 1778 to 1779, and from 1780 to 1783 again served in the Continental Congress. In that body, he became an active defender of the rights of states.

A close friend to Thomas Jefferson, Jones became a radical delegate to the Virginia Constitutional ratifying convention. In 1787 he once again served in the House of Burgesses where he soon parted ways with his old friend James Madison. In an October 29, 1787, letter to Madison, he stated that he had "many objections to the Constitution." Further, "I should have been pleased to see a declaration of rights accompany this Constitution" (Jensen and Kaminski, 508–509). In the convention, at first Jones took the position that the new proposed Constitution protected personal rights. Jones reported to the Federalist Madison that he worried about the opposition to the Constitution in the state. But he soon aligned himself with Patrick Henry (q.v.) and assisted in the strategy to draw up amendments to the Constitution. Jones had a brilliant legal mind, and he often talked with George Mason (q.v.) about the proposed Bill of Rights and no doubt joined the group that drew up that document. Also embittered over what he believed was Madison's betrayal of the rights of Virginians, Jones became an open opponent of the Constitution. He voted against ratification.

In 1789 Jones again became a judge of the Virginia General Court. He sided with the Jeffersonian forces during the Washington administration. Jones died at his home in Fredericksburg, Virginia, on October 26, 1805.

REFERENCES

Worthington C. Ford (ed.), *Letters of Joseph Jones of Virginia, 1777–1787* (Washington: Department of State, 1889); Jensen and Kaminski, *Documentary History*, vol. 13; George Morgan, *Life of James Monroe* (Boston: Small, Maynard and Co., 1921).

SAMUEL JONES *(July 26, 1734–November 25, 1819)* was born at Fort Hill, Long Island, New York. He was the son of William Jones, whose father had come to the colonies from Ireland, having been a privateer in Jamaica. His mother was Phoebe (Jackson), who came from the Dutch community on Long Island. The young Jones grew up in Hempstead, Long Island. He received little schooling, although one of his teachers was the young Samuel Seabury. Jones became a merchant marine sailor. Ambitious, he studied law under Judge William Smith, an ally of the rising young New York political star George Clinton (q.v.). Jones soon developed a successful law practice in New York City. In 1765 he married Eleanor, daughter of Cornelius Tuck, a well-to-do merchant in the city. Upon her death in 1768, he married Cornelia Herring (Horing), a member of the Bogart clan of powerful early Dutch settlers.

Both of Jones's marriages proved fortunate. His first father-in-law hired him as his lawyer and brought him into the still-powerful Dutch trade organization of New York City. His second father-in-law was a member of the colonial legislature and a real estate broker, and also was well connected to the Clinton forces. Jones himself bought land and became quite successful. In 1774 he joined other business leaders in the City Committee of Correspondence, where he supported nonintercourse with Great Britain. Jones favored resistance to England. He belonged to the New York Committee of One Hundred, which supported the Continental Congress. In 1776, to protect his financial interests from British invaders, he moved to Orange County, Connecticut. When New York City once again became safe, he moved back to practice law.

Along with his colleague Richard Varick, in 1782 Jones collected and published the legal statutes for New York state. Their book became an important source for the codification of state laws. From 1786 to 1790, he represented Queen's County in the New York General Assembly. Although considered a conservative in politics, Jones became a close ally of the radical Governor George Clinton.

As a Clintonian leader, Jones was elected to the New York Constitutional ratification convention. At Albany he actively opposed ratification of the Constitution. Jones's grounds for opposition centered on his worries that New York would lose trade advantage by joining a powerful federal union. At first he hoped to amend the Constitution, especially to abolish the proposed Supreme Court. His nine proposed amendments related to the powers of the courts, because as a lawyer-businessman he opposed the federal government's right to bring suit against a state. Jones also resisted any right for the federal government to interfere with state roads. But, after Jones realized that the other states were bent on ratification, and after coming under the influence or pressures of Alexander Hamilton's promise of amendments, he joined Melancton Smith (q.v.) to vote for ratification. Unlike others who changed their vote on the Constitution, however, Jones kept his ties to Governor Clinton. His Antifederalist friend General John Lamb (q.v.) also accepted his explanation for changing his vote. This kept Jones in touch with the growing Republican forces in the city.

These connections with old allies allowed Jones to join the New York Federal Republicans and to remain in public life. From 1789 to 1796, he served as recorder of New York City. From 1791 until 1797, he held office in the New York State Senate as a Clinton loyalist. In 1796, Jones drafted the law to regulate the office of state comptroller, and Clinton named him to that office in 1797. But by 1807 Jones had become a Federalist. He lost his bid in 1806 for the state senate to DeWitt Clinton and retired from public life.

No doubt the movements of Jones through the political spectrum were connected to the business world of New York City. The Federalist Chancellor James Kent regarded him as extremely intelligent, a person of moderation, a scholar of the common law, and skilled in the important technical tools of property law. Jones died at his Long Island home on November 25, 1819. Certainly his Antifederalism was of the business kind, as Jones feared a too-powerful national government's interference in municipal trade, land speculation, and, especially, a state's legal rights to adjudicate its own issues and needs.

REFERENCES

Bailyn, *Debate*, vol. 2; William A. Duer, *Reminiscences of an Old New Yorker* (New York: W. L. Andrews, 1867); Elliot, *Debates*, vol. 2; John Henry Jones, *The Jones Family of Long Island* (New York: Tobias A. Wright, 1907); Jackson Turner Main, *The Antifederalists* (Chapel Hill: University of North Carolina Press, 1961); Alfred Young, *The Democratic Republicans of New York* (Chapel Hill: University of North Carolina Press, 1967).

WILLIE JONES *(?, 1741–June 18, 1801)* was born in Surry County, Virginia. His father, Robin Jones, had emigrated from Wales to Virginia to practice law. He had been to Eton and then studied law in London. Young Jones's mother, Sarah Cobb, was born in Virginia. Robin Jones first came to Virginia during the 1730s as an agent for English business and then in the 1750s settled on a large estate on the Roanoke River in Northampton County. He next moved to North Carolina and became the richest landowner in the Halifax region. This successful leader also served as attorney general of North Carolina. Young Jones went to Eton also, and then traveled throughout Europe on the so-called grand tour. While there he soaked up many ideas from the late Enlightenment, especially those on liberty and freedom. Back home Jones became part of the wealthy planter idle rich. He lived in Halifax and built a magnificent plantation home, "The Grove." In 1776 he married Mary Montfort, connected to the powerful political and social Ashe family. They had thirteen children.

This rich planter owned over 1,000 acres of prime land and at least 120 slaves. Jones assisted Governor Thomas Tryon in his campaign against the North Carolina Regulators, the western radical farmers who wanted a full role in the North Carolina legislature. He first represented Halifax County in the colonial legislature in 1767, and again in 1771. In 1774 Jones joined the radical Committee of Public Safety and chaired the Halifax Committee. He gained election to the provincial congress in 1774 and served until 1779. By that time, it had become the North Carolina State House. He assisted in drafting the first North Carolina State Constitution and probably served as its principal author. In 1780, he was elected to the Continental Congress, where he became the superintendent of Indian affairs for the southern states. Jones served in the state senate in 1782, 1784, and 1788. He headed the Council of State in 1781 and 1787. Wealthy but radical in his politics, Jones became the state's most powerful political leader. According to Cadwallader Jones, "It was said of Willie Jones that he could draw a bill in better language than any other man of his day" (7).

Elected from the state to the Philadelphia Constitutional Convention of 1787, Jones refused to attend. A staunch defender of the rights of states, Jones assumed the leadership of the opposition to ratification in the first North Carolina convention of 1788 at Hillsborough. He attempted to force an up or down vote on the Constitution without debate, but lost that bid. Jones spoke infrequently, but led the opposition along with his lieutenants, Joseph McDowell (q.v.), Samuel Spencer (q.v.), and the Reverend David Caldwell (q.v.). Jones desired to defeat the Constitution outright. When other states ratified, Jones knew that he must fight a rear guard action to delay and to amend. Although his hero, Thomas Jefferson, from his post in France conditionally supported ratification, Jones used the writings of Jefferson on liberty and freedom to draw up a bill of rights to be added to the Constitution. Jones failed to get his ideas into the North Carolina debates. He did, however, succeed in persuading North Carolinians to reject the Constitution in 1788.

Even after a number of states had ratified and the new government had been called, Jones supported delay and called for a new convention for 1789. He told friends that North Carolina would not be damaged by remaining for a time outside of the new federal government. Besides, Virginians who supported amending the new Constitution, he said, wanted North Carolina in the Union at some later date. Jones also understood the politics of slave-owning sectionalism, and he commented that both South Carolina and Georgia needed North Carolina as an ally. Elected to the second state ratifying convention in 1789, Jones refused to attend. It seems he sensed other delegates' desire to vote to ratify, and he did not want to associate with the ratification forces. Another reason he refused service is that much animosity had sprung up against him for keeping North Carolina out of the federal Union. Many of his more practical friends had deserted him, especially after Jones talked of delaying North Carolina's joining the Union for another six or so years. Samuel A. Ashe quoted him as saying: "Gentlemen need not be in such haste. If left eighteen months or two years without offices, it is no great cause of alarm" (93).

This rich and stubborn republican retired to his plantation in 1789 but continued his interest in reform politics. He served ably on the Board of Trustees of the fledgling University of North Carolina. Jones helped to finance and construct the new North Carolina state house in the more centrally located Raleigh. In 1796 he lost a bid to become a Jeffersonian presidential elector. Although he kept his coastal plantation house, Jones resided in Raleigh. He died there on June 18, 1801. He epitomized the wealthy radical Antifederalist who believed in the ideals of liberty set forth by Thomas Jefferson. William Powell, his most recent analyst, says of Jones that "he was no demagogue or office seeker, but was instead a statesman whose guiding principles were the independence of sovereign people and the social and economic well-being of the masses" (337).

REFERENCES

William C. Allen, *History of Halifax County* (Boston: The Cornhill Co., 1918); Samuel A. Ashe, *History of North Carolina* (Raleigh, N.C.: Edwards and Broughton Printing Co., 1925), vol. 2; Elliot, *Debates*, vol. 4; Delbert H. Gilpatrick, *Jeffersonian Democracy in North Carolina* (New York: Columbia University Press, 1931); Cadwalladar Jones, *A Genealogical History* (Columbia, S.C.: Bryan Printing Co., 1899); William S. Powell, *Dictionary of North Carolina Biography* (Chapel Hill: University of North Carolina Press, 1988), vol. 3; Blackwell P. Robinson, "Willie Jones of Halifax" (MA thesis, Duke University, 1939); Robert Rutland, *Ordeal of the Constitution* (Norman: University of Oklahoma Press, 1965); Storing, *Complete*, vol. 2; Louise Irby Trenholme, *The Ratification of the Federal Constitution in North Carolina* (New York: Columbia University Press, 1932).

THOMAS (JAMES) JOSLYN was from West Greenwich, Kent County, Rhode Island. He probably was the son of Israel Joslyn (Joslin) and Sarah Brown. Later scholars transposed his name, signaling how little is known about his life. It is known that he joined Rhode Island's most famous Antifederalist, Jonathan J. Hazard (q.v.), in the leadership of the antiratification cause. Joslyn also had much political experience representing the farmers of his state. He was a key country party spokesman, and he sponsored in the state legislature in March 1787 a measure to make the village of Newport, populated with a large number of Antifederalists, into a town. He also led in the legislature the faction that wanted to redeem the state debt.

During the struggle over ratification, Joslyn wrote a bill to submit the proposed Constitution to the people of the state for a popular referendum. This radical democratic believer in the people failed in that measure. Joslyn believed that in town meetings the genius of the people was best reflected. He voted against ratification of the Constitution. Along wth his ally, Hazard, the state convention appointed Joslyn to inform the Continental Congress of the state's reasons for voting against the Constitution.

REFERENCES

Bailyn, *Debate*, vol. 2; Steven R. Boyd, *The Politics of Opposition* (Millwood, N.Y.: KTO Press, 1979); Irwin H. Polishook, *Rhode Island and the Union* (Evanston, Ill.: Northwestern University Press, 1969).

$\mathcal{K}$

MARTIN (KINGSLEY) KINSLEY *(June 2, 1754–June 20, 1835)* was born in Bridgewater, Massachusetts. He graduated from Harvard College in 1778, and then studied medicine. During the Revolutionary War, this patriot collected supplies for the Continental Army.

After the Revolution, Kinsley entered Massachusetts state politics. He moved to Hardwick in Worcester County and there became town treasurer and a state legislator in 1781 and in 1788. Kinsley also serve as a major in the militia that had supported the Shays's Rebellion.

In the Massachusetts state ratifying convention of 1788 Kinsley represented Hardwick County. His close friend and fellow Antifederalist, Jonathan Grout (q.v.), served with him. Kinsley made an important address to the convention on January 21, 1788, called "The Excessive Powers of Congress." He began with the assertion that "I will examine what powers we have given to our masters" (Elliot, 162). Kinsley feared that with federal government control of the army, the people of Massachusetts had no troops or arms with which to defend themselves. In that address, Kinsley also argued against the loss of annual elections, the lack of office rotation, and the people's inability to recall a failed politician. He invoked the history of the English parliaments, first chosen yearly, then stretched out over many years, until the political thinkers of England began to worry about too much parliamentary authority (162). Kinsley drew on his Revolutionary War experience to suggest that some people held too much power for too long. The result of holding office tenure for some time contributed to the rise of dictators. "From this duration," Bailyn quotes him, "bribery and corruption are introduced." Kinsley ended his speech rhetorically: "how do we call on accountability now" (900–903). He added to this his concern about one federal center of government, and said that the state centers of power would suffer as a result. This staunch Antifederalist student of the powers of governance voted against ratification of the Constitution.

After the failure to defeat the Constitution, Kinsley returned to state politics to continue his arguments in support of the prerogatives of local government. He again served as town treasurer of Hardwick until 1792. Kinsley was in the state legislature in 1790–1792, 1794–1796, 1801–1804, and 1806. He had moved to Hampden in the Maine territory in 1797 and served in office from there. Kinsley also was a member of the Massachusetts executive council in 1810 and 1811. He then served as judge of probate until he entered the state senate in 1814. He served as a Republican in the federal congress in 1819–1821 but lost his seat in 1820. This Antifederalist died in Roxbury, Massachusetts, on June 20, 1835.

REFERENCES

Bailyn, *Debate*, vol. 1; Elliot, *Debates*, vol. 2; Samuel B. Harding, *The Contest over the Ratification of the Federal Constitution in the State of Massachusetts* (Cambridge: Harvard University Press, 1896); David J. Siemers, *Ratifying the Republic* (Stanford: Stanford University Press, 2002).

L

JOHN LAMB *(January 1, 1735–May 31, 1800)* was born in New York City. His father, Anthony, had entered the colonies from England in 1724, perhaps having been transported as a criminal. His mother, of the Horn family of Dutch merchants, was from New York City. Although the younger Lamb had little early education, he spoke French and German, useful languages for a citizen of New York. He worked with his father in making optical instruments. Lamb was an excellent mathematician. In 1755 Lamb married Catherine (Jardine), a Huguenot, and they had three children. In 1760 he became a wine merchant in Manhattan.

During the 1760s, Lamb joined with the radical New York revolutionaries. He rejected the British Military Act and supported the oppressed merchants of Massachusetts. Lamb published a number of radical pamphlets and handbills as a member of the Sons of Liberty. After the battle of Lexington, he led the troops that took over the custom house in New York. Lamb sent his family to Connecticut during the war to escape occupied New York. He then entered the Continental Army, became a captain, and joined in the invasion of Canada. Captured there, the British later exchanged him. In a dispute with General Horatio Gates in 1779, he resigned his commission, but General George Washington refused his resignation. Lamb also came to regard the war as costing too much. But he persevered, and his technical skills allowed him to become a surveyor of ordinance. General Washington placed him in charge of the defenses of West Point, New York, in 1780. Lamb became an artillery commander in Yorktown in 1780 and fought in the decisive battle there in the autumn of 1781. There is some question as to whether he actually was brevetted general, but after the war people always referred to Lamb as general.

After the war ended, Lamb became collector of the port of New York in 1784, a patronage plum. He had lost an eye during the war and had developed serious gout. Lamb also took advantage of the fluid trading times to become moderately wealthy, and he then purchased confiscated Tory lands. He claimed that the war had taught him about excessive government expenses, and he came to regard the postwar federal government as wasteful. Lamb also served in the New York state legislature.

Although not elected as a member, during the state's ratification convention Lamb took an active part in the proceedings. He corresponded with other Antifederalists, especially the Virginians Richard Henry Lee (q.v.) and William Grayson (q.v.). That correspondence led to his collection of many letters and pamphlets, which he printed along with John Greenleaf (q.v.) in New York newspapers. Some scholars believe that Lamb may have coauthored *The Federal Farmer.* (There is much confusion over who wrote this most important Antifederalist work. The best evidence points toward Melancton Smith [q.v.], a friend and ally of Lamb's.) Clarence Minor, an able student of the Constitutional struggles in New York, says Lamb's use of the circular letter "was the chief weapon which the Antifederalists seem to have relied upon to influence public opinion" (125). In fact, Lamb's major contribution to the anti-Constitution movement was as a purveyor of Antifederalist propaganda. For their efforts, both Lamb and the newspaper editor Greenleaf often received threats from Federalist thugs. Then, Federalists regarded Lamb as a violent man.

After the state ratified the Constitution, Lamb became a leader of a group that wanted to call a second convention. Along with his friends Melancton Smith and Samuel Jones (q.v.), in October 1788 he formed the New York Federal Republican Party. His son-in-law, Charles Tillinghast (q.v.), also assisted the party. The organization became a wing of Governor George Clinton's (q.v.) political group, which continued to oppose the outcome of ratification of the federal Constitution. Lamb opened correspondence with allies in North Carolina and Maryland in hopes of persuading them to support calling a second constitutional convention. Nothing came of the effort, though the Lamb party continued to have some power in New York municipal politics. As president, George Washington remembered his old friend, despite his opposition to the new government, and named him collector of New York. Once again Lamb held a powerful job, but shortage of funds and local unrest led him to resign the position in 1797. Accused of stealing from the job, although a subordinate was probably guilty, Lamb died in poverty in New York City, on May 31, 1800.

REFERENCES

Linda Grant De Pauw, *The Eleventh Pillar* (Ithaca, N.Y.: Cornell University Press, 1966); Alexander Flick (ed.), *History of the State of New York* (New York: Columbia University Press, 1933); Jensen and Kaminski, *Documentary History*, vol. 14; Jacob Judd and Irwin H. Polishook (eds.), *Aspects of Early New York Society and Politics* (Tarrytown, N.Y.: Sleepy Hollow Restorations, 1974); Isaac Q. Leake, *Memorial of the Life and Times of John Lamb* (Glendale, N.Y.: Benchmark Publication Co., 1970); Clarence E. Miner, *The Ratification of the Federal Constitution by the State of New York* (New York: Columbia University Press, 1921); Storing, *Complete*, vols. 2 and 6.

JOHN LANSING *(January 30, 1754–?, 1829)* was born in Albany, New York. His father was Gerritt Jacob Lansing, whose family came to New York from the Netherlands in the 1640s. His mother was Jannetje (Waters). The family owned large tracts of land. Young John received a splendid private education and then studied law with the famous lawyer Robert Yates (q.v.) in Albany, and later with James Duane in New York City. Lamb learned much about political theory and politics from Yates, who was later a fellow delegate to the federal convention of 1787 in Philadelphia. He began the practice of law in Albany in 1775. In 1781 Lansing married Cornelia Ray of New York City. They had ten children.

An ardent young patriot, Lansing became a military secretary to General Philip Schuyler. Yates soon brought Lansing into politics, as a member of the powerful George Clinton (q.v.) machine. Lansing served in the New York State General Assembly during the war years 1780 to 1782.

When the war ended, Lansing continued in public life. He served in the assembly from 1783 to 1784, and again in 1786 and 1788. In the latter two years, he held the powerful position of speaker of the Assembly. He also was a member in 1786 of the New York committee to settle territorial disputes with Massachusetts. From 1786 to 1790, he served as mayor of Albany. Lansing in addition held national office as a member of the Continental Congress in 1784 and 1785. He supported the idea of small government under the Articles of Confederation. In 1787, along with Yates and Alexander Hamilton, he was chosen a New York delegate to the Constitutional Convention. On July 10, 1787, after having opposed most of the articles proposed for the new Constitution, he left Philadelphia with Yates and refused to vote on the Constitution. Lansing had supported the New Jersey small state plan but rejected the Connecticut compromise. Lansing and Yates also kept Governor Clinton apprised of events in Philadelphia, as both wrote down their memories of the proceedings. Published much later, Lansing's account of the convention is a major Antifederalist document. Thanks to the editing of the late eminent historian Joseph Strayer, history now knows just how much leaders like Lansing feared the power of states like Virginia and Pennsylvania. As Strayer said, "Lansing's notes throw new light on these state jealousies" (19). Of course, when Lansing and Yates left the convention, New York abdicated its right to a vote for the Constitution.

In the months before the New York ratification convention met, Lansing and Yates wrote "Reasons of Dissent," a report on the activities at the federal convention, which they later published in the *New York Journal* of January 14, 1788. In that report to Governor George Clinton, Lansing and Yates said that they objected to the Philadelphia convention's actions because its members had exceeded the authority to suggest revisions of the Articles of Confederation, subverted state powers, and proposed a federal government over the unmanageably large country. They summed up why they left the Philadelphia convention in this way: "A persuasion that our further attendance would be fruitless, and unavailing, rendered us less solicitious to return" (Storing, vol. 2, 18).

As a member of the New York ratifying convention, Lansing opposed the Constitution and actively debated its faults. His elaborate notes taken in Philadelphia no doubt assisted him in his arguments. Certainly he knew Hamilton's position and spoke often against it. But Lansing soon heard the news that Virginia and New Hampshire had voted to ratify, thus making it the law of the land. What New York did he now found superfluous. He knew that his state must go along, so he changed his tactics and demanded revisions to the federal Constitution. On July 7, 1788, he proposed a bill of rights be added. Governor George Clinton, Melancton Smith (q.v.), and Lansing claimed there could be no compromise over the necessity of a bill of rights or the explicit protection of individual freedoms. On July 10, Lansing offered a proposal to set up a procedure to amend the Constitution under certain conditions. The flaw in the Constitution that bothered him the most, he claimed, was that the federal government could now command the state militia without state government support. To him that appeared like the way Britain controlled the colonial militias, and he would not have it. On July 23, he proposed that New York ratify if the amendments were accepted. On July 24, Lansing offered to his fellow delegates a proposition that ratification include New York's right to secede from the Union if the early federal congresses did not amend the Constitution with a statement of personal rights. Each of his requests was voted down, and Lansing voted against New York's ratification of the Constitution.

In addition to his concerns for personal and public rights, this brilliant legal mind had other reasons for his opposition to the proposed Constitution. Like many of his friends, Lansing, too, was concerned with the future structure of the government. "We ought, therefore," he said on June 20, 1788, "to be extremely cautious how we establish a government which may give distinct interests to the rulers and governed, so as to induce the former to pursuits adverse to their happiness in the United States" (Elliot, 374). Lansing wanted powers explicitly delegated to the various states, to deprive the federal government of excessive authority. When the Federalists responded that they feared the breakup of the Union if they did not get the authority they wanted, Lansing said local government was all important in a federal republic. On elections controlled by the federal Congress, he reminded his fellow delegates that the Dutch government had once had elections but now had a hereditary monarchy. If the president controlled the taxing privileges, what, he asked, would happen to local authority over the purse? Lansing also revealed that in Philadelphia Hamilton had supported the idea that the country's economic elite make up the membership of the federal Senate to serve as a check on democratic government. Lansing said he accepted a form of democracy in order to forestall the day when the Senate would become hereditary. He allowed that the Senate "numbers [are] so exceedingly small, that they may easily feel their interests distinct from those of the community" (Elliot, 376, 289–291). Thus had a man of political moderation and business success been radicalized by the views of Hamilton and his Federalist friends.

Perhaps these specific fears of elite domination explain why, unlike some other New York state Antifederalists, Lansing refused to desert the Clinton faction and accept Federalist promises. Soon all of the Antifederalists had to make compromises with the new government. Yet, Lansing seemed unhurt in politics by being on the losing side at the ratification convention. In 1790 he became a judge of the New York Supreme Court, a post he held until 1801. He succeeded Yates as chief justice in 1798. In 1790 Lansing helped to settle the border dispute with Vermont. From 1801 until 1814, he served as chancellor of the state of New York. In that position he rejected the Robert Fulton and Robert Livingston political faction's proposal for a steamboat monopoly on the Hudson River. In 1804 Lansing ran as the Jeffersonian Republican candidate for governor but withdrew rather than turn against Governor George Clinton. However, he lamented the death of Alexander Hamilton and wondered whether he could any longer be an ally of the Aaron Burr Republican Party.

In 1814 Lansing retired from public life and returned to his practice of law in Albany. He became regent of the University of the State of New York in 1817. In that capacity, he supported the growth of Columbia College. On December 12, 1829, while on a visit to New York City he diaappeared. His body never has been recovered, and it is thought that either he was murdered or, more likely, fell into the Hudson River and was swept out to sea. Thanks to Joseph Strayer, Lansing has left an important legacy in his notes on the Constitutional Convention, as in them is contained one of the most powerful of Antifederalist arguments.

REFERENCES

Bailyn, *Debate*, vol. 2; Elliot, *Debates*, vol. 2; Jabez D. Hammond, *The History of Political Parties in the State of New York* (Cooperstown, N.Y.: Phinney, 1845); Clarence E. Miner, *The Ratification of the Federal Constitution by the State of New York* (New York: AMS Press, 1968); Claude G. Munsell, *The Lansing Family* (New York: Private Print, 1916); Jonathan Pearson, *Genealogy of Settlers of Albany* (Albany, N.Y.: J. Munsell, 1872); Storing, *Complete*, vols. 2 and 4; Joseph R. Strayer, *Delegate from New York; or Proceedings of the Federal Convention of 1787* (Princeton: Princeton University Press, 1939).

HUGH LEDLIE *(c. 1720–c. 1798)* was born in Windham County, Connecticut. Although little is known about his youth, he became one of the few important Connecticut Antifederalists. It is known that he was a captain of militia in the French and Indian War. Ledlie moved to Hartford, Connecticut about 1770, where he became a shopkeeper. He soon entered politics, and his enemies came to refer to him as a "wild" Irishman. Ledlie proved them correct as he joined the revolutionary cause with a vengeance. He joined the Windham Sons of Liberty and ardently resisted the British Stamp tax, even callling for destruction of the local custom house. Ledlie also served in the military during the American Revolution, although it is unlikely he left Connecticut.

As a member of the Connecticut convention of 1783, Ledlie studied the power of the federal Congress. In the state legislature, he refused to give any aid to ex–Connecticut Tories. He joined the state's radicals and proposed a bill to pay the state debts through state government financing. In state government, Ledlie strongly supported the rights of local jurisdictions, and he attended the Middletown convention of 1783, in which a number of the state's radicals sought more rights for local governments.

Elected from Hartford to the state ratification convention for the proposed federal Constitution, Ledlie soon became a leader of the Antifederalists. He feared that Federalists controlled the state newspapers and that the opposition did not receive a full hearing. Along with the other members of the minority anti-Constitution forces, he worried over threats against his life. Ledlie accused the Federalists of offering political positions to those who supported ratification of the Constitution, thus undermining the minority coalition of those who opposed the Constitution. He wrote an important letter to John Lamb (q.v.) of New York in January 1788, in which he described how difficult it was for Antifederalists to get their views into print. He said that Connecticut Federalists destroyed Antifederalist pamphlets. Lamb had his letter printed in the New York press. But the letter did little good, as the pro-Constitution forces in Connecticut overwhelmingly defeated their opponents at the convention.

It is thought that Ledlie retired from public life after the convention, a victim of Federalist state power. He is presumed to have died in Hartford in 1798.

REFERENCES

Jensen and Kaminski, *Documentary History*, vols. 3 and 14; Isaac Q. Leake, *Memorial of the Life of John Lamb* (Glendale, N.Y.: Benchmark Publication Co., 1970); Jackson Turner Main, *The Antifederalists* (Chapel Hill: University of North Carolina Press, 1961); Robert A. Rutland, *Ordeal of the Constitution* (Norman: University of Oklahoma Press, 1965); Oscar Zeichner, *Connecticut's Years of Controversy* (Chapel Hill: University of North Carolina Press, 1949).

ARTHUR LEE *(December 21, 1740–December 12, 1792)* was born at Stratford Hall, the ancestral home of the Lee family in Westmoreland County, Virginia. His father, Thomas Sim Lee, the wealthiest planter in Virginia's northern neck, built Stratford Hall in the 1720s. His mother, Hannah (Ludwell), was from a prominent Virginia family. Arthur received the proper training of a man from whose station in life much was expected. His father died when Arthur was young, and the youth looked to his older brother Richard Henry Lee (q.v.) to decide his future. At home he read the great classics in his brother's library. Lee then went to the prestigious Eton College, England's most famous preparatory school for the wealthy, and to the University of Edinburgh, a center of Enlightenment learning, to study medicine. He received the M.D. in 1764 and practiced medicine in Williamsburg, Virginia, until 1767. Lee had been elected to the Royal Society of Medicine in 1766. He then returned to London in 1768 to study law, and he joined the English bar in 1775. Lee never married, instead leading the itinerant life of the mind. His biographer Louis Potts says of him: "The course of his life was littered with alternate career goals and alienated relationships" (10). Certainly, as the youngest and pampered child of great wealth and family heritage, he had the leisure to pursue the life of learning.

But the American Revolution intervened in his plans. Even though he at one time had decided to live in England, he became a critic of British policies toward the colonies. In 1768, he wrote the *Monitor's Letters,* critical of British suppression of American trade. In 1769 Lee published the *Junius Letters*, also very critical of English oppression of colonial rights. As an agent for the colony of Massachusetts in London, he witnessed firsthand the damaging results of such policies on colonial trade. In 1774 his vehement *Appeal to Justice and Interests of the People of Great Britain* stood as a wringing defense of the American supporter in Parliament John Wilkes.

As the war began, Lee became the Continental Congress's commissioner to negotiate a treaty with France. In 1777 he went to Spain and then on to Berlin to gain support for the Revolution. He became embroiled in a scandal concerning American diplomacy and was summoned home, his name forever tarnished. But being a Lee, upon return to Virginia in 1781 he gained election to the House of Burgesses.

From 1781 until 1784, Lee served ably in the Continental Congress. However, he had little use for any kind of national political system. In 1782, he voted to reject the right of the Confederation to set permanent taxes on the states. His peers in government named Lee to the committee to negotiate the Treaty of Fort Stanwix of 1784, which opened Indian territory to western interests. While in Congress, Lee made a close friend of the future Rhode Island Antifederalist David Howell (q.v.). In 1785, Governor Patrick Henry of Virginia (q.v.) appointed him to the state treasury board. Lee rekindled his ties with local leaders and no doubt came once again under the influence of his elder brother, Richard Henry Lee. During the last years of the Confederation government, Lee temporarily forsook his absolute defense of local rights and began to advocate reforms in the Articles of Confederation, in the belief that his own state stood to gain from a better governed national government.

When the Philadeliphia Constitutional reform convention met in the summer of 1787, Lee seemed to equivocate over its purpose. He did not run for election to the state ratifying convention. His biographer Louis Potts states that Lee had little interest in reform, save that he opposed direct democracy and believed in a British form of Whig oligarchy that he found favorable to planter interests (283). Since Lee possessed little faith in people or government of any kind, Potts suggests he lacked interest even in state government prerogatives (276).

Nevertheless, Lee became one of the most significant of Antifederalist thinkers. A close reading of his attack on staunch Pennsylvania Federalist James Wilson's defense of the Constitution establishes his importance as a theoretician of the cause. Published in Thomas Greenleaf's (q.v.) *New York Journal* in November and December 1787, Lee's critique of Wilson was reprinted in Massachusetts, Pennsylvania, and Virginia, and certainly influenced his brother's and other Antifederalists' objections to the Constitution. The intelligent, well-educated, elitist Lee wrote for his peers alone, often lapsing into French and Latin and quoting Montesquieu and ancient Greek political philosophers in his discourse. In those "Cincinnatus" letters, he pointed out that Wilson had distorted the shortcomings of the Articles of Confederation and covered up the real threat of the proposed Constitution to individual liberty. Lee demanded that the Constitution include a declaration of rights. He wrote that he refused to "sacrifice the liberties of the people to the power and domination of a few" (Bailyn, 92). He called for restrictions on federal powers, and feared that the so-called simple means of funding the government by an import tariff would fail to gain needed revenues and also disrupt the flow of staple crops abroad. A strong government in need of revenue would resort to personal income tax and control over citizen business activity and wealth, Lee claimed. He also questioned the purpose of a standing army and worried about its use by a strong executive. Lee concluded "Cincinnatus" with this warning: "With magnificent promises you have bought golden opinions of all sorts of people, and with gold you must answer them" (Bailyn, 95). He believed that he had made an unanswerable case against the Constitution.

It is Saul Cornell who best summarizes Lee's major concerns over the nature of leadership as proposed in the Constitution. Even if no Democrat, Cornell points out, Lee nevertheless claimed the proposed House of Representatives, the democratic body, had too little power. The Senate, said Lee, the aristocratic body, had such powers as to lead to corruption in the elite. Indeed, the so-called democratic House was not democratic enough for Lee, because too few members were elected to it for the number of people it served. In addition, Lee's call for a bill of rights was designed to protect community interest, especially in the right to trial by jury. Cornell says that in Lee's proposed alternate, "the people retained the right to protect themselves and set restrictions on the exercise of individual liberty when the goal of the community demanded such limitations" (126).

After ratification of the federal Constitution in Virginia, Lee lost his position on the state treasury board because he had angered the Federalists. Richard Henry Lee attempted to get his younger brother another position in

Virginia, but Patrick Henry, believing him feckless and tainted by earlier foreign intrigues, denied him his powerful assistance. Arthur Lee then retired to his plantation, Landsdowne, in Middlesex County. He died there on December 12, 1792.

On the surface his career appears to have been one of a waste of talent with little to show for his sometimes strident efforts. That would be a false judgement. The author of "Cincinnatus" left a major statement of Antifederalist values and revealed most clearly in his writings much of what the members of that failed political movement believed. In dealing with the problem of quality leadership turning avaricious, he offered a balance between talent and democratic decision making. In speaking for personal interest above the state and nation, Lee offered an important idea about the very nature of government's purpose, its responsibility to the personal freedoms of each citizen.

REFERENCES

Charles H. Ambler, *Sectionalism in Virginia, 1776–1861* (New York: Russell and Russell, 1964); Bailyn, *Debate,* vol. 1; Richard Beeman, *The Old Dominion and the New Nation* (Lexington: University Press of Kentucky, 1972); Saul Cornell, *The Other Founder* (Chapel Hill: University of North Carolina Press, 1999); Richard Henry Lee, *Life of Arthur Lee,* 2 vols. (Boston: Wells and Lilly, 1829); Louis W. Potts, *Arthur Lee: A Virtuous Revolutionary* (Baton Rouge: Louisiana State University Press, 1981); Myra L. Rich, "The Experimental Years" (PhD diss., Yale University, 1966); Storing, *Complete,* vol. 6.
Arthur Lee's papers are at the Widener Library, Harvard University.

RICHARD HENRY LEE *(January 20, 1732–June 19, 1794)* was born at Stratford Hall, in Westmoreland County, Virginia. He was the son of the wealthy Northern Neck planter Thomas Sim Lee and Hannah (Ludwell), who was also from a wealthy Virginia planting family. Lee received an education from private tutors, and at the Wakefield Academy in Yorkshire, England. In 1752 he studied law back in Virginia but never actually practiced. Instead he became a gentleman planter, surrounded by books and by retainers. In 1757 he married Anne Aylett, the daughter of a planter, and established his residence at Chantilly, in Westmoreland County. Upon his first wife's death in 1768, Lee married Anne Prichard. He had a large family, but none of his children rose to the importance in public affairs that he had.

Planters of Lee's position and wealth often had a taste for public life. He had read widely in political thought, history, and economics, and was prepared to rise in colony affairs. Lee followed the expected route of service, beginning at the local level, and he became justice of the peace for Westmoreland County in 1757. In 1758 the progressive Lee entered the House of Burgesses, where he advocated checking the growth of slavery. Lee and other Tidewater tobacco planters understood that Virginia's economy could not find work for all of the slaves that lived there. The dilemma over the future of slave labor and the direction of population growth in Virginia would influence the later political activities of Lee and a number of his fellow leaders. He also became an ally of Patrick Henry (q.v.), assisting this western leader in the rejection of the Two Penny Act. In doing so, Lee ran afoul of the royal government. He had further troubles when he called for an investigation of the royal treasury in Virginia. In 1764 he opposed the expansion of taxes in the colonies. In 1765, Lee sent a forceful letter to King George III about the unfairness of the Stamp Act, and then led the Westmoreland County boycott of British imports. He next supported the formation of the Virginia Committee of Correspondence, the first venture to link all of the colonies in a potentially revolutionary movement.

As the American Revolution approached, Lee took a leadership position in favor of a separate Virginia. He had lost much in the tobacco boycotts and in the transfer of his wealth from tobacco to wheat, and had come to believe that only in a separate nation could Virginia's old elite continue its place in public and private life. As a delegate to the First Continental Congress in 1774, he formed a strong personal and intellectual friendship with the Massachusetts radical Samuel Adams (q.v.), who influenced his political views for the remainder of his life. Lee also developed close ties to another Virginia radical revolutionary, George Mason (q.v.). Active on various congressional committees, in March 1776 he declared that the king had become the principal source of the colonies' troubles. His argument later became the basis for justifying revolution that Jefferson stated in the Declaration of Independence. Lee signed that most momentous document. He also played a part in writing the Articles of Confederation. Most importantly, he helped to pave the way for new states to join the Union by persuading Virginia to relinquish claims to western lands. During the war, he worked with his brother Arthur Lee (q.v.) on issues of foreign policy. In 1779 he resigned from the Continental Congress. In 1780 Lee became a member of the Virginia House of Delegates, where he took a strong stand in favor of the rights of states in the new nation.

After the Revolution had ended, Lee continued to serve in the new state government. He resigned in 1783 once again to reenter the Continental Congress, and in 1784 his peers named him its president. He assisted in drawing up the ordinances that rejected the advance of slavery into the northwest. From his experiences in national government, he understood that the Articles of Confederation were defective. But he expressed fears that any changes to the Articles might give too much power to the federal Congress. So, when elected a delegate to the Philadelphia Convention of 1787 to revise the Articles, he declined stating that he opposed changes to that document. As a member of the Continental Congress, Lee voted against sending the proposed new Constitution to the states for ratification.

When the Virginia convention to debate ratification met, Lee took an active role. Before that he had corresponded with Samuel Adams and other friends from the Revolution as to how best to defeat the Constitution. He also began to write in opposition to ratification. For years historians believed that he had been the author of the famous Antifederalist *Letters of an American Farmer.* Most likely they were drafted by Melancton Smith (q.v.), a New York friend of his, with much input from the Virginian. The *Letters*, however, certainly reflected Lee's views on the problems with the proposed Constitution. He had written early in October 1787 that he regarded the Constitution as a threat to civil liberties. To his Virginia friends, soon to go to the convention, Lee expressed his fears of the loss of a free press, the absence of jury trial, and a judiciary dependent on the federal government. Much of his worries about individual liberties also informed his comments about too powerful a central government.

This Virginia leader's major concerns with the Constitution are contained in the letters he wrote to other Antifederalists during the ratification period. Even before the Constitution had been sent to the states, Lee stated that he wanted to amend the document to reflect the concerns of the citizenry over the lack of a bill of rights and the excessive powers of government. On September 27, 1787, he called for "the new Constitution to be so amended as to place the right of representation in the senate on the same ground that is placed in the House of delegates thereby securing equality of representation in its Legislature" (Jensen and Kaminski, 240). To Governor Edmund Randolph of Virginia he wrote on October 16, 1787, that he feared "a dangerous oligarchy" had been created in the proposed House of Representatives (Bailyn, vol. 1, 465, also see 466–472). Lee even advocated calling a second Constitutional Convention to amend the powers given to the federal Congress. He also feared the power of an excessive majority and asked what happened to the defense of minority rights. Most of all, Lee focused on just how a government representing so many different and conflicting interests could manage to function at all. On May 26, 1788, he suggested that "the almost infinite variety of climates, soils, productions, manners, customs and interests renders this still more difficult for the general government" to provide for all of the different interests in the country (Bailyn, vol. 2, 462). Other letters, such as one of May 7, 1788, to George Mason, printed and then circulated throughout the states, focused on the dangers of the new government to civil liberties (Ballagh, 380). With such comments to his friend Elbridge Gerry (q.v.) of Massachusetts, and to others from Pennsylvania, he was able to spread his concerns among many important Antifederalists. In these ways, Lee had used his pen to attempt to influence the outcome of the ratification conventions in a number of states.

After he realized the Constitution would be ratified, Lee reverted to an earlier argument, asking that amendments be guaranteed before ratification took place. He also supported the call for a second national convention to revise the proposed Constitution. But, to avoid violence, Lee soon acquiesced before the inevitable. He calmed his local constituents who were bent on disrupting the convention and later refused to participate in the new government. He set an example for them by accepting public office himself. Realizing Lee's symbolic importance to the cause, Patrick Henry maneuvered to send him to the first United States Senate instead of the Federalist leader James Madison. In the first Senate, Lee became a leader of those who demanded the Bill of Rights. He served ably as an opponent of what he thought were attempts to strengthen further the federal government.

On June 19, 1794, Lee died at Chantilly, his plantation in Westmoreland County. To the end of his life he was a mixture of conservative and radical Antifederalist. For example, he forecast slavery's end, but also wrote that the right to hold slaves was sacred. Lee's concerns with the new, stronger federal government were in part out of fear that free and slave states could not coexist, and that the free states controlled the new government. Also, as a member of Virginia's talented plantation elite, he expected the most able leaders to take their rightful place in the new republic. He wondered whether they would join such a new central government. No Democrat, he still believed that elected officials ought to be close to their constituents, just as he was with the people of Westmoreland County. Pauline Maier captured Lee's beliefs most ably when she called him an old revolutionary committed to the protection of the values of the American Revolution, and fearful of the Constitution. Referring to Lee, George Mason, and Samuel Adams, Maier stated: "The Revolution of 1787 lay beyond the Old Revolutionaries' capacity for innovation and very often for understanding" (294). "Theirs," she says, "were the traditional politics of consensus, the old quest for unanimity" (298).

REFERENCES

Bailyn, *Debate*, vols. 1 and 2; James C. Ballagh (ed.), *The Letters of Richard Henry Lee* (New York: Macmillan Co., 1911), vol. 2; Oliver P. Chitwood, *Richard Henry Lee* (Morgantown: West Virginia University Press, 1967); Jensen and Kaminski, *Documentary History*, vol. 13; Richard Henry Lee, *Memoirs of the Life of Richard Henry Lee* (Philadelphia: Cary and Lea, 1825); Charles Ramsdell Lingley, *The Transition in Virginia from Colony to Commonwealth* (New York: Columbia University Press, 1910); Pauline Maier, *The Old Revolutionaries* (New York: Alfred Knopf, 1969).

WILLIAM LENOIR *(May 20, 1751–May 6, 1839)* was born in Brunswick County, Virginia. The youngest child in a family of ten children, he was the son of Thomas and Mourning (Crawley) Lenoir. In 1759 his father sold the Virginia plantation and the family moved to Tar River, Tarboro, Edgecombe County, North Carolina. His father died in 1765. The young Lenoir received little education save what he acquired on his own. All his life he would lament his lack of formal education. He taught himself the land surveying business and rose to become a successful surveyor and land dealer. Lenoir conducted a school in Virginia in 1769, and in Halifax County, North Carolina in 1770. In 1771 he married Ann Ballard of Halifax, North Carolina. In 1775 they moved to Wilkes County, in western North Carolina, and he became a successful farmer. He was a Quaker.

Early a patriot, in 1775 Lenoir signed the "Association Paper" in support of revolution against Great Britain. He belonged to the local Committee of Safety. In 1776 he supported General Griffith Rutherford (q.v.) in the west in the war against the Cherokee. Lenoir helped in the bitter civil conflict with western Carolina Tories. He became a captain at the battle of Kings Mountain, and a hero at the struggle at Haw River in 1781. Lenoir later became a major general of militia.

Military service plus success as a farmer sent Lenoir into public life. He served as a justice of the peace in 1776. In 1778 he became county clerk of Wilkes County. For many years Lenoir represented his fellow Wilkes County citizens in the state legislature, including 1781 to 1784 in the state house, and 1787 and 1788 in the state senate. There he learned much about political governance, and he understood the issues of importance to his local district and to the state. Lenoir also held the positions of county register and county surveyor, and served as a member of the committee of affidavits, chair of the county court, and clerk of Wilkes County. Clearly, Lenoir had much experience in county and state governance as he began the most momentous political struggle of his life.

Prominent in the Antifederalist cause in both North Carolina state ratifying conventions, Lenoir spoke little but effectively, and gained respect among his peers. He became a major leader of the state's western political forces. Accordingly, just as the convention met, the state legislature chose him as one of five delegates to meet and offer resolutions to amend the federal Constitution. At both conventions, Lenoir used that experience to support writing a bill of rights, as he wanted a Constitution devoted to the protection of the rights of the states and the people. Louise I. Trenholme, the best authority on the state ratifying convention, says of his role and feelings in the conventions: "William Lenoir, an Antifederalist who was in both conventions, wrote forty-five years later that the state had finally adopted the constitution merely as an alternative less fatal than absolute severence from the adjoining states; and those who had yielded from necessity still regarded the central government with great jealousy" (242). Needless to say, Lenoir voted against the Constitution in both state conventions.

At the convention Lenoir spoke thoughtfully about his fears for the state. Rather than amend the Confederation Constitution, the Federalists, he claimed, destroyed it. He worried about the absence of freedom of speech in the Constitution, and insisted that in the proposed new federal city the centralists planned to control the press (Bailyn, 913). Infringement on the rights to religious liberty, too, he regarded a threat. Lenoir foresaw ecclesiastical courts directed to dictate people's faith (Elliot, 201–206). Lenoir also spoke out against the powers the Constitution gave to central government officials. Too much power accrued to the president, as even the supposedly independent national senate, he said, was under executive control. A sinister section-alism also entered his argument as Lenoir insisted the Constitution oppressed the slave states. Yet, unlike many other southerners, he asked serious ques-tions about the efficacy of the three-fifths Clause. Instead of strengthening the slave states, the clause meant further taxation, thus oppressing the poor, marginal western slaveholders, and perhaps destroying their opportunities to acquire slaves. "Therefore," he insisted in his opposition to the Constitution, "it is necessary for us to secure our rights and liberties as far as we can" (El-liot, 204–205).

After the Constitutional struggle, Lenoir returned to farming and to pub-lic life. In 1790, he owned twelve slaves and 4,500 acres of fine land. He also practiced as a blacksmith. Lenoir became an original trustee of the University of North Carolina in 1789 and, despite his lack of education, for a time served as chairman of the board. He reentered the state senate in 1790 and served until 1795, all of that time as speaker of the senate. He was also a member of the Council of State. In the last years of his life, Lenoir achieved his goal of enough financial success to begin his real education. He devoted himself to reading and studying, especially history and the law. His deep studies con-vinced this leader of the local people and state interests that the United States government would soon break up because of conflict over the powers of the federal government. Lenoir died at Fort Defiance, Wilkes County, North Car-olina, May 6, 1839, at the age of eighty-eight.

REFERENCES

Bailyn, *Debate*, vol. 2; Henry G. Connor, "Conventions of 1788–89," *North Car-olina Booklet*, 1918, vol. 4, no. 4; Elliot, *Debates*, vol. 4; Louise Irby Trenholme, *The Ratification of the Federal Constitution in North Carolina* (New York: Columbia Uni-versity Press, 1932); John H. Wheeler, *Historical Sketches of North Carolina* (1851 repr., Baltimore: Regional Publishing Co., 1964), vols. 1 and 2.

JAMES LINCOLN *(?–November 1791)* was from the Ninety-six Dis-trict, later named Abbeville County, of South Carolina. Little is known about his early life save that he farmed and also had a political career. Lincoln joined the Mount Sion Society, a religious organization, in 1780. He supported the founding of public schools in his region of the young state. He entered pub-lic life as justice of the peace and a county court judge from Abbeville County in 1786 and 1791, two powerful local political offices. Lincoln also served in the South Carolina General Assembly in 1787 and 1788, where he made many political friends.

Although facts about his life are sparse, enough is known to reveal how im-portant was Lincoln's role in the South Carolina federal Constitution ratify-ing convention. He developed close ties with Thomas Sumter (q.v.) and became an ally of the leader Rawlins Lowndes (q.v.). Elected to the state con-vention from Ninety-six District along with Arthur Simkins and Joseph Calhoun (q.v.), Lenoir joined the Antifederalists. Although he apologized to the convention for his lack of rhetorical skills, he nevertheless spoke forcefully and usefully for his cause. Lincoln lamented the absence of a bill of rights in the proposed Constitution and declared he could vote for no document that did not protect the rights of the people. He also claimed that the Constitution's writers planned to turn the country into an aristocracy, to take power away from the people and their leaders and place it in the hands of men miles away. He also feared that the chief executive could hold office for life, amounting to a form of kingship which he deplored (Elliot, 312–315). In addition, Lincoln lamented the lack of a free press and, as a member of the Antifederalist minority, wondered whether the opposition could get a fair hearing in heavily Federalist Charleston. Jackson Turner Main quotes him in the *Charleston Daily Advertiser* of February 1, 1788, thusly: "What have you been contending for these ten past years? Liberty. What is Liberty? The power of governing yourselves. If you adopt the constitution have you this power? No" (133).

After the convention, where he had voted against the Constitution, Lincoln returned to his western farm and to public life. He again served in the general assembly in 1789 and 1790. Lincoln died in November 1791 while on a visit to Savannah, Georgia, where he had gone to talk to fellow states' rights proponents. He is buried in Abbeville County.

REFERENCES

N. Louise Bailey and Elizabeth Ivey Cooper (eds.), *Biographical Dictionary of the South Carolina House of Representatives* (Columbia: University of South Carolina Press, 1981), vol. 3; Steven R. Boyd, *The Politics of Opposition* (Millwood, N.Y.: KTO Press, 1979); Elliot, *Debates*, vol. 4; Jack P. Greene, *The Nature of Colonial Constitutions* (Columbia: University of South Carolina Press, 1970); Anne King Gregorie, *Thomas Sumter* (Columbia: Publications of the South Carolina Historical Association, 1902, 1907); Jackson Turner Main, *The Antifederalists* (Chapel Hill: University of North Carolina Press, 1961); George C. Rogers, *Evolution of a Federalist* (Columbia: University of South Carolina Press, 1962); Robert A. Rutland, *Birth of the Bill of Rights* (Chapel Hill: University of North Carolina Press, 1955); Carl J. Vipperman, *The Rise of Rawlins Lowndes* (Columbia: University of South Carolina Press, 1978).

GILBERT LIVINGSTON *(?, 1742–?, 1806)* was born near Poughkeepsie, in Dutchess County, New York. He was the son of Dutchess County Clerk Henry Livingston and Susanna (Conklin), and was one of thirteen children. Young Livingston was the great-grandson of the first Robert Livingston, a wealthy and powerful political leader in provincial New York. Gilbert's father served in the provincial association and the colonial assembly. The family was Dutch Reformed, having strong connections to the old Dutch families of colonial New York. Henry Livingston, however, only belonged to the middle class of landowners. The younger Livingston owned a small farm with a few tenants, and practiced law. He was highly regarded as a lawyer. Liv-

ingston also ran a mercantile business in Poughkeepsie with the brother of Melancton Smith (q.v.). He married Catherine Crannell, who had a similar background as his.

During the American Revolution, Livingston and Peter Tappan, his brother-in-law, became shipbuilders. But without great wealth, Livingston decided the way to success was through politics. In the war, he chaired an important committee on military affairs for his friend, relative by marriage, and ally, Governor George Clinton (q.v.), to ensure against wartime inflation. Livingston served in the provincial congress in 1775, and the state assembly from 1777 to 1778 and again in 1788 and 1789. There Livingston supported the tenants' cause, and he opposed land price fixing. He also spoke out against what he called renewed Tory conspiracies to take over state government. He held the post of county surrogate from 1778 to 1785, and again from 1787 until 1794. Livingston was the law partner of the Federalist James Kent. He also was in the postwar mercantile business. Of the leaders from the old families, only Jeremiah Van Rensselaer (q.v.) and Livingston broke away to become Antifederalist opponents of the federal Constitution.

At the state ratification convention Livingston spoke for state authority and against federal powers. He claimed there was no safety under the Constitution for state interests. There was no way to stop the powers of the proposed United States Senate, he said, as its members would be "strangers to the condition of the common people" (Bailyn, 789–791). This Dutchess County leader in the convention also spoke eloquently about human nature and power. He said to his fellow delegates, "indeed, if it were not for the depravity of human nature, we should stand in need of no government at all" (Elliot, 389). Livingston insisted he opposed the Constitution unless there were serious amendments. Linda G. DePauw quotes him as saying: "I will steadily persevere, in every possible means to procure this desirable object, a revision of the Constitition" (254).

Yet Livingston at the last joined his fellow Dutchess County delegate Melancton Smith (q.v.) and voted to adopt the Constitution. He had been persuaded that New York had to join the majority of the states who had ratified, and that the Constitution would indeed be amended. Perhaps Livingston also believed in the need for some sort of government to govern the people, and worried that without the Constitution, the country could degenerate into anarchy. In a local newspaper of July 29, 1788, he referred to his switch as the most difficult political decision of his life.

After Livingston's vote for the Constitution, Governor Clinton broke with him. But Livingston continued his law practice and mercantile business, and served again in politics. He held office in the state house during the 1790s and rejoined the Clinton forces. He became surrogate of Dutchess County once again. In 1800 Livingston was a presidential elector on the Jeffersonian Republican ticket. He served as Dutchess County Clerk and county surrogate in 1804. In 1806 Livingston died in Dutchess County. He believed that his actions at the convention had been justified after the Bill of Rights had been passed. Livingston called himself an Antifederalist until he died.

REFERENCES

Bailyn, *Debate*, vol. 2; George Dangerfield, *Chancellor Robert Livingston* (New York: Harcourt, Brace, 1960); Linda Grant De Pauw, *The Eleventh Pillar* (Ithaca, N.Y.: Cornell University Press, 1966); Elliot, *Debates*, vol. 2; Joan Gordon, "Kinship and Class: The Livingstons of New York" (PhD diss., Columbia University, 1959); Staughton Lynd, *Antifederalism in Dutchess County* (Chicago: Loyola University Press, 1962); Henry Noble MacCracken, *Old Dutchess Forever* (New York: Hastings House, 1956); Nathaniel Sylvester, *History of Ulster County* (Philadelphia: Everts and Peck, 1880). Livingston's Papers are in the New York Public Library.

MATTHEW (LOCK) LOCKE *(?, 1730–September 7, 1801)* was born in northern Ireland to John and Elizabeth Locke. He came to Lancaster County, Pennsylvania, in the 1740s. His father died in 1744, and his mother remarried and moved to Anson County, North Carolina, in 1752. Locke married Elizabeth Brandon in 1749, and later Elizabeth Gastelowe of Philadelphia. It is known that he settled in Rowan County, North Carolina, just after 1752. He was a wagonmaster, and eventually owned his own wagon line. Locke became a justice of the peace and later a vestryman in the Episcopal church. He also farmed a grant of some 600 acres of land in Rowan County.

The path to political preferment came from Locke's service as justice of the peace and as vestryman. He entered the provincial congress in 1770 and served there until 1775. He became an expert on public finances. Locke served on a committee with the radical Herman Husband to receive and return fees to small farmers. In 1771 he was named Rowan County officer to deal with the Regulators. He was also elected treasury commissioner of the colony the same year. In 1774 Locke joined the Rowan County Committee of Safety, and became a patriot. In 1775 he was paymaster of troops of the Salisbury District. Locke also headed a movement to purchase weapons for the Rowan County militia. In 1776 Locke entered the state legislature, where he served until 1781. A delegate to the 1776 state convention that drew up the first North Carolina Constitution, Locke all his life held fond memories of participating in that dramatic moment in the quest for personal and political freedom. He felt most strongly about his support of the provision to establish religious freedom in the state.

After the Revolution, Locke entered the state senate, and he served there in 1782, 1784, and 1785. As a member of the state senate, he supported the movement for universal manhood suffrage, arguing against the requirement to own property in order to vote. In 1784 he became close to Timothy Bloodworth (q.v.), a future Antifederalist, as they both voted in favor of a state over a federal taxing system. In 1784 he became a trustee of the Salisbury Academy. By 1785 Locke's experience in public life and his positions in support of western farmers made him the leader of the state's western farmer debtor party. Also an ally of General Griffith Rutherford (q.v.), he replaced that leader as major general of the state militia. Locke served in the Continental Congress in 1788.

By the late 1780s, Locke owned much land in Rowan County, North Carolina, as well as in Iredell County, Tennessee. He thus had a stake in protecting western land interests. Locke's reputation led the people of the west to elect him to the first state Constitution ratifying convention in 1788 as a staunch Antifederalist. In the first state convention, he voted against ratification. Locke had spoken out that the "Constitution, if adopted as it stood, would render the people poor and miserable" (Elliot, 239). If the convention voted against ratification, he said, "the worst that could happen would be, that we should be thrown out of the Union" (Elliot, 239). He said that he continued to support the rights of poor farmers. Locke served on the important committee to call a second state convention in Hillsborough for 1789. But he lost his bid for election to that convention. Perhaps he lost because he had become too radical even for his region of North Carolina.

After his defeat for the convention, Locke returned to the state legislature where he continued in the cause of Antifederalism. He was elected as a Republican to the United States House in 1793 and served until 1799. Locke lost his bid for reelection in 1798. Opponents considered him an extreme Jeffersonian Republican and a supporter of Nathaniel Macon, the radical state's rights North Carolinian. A man with what he called rural values, proud of his lack of education, and with a religious obligation to the ordinary people, Locke's radicalism made an impression in the House of Representatives. He even opposed congressional praise for President George Washington's farewell address. Locke also spoke out against the quasi war with France in 1798, in the belief that his followers had supported the French Revolution. His famous speech in Congress in 1796 in which he opposed paying the states' debts to the nation made him a hero of the people in debtor states. Allies in the state legislature nominated him for the United States Senate in 1800, but Locke did not get a majority vote. The state and the times had changed. Locke retired to his large farm and died in Salisbury, Rowan County, North Carolina, on September 7, 1801.

REFERENCES

Samuel A. Ashe, *History of North Carolina* (Raleigh, N.C.: Edwards and Broughton Printing Co., 1925), vol. 2; Randall Capps, *The Rowan Story* (Bowling Green, Ky.: Homestead Press, 1976); R.D.W. Connor (ed.), *Documentary History of the University of North Carolina* (Chapel Hill: University of North Carolina Press, 1953); Elliot, *Debates*, vol. 4; Adelaide L. Fries (ed.), *Records of North Carolina Moravians* (Raleigh, N.C.: Edwards and Broughton Printing Co., 1922); Norman K. Risjord, *Chesapeake Politics* (New York: Columbia University Press, 1978); Jethro Rumple,

History of Rowan County (Baltimore: Regional Publishing Company, 1974); John H. Wheeler, *Memorial of North Carolina* (Baltimore: Regional Publishing Company, 1964), vol. 2.

RAWLINS LOWNDES *(January 1721–August 24, 1800)* was born on the island of St. Kitts in the British West Indies. His father, Charles, had emigrated to St. Kitts from England, and married Ruth (Rawlins), daughter of a West Indian planter. The marriage soon broke up, and the elder Lowndes brought his son to Charleston in 1730. Charles was sent to prison for indebtedness, and committed suicide there in 1735. The Charleston lawyer and businessman Robert Hall recognized the talents of this young man and adopted him. Under Hall's tutelage Lowndes studied law. Early seen as a leader, Lowndes served as deputy provost marshall of the Charleston District from 1742 to 1752. Accepted into Charleston society, in 1748 he married Amarinthea Elliott, daughter of a rice planter. He became a planter himself in St. Bartholomew Parish. Lowndes married two more times, in 1750 to Martha Cartwright, and in 1773 to Sarah Jones. He had a large family.

While provost marshall, Lowndes was elected to the colonial South Carolina legislature in 1749. He continued to practice law. Respected by his peers in the legislature, he served as speaker of that body from 1763 to 1765, and again from 1772 to 1775. He became president of the prestigious St. Cecilia Society in 1772. (That social society only allowed members to join through connections in the mother's line, in order to keep out poor adventurers like Lowndes. The rules did not seem to apply to him.) Lowndes also served as a judge of the Court of Common Pleas from 1766 to 1772. In 1766 he spoke out that the British Stamp Act violated the rights of loyal Englishmen, and he refused to render verdicts against anyone arrested in violation of that act. In 1775 the royal governor removed him from the court, calling him an enemy of England. He resisted English aggression, but, cautiously, he opposed open rebellion. Lowndes came to support the First Continental Congress but did not yet advocate independence.

Elected to the South Carolina provisional congress in 1775, Lowndes became its president. He then supported the appointment of a committee of safety and joined it. Lowndes argued against taxation without legislative representation. Still, he feared the consequences of rebellion. But when South Carolina declared independence in March 1776, Lowndes joined the legislative council. He supported the creation of the state constitution of 1776. In 1778 he became president of the new state government of South Carolina. Upon hearing that England planned to invade South Carolina, Lowndes decreed that the state refuse any trade with that country. He supported the Continental Army's defense of the Carolinas and helped to resist the British siege of Charleston. Raids on his rice plantation reduced his income. It is said that he either signed an oath of loyalty or neutrality to England in those hectic days of British occupation. Nevertheless, he was elected as a patriot to the state senate from his home parish. When the war came to an end, he was elected to the general assembly and served until 1790, when the delegates voted to remove the capital to Columbia.

Active in local affairs, a supporter of the development of new schools, and a promoter of new business, Lowndes also served as a warden of the Episcopal church. During the struggle over the federal Constitution, he became an ardent localist, arguing in defense of rights for the southern minority. In January 1788, he took part in the state legislative debates as a vigorous opponent of South Carolina ratifying the Constitution as written. He objected to what he believed was a threat to slavery in the Constitution. Lowndes also resisted congressional power to regulate commerce, believing national authority restricted the prerogatives of local rice exporters. He claimed not to have sought fame or preferment in the debates, but had acted in a manner fair to all. His biographer George Chase stated that Lowndes had wanted to "point out those dangers to which [his] fellow citizens [were] exposed" (17). Indeed, he regarded the Constitution as ruinous to liberty. But that cautious man refused to run for the state ratifying convention, perhaps because he understood that a majority of his friends supported the new document. After all, he said, the members of the legislature knew his worries. During the convention, he worked with the Antifederalists to oppose ratification.

A look at Lowndes's opinions on the Constitution in his own words reveals even more about his opposition to that document. In his debate with Edmund Rutledge in the state legislature on January 16, 1788, Lowndes argued that he opposed what others called an experiment in liberal government. He found the proposed document injurious to southern interests, fearing the northern states planned to dominate the new government. The northern states, he said, had prejudices against slavery and ideas different than the southern people (Bailyn, 19–25). On January 18, 1788, Lowndes stated that "without negroes this state would degenerate into one of the most contemptible in the union" (Storing, 150). Lowndes went on to to show where the Constitution was faulty in political structure. How, he asked, were the congressmen from South Carolina to be chosen? If all came from Charleston, as the Federalists threatened, the rest of the state had little reason to support that seaport's interests. The argument for checks on federal power he found inconclusive. Too many checks he found confusing and unsupportive of government's needs. The powers given to the president, he allowed, meant the possiblity of a monarchical government. He concluded that he wanted on his tombstone, "here lies the man that opposed the constitution, because it was ruinous to the liberty of America" (Storing, 153–157).

After the state had ratified the Constitution, Lowndes refused to speak further against it. Still, after he retired to his plantation in 1790, Lowndes claimed he had never given support to the Federalists, whom he insisted used the central government to usurp local and state rights. Lowndes died in Charleston on August 24, 1800, and is buried at St. Philip's churchyard. George B. Chase, Lowndes's biographer, stated that that solon's friends regarded him as clear, logical, discriminating, and succinct in his opinions. Certainly, the high regard for Lowndes in Charleston society meant his constituents rarely questioned his decisions, even when many of them disagreed with him. Lowndes fits the category of a conservative republican and a defender of southern slavery, who stands out as a symbol of the sectionalist Antifederalists.

REFERENCES

N. Louise Bailey and Elizabeth Ivey Cooper (eds.), *Biographical Dictionary of the South Carolina House of Representatives* (Columbia: University of South Carolina Press, 1981), vol. 2; Bailyn, *Debate*, vol. 1; George B. Chase, *Lowndes of South Carolina: An Historical and Genealogical Memoir* (Boston: A. Williams and Co., 1876); Elliot, *Debates*, vol. 4; W. Eugene Sirmans, *Colonial South Carolina* (Chapel Hill; University of North Carolina Press, 1966); Storing, *Complete*, vol. 4; Carl J. Vipperman, *The Rise of Rawlin Lowndes* (Columbia: University of South Carolina Press, 1978).

M

FRANÇOIS XAVIER MARTIN *(?–December 10, 1846)* was born in Marseilles, France, and as a youth went to Martinique. He received an excellent Catholic school education. He eventually moved to New Bern, Craven County, North Carolina, where he worked for his uncle. In New Bern, Martin also taught French to planter children, worked as a letter carrier, and trained in a print shop.

During the North Carolina federal Constitution ratification controversy, Martin owned and edited an Antifederalist newspaper, *The North Carolina Gazette*, which he had begun in 1785. He edited the paper, whose name he changed to *Martin's North Carolina Gazette* in 1787, until 1798. Martin avidly supported the small state ideals of the Antifederalists. He served that cause well, publishing Antifederalist pamphlets and providing materials for debate to the state Constitutional convention's Antifederalist members.

After the state ratification conventions, Martin continued to rise in the publication business. Perhaps for his loyalty to the Antifederalist cause, he received the lucrative contract to publish the acts of the assembly. Martin became one of the state's early book publishers. In 1804 he edited and published *The Public Acts of the General Assembly of North Carolina*. Martin also served in the North Carolina state legislature in 1806.

In 1809 President James Madison named this ardent Republican a judge in the Mississippi territory. In 1810 Martin moved to the Louisiana territory to become a judge. In 1812 he became the first attorney general of the state of Louisiana. In 1815 Martin became a member of the Louisiana Supreme Court, a post he held until 1846. Martin also wrote history. In 1827 he published a two-volume history of Louisiana. In 1829 he became the second person to publish a history of the state of North Carolina, in two volumes. Martin's work on North Carolina is especially interesting. In that important work he discussed the localist cause in depth and set out the reasons why the state had developed such a strong Antifederalist position.

A curious and fascinating man of letters, Martin never married, seemingly having spent most of his time in ardent political, ideological, and legal pursuits. In the 1830s, he went blind. Though he continued to serve on the state bench, he gradually lost all of his income and began to appear in public as a beggar. Martin died in New Orleans, Lousiana, on December 10, 1846. Although certainly not to be considered as a major Antifederalist leader, his work as a publicist for the cause and his history of those events make him an important North Carolina localist.

REFERENCES

Samuel A. Ashe, et al., *Biographical History of North Carolina* (Greensboro, N.C.: Charles L. Van Nappen, 1917), vol. 2; François X. Martin, *History of North Carolina from the Earliest Period* (New Orleans: Printed by A. P. Penniman and Co., 1829); William S. Powell (ed.), *Dictionary of North Carolina Biography* (Chapel Hill: University of North Carolina Press, 1975), vol. 4; Wilfred B. Yearns, "François X. Martin and His History of North Carolina," *North Carolina Historical Review* 36 (1959): 17–27.

LUTHER MARTIN *(February 9, 1744–July 10, 1826)* probably was born in New Brunswick, New Jersey. (There is some disagreement over the details of his early life before he came to Maryland.) His father was the poor farmer Benjamin Martin, and his mother was named Hannah. Young Martin managed to attend the grammar school of the College of New Jersey. He held a scholarship from 1762 to 1766 to the College of New Jersey (Princeton) and was an honor student. Like other bright, talented, and ambitious poor young men, he then taught school. Perhaps realizing he had no business or political future in his home state, Martin took a teaching position in Queenstown, Queen Anne's County, Maryland, instructing the children of wealthy planters. In 1769 he moved to Somerset County, Maryland, to study law. In 1770 Martin became superintendent of the grammar school at Onancock, Accomac County, Virginia. In 1771 he joined the Virginia bar in Williamsburg. Finally, Martin was able to begin his chosen career and his path to success, and he settled in Somerset County, Maryland, on the eastern shore. He became a most successful lawyer.

During the period of revolutionary turmoil, Martin entered politics, already highly regarded as a student of parliamentary and legal procedure. In 1774 he joined the Maryland patriot commission. In 1777 he wrote *An Address to the Inhabitants of the Peninsula* in which he delineated the reasons why Maryland had supported the Revolution and why it should affirm the Articles of Confederation. Marylanders on the Chesapeake Bay, he said, had experienced much devastation of their land from British invasion, and many felt the new government had done little to aid them. In addition, Martin wrote, Maryland's government had serious reservations about Virginia's enormous western land claims and worried whether Marylanders would ever be able to settle in the west. But, under the Articles of Confederation, Virginia had to give up those claims. Aside from his writing, Martin politicked among many of his friends for their support of the new nation, which raised him in the public eye. Elected attorney general of Maryland near the end of the Revolution, Martin, who made a career of cultivating powerful leaders, developed a friendship with the political leader Samuel Chase (q.v.). Martin prosecuted loyalists in Baltimore and assisted in the mass confiscation and resale of their lands. Along with some future Antifederalist leaders, including Chase, he profited from favored terms to purchase for himself some of those lands, especially rich property in the docklands of Baltimore harbor.

In 1785 Martin gained election to the Continental Congress. There he supported the government of the Articles of Confederation. Martin, perhaps because of his role in Maryland state politics, became a defender of the rights of small states and their veto powers of money bills. He continued as attorney general of Maryland. Elected as a delegate to the Philadelphia Constitutional Convention, this flamboyant and gifted orator spoke often there about the rights of states. He opposed the Virginia large state plan and defended the New Jersey small state plan. An ally of the New Yorkers John Lansing (q.v.) and Abraham Yates (q.v.), Martin assisted them and others in drafting the small state plan. Often Martin spoke out unadvisedly about fellow delegates' personal motives, suggesting a number were determined to create a central government to favor themselves and their wealthy allies. He earned the emnity of a number of delegates. Along with his fellow Maryland delegate, John Francis Mercer (q.v.), he walked out of the convention and refused to sign the Constitution. June F. Essary said Martin had become the "determined champion of the State's rights cause" (60).

Back in Maryland, in the House of Delegates, Martin attacked the Constitution and called on the state legislature to support a state convention opposed to ratification. As a member of the Maryland ratifying convention, Martin voted against ratification. Hindered by a throat infection, this eloquent lawyer spoke only occasionally at the convention. Instead, he allowed his pen to represent his views. In 1788 Martin published the address *The Genuine Information*, in which he reported on the events at the Philadelphia convention. He circulated it widely in pamphlet form among Antifederalists in Pennsylvania and Massachusetts, as he joined the ranks of the national leaders in opposition to the Constitution. Martin's pamphlet became a major statement for the cause.

Saul Cornell says Martin represented the elite branch of the Antifederalists because he had become a successful lawyer and Maryland attorney general. But Martin actually was descended from modest circumstances, and his *Genuine Information* reflects his past. According to Cornell, Martin "lent credence to the Antifederalist accusation that the Convention delegates planned a consolidated government" (51). That view of a wronged people and a suspicion of power obviously reflected his roots in poverty. Martin also wrote against the taxing powers of the proposed federal government, fearing the states without claims to western land could not raise sufficient tax revenue through sale of public land. He promulgated a clear theory of state rights.

Who should have power? he asked. He believed it should be the people through their local representatives. Then Martin expounded on his theory of localism, in which he even called for making new states out of parts of larger states when the population reached a certain number. Local government, closest to the people, best knew their needs, said he, and therefore must be the foremost power in the new government. He also opposed the means of election and powers given to the president as designed in the Constitution, suggesting that the small states would have no say in that selection. In a most radical mode, Martin spoke out about the principles of the American Revolution, claiming the people had resisted arbitrary powers by resorting to arms. "The time may come," he allowed, "when it shall be the duty of a State, in order to preserve itself from the oppression of the general government, to have recourse to the sword" (Storing, 71). Martin, a lawyer and land speculator, also spoke in favor of trial by jury. He wanted to maintain the right of ordinary citizens to have their cases heard by a jury of their peers.

In addition, Martin, faithful to his position at the Philadelphia convention, took a strong stand against the powers of the larger states, especially Virginia. He believed the three-fifths clause allowing slaves to be counted in the federal census made Virginia and the other large slave states too powerful in the new government. He also resisted reopening the slave trade. Congress, Martin claimed, encouraged "that most infamous traffic." The states thus "cruelly and wantonly sport with the rights of their fellow creatures" making "a solemn mockery of, and insult to, that God whose protection we had thus implored" and rendering "us contemptible to every true friend of liberty in the world." For Martin slavery was inconsistent "with the genius of republicanism" (Storing, 61–62). He joined eleven other Maryland Antifederalists in voting against ratification of the Constitution.

Despite these radical pronouncements calling for resistance and questioning slavery in a slave state, and despite his vote with the minority, Martin became a hero to Marylanders for his defense of local rights. He could have had any office in the state. Martin chose to remain as attorney general, a position he held off and on for twenty-nine years. He also became chief justice of the Court of Oyer and Terminor from 1813 to 1816. After 1800 Martin and his friend and ally Samuel Chase turned against President Thomas Jefferson, and for a time sided with the powerful Maryland Federalists. Believing Jefferson's foreign policy would wreck Baltimore trade, they opposed his policies. In 1804 Martin was Chase's chief counsel in the criminal proceedings to remove him as a justice of the United States Supreme Court. He helped to acquit his old friend. In 1807 Martin served as Aaron Burr's lawyer in his treason trial. His support for Burr forever indebted that difficult man to him.

In 1819 Martin again became attorney general of Maryland. He pled for the state in the famous *McCulloch v. Maryland* case. In that case Martin returned to his old Antifederalist state rights position. All of this time Martin himself was living on the slightly shady side of the law. In constant litigation, he drank heavily (many have seen Martin as a lifelong drunk and accordingly have belittled his accomplishments), made more enemies, and eventually lost his money and property. In 1820, Martin had a debilitating stroke from which he never recovered. In 1783 he had married Marie Cresap, from a fine Maryland family, and she would take care of him in his dying days. Aaron Burr also came to Martin's rescue, took him in, and supported him for the remainder of his life. On July 10, 1826, Martin died in New York City. He is buried in Trinity churchyard in lower Manhattan. Martin's *Genuine Information* remains one of the most important of Antifederalist statements against the centralist and arbitrary powers that he believed were so damaging to local government and to the needs of the people.

REFERENCES

Bailyn, *Debate*, vol. 2; *Biographical Cyclopedia of Representative Men of Maryland and the District of Columbia* (Baltimore: National Publishing Co., 1879); Henry E. Buchholz, *Governors of Maryland* (Baltimore: Williams and Wilkinson Co., 1908); Paul S. Clarkson and Samuel Jett, *Luther Martin* (Baltimore: The Johns Hopkins University Press, 1970); Saul Cornell, *The Other Founders* (Chapel Hill: University of North Carolina Press, 1999); Jesse Frederick Essary, *Maryland in National Politics* (Baltimore: John Murphy Co., 1915); Henry P. Goddard, *Luther Martin: The Federal Bulldog* (Baltimore: John Murphy Co., 1887); Horace H. Hagan, *Eight Great American Lawyers* (Oklahoma City: Harlow, 1923); Luther Martin, *Modern Gratitude: An Autobiography* (Baltimore: self-published, 1802); Storing, *Complete*, vol. 2; Charles Warren, *The Making of the Constitution* (Boston: Little, Brown and Co., 1929).

GEORGE MASON *(?, 1725–October 7, 1792)* was born in the Northern Neck of Virginia, near the Potomac River. His father, George Mason, was a prominent Virginia planter. His mother was Anne (Thomason). His uncle, the wealthy John Mercer of Marlborough, Virginia, became his guardian after the elder Mason was killed in an accident. Mason was educated at home with private tutors. He received training in history, the science of government, and the law. In 1750 Mason married Ann Eileck of Maryland, thus uniting two wealthy families. In 1780 he married Sarah Brent.

Following the pattern of some wealthy planters, Mason became devoted to local public affairs. Unlike a number of his peers, however, he never seemed to have had the taste for the political life on a larger stage. A prominent and faithful member of the Church of England, he served as vestryman of Truro Parish, near the Potomac, from 1748 until 1785. Mason supervised the building of the beautiful Pohick Church near his home. He served a term in the Virginia House of Burgesses in 1759, but resigned, preferring private political contemplation to the raucous activities of government and what he believed was an excessive display of public discourse. Shrewd in business—meaning land speculation—and planting already having begun to decline along the Potomac, he became an investor in the Ohio Company in 1752 and served as its treasurer in 1773. After he decided to give up thoughts of removing across the river to Maryland, Mason doted on the plantation home he designed, Gunston Hall, one of Virginia's most beautiful colonial homes, only eighteen miles from present-day Washington, on the banks of the Potomac not far from the home of his great friend George Washington.

In his capacity as a local leader, Mason had learned much about human political nature and public life. Out of loyalty to local rights he slowly joined the revolutionary cause. In 1766, in the open letter "The Virginia Planter," written to London merchants, he voiced opposition to the Stamp Act tax and wanted England to repeal the Declaratory Act. In 1769 Mason organized a boycott of British goods, and supported nonimportation and nonexportation with England. His home, Gunston Hall, became a meeting house for moderate revolutionaries. Mason talked with Washington in 1774 about how to aid the port of Boston to resist British oppression. That same year, he wrote the *Fairfax Resolves* in which he united the problems of Boston with those of each of the other colonies. He assisted in the military organization of Virginia as a member of the Committee of Safety.

In 1776 Mason framed the *Virginia Declaration of Rights*, a document that would become part of that state's first constitution, and a major influence on the future Bill of Rights. His famous declaration made the shy Mason into one of the new country's greatest defenders of individual rights. In that document he caught the eye of Richard Henry Lee (q.v.), who would become his collaborator in defense of local rights. Although a staunch defender of his Episcopal Church, Mason helped to disestablish the Church of England in Virginia. He believed in the individual conscience of faith and resisted state-supported religion. From 1776 to 1780, he served as a member of the Virginia state legislature, the House of Delegates. He helped reorganize the laws of Virginia, assisted in drafting the first state constitution, and worked out a compromise on the western boundary of Virginia, which endeared him to the smaller states. After the Revolution, Mason retired from government, with a distaste over what he believed was the government's failure in the war effort.

Meanwhile, he helped Thomas Jefferson draw up the ordinances concerning the northwest, and wrote a provision that no slaves be taken there. In 1786 he was persuaded to return to the Virginia legislature. Mason served as a delegate to the important Mount Vernon meeting that planned the 1786 Annapolis convention. When appointed to that convention, however, he refused to attend. He along with others hoped that the federal Congress could regulate trade and protect the interests of the young nation. But the war had taught him that the Articles of Confederation were just too weak to provide a government for all of the people. Elected to the Constitutional Convention of 1787, he attended because he believed the Articles needed amending. At first he supported James Madison's nationalist forces and favored the large state plan. Mason also said that he thought the new government had the right and ought to control and even prevent the slave trade. (Like many a revolutionary Virginian who understood that slavery was in decline, Mason also believed in the meaning of liberty as he understood it. His views of the future of slavery certainly make him an ambivalent Virginian.) Mason spoke often and made many contributions to the shape of the new Constitution. But he soon became disenchanted with the proceedings, found fault with the proposed document, and refused to sign the Constitution. On September 10, 1787, he joined with Elbridge Gerry (q.v.) to call for a second convention to rewrite the Constitution. When they failed, he walked out.

Even before the debates of the Constitution had ended, Mason set down his *Objections to the Federal Constitution*, destined to become a major Antifederalist statement, cited and used by Antifederalists throughout the nation. No doubt, his correspondence with Richard Henry Lee had sharpened his views on why he opposed the proposed Constitution. In the *Objections*, Mason proposed creating a presidential office that had few central powers, unlike what the Constitution allowed. He called the lower house too small to adequately represent the interests of its members' constituencies. He rejected the Senate's powers to control money bills, desired a privy council, and believed the federal judiciary had been given too much power. Unlike his friend Lee, Mason also made a formal protest against foreign slave trade and found fault with allowing that trade to continue until 1808. Above all in the *Objections*, Mason devoted his major arguments against the Constitution to its lack of a document like the Virginia Declaration of Rights. For him, the Constitution simply had no bill of rights to protect the sacred right of revolution, and the rights of individual freedom and liberty, as set down by the American Revolution.

After leaving the convention, Mason went home to Virginia to make plans with Patrick Henry (q.v.) and Richard Henry Lee to defeat the Constitution. He had joined the opposition against his great friend George Washington. Elected to the state ratification convention of 1788, Mason became a leading spokesman for its rejection. Fearing that the Antifederalists did not have the votes to defeat the Constitution, Mason proposed a clause-by-clause discussion of the document to buy the time to build a majority coalition of leaders aggrieved by certain parts of the Constitution. When Mason's movement to point out the flaws failed, he joined with Patrick Henry to draft a bill of rights, some twenty rights in all, based largely on his previous work on Virginia rights. On June 25, 1788, Mason was one of the delegates who voted against the Constitution because the new government had not guaranteed individual rights.

A closer look at Mason's actual words reveals more of why he opposed the Constitution. In October 1787, Mason wrote "Objections to the Constitution," which he had printed in the *Virginia Journal*. In that essay, he objected to the close connection the Constitution had made between the president and the Senate. In Mason's view, the result was that state powers were lost to the federal government, especially the right to protect its trade interests. Thus the government would become monarchical, or a corrupt and oppressive aristocracy (Bailyn, 349). On June 4, 1788, Mason made a major speech in the state ratifying convention in which he declared that federal power "is calculated to annihilate totally the state governments." He stated, "there never was a Government over a very extensive country, without destroying the liberties of the people." Simply put, "the members cannot possibly know the situation and circumstances of this immense continent" (Storing, 256). These fears led Mason to his supreme effort of demanding a bill of rights be included in the Constitution to ward off the dangers of excessive federal power over popular liberty (Storing, 259). In this way, Mason came to his finest collusion with Patrick Henry. Both men would be known as the authors of the Bill of Rights.

In March 1789, Mason called for a new Constitutional convention to revise the flawed document. Failing in that he retired to Gunston Hall. But his contributions to the cause of liberty were not yet over. Madison, in drafting a bill of rights, used Mason's writings and attributed his own efforts to Mason. Mason died in October 7, 1792, at his home, still believing that the first ten amendments to the Constitution were not enough to protect rights.

As a speculator in western lands, Mason believed—somewhat like Thomas Jefferson—that the west was the gateway to freedom. A southern slaveholder, this revolutionary freedom lover opposed the growth of slavery and freed his own slaves. An elite planter in every fiber of his body, he supported the people's rights to choose their leaders and to decide what power to give them. Perhaps above all, it was his view of revolution, and his connection to that generation of leaders, that led him to believe in the sanctity of personal freedom and therefore the necessity for any government to codify carefully the rights of a free people.

REFERENCES

Bailyn, *Debate,* vol. 1; Helen Hill Miller, *George Mason Constitutionalist* (Cambridge: Harvard University Press, 1938); Josephine F. Pacheco (ed.), *Antifederalism: The Legacy of George Mason* (Fairfax, Va.: George Mason University Press, 1992); Kate Mason Rowland, *Life of George Mason* (New York: Russell and Russell, 1964); Robert A. Rutland, *George Mason Reluctant Statesman* (Williamsburg, Va.: Holt, Rinehart, and Winston, 1961); Storing, *Complete,* vol. 5.
Mason's papers are in the Manuscript Division of the Library of Congress.

STEVENS THOMSON MASON *(December 29, 1760–May 10, 1803)* was born at the plantation Chippawamsic in Stafford County, Virginia. He was the son of the wealthy planter Thomson Mason and his wife Mary King (Barnes). The scion of Northern Neck, Virginia, political power, the younger Mason received an excellent preparatory education, then went to the College of William and Mary. He studied law and began a practice in Dumfries, Prince William County, Virginia. He married Mary Elizabeth Armistead of Louisa County, Virginia, the daughter of another successful planter. They had four children. His father, Thomas, was brother of George Mason (q.v.), perhaps the most important Antifederalist in the Northern Neck region. Stevens's father wrote in 1783 "A British American," an Antifederalist pamphlet that very much influenced his son.

As a young man, Mason's family connections landed him a prime Revolutionary War position as an aide to General George Washington. He would eventually, at a young age, become a brigadier general of the Virginia militia. Mason also early entered state politics, becoming a member of the Virginia House of Delegates in 1783 and again in 1794. He served in the state senate from 1787 until 1790, where he impressed his uncle and other later Antifederalist leaders with his strong commitment to local rights and his hostility toward aristocratic leaders. After the Revolution, he moved to Loudoun County, Virginia, to his plantation, Raspberry Plain, from which place he ably represented his constituents.

Even though only twenty-eight, Mason became an Antifederalist leader through his abilities and his family connections. He was a delegate from London County to the state ratifying convention of 1788. At the convention he supported his famous uncle in the cause of a bill of rights. Like his uncle, Mason voted against ratification.

As a member of the postconvention House of Delegates, Mason opposed the state legislature's attempt to write a bill of rights for the federal Congress as too shallow and inconclusive on major issues of civil liberties. He soon had the opportunity to make his presence felt in national politics when the state legislature appointed him to the United States Senate in 1794, after James Monroe (q.v.) had resigned to take a diplomatic post. Mason won his own term in 1797 and served as a Jeffersonian Republican until 1803. Determined not to offend his fellow Virginian, President George Washington, he nevertheless found fault with Jay's Treaty of 1794 and made his views public, to the utter chagrin of the Federalists. The Federalists wanted to censor him, but leaders from Virginia fought to defend his right to release that document. Mason joined other Republicans and opposed the Alien and Sedition acts of 1798 and supported the bill to repeal the Judiciary Act of 1801. When Thomas Jefferson became president, he made Mason the leader of the Senate. Mason died all too young in Philadelphia, Pennsylvania, on May 10, 1803. He is buried at Raspberry Plain in Loudon County, Virginia. To attest to the importance in Virginia of this leader, the Episcopal bishop of the state conducted the funeral, and it was filled with the pomp accorded to the state's planter-political elite.

REFERENCES

Hugh Blair Grigsby, *The History of the Virginia Federal Convention of 1788* (1890; repr., New York: Da Capo Press, 1969), vol. 2; Lawton T. Hemans, *Life and Times of Stephens Thomson Mason* (Lansing: Michigan Historical Commission, 1920); Daniel P. Jordan, *Political Leaders in Jefferson's Virginia* (Charlottesville: University Press of Virginia, 1983); Kate Mason Rowland, *Life of George Mason* (New York: Russell and

Russell, 1964); Norman K. Risjord, *Chesapeake Politics* (New York: Columbia University Press, 1979).

BLAIR M. McCLENACHAN *(?–May 8, 1812)* was probably the son of an immigrant from northern Ireland, the Episcopal priest William Mc-Clenachan. Some believe he was born in Ireland. McClenachan became a prominent Philadelphia merchant. During the American Revolution, he ran a privateer and became wealthy in illegal trade. A strong patriot, McClenachan founded and subsidized the First Troops of the Philadelphia Cavalry. He worked with the nationalist Robert Morris to raise salaries for the Continental Army. McClenachan became a subscriber and later a director of the Bank of Pennsylvania in 1780.

After the war, McClenachan assumed leadership of the Philadelphia Constitutionalist Party, the party of the ordinary people, and he developed ties to the localists Davd Redick (q.v.) and James Hutchinson (q.v.). He turned on his fellow Philadelphia businessmen who opposed reforms for the working classes. Nevertheless, McClenachan grew wealthy in the mercantile business, as he became the powerful owner of a merchant fleet. Yet, for a short time this flamboyant business buccaneer went to jail because of his accumulated debts. Perhaps the way he lived on the edge of the business world and his poverty-ridden youth led McClenachan to join the Antifederalist cause in his adopted city. Although not a member of the state ratifying convention—few Philadelphia Antifederalists were elected—McClenachan chaired the meeting at Harrisburg, Pennsylvania, of September 1788 that called for a second state convention to address concerns with the federal Constitution. He was known in that convention as an ally of the radical John Hanna (q.v.).

Durng the Federalist era, McClenachan headed the Philadelphia Gallic Party and served as president of the Democratic Society. Pro-French, in 1794 he opposed the Jay Treaty. From 1790 until 1795, he served in the Pennsylvania State Assembly. McClenachan also gained election to the United States Congress and served as a Republican there from 1797 until 1799. He also was commissioner of United States loans for a time. McClenachan married and had a large family. He died in Philadelphia at an old age, on May 8, 1812. He is buried in St. Paul's cemetery.

REFERENCES

Steven R. Boyd, *The Politics of Opposition* (Millwood, N.Y.: KTO Press, 1979); Harold Donald Eberlein and Horace Mather Lippincott, *The Colonial Homes of Philadelphia* (Philadelphia: J. B. Lippincott Co., 1912); Elliot, *Debates*, vol. 2; John Bach McMaster and Frederick D. Stone, *Pennsylvania and the Federal Constitution, 1787–1788* (New York: Da Capo Press, 1970); Henry Simpson, *The Lives of Eminent Philadelphians* (Philadelphia: William Brotherhead, 1859).

JOSEPH McDOWELL *(February 15, 1756–July 11, 1801)* was born in Winchester, Virginia. His father, Joseph, born in Tyrone County, Ireland, was a small farmer in western Virginia who decided to seek his fortune in North Carolina, having been given a grant of land in Anson County. He settled his family in Morgantown, Burke County, in the western part of the colony. Joseph's mother was Margaret (O'Neal). The family moved back and forth between North Carolina and Virginia as Joseph's father tried to make a living. Young Joseph attended local schools, then went back to Virginia to study in Winchester. He attended Augusta Academy (later renamed Washington College) in Lexington, Virginia. McDowell settled into a life as a farmer and trader in North Carolina. In 1780, he married Margaret Moffett of Virginia. They had eight children.

Close to his older brother Charles, McDowell was imbued with the spirit of revolutionary resistance. He fought in his brother's regiment in the Revolution, first against the Cherokee Indian loyalists in 1776. He then participated in the major defenses of North and South Carolina, fighting at the battles of King's Mountain and at Cowpens in 1781. McDowell rose to the rank of colonel and later claimed to have been promoted to general. During the war McDowell served under Griffith Rutherford (q.v.) and made a close friend of Matthew Locke (q.v.), two men who no doubt influenced his later support of the Antifederalists.

After the war, this young revolutionary hero entered the North Carolina state legislature and served there from 1780 to 1789. McDowell developed a lucrative law practice in Burke County. In the state house, he came under the influence of the leader Willie Jones (q.v.) and became an ardent defender of local rights. In 1786 he served on the Council of State. The state legislature selected McDowell for membership in the Philadelphia Constitutional Convention in the summer of 1787. Perhaps sensing the delegates planned radical changes to the Articles of Confederation, this committed localist refused to attend.

When elected to the first and then second North Carolina state ratification conventions, McDowell readily joined the Antifederalists and embraced their state's rights, anti–federal government views. He became a major figure in the state debates, speaking forcefully on behalf of local rights. McDowell often addressed matters concerning his state's interests. He rejected the proposal to give the federal Congress taxing and moneymaking powers, preferring that North Carolina print its own paper money. He also made comparisons between the proposed new government and the activities of Great Britain. Especially did he fear taking away the "great safeguard of liberty, the trial by jury" (Elliot, 88). "We are," he claimed, "giving away our dear-bought rights" (150). This excellent lawyer and judge of government affairs said he regarded the Constitution as too complicated for the ordinary citizen, and thought it filled with ambiguities. He wanted to amend the Constitution before the state voted on it. "I have," he said, "much information from friends in other states who demand a bill of rights" (210). Furthermore, "[a] bill of rights ought to have been asserted, to ascertain our most valuable and unalienable rights" (211). McDowell also wondered how such disparate interests among the states could make a nation. "They differ," he said, "in climate, soil, customs, manners, etc." (211). McDowell concluded his arguments with the ringing assertion: "I never will agree to a government that tends to the destruction of the liberty of the people" (Elliot, 212). Indeed, he voted against ratification in both state conventions.

After the state rejected the Constitution in 1788, McDowell traveled north with other North Carolina Antifederalists to lobby for a second federal Constitutional Convention. He failed to achieve his purpose. In the second state convention, McDowell led the Antifederalists from his section of the state. When North Carolina finally joined the Union, McDowell became a leader of the state's Democratic-Republicans, but especially of the people in the west. In 1789 he joined a number of other Antifederalists to serve on the Board of Trustees of the new University of North Carolina. Elected to the fifth federal Congress, he held office from 1797 to 1799. Like other loyal Jeffersonians, McDowell voted against the Alien and the Sedition acts of 1798. He declined reelection to Congress in 1798. McDowell worked in the federal Congress and with the state legislature on committees to create boundaries between Kentucky and Tennessee. He moved to Kentucky in 1800 but returned to Burke County, North Carolina, in 1801. He died in Morgantown, North Carolina, on July 11, 1801. There is some thought that he actually died in Rockbridge County, Virginia. Nevertheless, he is buried at his beloved "Quaker Meadows" near Morgantown.

REFERENCES

Samuel A. Ashe, *Biographical History of North Carolina* (Greensboro, N.C.: Charles L. Van Nappen, 1917), vol. 7; Bailyn, *Debate*, vol. 2; Elliot, *Debates*, vol. 4; C.L. Hunter, *Sketches of Western North Carolina, Historical and Biographical* (Raleigh, N.C.: The Raleigh News and Steam Job, 1877); John Hugh McDowell, *The Mc-Dowells, Erwins, Irwins, and Connections* (Memphis: C.B. Johnston, 1918); Edwin W. Phifer, *Burke: The History of a North Carolina County* (Morgantown, N.C.: Phifer, 1980); Louise Irby Trenholme, *The Ratification of the Federal Constitution in North Carolina* (New York: Columbia University Press, 1932); John H. Wheeler, *Historical Sketches of North Carolina*, 2 vols. (1851; repr., Baltimore: Regional Publishing Co., 1964).

DUNCAN (McFARLAND) McFARLAN   *(?–September 17, 1816)* was born at Laurel Hill, Scotland County, North Carolina. He received a common school education. McFarlan farmed in Richmond County. Young and aggressive, he gained election to the state ratification convention of 1788 and voted against ratification. He served in the state house in 1792, and the state senate in 1793, 1795, 1800, and from 1807 until 1809. McFarlan ran and lost for the federal house in 1802 but was elected in 1805 and served for one term. He later farmed and was a merchant. McFarlan died at his farm in Laurel Hill, North Carolina, on September 17, 1816.

Hugh Leffler described McFarlan as a brutish and violent farmer: "Duncan McFarland of the Fayetteville District had fist fights, was convicted of rape, charged with toryism, murder, perjury, hog-stealing, forgery, and witchcraft: he was rotten-egged in the 1804 campaign; yet he served six terms in the General Assembly and one term in Congress" (286).

REFERENCES

Delbert H. Gilpatrick, *Jeffersonian Democracy in North Carolina* (New York: Columbia University Press, 1931); Hugh T. Lefler and John T. Newsome, *North Carolina* (Chapel Hill: University of North Carolina Press, 1963); David J. Siemers, *Ratifying the Republic* (Stanford: Stanford University Press, 2002); John H. Wheeler, *Historical Sketches of North Carolina* (1851; repr. Baltimore: Regional Publishing Co., 1964), vol. 2.

LACHLAN McINTOSH *(March 5, 1727–February 20, 1806)* was born in Badenock, Inverness-Shue, Scotland to John Mohr McIntosh, who emigrated with his family to Darien, Georgia, in 1736, and Magaret (Fraser). Young McIntosh received a local education, farmed and hunted, and hungered for the opportunity to rise in life. In 1748 he moved to Charleston, South Carolina, where he clerked for the wealthy merchant and planter Henry Laurens. There he married Sarah Threadcraft. They had seven children.

During the early 1770s, McIntosh returned to Georgia, where he became a large rice planter. Elected to the provisional legislature from the Savannah parish of St. Andrew, he supported the revolutionary cause. In 1776 he became a colonel of Georgia troops, and that same year he was promoted to brigadier general in the Continental Army. Unfortunately for his political and military career, in 1777 McIntosh fought a duel with the political leader Button Gwinnett and killed him. Close political and military friends immediately transferred McIntosh to General George Washington's headquarters at Valley Forge to get him away from the anger raised over Gwinnett's death. In 1778 he commanded the western department at Fort Pitt but lost that command in 1779. McIntosh then transferred to a South Carolina regiment, fought in defense of Savannah, and was made a prisoner of war. McIntosh and other small planters saw the British devastation of their homeland and wondered just which side could best protect their interests.

The aftermath of war found McIntosh poor and out of work, as he had lost everything in the British destruction of Georgia and in the resultant disruption of slave life. He was a forgotten and tarnished military hero. McIntosh managed to get a job as an overseer on his older brother's estate. He joined the Society of Cincinnati and became president of the Georgia chapter. That organization of ex-wartime officers became his entree back into political life. In 1784 he gained election to the Continental Congress. But he never went north to take up his post. Instead, McIntosh became part of a commission to settle a border dispute between Georgia and South Carolina. His service in that controversy, one of moderation and compromise, restored him in the eyes of local leaders. McIntosh acquired good rice land and became a planter in Camden County, Georgia.

When the Georgia assembly called a state convention in October 1787 to ratify the new proposed federal Constitution, few in the state rose to oppose ratification. Sparsely settled and poor, Georgia required national military protection from Indians on its border, making the new national government necessary to that state. In the state ratifying convention, all delegates voted for the Constitution.

Georgia's only opponent to immediate and unconditional ratification was the old military hero Lachlan McIntosh. He wrote a long and cogent letter of his opposition views to a convention delegate on December 17, 1787. McIntosh said he did not object to ratification, but he wanted the delegates to support the call for a second Constitutional Convention because he feared the southern states' interests were not protected in the proposed Constitution. He feared that the slave states would be in a minority in the new nation, and that a strong federal government would override those states' rights. McIntosh knew that the country needed a stronger central government, but he had learned from his friend Elbridge Gerry (q.v.) and from reading the "Centinel" letters that the new nation needed to guard against oppressive majority interests. A part of that majority, McIntosh believed, planned to exercise its right to raise funds from an import tariff, which would be dangerous to slave states' business interests and especially to the needs of a declining rice exporting community. He ended his tale of fear by echoing the Jeffersonian idea that the Constitution should be allowed a trial period of twenty years before a revolution of the people overthrew it.

During the post-ratification period, the once frustrated old leader became preoccupied with planting and trade and little concerned with public life. McIntosh never reentered politics, perhaps because his equivocation on ratification hurt him in Georgia. He died on February 20, 1806, in Savannah, Georgia. His small legacy as the Georgia leader who desired a full debate and delay on ratification stands as its single voice supportive of the Antifederalist position.

REFERENCES

Kenneth Coleman, *The American Revolution in Georgia* (Athens: University of Georgia Press, 1958); Kenneth Coleman and Charles Stephen Gurr, *Dictionary of Georgia Biography* (Athens: University of Georgia Press, 1983), vol. 2; Lilla M. Hawes (ed.), *Papers of Lachlan McIntosh, 1774–1779* (Savannah: Georgia Historical Society, 1957); Harvey H. Jackson, *Lachlan McIntosh and the Politics of Revolutionary Georgia* (Athens: University of Georgia Press, 1979).
The McIntosh papers can be found at the Georgia Historical Society in Athens.

ALEXANDER MEBANE *(November 26, 1744–July 5, 1795)* was born in Pennsylvania, one of twelve children of Alexander and Mary (Tinn) Mebane, wealthy immigrants from northern Ireland. The elder Mebane had come to Pennsylvania to be a justice of the peace. Mebane moved with his parents to Hawfields, North Carolina, during the 1750s. The son of a now successful planter, he attended the schools of Orange County, North Carolina. This stern and practical man married Mary Armstrong of North Carolina in 1767. He was a delegate to the provincial congress and then the first state legislature in 1776. Mebane also went to Halifax, North Carolina, to assist in drafting the first state constitution, a document he continued to support even when others wanted to change it.

During the Revolution, Mebane served his state in public office. He was a justice of the peace in Orange County in 1776, and sheriff there from 1777 to 1780. The North Carolina General Assembly named Mebane a colonel of militia. He participated in the defense of his state against the British invasion. Mebane also collected and distributed supplies to North Carolina troops. He sent his wife and children out of the state to protect them from Tory marauders. Tories burned out his family's plantation during the war.

When the war came to an end, Mebane continued in public life. He was auditor of the Hillsborough District in 1783 and 1784. Mebane served in the state legislature in 1783 and 1784, and again from 1787 until 1792. In 1788 he became a colonel of militia of the Hillsborough District, and in 1789, its general. His constituents elected him in 1788 and 1789 to both state ratifying conventions for the federal Constitution. At the convention he joined his brother, William, and Absalom Tatom (q.v) of Hillsborough to argue against ratification. He voted against ratification at both conventions, saying little but siding with those who feared federal encroachment on local prerogatives. Mebane served as auditor of the first convention and called for a bill of rights. At the second state convention he tried to get the Constitution amended but lost his bid.

After the convention, Mebane became one of the original trustees, along with many other Antifederalists, of the University of North Carolina. He assisted in the selection of Chapel Hill for the University site, and he helped to lay out that most beautiful little town. Considered a prominent state leader, he gained election to the federal Congress in 1793, and, although ill, he ably served the small government Antifederalist cause in Congress until he left office. Mebane died at Hawfields, Orange County, North Carolina, on July 5, 1795. In 1793, he had married as his second wife Anne Claypole of Philadelphia, who survived him. Writing of Mebane some years later, Eli Caruthers said, "he was distinguished for his sound practical sense, his unblemished integrity and unblinding firmness" (365).

REFERENCES

Eli Washington Caruthers, *Revolutionary Incidents and Sketches of Character* (Philadelphia: Hayer and Zell, 1854); Hugh T. Lefler and Paul Wager (eds.), *Orange County, 1752–1792* (Chapel Hill: Orange Print Shop, 1953); David J. Siemers, *Ratifying the Republic* (Stanford: Stanford University Press, 2002); Louise Irby Trenholme, *The Ratification of the Federal Constitution in North Carolina* (New York: Columbia University Press, 1932); John H. Wheeler, *Historical Sketches of North Carolina*, 2 vols. (1851; repr., Baltimore: Regional Publishing Co., 1964).

JOHN FRANCIS MERCER *(May 17, 1759–August 30, 1821)* was born on his father's plantation, Marlborough, in Stafford County, Virginia. His father, Robert Mercer, had come to Virginia in 1740 from northern Ireland, became a wealthy planter and merchant, and had strong ties to the George Mason (q.v.) family of Potomac River wealth as well as to a Maryland branch of the Mercer and Garnett families. John F. Mercer's mother was Ann Roy. His brother, James Mercer, was a Revolutionary War leader in Virginia. Young Mercer had an excellent preparation for college in local private schools, and in 1775 he graduated from the College of William and Mary. In 1785 he married Sophia Sprigg, from a wealthy family in Anne Arundel County, Maryland.

Mercer had planned to study law but the American Revolution interrupted his career path. At the young age of seventeen, he enlisted in the army as lieutenant in the Third Virginia regiment of the Continental Army. By 1777 he was a captain and aide to General Charles Lee. Wounded in combat at the battle of Monmouth, New Jersey, in 1778, Mercer then resigned his commission in 1779. He had lost rank for supporting the disgraced Charles Lee. Back in the army in 1780 as a lieutenant colonel, Mercer commanded a home brigade at Guilford, North Carolina, and at the decisive battle of the war at Yorktown, Virginia, in October 1781.

During the short time Mercer was out of the army, he had studied law with Thomas Jefferson. Jefferson shaped many of Mercer's later political views and admired the young man. Mercer began his law practice after the Revolution in Fredericksburg, Virginia. He served in the Virginia House of Delegates in 1782, and again in 1785 and 1786. From 1782 to 1785, Mercer represented Virginia in the Continental Congress. After he married, Mercer moved to his wife's estate, Cedar Park, in Anne Arundel County, Maryland. Though Mercer never gave up his political ties gained in youth in Virginia, the rest of his public career would be played out on the Maryland stage.

Of course, his political ties along the Potomac and his family fame catapulted him into prominence in Maryland. The Maryland legislature chose him as a member of the Constitutional Convention at Philadelphia in the summer of 1787. There he spoke often against the centralizing tendencies of the Constitution as proposed. Aggrieved over the ultraconservative political views of some of the delegates, Mercer claimed that at least twenty of them favored turning the country into a monarchy. He became a close ally and personal friend of Luther Martin (q.v.), and he joined that leader in leaving the convention and refusing to sign the Constitution. In 1788, also now a fast friend and supporter of the Antifederalist Samuel Chase (q.v.), Mercer gained election to the Maryland ratification convention. Again he spoke out against ratification of the Constitution, as he used information from his old Virginia friends and his experiences in Philadelphia to point out the dangers of that document to local rights. Mercer voted against ratification of the Constitution.

A major contributor to the debate on the Constitition, Mercer published "Essays by a Farmer" in the *Maryland Gazette* in February and March 1788. The work later was printed as a pamphlet. In that wide-ranging effort Mercer displayed his skills on governance as well as his sense of doom as he waxed eloquent in denunciation of the creation of arbitrary government. Of course, true to political form, Mercer claimed that he did not want to harm the people, and that he would "rather conciliate than divide." Still, he had to speak out, and he used his own keen understanding of past laws and political customs to make his case in oppositon. Mercer displayed his hatred of the English ultraconservative Robert Filmer whom he believed influenced Federalists to create a paternalistic government in which they claimed to know what was best for the ordinary people. He identified with the origins of the natural rights of the people, a gift he believed could be found in works as early as the Magna Carta and later in the writings of the great jurist Henry Bracton. Mercer went on to state in detail his fears of a patriarchal government. He also spoke out in favor of trial by jury. Mercer next discussed the kind of leadershp the Constitution created, and suggested it led to hereditary authority. His hero was the Italian Renaissance political theorist Niccolò Machiavelli whom he believed "deliver[ed] his deliberate opinion in favour of the body of the people, as the only safe depository of liberty and power" (Storing, 49). "The minions who circle around the court of the dictator only strengthened the ruler, at the expense of popular rights," (49) Mercer stated. Moral virtues and responsible leadership could not exist in a large territory. For Mercer, "division of Europe into small independent states preserves a degree of social happiness," (65) a lesson in history applicable to his new country's present situation. Finally, for this thoughtful man, the fear that such central government would sap the morale, even "the manly vigor" (69) of the people meant certain decline of the republican ideal he so cherished (69). His views of history, of venal human nature, and of smug paternalism, Mercer concluded, explained his opposition to the proposed Constitution.

Despite the state's overwhelming support for the Constitution, Mercer ran for the first federal Congress as an Antifederalist. He lost his bid for election. Without hesitation, Mercer joined the fledgling minority Republican faction in Maryland and gained election to the Maryland House of Delegates. He served there in 1788 and 1789, and again from 1791 until 1792. In 1791 he was elected to the United States House of Representatives and held office until his resignation in 1794. His major interest, however, was in Maryland reform politics, as he sought to expand suffrage for the many farmers of the state. He served in the state house again from 1800 until 1801. In 1801 Mercer was elected Jeffersonian Republican governor of Maryland. He held office as governor until 1803. Back in the House of Delegates after a short retirement, he served from 1803 until 1806. Mercer temporarily broke with the Republican Party over the War of 1812 because he believed that the Republican embargo injured the commercial interests of his adopted state.

Until he died, Mercer's politics remained that of the young idealistic Jeffersonian and Revolutionary War soldier. He returned to his plantation, Cedar Point, after his term in office, where he died on August 30, 1821. Mercer is remembered in the state's history as the governor who championed democratic rule in Maryland. H. E. Buchholz said of Mercer: "his administration is noteworthy for radical reforms in the governmental institutions of Maryland" (55). As governor, Mercer had broken the old freehold laws of ownership that had restricted voting. His public life, thus, reveals the wealthy Antifederalist as social reformer.

REFERENCES

Henry E. Buchholz, *Governors of Maryland* (Baltimore: Williams and Wilkins Co., 1908); James Mercer Garnett, *Genealogy of the Mercer-Garnett Family* (Richmond, Va: Whittet and Shepperson Printers, 1910); James Mercer Garnett, "John F. Mercer," *Maryland Historical Magazine,* 12 (September 1907): 235–248; F. B. Heitman, *Historical Register of Officers of the Continental Army* (Baltimore: Geneaological Publishing Co., 1967); Storing, *Complete*, vol. 5.

JAMES MONROE *(April 28, 1758–July 4, 1831)* was born in Westmoreland County, Virginia. He was the son of Spence Monroe, a Potomac River tobacco planter, and Elizabeth Jones, a cousin of James's future Virginia Antifederalist ally Joseph Jones (q.v.). Young Monroe received the quality education reserved for the privileged planter class. He attended the school of Archibald Campbell to prepare him for college. Monroe entered the College of William and Mary in 1776 but dropped out to enlist as a lieutenant in the Virginia Continental Army. A perceptive, intelligent, ambitious, and shrewd young man raised in the surroundings of practiced Virginia public leaders, he became a dedicated follower of Thomas Jefferson. Monroe would serve his country as an opponent of the Constitution, a United States Senator, diplomat extraordinary, and as President of the United States from 1817 until 1825. His career as an Antifederalist thinker was marked by the caution needed to retain the good favor of Virginia's great Federalist statesmen.

Young Monroe emerged from the American Revolution a military hero. He served with General George Washington at the battles of Harlem Heights and White Plains, New York. In New Jersey, he was wounded in the battle for Trenton. From 1777 to 1778, he served as Washington's aide. He fought at Brandywine, Germantown, and Monmouth. Mustered out of the army in 1780, Monroe took up the study of law from 1780 to 1783, becoming Thomas Jefferson's law clerk.

In 1782, the rising young lawyer entered the Virginia state legislature. From 1783 until 1786, he served ably as a national leader in the Continental Congress. A moderate in politics, Monroe called for a stronger Congress, especially in the regulation of interstate commerce. But he also was a committed localist, who was particularly interested in southern states' western land claims. Accordingly, he opposed John Jay's negotiations with the Spanish government over navigation of the Mississippi River. In 1786 he attended the Annapolis Convention, at James Madison's request. Monroe left federal government service in 1787 and returned to become a member of the Virginia House of Burgesses.

On the eve of the Philadelphia Constitutional Convention, in private letters to close friends Joseph Jones and Richard Henry Lee (q.v.)—he had grown up near the ancestral Lee home, Stratford Hall—Monroe said that he knew the Articles of Confederation were imperfect because they could not regulate commerce or defend the western frontier. Elected to the Virginia Constitutional ratifying convention from his new home in Spotsylvania County, where many Northern Neck leaders had moved because of the decline of tobacco lands, and coming now from the Fredericksburg area, he knew that he must be careful how he represented such a bastion of Federalism. Also, he lived in a state where its great leaders were divided on the Constitution. He thus seemed torn over the best course of action. He at first described himself in public as neutral on ratification. But Monroe soon made up his political mind and became a lieutenant to the Antifederalist leaders Patrick Henry (q.v.) and William Grayson (q.v.). He had chosen to work to defeat the Constitution, and he spoke often at the convention in opposition to ratification. Monroe also drafted a long commentary against the Constitution but refused to circulate it, fearing the Federalists would someday use it against him. Monroe voted against ratification.

Monroe's speeches and writings, particularly the secret commentary "Observations on the Federal Government," show how a committed nationalist also could find fault with the Constitution as proposed. In July 1787, he told Jefferson that he wanted to remain noncommittal. In his own writings, Monroe seemed to debate with himself over the best course of action. His first view was that he desired a stronger federal government. However, his major speeches at the state convention reveal Monroe's reasons for finally voting against ratification. On June 10, 1788, he applied a historical analogy to his growing fears over federal power. Monroe's experience in the American Revolution, he said, had taught him to suspect excessive use of authority like that used by the British. He then asked the delegates to support a means to amend the document. On June 13, he used the failed Jay's Treaty as an example to show how a few powerful states could overwhelm the others since the new Constitution no longer required unanimous consent to legislation so important to the minority. On June 14, he asked, with a supposedly unassuming but damaging question, why the proposed federal Congress had the powers to set the time, place, and manner of all elections, federal and state. On June 18, Monroe spoke against the electoral college, fearing its antirepublicanism and susceptibility to bribery, and called for direct election of the president. On the last day before the state convention's vote, Monore seized on the lack of a bill of individual rights in the Constitution as his excuse for voting against ratification. Stuart G. Brown maintains that Monroe's "stand for civil liberties and for the common man of the west built on his base of popularity much more effectively than a narrow state's rights stand would have done" (32).

Herbert Storing believes that Monroe's work, "Some Observations on the Constitution," though circulated only privately among friends, had a profound influence on the Virginia Antifederalist cause. In that secret paper, Monroe again stated that he believed the Articles of Confederation weak and in need of revision. The proposed Constitution, however, for this future national leader, had gone too far in making a central government. Size disturbed him, as he joined the outcry in opposition to creating such a large republic. He also feared the making of a monarchy as a result of the powers granted to the presidency and to the Senate. Above all, he again and again warned that just men needed to support personal rights, but unfaithful guardians abounded. How, he asked, does the country guard against abuse of power? He called for a middle course between central and state power, something the Federalists said they supported but, he claimed, in actuality did not. What Monroe wanted was for the state governments to have specific duties, clearly laid out in the new government. He concluded this perceptive paper with the assertion that the unseemly rush to ratify the Constitution hid a Federalist leadership unconcerned with the rights of the states (Storing, 287–306).

Unlike a number of Virginia's Antifederalists, the cautious compromiser Monroe quickly accepted the new Constitution, though he continued to call for a bill of rights. In 1789 he lost in a contest against James Madison for Congress but earned the gratitude of the Antifederalists for running against their then-enemy. His reward was elevation to the United States Senate in 1790, where he took the Republican anti–United States Bank position and became a most cautious critic of the Washington administration, but of course not of the great Virginian himself. In 1794 President Washington named him minister to France but had to recall him in 1796 because of a failed mission. Monroe defended his activities in 1797 with *A View of the Conduct of the Executive.* From 1799 until 1802, he served as Virginia's Republican governor. Jefferson sent his now loyal localist to France in 1803 to secure free navigation of the Mississippi River, and Monroe became a key negotiator in the purchase of Louisiana.

In 1808 the committed anti–federal government advocate joined Virginia's radical Tertium Quids, John Randolph of Roanoke, and John Taylor of Caroline, in an attempt to defeat James Madison for president. But Monroe, who philosophically may have been a state's rights advocate, soon converted to nationalism and supported Madison to avoid splitting the southern Republicans. He served in the state legislature in 1810, as Virginia governor again in 1811, and protected his national image as Madison's secretary of state from 1812 to 1816. Always an expansionist, he supported the War of 1812 and the south-erners who in 1813 wanted to annex east Florida. As president of the United States from 1817 until 1825, Monroe presided over a nation with decidedly sectionalist inclinations. He continued to favor expansion, opposed excessive government expenses—in 1822 he published his *Views on the Subject of Internal Improvements*—and signed the Missouri Compromise bill, which expanded slavery into that new state. Most connected to his nationalist reputation was the Monroe Doctrine, a foreign policy manifesto. A careful look at that document suggests that Monroe continued as a localist with a committed interest in protecting southwestern expansion from foreign interests.

After he left office, Monroe wanted to retire from public life. He did, how-ever, accept election with a number of his state's great leaders to the Virginia Constitutional Convention of 1829. Monroe presided over that convention and opposed giving additional voting power to the state's western parts, re-taining his specific localist defense of eastern and middle Virginia slaveown-ers. In 1830 he moved to New York City and died there on July 4, 1831, five years to the day after the death of his hero, Thomas Jefferson. Monroe was a gifted student of politics, a leader who survived the conflicting national and localist tensions in his own state. As a national leader, he gained a reputation of supporting the growth of national government, but sustained his follow-ing in Virginia by seeming to be a state's rights advocate when necessary. Was he the Antifederalist as political opportunist, or was he an Antifederalist with mixed views over the Constitution's support of national political power? Suf-fice it to say, Monroe's later life has not left as clear a message to history as his Antifederalist private views had announced.

REFERENCES

Harry Ammon, *James Monroe* (New York: McGraw Hill, 1971); Stuart Gerry Brown (ed.), *Autobiography of James Monroe* (Syracuse: Syracuse University Press, 1959); W. P. Cresson, *James Monroe* (Chapel Hill: University of North Carolina Press, 1946); Daniel Coit Gilman, *James Monroe* (New York: Houghton Miflin, 1893); Stanislaus M. Hamilton (ed.), *Writings of James Monroe* (New York: G. P. Putnam's Sons, 1898–1903), vol. 1; Daniel Preston (ed.), *The Papers of James Monroe* (Westport, Conn.: Greenwood Press, 2003–), vol. 1; Storing, *Complete*, vol. 5.
Monroe's papers are at the Library of Congress and the New York Public Library.

N

SAMUEL NASSON *(February 14, 1744–August 28, 1800)* was born in New Hampshire. Little is known about his early life save that he received a primary education, as did most young men raised in a Congregational household. As a young adult he removed to York County, in the Maine territory of Massachusetts. He was a saddler and then a storekeeper in York. Nasson married Mary Ball Shore and later Mrs. Joanna Tilden Moulton.

During the American Revolution, Nasson became the quartermaster of his Maine regiment and later was made captain. In the Continental Army he took part in the defense of Boston and the battle of Long Island in 1776. He rose to the rank of major. After the war, Nasson became a successful merchant in Sanford, Maine, territory. He became selectman, town clerk, and town treasurer, as he rose in the local political hierarchy. In 1787 Nasson gained election to the Massachusetts General Court, but was defeated for reelection to the legislature in 1789.

It was Nasson who stirred the people of Sanford to elect a delegate to the Massachusetts state ratifying convention. He became the delegate from his town. Nasson served as a staunch Antifederalist, and in the convention moved that the Constitution be discussed line by line. He lost that bid. Bernard Bailyn points out that Nasson opposed any compromise on the Constitution without guaranteed amendments (1029). Nasson's convention speech, later published as the pamphlet "Pathetick Apostrophe," of February 1, 1788, made him one of the Maine territory's most important Antifederalists.

In that speech he declared that the state's very liberty was at stake, as he feared the new Constitution created a federal government much like that of the hated Great Britain. Nasson declared: "When I give up any of my natural rights, it is for the security of the rest: But there is not one right secured, although many are neglected" (Bailyn, 926). He said that he spoke out of duty to his constituents, to defend their "liberty and safety." In the debates he went on to advocate for a bill of rights. Nasson also remonstrated against the three-fifths clause, maintaining that the southern states gained too much power from its passage. The inequity of it all bothered Nasson; he believed the northern poor workers and voters lost when slaves were used by wealthy planters as labor and as part of the population count for political power (Elliot, 134). He rejected six-year senator terms: "I think, sir, that rulers ought, at short periods, to return to private life, that they may know how to feel for and regard their fellow creatures" (135). Nasson also believed the federal powers to tax and to raise an army were dangerous. Armies, he said, "are too frequently used for no other purpose than dragooning the people into slavery." (135). Using his knowledge of the recent American Revolution, Nasson referred his fellow Massachusetts delegates to the Boston Massacre in 1770 that resulted from the forced boarding of British troops. Standing armies, paid for by the people, were, for Nasson, "the bane of republican governments" (Elliot, 136). Needless to say, Nasson voted against the Constitution.

After the announcement of the convention's vote, Nasson joined those who suggested that the Antifederalist delegates should support the results. In this his feeling was similar to that of his fellow Mainer, William Widgery (q.v.). Yet, Nasson also admonished another Antifederalist delegate, Nathaniel Barrell (q.v.), for too quickly accepting the Federalist vote at the convention. Although Nasson lost his bid for reelection to the General Court in 1789, he held no animosity toward the opposition. He even praised Govenor John Hancock when the governor returned to the defense of local rights. Nasson went back to the Maine territory and retired from politics to continue his business interests. Along with Widgery, he served as a presidential elector in 1796 on the Republican ticket. Nasson died in Sanford, Maine territory, on August 28, 1800.

REFERENCES

Bailyn, *Debate*, vol. 1; Elliot, *Debates*, vol. 2; Van Beck Hall, *Politics Without Parties: Massachusetts, 1780–1791* (Pittsburgh: University of Pittsburgh Press, 1972); Samuel B. Harding, *The Contest over the Ratification of the Federal Constitution in the State of Massachusetts* (Cambridge: Harvard University Press, 1896); Thomas H. O'Connor and Alan Rogers, *This Momentous Affair: Massachusetts and the Ratification of the Constitition* (Cambridge: Harvard University Press, 1987).

THOMAS NELSON *(December 26, 1738–January 4, 1789)* was born in Yorktown, Virginia, the eldest son of the wealthy planter William Nelson and his wife Elizabeth (Burwell). The most powerful families in Virginia often sent children abroad for education, and young Thomas was no exception. He attended the Hackney School in England, and marticulated from 1758 until 1761 at Christ's College, Cambridge. Nelson then returned home to become a gentleman planter. In 1762, he married Lucy Grimes, who was connected to the powerful Randolph family. They had eleven children.

Like many of his position, Nelson soon entered local government, first as a justice of the peace. He became a member of the colonial Virginia Burgesses in 1761 and joined the Virginia council in 1764. Nelson served in the

Burgesses continuously from 1761 until 1776. A friend of the radical Patrick Henry (q.v.), Nelson early became a revolutionary. He held the rank of colonel in the Second Virginia Regiment in 1775. Nelson helped to draft the Virginia Declaration of Freedom. In 1775 he was elected to the Continental Congress, and he signed the Declaration of Independence in 1776. Nelson also served on the committee to draft the Articles of Confederation. He became sick and resigned from Congress in 1777. Nelson then reentered military service as brigadier general of Virginia militia and went to Philadelphia in 1778. He served again in the House of Delegates from 1777 until 1781. Elected a member of the Continental Congress in 1779, Nelson again became sick and returned to Virginia. This state leader was elevated to governor of Virginia in 1781, commanded the Virginia militia, and was with General George Washington at Yorktown. He resigned as governor in 1781.

Broke after the war, at least when compared to his prewar wealth, Nelson moved to Hancock County, Virginia, to farm, but he never recouped his fortune. Back in the House of Delegates from 1782 until 1784, and from 1786 until 1788, Nelson became the ally of William Grayson (q.v.). Together, they led the local rights faction in the legislature. In 1787 Nelson declined, along with Richard Henry Lee (q.v.), to accept election to the Constitutional Convention in Philadelphia. In the state legislature of 1788, Nelson took an active part with the Antifederalists to oppose calling the state ratifying convention, and the conservative York County did not send him to the convention.

For many Virginians, Nelson served as a model of the patriot hero and wealthy planter who preferred local and state government over federal authority. He died of asthma in Yorktown, Virginia, on January 4, 1789. Perhaps more than any other leader, Nelson's life symbolizes the public servant as defender of local rights. Certainly, Federalist leaders like James Madison feared the opposition's use of the career and opinions of this famous and beloved old leader to make its case against the Constitution.

REFERENCES

Emory Evans, *Thomas Nelson of Yorktown* (Charlottesville: University of Virginia Press, 1975); Jensen and Kaminski, *Documentary History*, vol. 4; *Letters of Thomas Nelson* (Richmond: Virginia Historical Society Publications, 1884); William Meade, *Old Churches and Families of Virginia*, 2 vols. (Philadelphia: J. P. Lippincott, 1861); Norman K. Risjord, *Chesapeake Politics* (New York: Columbia University Press, 1979); Storing, *Complete*, vol. 2.

JOHN NICHOLSON *(?, 1757–December 5, 1800)* was born in Wales to William and Sarah Nicholson. As a youth, John emigrated with his brother Samuel to Pennsylvania. He first settled near Charlestown, then moved to Carlisle, Pennsylvania, where he became a tradesman and a merchant. Just before the outbreak of the American Revolution, Nicholson moved

to Cumberland County, Pennsylvania. There he became a successful land speculator.

The Revolution made him famous in his adopted state. Nicholson joined the Continental Army in 1775 and served as a sergeant of the First Pennsylvania Regiment. In 1778, he became a clerk of the Chamber of Accounts of the Board of Treasury of the Continental Congress. In that office he defended a number of military officers he felt had been unjustly accused of profiteering from war purchases. Some of those men became his close friends and political allies. Nicholson resigned from national office in 1781 to become Pennsylvania state commissioner of accounts auditor. As liquidator of Tory estates in 1781, he allied himself with Robert Morris, treasurer of the Continental Congress.

When the war ended, the many skills Nicholson had learned about accounting and purchasing made him valuable to his state government. In 1782 the governor named him comptroller general of Pennsylvania. In 1785 Nicholson became state receiver general of taxes. Nicholson also continued to confiscate and resell the estates of Pennsylvania's Tories, and he enhanced his personal landholdings in that fashion. In those various state positions, Nicholson had also been able to assist his friends in acquiring land and getting government contracts. He obtained the secretaryship of the state senate for George Bryan (q.v.), son of the state's leading Antifederalist politician, Samuel Bryan (q.v.). After he left public office, Nicholson became a manufacturer, acquiring for himself lucrative state contracts.

But his real love was politics and its gains and intrigues. Nicholson had personal investments in western Pennsylvania, a section that was heavily Antifederalist. He believed the federal government as proposed in the Philadelphia convention threatened those localist western interests. Nicholson allied himself with those westerners, as he offered them propositions to amend the Constitution. During the crisis over ratification, Nicholson organized a petition campaign against the Constitution. He wrote an important pamphlet, *A Review of the Proposed Constitution,* which he published in December 1787. In that pamphlet, Nicholson wrote that "liberties, lives and property" would be lost if the people did not petition the convention to amend the Constitution. His principal concern was with the enormous centralizing powers proposed for the federal government. Nicholson also worried about religious rights of the various denominations fearing that the Constitution implied support for only one national church (Jensen and Kaminski, 710–711).

After the state convention ratified the federal Constitution, Nicholson continued his Antifederalist activities. He joined in the call for a second state convention, and he supported the Antifederalist meeting in the spring of 1788 in Harrisburg. Nicholson opposed Alexander Hamilton's national financial maneuvers. He supported the Bank of Pennsylvania over a national bank. But when his state's political organization, the Democratic-Republican Society, split during the 1790s, Nicholson joined the Federalists. His large landholdings had been threatened in the Whiskey Rebellion, and he supported President George Washington's call for troops to put down insurrection. Nicholson also had become a partner of the Federalist Robert Morris in land speculation. But the Federalist decision on Jay's Treaty in 1795 sent him back into the arms of his western Antifederalist allies. He then became a Republican ally of the radical Samuel Bryan.

That Nicholson's life would later come to a sad end reveals the plight of some rising middling businessmen who may have bent the laws for personal gain. In 1793 the Pennsylvania House impeached him from his state position on charges that he had printed faulty loan certificates. But in 1794 the state senate acquitted and reinstated him. Nicholson resigned from office to become a partner of the arch-Federalist Robert Morris, and for a time he grew wealthy. Nicholson used his gain to give handouts to ambitious men down on their luck. He bought lots in Washington, D.C., and in 1795 formed the North American Land Company. An opponent of slavery, he fought its extension into the northwest. In Pennsylvania, Nicholson aided the immigrant Irish population, probably enhancing his own political position. He even employed ambitious young businessmen in his button factory. This support of the poor and the oppressed came crashing down in 1798 when Morris was arrested for debt. Nicholson followed his mentor into prison in 1800. Nicholson had speculated on land ventures in Georgia, Kentucky, and Virginia. He went broke in those investments. Nicholson died in a Philadelphia debtors' prison on December 5, 1800, supposedly leaving debts of twelve million dollars and four million acres of land liens. He left a wife and eight children. His biographer, Robert Arbuckle, believed that the "failure to accept his limitations was the chief cause of his downfall" (204).

In his Antifederalist opposition to federal encroachment on state economic interests, Nicholson belongs to a category of the procommercial wing of his party. There he took a consistent position in supporting the growth of the west as a place of opportunity, and he shared his gain with allies and was fiercely independent, all of which contributed to his worries about how excessive government interference limited individual opportunity.

REFERENCES

Robert D. Arbuckle, *Pennsylvania Speculator and Patriot: Entrepreneurial John Nicholson, 1757–1800* (University Park: Pennsylvania State University Press, 1975); Steven R. Boyd, *The Politics of Opposition* (Millwood, N.Y.: KTO Press, 1979); Saul Cornell, *The Other Founders* (Chapel Hill: University of North Carolina Press, 1999); Franklin Ellis, *History of Fayette County, Pennsylvania* (Philadelphia: L. H. Everts, 1882); Jensen and Kaminski, *Documentary History*, vol. 2; Harry M. Tinkcom, *Republicans and Federalists in Pennsylvania, 1790–1801* (Harrisburg: Pennsylvania Historical and Museum Commission, 1950).

O

SAMUEL OSGOOD *(February 3/14, 1747/48–August 12, 1813)*
was born at Andover, Massachusetts. He was the son of Captain Peter Osgood and Sarah (Johnson). Osgood received a private education and graduated in the class of 1770 at Harvard College. He then went into business with
his older brother Peter (later a member of the Massachusetts Constitutional
ratifying convention who voted against the Constitution). They developed a
successful trade business. In 1775 he married Martha Brandon, who died a
few years later. In 1786 Osgood married Maria Franklin, from a family connected to George Clinton (q.v.) of New York.

Becoming an ardent patriot, Osgood served in the Essex Convention of
1774 that drafted the Essex Resolves. He was elected to the provincial congress in 1775. Osgood also held office as captain of the Andover Minutemen,
and rose to major and then colonel under General Artemas Ward. Elected to
the Massachusetts Constitutional Convention of 1779–1780, Osgood helped
to draft that revised state constitution. Osgood served in the Massachusetts
State Senate in 1780. He became a director of the Bank of North America in
1781. From 1781 until 1784, the state legislature sent Osgood to the Continental Congress. There he took an extreme state and localist position, even
opposing the powers of federal Congress to tax the states. He served on important committees and spoke often on money bills. Previously, he had made
friends with the radical Samuel Adams (q.v.), and in the Congress he developed a lasting attachment to Richard Henry Lee (q.v.) and his ideals. All of
those members had experience with large, oppressive government, and their
worries about federal power were related to their fears that large central government created an aristocracy. In the Congress, Osgood vigorously opposed
all financial schemes of Robert Morris. In that struggle over money he also
became an ally of Elbridge Gerry (q.v.) and Abraham Clark (q.v.), two future
Antifederalists. In 1785 Osgood's fellow delegates named him commissioner
to the treasury. In that position, he forged an alliance with that brilliant and
perverse Virginian, Arthur Lee (q.v.). Osgood, along with his friends, attacked
the policy of Treasurer Noah Webster.

In the events building up to the ratification convention in Massachusetts, Osgood took an extreme Antifederalist position. Osgood did not serve in the Massachusetts convention because he had business that took him to New York City. But he worked with the New York and Massachusetts Antifederalists to try to defeat the Constitution. On January 5, 1788, he wrote a celebrated letter to Samuel Adams (q.v.), which circulated through Antifederalist groups. In the letter, Osgood rejected the Constitution because it had no bill of personal rights to protect the liberties of Americans. He also felt the government's proposed reserved rights threatened the prerogatives of state legislatures. He told Adams, "I believe if the new government should take place, it would prove true, that the first rebellion against it would break out in the Town of Boston," (266) because Bostonians would feel underrepresented in the new federal Congress. To Adams he exclaimed, "What inexhaustible Fountain of Corruption are we opening?" (266). Osgood was referring specifically to the location of the federal government, where graft and corruption could even destroy Philadelphia, the proposed seat of government (Bailyn, 267). No doubt his fears found their way into the arguments of his many Antifederalist friends.

After the Constitution had been ratified in both Massachusetts and New York, Osgood realized that it could not be stopped in the rest of the country. To Elbridge Gerry he wrote in 1789 that the first federal Congress should behave like another Constitutional Convention and make major reforms to the Constitution. Osgood remained in New York in the merchant business and grew close to DeWitt Clinton (q.v.). He became part of the poltical circle around Governor George Clinton and Melancton Smith (q.v.). Because of his talents in government, President George Washington made this Antifederalist postmaster general of the United States. By 1800, however, Osgood had returned to state and local government in New York. As leader of the local government forces, he became the speaker of the state assembly. Osgood remained faithful to the Antifederalist cause. President Thomas Jefferson named him supervisor of internal revenue for the district of New York in 1802. From 1803 until 1813, Osgood served as official of the port of New York. He died in New York City on August 12, 1813.

REFERENCES

Bailyn, *Debate*, vol. 1; Edmund Cody Burnett, *History of the Continental Congress* (New York: Macmillan Co., 1941); Samuel P. Harding, *The Contest over the Ratification of the Federal Constitution in the State of Massachusetts* (Cambridge: Harvard University Press, 1896); Jackson Turner Main, *The Antifederalists* (Chapel Hill: University of North Carolina Press, 1961); Ira Osgood and Ellen Putnam, *A Geneaology of the Descendents of John Christopher and William Osgood* (Salem, Mass.: Printed at the Salem Press, 1894); Robert A. Rutland, *Ordeal of the Constitution* (Norman: University of Oklahoma Press, 1965).

Osgood's papers are in the New York Public Library, and the Massachusetts Historical Society in Boston.

ELEAZOR OSWALD *(1755–1795)* was born in England and came to New York City in 1770. He apprenticed with John Holt at the New York *Journal.* Oswald had considerable writing talents, and he easily took to the newspaper business, even though he took offense at almost every perceived slight to his skills. In 1772 he married Holt's daughter, Elizabeth. For a time he lived and worked in New Haven, Connecticut.

An ardent patriot, from 1775 until 1779 he served in the Continental Army under John Lamb (q.v.) and rose to the rank of lieutenant colonel. From 1779 until 1781, he published the Baltimore *Maryland Journal,* a vigorous revolutionary newspaper. As the war came to an end, Oswald moved to Philadelphia in 1782 where he started the *Independent Gazetteer.* In 1783 Oswald ran the London Coffee Shop, where many of the leaders of the Philadelphia radical Constitutionalist Party congregated. He became friends with the local politicals who would lead the Antifederalist cause in Pennsylvania, including the gifted writers and political strategists George Bryan (q.v.) and Samuel Bryan (q.v.). He also helped his father-in-law, John Holt, revive and operate the New York *Journal.* In 1787 Oswald sold his share in the *Journal* to Thomas Greenleaf (q.v.), because he had transferred most of his editorial work to Philadelphia. As Oswald became more of a leader in that city's republican force, he clashed with the opposition. In 1786, because he sensed a slight, which incited his uncontrollable temper, Oswald fought a duel with Matthew Carey, a leading nationalist newspaperman and publisher.

During the summer of 1787, Oswald published a number of articles critical of the supposed events going on at the Constitutional Convention in Philadelphia. He became, in the view of Greenleaf and Charles Tillinghast (q.v.), the leading Antifederalist printer in the country. At first Oswald had claimed neutrality on the Constitution, but he soon proved Tillinghast correct. Tillinghast wrote to Hugh Hughes (q.v.) that Oswald dared to print the addresses of the Antifederalist members of the Constitutional Convention. For his actions, Federalist enemies withdrew their subscriptions to his newspaper. But Oswald persevered. Now a staunch Antifederalist, he printed many of the state's Antifederalist pamphlets, including "Centinal," "An Old Whig," and "Philadelphiensis." Those articles that had first appeared in his paper soon circulated throughout the states and became useful to the Antifederalist cause throughout the nation. Oswald also printed copies of the Pennsylvania "Dissent of the Minority," and made certain his friends obtained copies of that valuable Antifederalist document. John Lamb (q.v.) took a number of Oswald's pamphlets to New York and passed them on to follow Antifederalists. In 1788 hostile Federalists unjustly sued him for libel, and the Philadelphia court fined and imprisoned him.

Also an author of Antifederalist works, Oswald wrote an "Address to the Public," a ringing defense of freedom of the press. George Bryan defended his rights to publish works of opposition to the Constitution and, along with other Antifederalist leaders, managed to get Oswald released from prison. It is possible that Oswald contributed to the Bryans' "Centinel" articles. Certainly both the Bryans and Oswald took exception to those who desired to silence their right to oppose the Constitution. As the struggle to oppose the Constitution wound down, Oswald nevertheless attempted to influence events in Virginia and New York. Aside from his connection to John Lamb in New York, Oswald also communicated with George Mason (q.v.) and Richard Henry Lee (q.v.) in Virginia. He traveled to Virginia to deliver copies of "Centinel" and to work with the Antifederalist forces there. He also became a friend of William Grayson (q.v.). But all of those actions were for naught, and Oswald watched as the states finally ratified the Constitution.

For a time Oswald continued his Antifederalist newspaper but never regained the old circulation. He went to England in 1792, then to France in 1793, where he became a colonel in the French Revolutionary Army. The year 1793 also found him in Ireland, but he returned to the United States later that same year. Oswald probably went into debt. Still, he remained active in Democratic-Republican societies in New York and Philadelphia. He died in Philadelphia sometime in 1795. Oswald belongs to that group of radical Antifederalist defenders of civil liberties and freedom of speech who served as publicists for the cause.

REFERENCES

Joseph S. Foster, *In Pursuit of Equal Liberty: George Bryan and the Revolution in Pennsylvania* (University Park: Pennsylvania State University Press, 1994); Jensen and Kaminski, *Documentary History*, vols. 35–36; Robert A. Rutland, *Birth of the Bill of Rights* (Chapel Hill: University of North Carolina Press, 1955); Robert A. Rutland, *Ordeal of the Constitution* (Norman: University of Oklahoma Press, 1965); Storing, *Complete*, vol. 2.

$\mathcal{P}$

WILLIAM PACA *(October 31, 1740–October 13, 1799)* was born at Wye Hall in Harford County, Maryland. His father was the wealthy eastern shore planter John Paca, and his mother was Elizabeth (Smith). Paca received a private education at home and attended the College of Philadelphia, from which he received the M.A. in 1759. He then studied law with the eminent Annapolis lawyer Stephen Bodley, and at the Inner Temple in London. Paca began the practice of law in 1761. That same year he married the wealthy Mary Lloyd Chew, daughter of Benjamin Chew, a power in colonial Maryland politics. In 1777 he married Anne Harrison of Philadelphia. He settled in Annapolis, where he practiced law and entered public life.

In 1768 Paca became a member of the Maryland colonial legislature. There he soon formed a political bond with Samuel Chase (q.v.). From 1771 to 1774, Paca led the anti-Proprietary forces in Maryland. He also opposed the poll tax. A strong patriot, Paca belonged to the Maryland Committee of Correspondence. In 1774 he was elected to the First Continental Congress, in which he served from 1775 to 1779. Paca also signed the Declaration of Independence, and in August 1776, he wrote the Declaration and Charter of Rights, delineating Maryland's reaasons for supporting the Revolution.

Durng the Revolution, Paca personally paid to outfit Maryland's troops. He also helped to write the first Maryland State Constitution. Paca raised funds to construct and design the magnificant Maryland State House in Annapolis. In 1778 he became chief judge of the Maryland General Court. In 1780 he was elevated to the chief justiceship of the Court of Appeals. In that capacity, he heard many admiralty cases. Particularly vengeful toward Maryland's Tories, Paca supported the confiscation of their lands. As the war came to an end, the people of Maryland elected this revolutionary leader their governor in 1782.

During the Confederation period, Paca led the state as governor until 1785. He assisted many homecoming soldiers in acquiring property and jobs. Of course, like many other leaders, he speculated in Tory lands. Devoted to his state and to its growth, and loyal to his eastern shore heritage, Paca became a member of the Board of Trustees of Washington College, in Chestertown, Maryland, the nation's tenth oldest institution of higher learning. With his ally, Chase, Governor Paca championed debtor relief. He also fought for a paper money bill to help middling businessmen and farmers finance the growth of enterprise in the state. An advocate of a strong government to help finance the growth of the new nation and provide for needed military defense, he nevertheless declined election to the Philadelphia Constitutional Convention of 1787.

Along with Chase, Paca led the state's Antifederalist forces in the April 1788 state ratifying convention. He understood from the beginning that Maryland overwhelmingly supported the Constitution and he too favored a stronger government. But Paca wanted to amend the proposed Constitution, and he fought in the state convention for that right. He proposed some twenty-eight amendments, but the majority Federalists would not allow him to speak on the convention's floor. Knowing the importance of at least introducing his amendments as a matter of public record, Paca forged a deal with the Federalists to desert his fellow Antifederalists and vote for ratification if Federalists would allow him to present his amendments. Paca was the only Antifederalist leader, of twelve, who voted for the Constitution.

Although he appeared to have deserted the cause, Paca, the delegate from Harford County, left a legacy of his objections to the Constitution and an explanation for why he had succumbed to Federalist persuasion, which confirms his continued support for Antifederalist positions. His words in the convention on April 21, 1788, reveal his reservations about the proposed Constitution. What he had wanted to do was achieve changes in the document through amendment before ratification. Paca understood what power the Maryland Federalists had, but this Antifederalist was determined to create a public record of his dissent from the majority. He had chaired the Committee on the Bill of Rights, so he knew what he wanted to see changed in the Constitution. Paca's "Address of a Minority of the Maryland Ratifying Convention" revealed his devotion to an independent judiciary. In that address, Paca also voiced his desire to restrain the federal government's powers over the army, suggesting instead state sponsored militias. In his final statement to the convention, joined in by Chase, Luther Martin (q.v.), and William Pinkney (q.v.), Paca declared: "we consider the proposed form of national government as very defective" (Elliot, 549) because "[l]iberty and happiness of the people are in danger" (Elliot, 552). They concluded, "we neither fear censure nor wish applause" (Elliot, 549–556; also see Storing, 99).

Wealthy, refined, a man of great social status, the upper-class Paca also had superb political tactical skills and a keen understanding of the science of government. Brilliant and a gifted speaker, he fought and compromised to have the opportunity to present his views for the record. Paca's key contribution to the Antifederalist cause, then, were his amendments. Along with the proposals of George Mason (q.v.) of Virginia, his amendments made up the nucleus of the Bill of Rights. Paca's amendments showed that he desired guarantees of individual freedoms of behavior and conscience. Accordingly, he advocated the right to petition the legislature for personal grievances. He believed strongly in the right to trial by jury, especially a jury of one's peers. Paca wanted specific limitations on the right to search warrant and seizure. He also was a committed Episcopalian who wanted to prohibit the establishment of a national church. Because of his belief of religious freedom, he advocated separation of state and church. Fortunately, many of his proposed amendments have become part of the legal fabric of this society.

President George Washington in 1789 appointed Paca a federal district judge. Some said the Federalists had rewarded him for his vote in favor of the Constitution. But Samuel Chase knew better. Paca never deserted his Antifederalist supporters and friends. He died in Talbot County, Maryland, on October 13, 1799.

REFERENCES

Henry Ewald Buchholz, *Governors of Maryland* (Baltimore: Williams and Wilkins Co., 1908); Philip A. Crowl, "Antifederalism in Maryland," *William and Mary Quarterly* 3rd ser. (October 1947): 446–469; Elliot, *Debates*, vol. 2; Gregory Stiverson, *William Paca: A Biography* (Baltimore: The Johns Hopkins University Press, 1976); Storing, *Complete*, vol. 5; Oswald Tilghman, *History of Talbot County* (Baltimore: Williams and Wilkins Co., 1915), vol. 1.

NATHANIEL PEABODY *(March 1, 1741–June 27, 1823)* was born in Topsfield, Massachusetts. He was the son of Jacob Peabody, an eminent physician, whose family had come to New England in 1635. His mother, Susanna (Rogers), was the daughter of a minister from Boxford, Massachusetts. Young Nathaniel studied medicine with his father. He set up his own practice in 1761 in Plaistow, New Hampshire, and soon moved to Atkinson, New Hamsphire, where he developed a large practice. In 1763 he married Abigail Little of New Hampshire.

Aside from his lucrative medical practice, Peabody had political ambitions. He was elected justice of the peace of Rockingham County, New Hampshire, in the early 1770s. In 1774, Peabody expanded his political reputation by becoming a lieutenant colonel of colonial militia. A patriot and radical revolutionary, in 1774 he joined others in capturing the British magazine at Fort William and Mary. He participated in the war as a member of the Rhode Island expedition in 1778. That year Peabody also became adjutant general of the New Hampshire state militia.

Famed for his military service, Peabody made an even greater contribution to the war through his activities in New Hampshire and national politics. As a member of the state legislature, he rose to become one of the young state's most powerful political leaders. From 1776 until 1779, he served in the legislature. He held office there again from 1781 until 1785. The state legislature sent him to the Continental Congress from 1779 to 1780. Peabody headed the Congress's commission to study the medical treatment of wartime servicemen. A man possessed with little tact, perhaps too intelligent to suffer the excuses of people he thought foolish, and gifted with a quick and biting wit, he became an outspoken critic of the federal government's medical and military policies.

After the Revolution, he returned to the state legislature and became a leader among the forces in defense of state prerogatives. Peabody helped to write the state constitutions of 1781 and 1783. He declined appointment to the Continental Congress in 1785. In 1785 and 1786, Peabody led the state senate. He also became a general of the state militia. Through his political and military connections, he began discussions about a state medical society, in hopes of setting standards for the licensing of physicians.

Peabody took part in the proceedings to elect delegates to the New Hampshire state ratifying convention for the proposed federal Constitution of 1787. He attempted to persuade the state house of representatives to elect a large number of delegates to the convention, in hopes of representing all of the people and raising the dangers of the proposed Constitution. As a leader from the Merrimac Valley, he led a contingent of radical farmers opposed to ratification. Peabody and the farmers feared the taxing powers of the federal government, desired paper money, and called for debt relief. As a radical Antifederalist, he spoke often against the Constitution, but he himself refused to become a delegate to the convention. Enemies had diminished Peabody's reputation by using his many debts to declare him an irresponsible leader. Indeed, Peabody had become a debtor because he had overspeculated in land and because he had an extravagant lifestyle. Therefore, Peabody believed he could best influence delegates if he did not stand for election and thus avoid attacks on his good name. Despite his efforts among friends outside of the convention and his work on affecting public opinion, the state convention eventually approved the Constitution. Peabody acquiesced in the decision rather than be regarded as a malcontent.

In 1788, Peabody was defeated in his bid for election to the United States Senate. But in 1790 he achieved his dream when the legislature founded the state medical society. For his efforts on behalf of medical standards, Dartmouth College awarded him an honorary degree. Peabody also returned to public life as a delegate to the state constitutional convention of 1792. Loyal members of the legislature elected him speaker of that body in 1793. But creditors had him remanded to prison in Exeter, New Hampshire, and Peabody took forced retirement from public life in 1795.

When he left prison, he returned to the private practice of medicine. Though he never grew wealthy, Peabody repaid his debts and led a productive life. As he grew older, illness weakened him, but he persevered in his practice. He died at Exeter on June 27, 1823. James Thacker said of Peabody that he was shrewd and vigilant in defense of personal freedom. "From his knowledge of human nature and the selfish policy of nations, he foresaw approaching danger and raised his warning voice. His learning," said Thacker, "was always decidedly in favor of popular rights. In his politics he was a Democratic-Republican, and he freely adhered to that party" (420).

REFERENCES

Charles H. Bell, *History of the Town of Exeter, New Hampshire* (Exeter: The Quarter-Millenial Year, 1888); Jere R. Daniell, *Experiment in Republicanism: New Hampshire Politics and the American Revolution, 1741–1791* (Cambridge: Harvard University Press, 1970); Nathaniel J. Eisenman, "Ratification of the Federal Constitution by the State of New Hampshire" (PhD diss., Columbia University, 1937); James Thacker, *American Medical Biography* (1828; repr., New York; Milford House, 1967); William C. Todd, *Biography and Other Articles* (Boston: Lee and Shepard, 1901); Joseph B. Walker, *A History of the New Hampshire Convention* (Boston: Supples and Hurd, 1888).
The Historical Society of New Hampshire has Peabody's papers.

THOMAS PERSON *(January 19, 1733–November 16, 1800)* was born in Brunswick County, Virginia. His father, William, emigrated to North Carolina in 1740. His mother's name was Ann. Little is known about Person's early life save that he grew up in Granville County, North Carolina, on the Virginia border. He had probably received some primary education, for he gained success as a public speaker and knew enough mathematics to become a surveyor. Person worked as a surveyor for Lord Granville, and grew to be a well-to-do land speculator. Like many surveyors, he had the skills to discover good land for himself. He owned much property in frontier Tennessee. In 1760 Person married Johanna Thomas of Granville. They had no children.

For all his success in land speculation, Person's true love was politics, and he rose rapidly in colonial government. He became a justice of the peace in 1756, county sheriff in 1762, and in 1764 gained election to the North Carolina colonial assembly. Person rose in public life through his close ties to the western small farmers. He supported the Regulators and became a counselor and advisor to them. Colonial authorities arrested him after the battle of Alamance in 1771. Tried in colonial courts for perjury, Person managed to persuade a jury of his innocence. As far as the royal government was concerned, he was too much of a liability and rabble rouser to be allowed to remain in public life.

The ferment around the American Revolution revived Person's political career, as he became an ally of the war leader Willie Jones (q.v.). Elected as a delegate from Granville County to the colony's radical provisional congress, he voted to rebel against Great Britain. In 1776, he served on the state Council of Safety. There, he joined the committee to draft the Halifax resolution. Person then assisted in writing the first North Carolina State Constitution in 1776. That year he became a general of state militia. Also elected a justice of the peace, he worked to organize his local constituents for war. Person served for many years in the North Carolina House of Commons, including the war years from 1777 to 1782.

During the Confederation period after the war, he continued in the state house, as he rose to a position of leadership there in 1786, and again from 1788 until 1791. In 1784 Person gained election to the Continental Congress, but he refused to attend, saying that he distrusted federal government and preferred to serve in his own state. He did become a state senator in 1787. Also in that year, Person chaired the committee to settle North Carolina debts with the federal government. North Carolina, thanks to Person and others, emerged debt-free in the Confederation period. Those arduous negotiations over indebtedness explain just why Person so disliked federal interference in state affairs. At that time, Person owned over 90,000 acres of land and sixty-two slaves.

In the crisis over ratification of the Constitution of 1787, Person used his platform in the state senate to help organize the Antifederalist antiratification forces, especially among the state's westerners. As a delegate to the first ratifying convention at Hillsborough in 1788, Person attempted to cut off discussion on the Constitution and called for an up or down vote. In a procedural motion, he lost his bid, and so he then spoke out about why he opposed ratification. Above all, he feared federal taxation policies that he thought would put his own state in financial jeopardy. Person was convinced that the large and wealthy states would control the tax funds and use them for their own needs. He voted against ratification.

Person also had been in correspondence with New York Antifederalist John Lamb (q.v.), who urged him to continue opposition to ratification. Accordingly, Person opposed calling a second state convention and argued to keep North Carolina out of the Union. Others threatened him, accusing the westerner of stirring up the state's radicals. In the second ratifying convention, held at Fayetteville in 1789, Person continued to resist the ratification forces and behaved in an obstreperous manner. He spoke against the new president, George Washington, calling the nation's beloved general a tyrant. For his attacks on Washington, citizens of Tarboro burned him in effigy. Even his close friend Willie Jones (q.v.) believed Person had gone too far. Despite the clash with Jones, Person continued to work behind the scenes to rally his allies to reject the Constitution a second time. True to his beliefs, Person voted against ratification in the second state convention. At the convention, he had gained a reputation as a maneuverer in support of opposition rather than as an effective speaker.

Undeterred by personal attacks, Person continued to serve in the state senate through 1791, where he promoted republican policies. He gained election to the state house from 1793 to 1795 and again in 1797. Person also served as a trustee, as did many other Antifederalists, of the young University of North Carolina. He served as a trustee from 1789 until 1798, and took much pride in assisting that college to grow. To the end of his days a radical republican, Person remained popular with the state's farm community. He retired from public life in 1797. Person died in Franklin County, North Carolina, on November 16, 1800.

REFERENCES

Samuel A. Ashe, *Biographical History of North Carolina* (Greensboro, N.C.: Charles L. Van Nappen, 1917), vol. 3; Bailyn, *Debate*, vol. 2; Louise Irby Trenholme, *The Ratification of the Federal Constitution in North Carolina* (New York: Columbia University Press, 1932); John H. Wheeler, *Historical Sketches of North Carolina* (1851; repr., Baltimore: Regional Publishing Co., 1964), vol. 2.

WILLIAM PETRIKIN *(1761–1821)* was born in Scotland. While still living there, he married Elizabeth (McEwen). They emigrated to Pennsylvania, where they first settled in Muncy but later laid down roots in the mid-1780s in Carlisle, then considered a rural community. Petrikin earned his living as a tenant farmer and a mechanic. For a time he practiced as a tailor. Evidently he learned to read and to write, for he would have an important correspondence with Antifederalist John Nicholson (q.v.), and in 1787 he would write the important work *The Government of Nature Delineated*. Much too little of either his early or later life is known to make an adequate judgment of his learning, or his reasons for becoming an Antifederalist, aside from his own pronouncements.

Petrikin appears in this volume because, as Saul Cornell says, he best represents the lower-class Antifederalist. A follower of Samuel Bryan (q.v.), Petrikin assisted in leading the radical western Pennsylvania farmers. He feared that Federalists in his town controlled the newspapers and other forms of public communication, and he wanted a means to strike back. Nicholson sent him copies of the Bryans' "Centinel" essays, and Petrikin used them to develop themes in his own publications.

The Government of Nature Delineated, which Petrikin published himself in Carlisle in February 1788, is an outspoken and satirical defense of poor people's views of the wrongs in the Constitution. Fourteen hundred copies of that pamphlet circulated throughout the states. In it, Petrikin attacked the local aristocracy, which had not talent, he said, but family position. Those men had the means, thanks to the Constitution, to control elections and therefore gain office. He also found that taxes forced ordinary people to work long hours and thus limited their pursuit of political interests. Petrikin resisted the idea of a federal and even a state army, fearing that small farmers and laborers would be deprived of their own arms. He favored local militia because it allowed ordinary people to protect their rights. Likewise, Petrikin defended trial by jury of one's peers as the only means to protect the interests of the poor. He went beyond other Antifederalists to resist too much state power, and called for a direct democracy based on the will of the local people. Local interests for Petrikin were closest to direct representation for the people.

Incensed over Pennsylvania's—for him—too-rapid ratification of the Constitution, Petrikin incited the so-called Carlisle Riot of Christmastime 1787. When local Antifederalists counterdemonstrated against Federalist victory celebrations over ratification, there were pitched battles in the streets of Carlisle. Petrikin defended the rioters. When he was arrested, he refused to allow others to post bail for him, and he served with other rioters in jail in the winter of 1788. While in jail he wrote "One of the People," an explanation of the riot, for the *Carlisle Gazette.* He claimed the Federalists had caused the riot and that they had an agenda to use the threat of violence to "deprive all immigrants of their rights." Their object, he insisted, was to keep newcomers from entering Pennsylvania for fear they would join the radical forces (Elliot, 674–678). Petrikin also published "The Scourge" in late January 1788, a diatribe against those who wanted "by fraud and force, to cram down your throats a constitution which would immediately create them your rulers" (Elliot, 688). He attended Pennsylvania's radical Antifederalist convention held in Harrisburg in 1788. Upset when other Antifederalists made little effort to fight to reverse ratification, he lost heart in being able to stop the conservative forces in the state.

This radicalism surfaces again in letters written to Philadelphia's John Nicholson (q.v.), in which Petrikin broke with fellow westerner William Findley (q.v.) and other Antifederalists over the Whiskey Rebellion in 1795. Petrikin supported the Whiskey rebels and asserted that Federalist lawyers had determined to prosecute those western farmers to put down efforts of popular resistance to oppression. This radical soon began a peripatetic movement throughout the state's west, perhaps in search of another means to rise in political life. He became justice of the peace in Cumberland County in 1795. Sometime that same year, Petrikin moved to Mifflin County, Pennsylvania, and in 1800 he served as justice of the peace in Centre County. He held office as Centre County register and recorder from 1809 until 1821. He became county notary public in 1813. Petrikin died in Centre County, Pennsylvania, in 1821. Much more needs to be discovered about this most radical of Antifederalists. It is not even clear that he wrote his own publications, since many scholars believe him to have been semiliterate.

REFERENCES

Saul Cornell, "Aristocracy Assailed: The Ideology of Backcountry Antifederalism," *Journal of American History* 76, no. 4 (March 1990): 1148–1172; Saul Cornell, *The Other Founders* (Chapel Hill: University of North Carolina Press, 1999); Elliot, *Debates,* vol. 2; John Blair Linn, *History of Centre and Clinton Counties Pennsylvania* (Philadelphia: L. H. Everts, 1883); Thomas Slaughter, *The Whiskey Rebellion* (New York: Oxford University Press, 1986).

CHARLES PETTIT *(September 3, 1736–September 3, 1806)* was
born in Hunterdon County, New Jersey. He was the son of the French Huguenot John Pettit, a Philadelphia and New Jersey importer. He received a classical education and in 1770 was admitted to the New Jersey bar. Soon

political service appealed more to Pettit than did the practice of the law. He also worked with his father in the import business. In 1758 he married Sarah Reed, daughter of his father's business associate.

His interest in provincial politics led Pettit to become surrogate of his county in 1767. In 1769 he held office as deputy secretary of the province and for a time gained the confidence of the British authorities. In 1771 he became aide to Royal Governor William Franklin. But Pettit supported the colonial struggle against the British government, and in 1776 he served as an aide to revolutionary Governor William Livingston. Pettit held the office of secretary of the state from 1776 until 1778. He also attained the rank of colonel in the new state militia. Because of his background in merchant trade, Pettit served as quartermaster general of the Continental Army from 1778 until his resignation in 1781. Scrupulous in his business dealings, Pettit believed the government's military procurement system was corrupt.

After the war, Pettit moved to Philadelphia to become an importer and insurance agent, and to practice some law. He served in the Philadelphia city government from 1784 until 1785. Pettit devised the Pennsylvania funding system to alleviate state war debts. He also looked for ways to improve national commercial interests. From 1785 until 1788, Pettit served in the Continental Congress. He had become a supporter of the radical Constitutionalist Party, a rare alliance for a Philadelphia merchant.

Defeated for election to Pennsylvania's Constitution ratification Convention in 1787, Pettit nevertheless became a leader of Philadelphia's moderate Antifederalist forces. He opposed ratification of the Constitution but realized that Pennsylvania was strongly pro-Constitution, so he resolved to opt for amendments. After the Constitution had been ratified, Pettit attended the Antifederalist Harrisburg Convention of early 1788. At Harrisburg, he took the side of the moderates who wanted to amend the Constitution, and worked unsuccessfully to persuade Robert Whitehill (q.v.) that anarchy might ensue if the Harrisburg Convention took a radical stance. Saul Cornell, a careful student of the behavior of Pennsylvania's Antifederalist moderates, says that "Pettit and middling democrats hoped that the struggle for amendments might actually revitalize an alternative politics, to combat the politics that inspired Federalists" (139). He signed the protest of the Harrisburg convention.

After the state Constitutional crisis had subsided, Pettit attempted to run for the United States Congress but lost his bid for office. Remaining a moderate Antifederalist, he opposed the Carlisle rioters, suggesting their actions hurt the cause. Pettit next attempted to influence Pennsylvania delegates to the national Congress to support the Bill of Rights. He used his advocacy for personal rights to appeal to those in eastern Pennsylvania who had become wary of the Constitution supporters. Pettit believed that state government superseded both national government and local authorities, and he continued to speak out in favor of state prerogatives in the new nation. In 1788 he published *View of Principles. Operation, and Probable Effects of the Funding System on Pennsylvania*, a pamphlet designed to thwart what he believed were oppressive economic maneuvers by Secretary of Treasury Alexander Hamilton.

During the 1790s, Pettit became interested in the state's relationship to the national government. In 1790 he presented Pennsylvania Revolutionary War claims for reparations to the federal government. Pettit spoke against the Jay Treaty of 1795, believing it harmful to Pennsylvania's western trade interests. Despite these activities, his political career in Philadelphia never recovered from his support of Antifederalism. Still, Pettit managed some public service. He served as a trustee of the University of Pennsylvania, a post he held from 1791 until 1802. He also belonged to the American Philosophical Society. In the late 1790s, Pettit retired to his business interests, becoming president of the Insurance Company of North America, based in Philadelphia. He held that office from 1796 until his death in Philadelphia, on September 3, 1806.

REFERENCES

Saul Cornell, *The Other Founders* (Chapel Hill: University of North Carolina Press, 1999); Jensen and Kaminski, *Documentary History*, vol. 18; T. H. Montgomery, *History of the Insurance Company of North America* (Philadelphia: Press of Review Publishing and Printing Co., 1885).

WILLIAM PINKNEY *(March 17, 1764–February 25, 1822)* was born in Annapolis, Anne Arundel County, Maryland. He was the son of the loyalist Jonathan Pinkney, an immigrant from England, and Ann (Rind). William was forced to leave the prestigious King William's School in Maryland because of the revolutionary crisis, so he pursued a course of self-study. Unlike his father, the younger Pinkney supported the revolutionary cause. After the war, he became a medical student but soon dropped medicine to study law with Samuel Chase (q.v.). Pinkney joined the Maryland bar in Harford County in 1786. He was a brilliant student who had become devoted to Chase and his circle of friends. Pinkey belonged to the Episcopal Church.

This ardent young man belied his age and experience during the crisis of the state ratification of the Constitution. He was elected to the Maryland State House in 1788 and would serve there until 1792. Pinkney became a useful Chase lieutenant and legal advisor to the Antifederalist cause. He gained election to the state ratification convention as a delegate from Harford County. He was elected along with Baltimorian Luther Martin (q.v.) from that county because Baltimore was a center of Federalism. Though Pinkney did not speak much at the convention, his support for the Chase forces was quite important to the cause. Pinkney voted against ratification, and defended the rights of state over the new federal government. He signed the Maryland "Dissent of the Minority."

Maryland truly was Federalist country—only eleven of the delegates voted against ratification. This meant Pinkney faced a hostile public as he sought to further his political career. In 1789, he married Mary Ann Maria Rodgers, from a Maryland seafaring and merchant family. He continued his successful legal career. Elected to the federal Congress in 1790, the state's Federalists contested the election, and Pinkney then refused to serve. Pinkney served in the state senate in 1791. He gained election to the state executive council in 1792 and served until 1795. In 1796 President George Washington chose him to lead the team to adjust the country's claims for maritime losses to the British, which brought him to London from 1796 until 1804. Meanwhile, Pinkney had joined his hero Chase in going over to the Federalist side.

In 1804 Pinkney returned to Maryland to build his law practice in Baltimore. In 1805 he served as attorney general of Maryland, although he soon resigned from that office. Pinkney then returned to the Republican cause. In 1806 President Thomas Jefferson chose him to confront the British government over reparations. In 1811 President James Madison nominated this ardent Republican as attorney general, a post he held until 1814. During this period, Pinkney wrote his famous "Publius" pamphlet in support of the War of 1812. In it he spoke of the rights of the coastal states to trade fairly and safely on the high seas. He took part in the battle of Bladensburg in 1814 and was wounded.

Pinkney had a distinguished postwar career in Republican politics. He served in the federal Congress in 1815 and 1816. He was minister to Russia from 1816 until 1818. The state legislature, now pro-Republican, named him to the United States Senate in 1819, and he served ably there until 1822. As a member of the senate from a slave state, Pinkney supported the slave states in the Missouri crisis of 1819. All his life a defender of state rights, Pinckney argued in 1819 before the United States Supreme Court for the state of Maryland in the celebrated *McCulloch v. Maryland* case. Pinkney died in Washington, D.C., on February 25, 1822.

Flamboyant, vain, and lacking a sense of humor, Pinkney was a brilliant lawyer and a good political leader. Despite his switch to the Federalists for a few years, he mostly kept faith with the Antifederalist cause that he had championed in 1788. Though young during the crisis over ratification, he later rose in public life and continued his loyalty to small government.

REFERENCES

Robert Ireland, *The Legal Career of William Pinkney, 1764–1822* (New York: Garland Press, 1986); Edward C. Papenfuse, et al., *A Biographical Dictionary of the Maryland Legislature* (Baltimore: The Johns Hopkins University Press, 1985), vol. 2; William Pinkney, *Life of William Pinkney* (New York: D. Appleton, 1853); David J. Siemers, *Ratifying the Republic* (Stanford: Stanford University Press, 2002); Benjamin B. Steiner, "Maryland Adopts the Federal Constitution." Pts. 1 and 2. *American Historical Review* 5 (October 1899): 22–42; (January 1900): 207–224; Henry Wheaton,

Accounts of the Life, Writings, and Speeches of William Pinkney (New York: J.W. Palmer and Co., 1826).

SAMUEL JOHN POTTER *(June 29, 1753–October 14, 1804)* was born in South Kingston Township (formerly Little Rest), Rhode Island. He was the son of John and Mary (Perry) Potter, originally from Massachusetts. He received a preparatory education but forsook college to study law in a private office. He developed a successful law practice. As a member of a family with agrarian interests in the colony and the state, Potter strongly supported the revolutionary cause in defense of the rights of the people of Rhode Island. He fought in the Revolutionary War.

Potter also served in the second Rhode Island state Constitutional ratifying convention in March 1790 as a delegate from North Kingston. He rose to leadership among the Antifederalists, and he continued to oppose the Constitution even when the convention finally ratified it in May 1790. Potter's activities in the convention were not so much as an Antifederalist ideologue than as a political activist and organizer of the opposition. Still, he spoke of his localist beliefs and attacked the Constitution as creating too strong a federal government.

As leader of the so-called Radical Country Party, Potter served as deputy governor of Rhode Island from 1790 until 1803. Potter was also a Republican presidential elector in 1796. He served as a Republican in the United States Senate in 1803 and 1804, and supported the policies of Republican President Thomas Jefferson. Potter died in Washington, D.C., on October 14, 1804. His wife, Anne Segar, whom he married in 1788, survived him. Potter is buried in the family plot in Washington County, Rhode Island.

REFERENCES

Genealogies of Rhode Island Families (Baltimore: Genea Publishing Co., 1989), vol. 2; Irwin H. Polishook, *Rhode Island and the Union* (Evanston, Ill.: Northwestern University Press, 1969); Franklin Edward Potter (comp.), *Descendants of Nicholas Potter, of Lynn, Massachusetts* (Baltimore: Gateway Press, 1991); David J. Siemers, *Ratifying the Republic* (Stanford: Stanford University Press, 2002).

ℛ

DAVID REDICK *(?–September 28, 1805)* was born in Ireland, moved to the colonies before the Revolution to settle in Lancaster County, Pennsylvania, and came to the western part of the state in 1782. Redick became a surveyor in Lancaster, and with David Hoge surveyed the town of Washington. He also bought lots there. Redick was admitted to the Pennsylvania bar in 1782 and soon became a leading lawyer in his part of the state. He was a Mason and also a Presbyterian. Redick married the daughter of the large landowner Jonathan Hoge. They had three children.

A close ally of the radical William Findley (q.v.), Redick soon entered state politics. Elected to the state legislature from Washington County, he rose in radical circles and became an opponent of chartering the Bank of North America in 1785. A member of the Pennsylvania Supreme Executive Council in 1786, he became vice president of that body in 1788. In 1787 Redick served as an agent from Pennsylvania to negotiate with New York over Connecticut boundary claims. In that capacity he became a friend and ally of New York's governor, George Clinton (q.v.). He also was appointed surveyor of the Ten Islands in the Ohio and Allegheny rivers. Through dealings in surveying and land claims, Redick became a successful real estate owner.

As a leader of the western interests of the state, Redick opposed sending delegates from Pennsylvania to the Philadelphia Constitutional Convention of 1787. He was an associate and aide of the Antifederalist John Smilie (q.v.), like himself a leader of the Constitutionalist Party who refused to accept changes in the state constitution. Although he did not serve in the state ratifying convention, Redick's writings made him a major western Pennsylvania Antifederalist. He probably was the anonymous "Z" who wrote in opposition to Pennsylvania's ratification of the federal Constitution in *The Freeman's Journal* of August 22, 1787. Redick also published "The Loss of American Liberty," an Antifederalist article, on September 24, 1787. He insisted that supporters of the federal Constitution planned to override the defense of civil liberties that the Constitutionalist Party held so dear. In "The Loss of American Liberty," Redick declared, "in my opinion the day on which we adopt the present proposed plan of government, from that moment we may justly date the loss of American liberty" (Bailyn, 15). Redick also stated that he had "strong evidence that these people know it will not bear an examination and therefore wish to adopt it first and consider it afterward" (16). He concluded "Loss of American Liberty" with his opposition to any members from the federal Constitutional Convention serving in the state ratifying convention.

In a letter to fellow Antifederalist William Irvine, published in September 1787, Redick mused further on his opposition to the Constitution. In that letter he said he knew how unsafe it was to speak out against the Constitution in Pennsylvania, but he had to make his argument known. He feared the loss of liberty of the press, standing armies, and congressional taxing powers. Redick also wrote bitterly about the Federalist stranglehold on the state government. He wondered whether the Federalists planned to use the power to tax to keep Germans or Irish from coming to the state. Redick's hatred for the Quaker elite also surfaced in his bitter denunciation of how they controlled Philadelphia and pushed for passage of the Constitution. He concluded his long letter to Irvine with the charge that the Federalist agenda included plans to inhibit the rise of democracy in the new United States (Jensen and Kaminski, 135).

After the Pennsylvania Antifederalists lost their bid against ratification, Redick decided to remain in politics to pursue the cause of local rights. He was a delegate to the state constitutional convention in 1789 and 1790. Redick was elected to the American Philosphical Society in 1789. In 1791 he became prothonotary (chief clerk) of Washington County. Along with fellow westerner Findley, he attempted to defend the policies of the state's Whiskey rebels in 1794, while at the same time condemning their radical actions. He supported law and order, he said, but also wanted to keep President George Washington from sending troops to put down the rebellion. At that time, Redick was an ally of Thomas Jefferson and a strong Republican. Some scholars say that he became a Federalist in the late 1790s, but he seemed always a supporter of western farmer interests. Redick died in Washington County, Pennsylvania, on September 28, 1805.

REFERENCES

George D. Albert, *History of the County of Westmoreland Pennsylvania* (Philadelphia: L. H. Everts and Co., 1882); Bailyn, *Debate*, vol. 1; Steven R. Boyd, *The Politics of Opposition* (Millwood, N.Y.: KTO Press, 1979); Alfred Creigh, *History of Washington County* (Washington, Pa.; self-published; 1870); Boyd Crumrine (ed.), *History of Washington County, Pennsylvania* (Philadelphia: L. H. Everts and Co., 1884); Jensen and Kaminski, *Documentary History*, vol. 2; Jackson Turner Main, *The Antifederalists* (Chapel Hill: University of North Carolina Press, 1961).

CHARLES RIDGELY *(September 17, 1733–June 28, 1790)* was born in Baltimore County, Maryland. He was the son of Charles and Rachael

(Howard) Ridgely, his mother being the daughter of a powerful Baltimore political figure. Ridgely had little formal education, though by 1756 he was sailing in his merchant father's ships. In 1757 the French took him prisoner, accusing the young man of piracy. After he was released he soon became captain of his own ship. In 1760 this devout Episcopalian married Rebecca Dorsey, daughter of a prominent ironmaster. In 1761 Ridgely joined his father to found the Northampton Ironworks. He also became a merchant in Baltimore and eventually opened the firm Ridgely, Goodwin, and McClure, which remained in business until 1784.

A supporter of the American Revolution in Tory-dominated Baltimore, Ridgely served as an officer in the Continental Army. He also made cannon, shot, and kettles from pig iron for the Maryland troops. It is rumored with some evidence that he also ran a successful privateer out of the many inlets on the eastern shore of Maryland. During the war, Ridgely developed strong business and political ties to Samuel Chase (q.v.) and John F. Mercer (q.v.), both of whom were involved with him in the purchase of Tory lands after the Revolution. Ridgely also became quite successful as a trader in wheat and sugar. Along with Chase and other former revolutionaries, he bought much land along the docks of Baltimore. During the 1780s, Ridgely owned an ironworks in Anne Arundel County and became a partner with Samuel Chase in the Nottingham Iron Works in Baltimore County. Connected to the political boss of Baltimore County, Dr. Fred Ridgely, he served a number of terms in the state legislature.

This wealthy merchant also supported the Antifederalist cause in Maryland. He belonged to the Paper Money political faction in Maryland. Despite his success, Ridgely also had debts to British merchants. This combination of roles as a land speculator and supporter of inflationary paper money, and his indebtedness, led Ridgely to oppose stronger federal government interference into state and local affairs. He favored lower taxes and worried that the Constitution's proponents planned to raise taxes. Perhaps, most importantly, his business interests led Ridgely to advocate weak and decentralized government. As a member of the state ratification convention, he worked with Chase and others to defeat the proposed federal Constitution. Accordingly, he voted with the minority against ratification. Ridgely signed the "Dissent of the Minority."

After the convention, British merchants brought a lawsuit against Ridgely. Although members of his family, including the powerful political boss and first cousin Charles Ridgely of William (with whom he is often confused), continued in public life, Ridgely the merchant appears to have disappeared from public view. He died in Baltimore County, on June 28, 1790.

REFERENCES

Philp A. Crowl, "Antifederalism in Maryland," *The William and Mary Quarterly*, 3rd ser., 4 (October 1947): 446–469; Philip A. Crowl, *Maryland During and After the*

Revolution (Baltimore: The Johns Hopkins University Press, 1943); Edward Papen-fuse, et al., *A Biographical Dictionary of the Maryland Legislature* (Baltimore: The Johns Hopkins University Press, 1985); Melvin Yazama (ed.), *Representative Government and the Revolution: The Maryland Constitutional Crisis of 1787* (Baltimore: The Johns Hopkins University Press, 1975).

There are Ridgely family papers at the Maryland Historical Society in Baltimore.

SPENCER ROANE *(April 4, 1762–September 4, 1822)* was born
in Essex County, Virginia. His father was William Roane, a leader in the House of Burgesses and later a veteran of the Revolutionary War. His mother was a daughter of the wealthy Colonel Spencer Ball. Young Roane received a special private education from teachers imported from Scotland. His grandfather had been born in Scotland, and the family believed strongly in Scots-trained education. He graduated from the College of William and Mary. A brilliant young student, Roane belonged to the Phi Beta Kappa Society.

Following the pattern of other wealthy landowners, Roane also read law. He was elected to the Virginia House of Delegates in 1783 and 1784, where he roomed with the celebrated Richard Henry Lee (q.v.). At the young age of twenty-two Roane was elected to the Council of State and became a confidante of Governor Patrick Henry (q.v.). In 1786, he married Henry's daughter Anne, and, after her death, he married Elizabeth Hoskins in 1799. Roane also read George Mason's (q.v.) Declaration of Rights and was much impressed. He became a follower of his hero, Thomas Jefferson.

When Virginians chose delegates to the state ratification convention for the federal Constitution, Roane was not elected. Nevertheless, he became an important young leader of the Antifederalist cause. His major effort in behalf of Antifederalism was the radical "A Plain Dealer" of February 13, 1788, published in the *Virginia Independent Chronicle*. In that piece, Roane attacked Governor George Randolph for supporting the Constitution. He claimed that the Constitution deprived the state of its rights in the new nation. Though Roane insisted that Governor Randolph wanted to silence the opposition, he nevertheless planned to speak out. How, he asked, could the governor try to silence such leaders as Richard Henry Lee (q.v.), and oppose all those men of good will, those defenders of civil rights, who desired to amend the Constitution. Roane also accused the authors of the Constitution of seeking to perpetuate an aristocracy, as they made it nearly impossible to remove a poor or corrupt legislator. He declared, "the Constitution should be like Caesar's wife—not only good, but unsuspected" (Jensen and Kaminski, 364). After the delegates ratified the Constitution, Roane knew he had little choice but to join the new nation. Still, he insisted that the losers made up a respected and talented minority.

After the convention, Roane continued his political career. He served in the state senate in 1788 and 1789. In 1789 he became a judge of the general court. In 1794, Roane called for further revision of the federal Constitution. Also in 1794 the governor named him a judge of the supreme court of appeals, where he served with distinction for over twenty-seven years. A strict constructionist, a Jeffersonian Republican, and a committed small-government Antifederalist, Roane supported the Virginia Resolution of 1798. In 1804, he assisted in founding the Richmond *Enquirer,* a newspaper devoted to the rights of the states. A supporter of James Madison's administration, in 1811 Roane published the celebrated "Hampden," a diatribe against the Federalist principles of fellow Virginian John Marshall.

In 1802 Roane had moved from Essex to his plantation, Spring Garden, in Hanover County, Virginia. In 1815 he built a home in Richmond where he collected a large library dedicated to political philosophy. The young state righters of Virginia gathered there to discuss the country's future with the now-aging Antifederalist. He had become for them a symbol of small government. Roane died at Warm Springs, Virginia, on September 4, 1822.

REFERENCES

Richard Beeman, *The Old Dominion and the New Nation* (Lexington: University Press of Kentucky, 1972); Richard Beale Davis, *Intellectual Life in Jefferson's Virginia* (Knoxville: University of Tennessee Press, 1972); Paul L. Ford (ed.), *Essays on the Constitution* (Brooklyn, N.Y.: Historical Printing Club, 1892); Jensen and Kaminski, *Documentary History,* vol. 8; David J. Mays, *Sketch of Judge Spencer Roane* (Richmond, VA.: Richmond Press, Inc., Printers, 1929); Norman K. Risjord, *Chesapeake Politics* (New York: Columbia University Press, 1979); Robert A. Rutland, *Ordeal of the Constitution* (Norman: University of Oklahoma Press, 1965).

THOMAS RODNEY *(June 4, 1744–January 2, 1811)* was born in Kent County, Delaware. He was the son of Ceasar Rodney, a large farmer in Kent County. His mother was Elizabeth (Crawford). Rodney received an excellent private education. His father died young, and his mother then married Thomas Wilson, a Delaware farmer. Young Rodney then went to work for his brother, Ceasar, a later signer of the Declaration of Independence, on the family farm. In 1771 he married Elizabeth Fisher of Philadelphia, Pennsylvania.

In 1764 Rodney moved to Dover, Delaware, to become a county official. For a time, he owned a store in Philadelphia but soon returned to Kent County to farm and enter politics. He became a justice of the peace in Kent County in 1770 and held that position until 1774. Rodney entered the colonial assembly in 1775, and served until 1776. He was a member of the radical Committee of Correspondence in 1775 and 1776. A strong supporter of the Revolution, he was elected to the Council of Safety. In 1775 Rodney organized the county militia and became its colonel.

When war broke out in 1776, Rodney went to Bristol, Pennsylvania, to fight with General George Washington's Continental Army. He participated in the second battle of Trenton and the defense of Princeton, and took charge of the military headquarters at Morristown, New Jersey. Rodney then became an agent of the French government and negotiated for supplying French troops to fight for the American Revolution. Rodney also had an important civilian political role during the war. From 1778 until 1785, he was a judge of the Admiralty Court, where he assisted in deciding many cases of privateering and blockade running. Rodney was also a judge of common pleas. From 1778 untl 1788, he served as register of wills of Kent County.

During the Confederation period, Rodney held office in the Continental Congress, serving five terms altogether, including the years 1783 to 1787. While in the Continental Congress, Rodney kept a diary of his experiences. He seemed quite wary of any attempts in that body to circumvent the powers of the states. In 1786 and 1787, Rodney gained election to the Delaware House of Representatives. In 1787 his peers selected him as Speaker of the House.

Although he did not serve in Delaware's federal Constitutional ratifying convention, Rodney became a cautious opponent of ratification in a state overwhelmingly in support of the Constitution. Harold Hancock says that "Thomas Rodney was the only known Delaware politician who at first expressed doubts about whether the Constitution would provide better government. He thought that the proposed document did not promote national unity, gave the states too much power, and failed to provide an adequate balance among the different classes of society" (115). Rodney also wrote bitterly about the Antifederalist defections in nearby Pennsylvania, attributing those losses to Federalist bullies.

Though a staunch defender of individual rights, Rodney resented what he believed was a return of Delaware's wartime Tories to power in the Confederation period. He belonged to that branch of whiggish ideology that believed the people were losing power to a renewed aristocratic movement in the state and in the nation. Rodney had taken over leadership of the state's Republicans after his famous brother, Ceasar, had died prematurely in 1784. During the Federalist period, he continued to lead that organization and he supported the rising Jeffersonian Republicans in Delaware. Heavily in debt, Rodney served time in debtors' prison in 1791 and 1792. After he left prison, he achieved some degree of financial stability. In 1798, Rodney became president of the Delaware Agricultural Society. He was named an associate justice of the state supreme court in 1802. Perhaps sensing the power of the state's conservatives to control future appointments, Rodney accepted President Thomas Jefferson's offer of a judgeship in the Mississippi Territory in 1803. He settled in Natchez and ably performed the task of a frontier judge. Rodney died in Natchez, on January 2, 1811.

REFERENCES

Henry C. Conrad, *History of the State of Delaware* (Wilmington, Del.: Aldine, Publishing and Engraving Co., 1908), vol. 1; Harold Hancock, *The Loyalists of Revolutionary Delaware* (Newark: University of Delaware Press, 1977); J. M. McCarter and

B. F. Jackson, *Historiographical and Biographical Encyclopedia of Delaware* (Wilmington, Del.: Aldine, Publishing and Engraving Co., 1882); Jensen and Kaminski, *Documentary History*, vol. 2; J. Thomas Scharf, *History of Delaware: 1609–1888* (Philadelphia: L. J. Ricgard, 1888), vol. 1.

GRIFFITH RUTHERFORD *(c. 1720–August 10, 1805)* was born

in Ireland sometime around 1720. He was the son of John and Elizabeth (Griffith) Rutherford, who died at sea on their voyage to these shores. The ship first dropped off young Rutherford in Philadelphia, Pennsylvania, where he lived with relatives and worked on their farm. Rutherford received little education aside from what he taught himself. By the 1750s, he had emigrated to Halifax County, North Carolina. He became a landowner in Rowan County and owned eight slaves. Rutherford joined the Presbyterian church. In 1754 he married Elizabeth Graham. Adventuresome and a natural leader, Rutherford served in the French and Indian War. In 1760 he became captain of the Rowan County militia. In 1766 he represented Rowan County in the colonial assembly. From 1767 until 1769, Rutherford served as sheriff and justice of the peace of Rowan County. While in the assembly, he supported the North Carolina Regulators and in 1768 wanted to pardon those western farmers. He refused to fight against them in 1771. In 1772 Rutherford became colonel of the Rowan County militia.

An ardent Whig, Rutherford became a military hero in the Revolutionary War. A member of the Committee of Safety of the Salisbury District in 1775, he overcame his suspicions of the conservative eastern region to support unified revolutionary activity. He also served in the provisional congress in 1776 where he became an ally of Matthew Locke (q.v.). Rutherford assisted in writing the first North Carolina State Constitution. He served as a state senator from Rowan County from 1777 to 1787. But his major wartime contribution was in the military, where that natural leader rose to a position of some importance. Rutherford gained election as brigadier general in 1776, and he took part in the Cherokee war in the western part of the state. In 1776 he also fought Tories in the Cape Fear region. Wounded and captured in 1780 at the battle of Camden, after years of fighting Tories in the state's west, the British later exchanged him. He commanded North Carolina troops at the battle of Wilmington, and in 1781 he defeated the loyalists at the battle of Raft Swamp. In 1782 he again fought the Cherokee in the west.

After the war, Rutherford took an active part in opposing the restoration of Tory property. He continued to serve in the state senate from Rowan. As a member of the Council of State, he assisted in confiscating Tory lands. Rutherford ran for governor in 1783 but lost his bid, being considered too radical for the state's easterners. Rutherford joined the Antifederalist cause and opposed ratification of the federal Constitution. At the Hillsborough convention of 1788, he claimed to represent the western farmer interests that opposed a strong central government. But in 1789, the citizens of Rowan

County, fearing him too radical, refused to send him to the second state convention. Nevertheless, for a time Rutherford remained a power among the state's Antifederalists.

In 1792, no longer satisfied with either the politics of North Carolina or his opportunities there, the former military hero moved to Sumner County, Tennessee. As a land speculator, he had purchased much land in the Tennessee territory. In 1794 Rutherford became president of the new Tennessee state legislative council. A county in that state was named after him in 1803. Rutherford died on August 10, 1805, in Rutherford County, Tennessee, at the age of eighty-four.

REFERENCES

Samuel A. Ashe, *History of North Carolina* (Raleigh, N.C.: Edwards and Broughton Printing Co., 1925), vol. 1; Randall Capps, *The Rowan Story* (Bowling Green, Ky.: Homestead Press, 1976); Robert Claude Carpenter, "Griffith Rutherford: Frontier Military and Political Leader" (master's thesis, Wake Forest University, 1974); Hugh T. Lefler, *History of a Southern State: North Carolina* (Chapel Hill: University of North Carolina Press, 1963); Griffith J. McRee, *Life and Correspondence of James Iredell* (New York: Peter Smith, 1949); Louise Irby Trenholme, *The Ratification of the Federal Constitution in North Carolina* (New York: Columbia University Press, 1932); John H. Wheeler, *Historical Sketches of North Carolina*, 2 vols. (1851; repr., Baltimore: Regional Publishing Co., 1964).

The Rutherford manuscripts are in the archives of the North Carolina Historical Commission in Raleigh.

S

CORNELIUS SCHOONMAKER *(June 1745–1796)* was born at Shawangunk, Ulster County, New York. From a Dutch farming family, he had little schooling. But the ambitious Schoonmaker became a land surveyor, which led to his speculation in land and eventually to successful farming in Ulster county. He married Sarah Hoffman, and they had six children.

A patriot during the American Revolution, Schoonmaker served on the Ulster County Committee of Vigilance and Safety. He also was in the state legislature from 1777 until 1790, where he joined those loyal to the first state constitution. In the state legislature, Schoonmaker opposed the federal government's power to control imports, and favored paper money bills. He was a political lieutenant of Governor George Clinton (q.v.), and in January 1788 moved that the state legislature condemn the federal Constitutional Convention in Philadelphia as having exceeded its authority. Schoonmaker was elected to the state ratifying convention in 1788, and he took an active part in debate as an Antifederalist. At the convention, he spoke again to his claim that the Philadelphia convention had exceeded its mandate and that at best another convention had to be held to assess the will of the people. An ally of Melancton Smith (q.v.), Schoonmaker soon agreed with that solon that ratification of the Constitution was inevitable. But he broke with Smith and voted against ratification. Schoonmaker believed that the Federalists' promise of a bill of rights, which induced a few Antifederalists to vote for ratification, would not be delivered.

This Antifederalist continued in the state legislature to support Governor Clinton, and in 1789, he joined those who wanted to make the Federalist Rufus King a candidate for the federal Senate. In this act, Schoonmaker hoped to unite New York Federalists and Antifederalists. Soon he knew he had been mistaken. In 1789 Schoonmaker, a slaveowner, also tried to stop the New York Emancipation Bill. Elected to the federal Congress in 1791, he lost his bid for reelection to a Federalist in 1792. While in Congress, Schoonmaker allied himself with the Antifederalists, but most of his friends kept quiet in hopes that the Federalists would force unsound policies on the nation, thus destroying their small majority. He returned to the state assembly in 1795. Schoonmaker died in the spring of 1796 at his home in Shawangunk, New York.

REFERENCES

Steven R. Boyd, *The Politics of Opposition* (Millwood, N.Y.: KTO Press, 1979); *Commemorative Biographical Record of Ulster County, New York* (Chicago: J. H. Beers Co., 1896); Robert A. Rutland, *Birth of the Bill of Rights* (Chapel Hill: University of North Carolina Press, 1955); Eugene Wilder Spaulding, *New York in the Critical Period, 1783–1789* (New York: Columbia University Press, 1932); Nathaniel B. Sylvester, *History of Ulster County, New York* (Philadelphia: Everts and Peck, 1880); Alfred Young, *Democratic Republicans of New York* (Chapel Hill: University of North Carolina Press, 1967).

AMOS SINGLETARY *(September 1721–1806)* was born in Sutton, Massachusetts, to the farmer John Singletary and Mary (Greele). Tutored at home, Singletary never went to school. In 1742 he married Mary Curtis of Topsfield. He belonged to the Baptist church, as did his family. Singletary became a successful farmer in Worcester County, where he also owned a gristmill. It is possible that Singletary practiced law in the town of Sutton. He first entered politics as a justice of the peace, and he served often on the colonial general court. A supporter of the Revolution, Singletary held office in the provisional state legislature in 1775, and then four years in the state house and two terms in the state senate. In the legislature during the war, he became a leading opponent of the eastern Massachusetts banking and trade legislators, believing that those interests hurt the western farmers.

As an Antifederalist from Worcester County, Singletary spoke often in the state convention against ratification of the Constitution. He claimed to be a poor speaker, and he attacked the smooth and glib-tongued lawyers who supported the Federalist cause. Singletary feared that the Constitution's supporters "[would] swallow up all us little folks, like the great leviathan" (Harding, 77). Singletary also opposed a standing army and supported the calling of a militia for any need of military defense. At the convention, this wise westerner used his concerns about the army to dramatize fears of an aristocracy But Singletary's main arguments centered on service and political power in the proposed national congress. "We thought . . . we were giving great powers to we know not whom," said this westerner. Along with Phaneul Bishop (q.v.), he argued that electing senators for six years meant the possibility of life tenure. He worried about huge wages for national leaders (Elliot, 44). Singletary had supported the American Revolution, he said, in order to found a republican government. He feared that the Constitution as written repudiated republicanism. Singletary declared, if anyone in 1775 had suggested that such a powerful government be created in the new nation, the people would have resisted them (Elliot, 101). Singletary voted against ratification of the Constitution.

It is unclear whether Singletary took part in post-1789 politics. There is some indication that he had moved to Maine. Singletary died in 1806.

REFERENCES

William A. Benedict and Hiram A. Tracy, *History of Sutton* (Worcester, Mass.: Published for the town of Sutton, 1878); Elliot, *Debates*, vol. 2; Van Beck Hall, *Politics Without Parties: Massachusetts, 1780–1791* (Pittsburgh: University of Pittsburgh Press, 1972); Samuel B. Harding, *The Contest over the Ratification of the Federal Constitution in the State of Massachusetts* (Cambridge: Harvard University Press, 1896); William Durkee Williamson, *History of the State of Maine* (Hallowell, Maine: Glazier and Masters, 1832).

JOHN SMILIE *(1741/42–December 30, 1812)* was born in Ireland. Little is known about his early life save that he must have received a decent education there. He settled in Lancaster County, Pennsylvania, in 1760, and took up the occupation of school teacher in that colony's western section. Smilie also farmed for a time. He began in politics as leader of Lancaster County's radical revolutionaries. Smilie attended conferences of revolutionaries and served in the new state assembly in 1778, 1779, and 1780. Smilie also saw military service in the Revolutionary War, serving as a private in a Pennsylvania regiment in 1776 and 1777.

In 1781 Smilie moved to Westmoreland County and served that county in the state legislature, rising to become a member of the Supreme Executive Council (then a form of state senate). After his county divided, Smilie represented the new Fayette County. Altogether he represented western farmers in the state assembly for over thirty years. Russell Jennings Ferguson, author of a major study on early western Pennsylvania politics, said that Smilie "met his constituents on equal terms, talked with them about crops, Indians, and politics, and held their confidence" (43–44). Smilie served on the state Council of Censors in 1783 and 1784. In 1783, in the Council of Censors he opposed the forces in the state who wanted to revise the state constitution. In 1785 Smilie joined the radical leader William Findley (q.v.) in opposing the state bank powers. Those westerners believed the immigrant small farmers would lose out to eastern business interests in the struggle for loans from the bank. Smilie also served in the assembly from Fayette County from 1784 to 1786. He was on the state Supreme Executive Council from 1786 until 1789, thus placing him in Philadelphia during the Constitutional Convention.

When the state's leaders began the movement to ratify the proposed new federal Constitution in 1787, Smilie joined the opposition. He led Fayette County's struggle to stop ratification. Smilie made a major speech in the state convention against the new federal government. His most important argument against a strong federal government was that the Federalists wanted an aristocracy to control the central government. The leaders, he said, also planned to deprive ordinary people of a free press. He also stated that only local government could adequately provide for trial by jury. An ally of George

Bryan (q.v.), Smilie also wrote parts of the famous Antifederalist articles called "Old Whig," and perhaps even the prestigious "Centinel" pieces. When the convention voted to ratify, Smilie voted against. He signed "The Dissent," a protest against Federalist mob violence perpetrated on local Antifederalists.

Living in fear for his life, as did many opponents of the Federalists, Smilie nevertheless made important contributions to the Antifederalist cause. Aside from his great defense of a free press, he spoke out against altering the old government without clarity on the Federalist design of the actual powers in the new government. His own words convey the fears so many had of the proposed new government. "So loosely, so inaccurately are the powers which are enumerated in this constitution defined," said he, that he demanded the Federalists describe more clearly their design for the new federal government (Bailyn, 804–806). Smilie called for a full discussion of the proposed document, and the Federalists replied with silence, revealing their contempt for his views. Out of frustration he declared: "Because the people have a right to alter and abolish government, can it therefore be inferred that every step taken to secure that right would be superfluous and nugatory?" (Storing, 384). Smilie also mentioned in the state convention that he had corresponded with George Mason of Virginia (q.v.), and that the Virginians' main concern about the Constitution was that "there was no security for our rights in this Constitution" (Storing, 387). Like Mason and others, Smilie demanded a bill of rights, not only to protect personal rghts, but to offset the powers of the central government.

After the state's so early and ill-considered vote for ratification, Smilie helped to organize the Pennsylvania convention that met at Harrisburg in 1788. Though not present at the Harrisburg convention, Smilie nevertheless supported the movement there to amend the Constitution by adding a statement on individual rights. Smilie was also a member of the state consitutional convention of 1790. He remained in the Pennsylvania State Senate from 1790 to 1793, and resigned only to enter the United States House. Smilie served as a Jeffersonian Republican in the 1793–1795 term and again from 1799 until 1812. There, he defended expansion of western settlements and became an able leader of those who wanted a second war with England. Close to President James Madison, Smilie assisted in passing important anti-British Republican legislation. He died in Washington, D.C., on December 30, 1812.

REFERENCES

Douglas M. Arnold, *A Republican Revolution: Ideology and Politics in Pennsylvania, 1776–1790* (New York: Garland Press, 1989); Bailyn, *Debate*, vol. 1; Saul Cornell, *The Other Founders* (Chapel Hill: University of North Carolina Press, 1999); Russell Jennings Ferguson, *Early Western Pennsylvania Politics* (Pittsburgh: University of Pittsburgh Press, 1938); Storing, *Complete*, vol. 4.

JONATHAN BAYARD SMITH *(February 21, 1742–June 16, 1812)* was born in Philadelphia, Pennsylvania. He was the son of Samuel

Smith, who had moved to Philadelphia from New Hampshire and became a wealthy merchant. Young Smith had his primary education in England and graduated from the College of New Jersey (Princeton) in 1760. He too became a merchant. His first marriage was to Susannah Bayard of Maryland, daughter of a wealthy Federalist merchant. Smith later gained a connection to George Bryan (q.v.) by his second marriage.

A devoted patriot, Smith was secretary of the Philadelphia Committee of Safety from 1775 to 1777. He had been a member of the provisional congress of 1774 and was also its secretary. Smith was part of the group of leaders who threw out the Pennsylvania provisional government. He served in the Continental Congress in 1777 and 1778 and voted to ratify the Articles of Confederation. In 1778 he was a member of the committee to publish the congressional journals. He staunchly supported the Articles of Confederation. He resigned from the Congress to assist in the defense of Philadelphia in 1778. Smith served as a captain and then a colonel in the Brandywine campaign. He joined the Court of Common Pleas in 1778. In 1779 Smith helped to found the University of of Pennsylvania, and served on its board of trustees from 1779 to 1791. His staunch revolutionary liberalism led Smith to support the radical Constitutional Party in Philadelphia.

Part of the urban elite, Smith joined George Bryan in opposing calls for the state's federal Constitutional ratification convention. After the legislature called the convention, Smith failed in his bid for election to it because heavily Federalist Philadelphia opposed the Antifederalists there. He had previously lost in his attempt to replace James Wilson, the extreme Federalist, as prothonotary (chief clerk) of the city of Philadelphia. Nevertheless, Smith assisted the Antifederalist forces. Smith helped to draft Antifederalist pamphlets, and he circulated them throughout the state and even in New York. He was one of the wealthy leaders who put his resources to work in the cause of Antifederalism.

After the state ratified the Constitution, Smith returned to local politics. He was a city alderman from 1792 to 1794. He became auditor general of Pennsylvania in 1794 and held that post for two years. From 1779 until 1808, he served as a trustee of Princeton. In 1800, he supported Thomas Jefferson for president. In 1805, as a member of the reform convention, he opposed revisions in the state constitution. Smith belonged to the Masons and to Philadelphia's conservative Presbyterian Church. He also helped to found the Republican Society of the Sons of St. Tammany, as he assumed leadership among the city's immigrant population. His social status and brilliance elevated him to membership in the American Philosophical Society. William Findley (q.v.) had wanted his Antifederalist colleague to write a history of the cause. Although Smith had kept many documents from the Constitutional crisis, he never wrote that history. His son, Samuel Harrison Smith, also a Jeffersonian, founded the *National Intelligencer* in 1800. The elder Smith died in Philadelphia on June 16, 1812.

REFERENCES

Steven R. Boyd, *The Politics of Opposition* (Millwood, N.Y.: KTO Press, 1979); John Hill Martin, *Martin's Bench and Bar of Philadelphia* (Philadelphia: R. Welch and Co., 1883); James G. Wilson, "Col. Bayard and Bayard Family," *New York Genealogical and Biographical Record* (New York: Published by the Records Commission, 1885). The Smith family papers are at the Library of Congress.

MELANCTON SMITH *(May 7, 1744–July 29, 1798)* was born in Jamaica, Long Island, New York. His father, Samuel Smith, was a middling Long Island farmer. Smith's mother, Elizabeth (Bayles), gave him his primary education. For a time, Smith apprenticed in a retail store in Poughkeepsie, New York. He later owned a store there. A successful if not rich merchant, this staunch Presybterian also became a land speculator in Dutchess County, New York. His first wife, Mary, died in 1770, and he married Margaret Mott in 1771. They had three children.

In 1775 Smith represented Dutchess County as a delegate to the first provisional congress. He supported the Revolution and raised a regiment in Dutchess County, becoming captain of rangers, and later major of militia. He became a wartime ally of George Clinton (q.v.). In 1775 Smith was part of a commission to defeat Tory conspiracies against the fledgling New York revolutionaries. He examined loyalists and administered oaths of allegiance to citizens in southern New York State. From 1777 until 1779, he held the powerful post of high sheriff of Dutchess County. Smith also served as commissary agent for the state army.

After the war, Smith returned to his merchant occupation. He speculated in government securities and bonds, and purchased Tory lands. In 1782 he ably handled a dispute between the army and local contractors, and settled it to the satisfaction of both sides. Smith moved to New York City in 1784, continued in the mercantile business, and also practiced law. From 1785 to 1788, he served in the Continental Congress. Although he saw some failings in the federal government under the Articles of Confederation, Smith generally supported its policies.

Elected to the state ratifying convention from Dutchess County—New York City being Federalist—which was held in Poughkeepsie in 1788, Smith served as the manager of the Antifederalist forces. He proposed that the new Constitution was no better than the Articles of Confederation and sought at first to defeat it. If the Constitution was to be adopted, Smith said, then the state must guarantee a bill of rights delineating the liberties of the people who required protection from the new government. Once he realized that Virginia had ratified the Constitution, Smith knew New York had to go along. Smith moved that the state ratify with the provision that if the new government did not adopt a bill of rights after four years, New York would secede from the Union. In this maneuver he failed. Smith also had been in correspondence with Nathan Dane (q.v.) of Massachusetts and other eastern state moderates, and all of them had feared the consequences of refusing to go along with the majority of the states that had ratified the Constitution. Incurring the wrath of Antifederalist stalwart leader George Clinton, Smith voted for ratification. He said he believed amendments were forthcoming. Offering another view of Smith's action, Alfred Young suggested that he voted for the Constitution because he feared the breakup of New York State if it did not ratify. Alexander Hamilton had threatened to take New York City out of the state, and Smith believed him (Young, 114).

In his tortured way, Smith revealed in his words at the convention why he came round to vote for the Constitution. He claimed his most important problem with the Constitution was the number and quality of representatives. Smith insisted that the new representatives lacked experience in public life, especially in dealing with the interests of their local constituents. He called for a much larger House of Representatives, insisting that the leaders should not just come from the wealthy but from "those of the middling class of life" (Bailyn, 759). Because of the proposed structure of government, Smith feared the oppression of popular rights. He wondered how to guard against the rich and powerful's encroachment on personal rights. That reasoning led Smith to move to demand a bill of rights. Since, he said on June 20, 1788, there was no way to make a perfect government, a set of specific laws protecting rights could suffice to ward off the evils of this Constitution. On June 25, 1788, he called for amendments to create a bill of rights for the Constitution. By the end of the convention, in order to protect the people from large government and oppressive leaders, this Antifederalist had decided to vote in favor of ratification if the Federalists promised him reforms in the form of a bill of rights (Storing, 148–176).

Despite his desertion of his allies, in his writings Smith left a major legacy of the ideas behind the Antifederalist cause. Most important of his works remains the *Letters from the Federal Farmer*. Many scholars now believe that Smith had a role in drafting that work. Saul Cornell claims that "Smith now seems the most likely author of these essays" (89). Cornell believes that the Federal farmer's "discussion of liberty and rights was among the most lucid of any Antifederalist author" (89). The essays do bear the mark of many of the discussions Smith had with other middle-class Antifederalists, including Governor George Clinton. In *Letters*, other writings, and speeches, Smith described how state constitutions best supported individual liberties. He supported state police power and upheld the centrality of state legislatures in government. Smith also wrote about the importance of jury trials. The militia, said that Revolutionary War veteran, should not be a professional federal army but made up of every citizen of a state. *Federal Farmer* spoke for the middle range of wealth and power and worried about the poor and the power of an aristocracy, which was consistent with many of Smith's positions.

It is thought that Smith also assisted in writing the proconvention newspaper series called "Brutus," in which many of New York's and Virginia's Antifederalist views were outlined. James Madision believed Smith to have been an ally of Richard Henry Lee (q.v.), and that the Virginian discussed "Brutus" with Smith. As "Plebian," another commentator in the New York press, Smith added the important *An Address to the People of New York State.* "Plebian" demanded the right of trial by jury of one's peers. "Plebian" also insisted that the Constitution be amended before adoption. That his strategy failed in no way mitigates Smith's contributions to the necessity to protect the freedoms of ordinary, hardworking, moderately successful people.

Though Clinton turned on this articulate capitulator, after ratifcation Smith continued to agitate for Constitutional reform. In 1789 Smith sponsored the call for a second state Constitutional Convention to call on the new federal Congress to amend the constitution. In 1791, in the New York state legislature, Smith again became a Clinton ally. He assisted in the successful Clinton campaign to regain the governorship in 1792. Smith died July 29, 1798, in New York City during a yellow fever epidemic. If he was the author of the *Federal Farmer*, then he left a legacy, in Cornell's words, of siding "with the right of the community to regulate the behavior of individuals," not with the federal government (94).

REFERENCES

Bailyn, *Debate*, vol. 2; Robin Brooks, "Melancton Smith" (PhD diss., University of Rochester, 1964); Saul Cornell, *The Other Founders* (Chapel Hill: University of North Carolina Press, 1999); Frank Hasbrouck (ed.), *History of Dutchess County, New York* (Salem, Mass.: Higginson Book Co., 2000); Clarence E. Miner, *The Ratification of the Federal Constitution by the State of New York* (New York: AMS Press, 1968); Eugene Wilder Spaulding, *New York in the Critical Period* (New York: Columbia University Press, 1932); Storing, *Complete*, vol. 6; Robert H. Webking, "Melancton Smith and the Letters from the Federal Farmer," *William and Mary Quarterly* 44, no. 3 (July 1987): 510–528; Alfred Young, *Democratic Republicans of New York* (Chapel Hill: University of North Carolina Press, 1967).
There are Smith papers at the New York Historical Society, the New York Public Library, and the Library of Congress.

MERIWETHER SMITH *(?, 1730–January 25, 1790, or January 24, 1794)* was born at Bathurst, Essex County, Virginia. He was the son of Colonel Francis and Lucy (Meriwether) Smith. They had merged with the marriage two wealthy and prominent political Virginia planter families. His father was a member of the House of Burgesses. Smith received the education of a planter's son at home. In 1760 he married Alice Lee of Maryland, and in 1769 he married Elizabeth Daingerfield. Smith was a successful planter.

In 1766 this planter leader signed the Westmoreland Association memorandum in opposition to the Stamp Act. In 1769 he supported the boycott of British goods. In 1774 Smith joined the Essex County committee in support of separation from Great Britain. Smith became a member of the House of Delegates in 1775, having previously served in the colonial legislature. In the conventions of 1775 and 1776, he was on the committees to prepare the

Virginia Declaration of Rights. He drafted the section on independence. As a member of the Virginia House of Delegates in 1776, 1778, 1781, and 1782, and from 1785 to 1788, Smith rapidly became a leader. He served on the prestigious Council of State, especially in the crucial years 1782 to 1785. An expert on state finances, Smith also served in the Continental Congress from 1778 to 1780, and in 1781. This man of many eccentricities was an ardent Francophile. He had become an enemy of the South Carolinian ultranationalist Henry Laurens, and he supported the rights of states in the new government.

Despite his squabbles with many later political allies, including Richard Henry Lee (q.v.), Smith stood with the Antifederalist forces of the state in the ratifying convention. In the House of Delegates, he opposed giving Congress control over state commerce, and he continued his opposition in the state convention. In 1786 Smith had spoken out against Virginians attending the Annapolis convention. Chosen as a delegate, he declined to attend. James Madison regarded Smith as an enemy on matters of state cooperation and trade, and he was correct in this assessment. As a friend of Patrick Henry (q.v.), Smith joined him at the state ratifying convention in 1788 in opposition to the Constitution's method of paying foreign debts. Both men feared that a strong central government threatened Virginia's financial and trade interests. Smith voted against adoption of the Constitution.

After losing the struggle over ratification, Smith retired to his home in Essex County. There he died in either January 25, 1790, or January 24, 1794—the record is conflicting.

REFERENCES

Hugh Blair Grigsby, *The History of the Virginia Federal Convention of 1788* (New York: Da Capo Press, 1969); Jensen and Kaminski, *Documentary History*, vol. 8; Norman K. Risjord, *Chesapeake Politics* (New York: Columbia University Press, 1978); Robert A. Rutland, *Birth of the Bill of Rights* (Chapel Hill: University of North Carolina Press, 1955).
Some Smith letters are in the Library of Congress.

O'BRIEN SMITH *(?, 1756–April 27, 1811)* was born in Ireland. He inherited land in South Carolina from his uncle, James Parson, and came to the Ninety-six District after the Revolution, probably in the 1780s. Eventually Smith grew wealthy, owning over 9,000 acres and 170 slaves. He resided at the plantation Duharu near St. Bartholomew Parish. In 1785 he married a Miss Webb, and in 1786 Martha Shriving.

Due to his great landownership, Smith became a member of the exclusive South Carolina Society. He also belonged to the Charleston Library and Hibernian societies, and served as a director of the Bank of Charleston from 1805 until 1811. He entered political life around the time of the state ratification convention for the federal Constitution. Unlike many of his well-to-do friends in Carolina society, Smith became an Antifederalist. Elected a delegate to the ratification convention, Smith spoke out against the federal document. He desired to show his dislike for what others claimed was a British-inspired Constitution. Though too young to have participated actively in the American Revolution, Smith's connection with former patriots and their defense of personal liberties obviously swayed his opinions. He joined the minority in voting against the Constitution.

Continuing in public service, Smith served in the state legislature from 1789 until 1799. He became a state senator in 1800 and held office until he resigned in 1805. Smith gained election as a Republican in the federal Congress in 1805 and served for one term. He returned to the South Carolina House from 1808 until 1811. Smith died in Charleston, South Carolina, on April 27, 1811. He is buried at his plantation in St. Bartholomew Parish, Colleton County.

REFERENCES

N. Louise Bailey and Elizabeth Ivey Cooper (eds.), *Biographical Dictionary of the South Carolina House of Representatives* (Columbia: University of South Carolina Press, 1981), vol. 2; George C. Rogers, *Evolution of a Federalist: William L. Smith of South Carolina* (Columbia: University of South Carolina Press, 1962); Alexander S. Salley (ed.), *Journal of the Convention of South Carolina which Ratified the Constitution of the United States, 1788* (Atlanta: Foote and Davis, Co., 1928); David J. Siemers, *Ratifying the Republic* (Stanford: Stanford University Press, 2002).

SAMUEL SPENCER *(January 21, 1734–March 20, 1793)* was

born in East Haddam, Connecticut, to Samuel and Jerusha (Brainerd) Spencer. The family was prominent in New England Presbyterian circles, and Spencer graduated with the class of 1759 from the College of New Jersey (Princeton). He studied law and moved to North Carolina, settling in the early 1760s in Anson County. Spencer became a successful lawyer and landowner, and entered the colonial North Carolina General Assembly in 1766. That same year, he also served as clerk of court for Anson County, as his fellow citizens thought highly of his talents and Princeton education. Smith served in the provincial congress of 1774 and in the first North Carolina state legislature.

From 1768 to 1776, Spencer held rank as colonel in the Anson County militia. He fought against the Regulators at the battle of Alamance in 1771. At first he seemed hesitant to separate from Great Britain, due to his English ancestry. Soon Spencer joined those who supported revolution. He helped to write the first North Carolina State Constitution in 1776. During the American Revolution, he served as a colonel in the North Carolina militia. Spencer also was a judge in the state court system in 1777 and served on the state superior court from 1777 until 1793. He owned eighteen slaves and some 2,000 acres of land, elevating him to membership in the landed planter class. In 1776 he married Phillipa (some called her Sylbil) Pegues, from a prominent South Carolina family. They had four children.

In 1784 Princeton gave Spencer an honorary degree, which meant that he had received some notoriety in judicial circles. As one of the first three members of the superior court, Spencer often struggled with the state legislature over legislative prerogatives. As a judge Spencer became sensitive in his defense of personal rights and trial by jury. Along with Samuel Ashe (q.v.) and others, Spencer, representing Anson County, became a leader of the Antifederalists in the Hillsborough state ratifying convention of 1788. At that first North Carolina convention, he led those from his part of the state who rejected the federal Constitution. Spencer spoke often, most tellingly against the powers of the aristocracy over ordinary people. He voted against ratification at the first state convention.

Spencer served as president of the second North Carolina convention in 1789. He was appointed to the committee to prepare amendments to the Constitution. Spencer especially disliked the absence of a bill of rights, and opposed any attempt to establish a religious test for office holding. That led him to a spirited defense of individual religious conscience, as he resisted thought of the government's establishment of any religious denomination (Elliot, 200). He voted against ratification in the second convention, stating that by remaining out of the Union, North Carolina would put pressure on the national Congress to write into law a needed bill of rights.

In both conventions Spencer often debated his major opponent, the Federalist James Iredell. His views in those debates are worth a closer reading. In debate on July 25, 1788, Spencer spoke eloquently of his fears of the United States Senate's powers. He exclaimed that the Senate as designed appeared detached from the people. That the state legislatures selected senators did not protect the people from the excessive powers of that body, said Spencer. On July 28, 1788, Spencer claimed that the Senate had the authority to control the president, and that the idea of separation of powers seemed unable to protect the prerogatives of the various branches of government. He feared that the Senate's powers to make treaties meant it "swallows up all other powers, and renders that body a despotic aristocracy" (Bailyn, 881). Joining the argument of his ally, Judge Samuel Ashe, Spencer also spoke to the right to trial by jury. Spencer made a comparison with England, as he insisted that his major grievance with that country had been that Americans had to go to England for trial. He wanted local trials for local issues and wondered whether the new federal government wanted to abolish local legal rights (Bailyn, 890). In his concluding arguments, Spencer laid out his own code of government activities. He insisted that the people actually possessed all power, and that "those who administer the government are their servants" (Elliot, 200).

Louise Trenholme wrote that Spencer desired to control the excessive powers of the federal government, especially in regard to personal legal rights. Of

Spencer's role in the state conventions Trenholme said: "With a sincere interest in the welfare of the union, he wanted a federal government to be established, provided the rights of the states and of the people were safeguarded" (169). A lawyer accustomed to public debate, Spencer brought to the state conventions both learning and dignity.

In 1789 Spencer joined a number of other prominent former Antifederalists in becoming a trustee of the fledgling University of North Carolina. He later joined the Methodist Church. Spencer continued on the courts, doing his duty to his adopted state until the end of his life. He died at his plantation house in Anson County, North Carolina, on March 20, 1793.

REFERENCES

Bailyn, *Debate*, vol. 2; Lucy Abigail Brainerd, *Genealogy of the Brainerd-Brainard Family in America* (Hartford, Conn.: Lockwood and Brainard, Co., 1908), vol. 1; Elliot, *Debates*, vol. 4; James McLachlan (ed.), *Princetonians, 1748–1768: A Biographical Dictionary* (Princeton: Princeton University Press, 1976); Mary Louise Medley, *History of Anson County, 1750–1796* (Wadesboro, N.C.: Anson County Historical Society, 1976); William S. Powell, *Dictionary of North Carolina Biography* (Chapel Hill: University of North Carolina Press, 1979), vol. 4; Louise Irby Trenholme, *The Ratification of the Federal Constitution in North Carolina* (New York: Columbia University Press, 1932).

JOSEPH STANTON, JR. *(July 19, 1739–?, 1807)* was born in Charlestown, Rhode Island. His father, Colonel Joseph Stanton, was an officer in the French and Indian War, and his mother, Mary (Champlin), was from a wealthy Newport commercial family. Stanton trained in the law. He also had large landholdings and owned as many as forty slaves. Stanton had years of political service in his native colony and state. He served in the General Assemby from 1768 until 1775 and again from 1793 until 1801. Stanton went with his father on the military expedition of 1759 against Canada. During the American Revolution, he served as a colonel in the Revolutionary Army. He commanded Rhode Island troops and rose to the rank of general in the state militia. Stanton had also served on the radical Committee of Public Safety, that led Rhode Island to revolution. He was connected by marriage to the political leader and later Antifederalist Thomas Joslyn (q.v.).

A postwar leader of the Paper Money forces, Stanton rose to become a major figure in the Antifederalist cause. He assisted in forming the state's Antifederalist coalition. Stanton spoke out of his worries about the taxing measures in the Constitution, out of fear that the power to tax allowed the federal government to grow too powerful. He also opposed the poll tax because such a tax would deprive the ordinary people of their right to vote. Mysteriously, for a man who owned slaves, Stanton argued that the Constitution, by extending the life of importation of slaves to the country, encouraged the continuation of the slave trade. Perhaps sensing the end of slavery in the north, he wanted to sell his slaves and worried that the continued slave trade hurt his chances. At the convention Stanton moved to adjourn without voting on the Constitution. When his measure failed, he voted against ratification.

Former opponents of the Constitution often rose in post-convention Rhode Island politics—the state being a bastion of Antifederalist sentiment—and Stanton was no exception. The state legislature elected him to the United States Senate in 1790 as a Republican, and he served there until 1793. The Federalists hated him because of his support for reforms in the new federal government. He became a leader of the so-called Country Coalition in Congress. After service in the Senate, Stanton returned to state politics and held office in the state house from 1794 until 1800. A Jeffersonian Republican leader, he returned to national politics as a member of the House of Representatives in 1801, serving until 1807. Stanton strongly supported the policies of President Thomas Jefferson. He died in Charlestown, Rhode Island, in 1807. Stanton died poor, having lost money with the end of slavery.

REFERENCES

Biographical Cyclopedia of Representative Men of Rhode Island (Providence: National Biography Publishing, 1881); David S. Lovejoy, *Rhode Island Politics and the American Revolution* (Providence: Brown University Press, 1958); Irwin H. Polishook, *Rhode Island and the Union* (Evanston, Ill.: Northwestern University Press, 1969); *Representative Men and Old Families of Rhode Island* (Chicago: J. H. Beers and Co., 1908), vol. 2; William R. Staples, *Rhode Island Politics in the Continental Congress, 1765–1790* (New York: Da Capo Press, 1971).

WILLIAM FRANCIS STRUDWICK *(May 12, 1770–July 31, 1810)* was born at the plantation Stag's Park in New Hanover County, North Carolina. He was the son of Samuel and Martha (Williams) Strudwick. William's father had been born in England, then given a grant of land of nearly 40,000 acres near Wilmington, North Carolina, in 1764. Samuel became a member of the colonial governor's council, secretary of the province, and later clerk of the pleas court. He was pro-English in the American Revolution. Apparently, William had little education, instead settling into the life of a successful Cape Fear River planter. In 1793 he married Martha Sheppard, daughter of a wealthy planter. They had five children. Strudwick eventually owned more than 4,000 acres of land.

The younger Strudwick, perhaps due to his father's importance, early in life became a leader in his region of North Carolina. He supported the American Revolution. In 1789 Strudwick served as a delegate to the state ratification convention and voted against the Constitution. Strudwick also was a member of the North Carolina convention of 1790, where he again voted against ratification. He served in the state senate from 1792 until 1797. Strudwick replaced Absalom Tatom (q.v.) in the United States House in 1797 and served until 1799. By this time he had become a Federalist. Strudwick served again in the state house from 1801 until 1803. In 1804 he was executor of deeds in his county. He died on July 31, 1810 at Stag Park.

REFERENCES

John H. Hill, *Reminiscences of Some Old Cape Fear Families* (Goldsboro, N.C.: self-published, 1893); Hugh T. Lefler and Paul Wager (eds.), *Orange County, 1752–1952* (Chapel Hill: University of North Carolina Press, 1953); David J. Siemers, *Ratifying the Republic* (Stanford: Stanford University Press, 2002); Betsy L. Willis and James W. Strudwick (comps.), *Genealogy and Letters of Strudwick, Ashe, Young, and Allied Families* (Alexandria, Va: self-published, 1971).
There are Strudwick estate papers at the North Carolina State Archives, in Raleigh, North Carolina.

THOMAS SUMTER *(August 14, 1734–June 1, 1832)* was born near Charlottesville, in Hanover County, Virginia. His father, William Sumter, was a native of Wales who emigrated to Virginia to run a small mill. His mother, named Patience, was a midwife. The younger Sumter had only the rudiments of a local school education. The adventurous young man fought in General Edward Braddock's western campaign against the Indians and the French in 1755. He was later arrested for debts but managed to escape imprisonment. Sumter moved to Eutaw Springs, South Carolina, acquired land, and for a time ran a crossroads store. In 1767 he married Mary Cantey, daughter of the wealthy Joseph Cantey, a South Carolina planter.

A patriot, Sumter soon joined the Revolutionary cause. He served in the first two South Carolina provincial congresses. In 1776 he became a captain of rangers in the Cherokee campaign in the state's western region. That same year, Sumter was elevated to the rank of lieutenant colonel in a South Carolina regiment. He joined the Continental Army, fought in Georgia and Florida, and resigned his commission in 1778. After the fall of Charleston to the British in 1780, Sumter reentered the army. Elected a general after the Tarleton raiders burned his home, he went to North Carolina to fight at Rocky Mount in 1780. Severely wounded after the battle of Blackstock's Hill, he soon recovered and began to raise troops for further defense of western Carolina. His famous Sumter's Law, a promise to give confiscated Tory lands and slaves to Revolutionary War soldiers, helped him build a patriot army. He succeeded in defeating the British in the campaigns at Fort Granby and Quinby Bridge. In 1782 Sumter, now a legend and known throughout the state as the "Gamecock," resigned from the army.

Declining election to the Continental Congress in 1783, Sumter preferred service in the state legislature. Grateful citizens bestowed large amounts of land on this war hero. This entrepreneurial leader became a canal builder and a land speculator. Living the life of a landed gentleman, Sumter bred great race horses. In 1786 he led in setting the site for the capital of South Carolina at Columbia in the Piedmont. He had dreams of new water routes to the west, transportation routes that would help in the state's development. In addition to his financial successes, Sumter longed for a major role in the political life of his adopted state.

In the struggle over ratification of the Constitution, Sumter became a leader of the state's western farmers who opposed the Constitution. He took little part in the early discussions of the Constitution. Behind the scenes, however, he joined Rawlins Lowndes (q.v.) to oppose holding the state convention in Charleston, a place he considered a stronghold of Federalist conservatism. At the convention, believing the delegates were moving too rapidly toward ratification without adequate discussion and deliberation, on May 21, 1788, he moved to postpone voting until after Virginia had made its decision. His motion lost. On May 23, 1788, Sumter joined the minority in voting against ratification.

Sumter's reasons for opposing the Constitution were many and complicated, reflecting the voice of a large landholding slaveholder who also believed in the individual freedom gained from his and others' personal sacrifices in the Revolutionary War. He spoke against executive powers, because he feared the tendency toward monarchy in the absence of restrictions on terms allowed the president. In this view of executive power, Sumter joined with the radical Aedanus Burke (q.v.), an ally and major influence on his political positions. Because Sumter also defended middling western farmers ambitious for more land, and thus their need to borrow money at good rates, he wanted the states to have the right to coin and print paper money. Sumter also spoke against the clause in the Constitution that ended importation of slaves after 1808. Clearly, his plans for white freedom included the rights of the middle-class farmers to expand their slaveholdings.

After he voted against ratification of the Constitution, Sumter agreed to serve in the new government. In 1789, his last term in the state legislature, Sumter favored revising the state constitution to reflect the new federal laws. Elected to the first federal House of Representatives, he served continuously from 1789 to 1793. Loyal to his South, Sumter voted to place the federal capital on the banks of the Potomac River. A fearful Antifederalist, he resisted the Federalist scheme to assume state debts. Federalists defeated him for election in 1793, but he again was elected to the United States House in 1796. A man of Jeffersonian principles, especially of the rights of states, in 1801 the state legislature sent this famed patriot to the United States Senate. In 1810 President James Madison appointed him minister to Brazil, and he resigned from the Senate.

In 1812, nearly broke from years of sacrifice in public service, Sumter retired to private life. He died June 1, 1832, near his beloved Statesburg, South Carolina, the last surviving general of the American Revolution. Sumter was a proud leader who often fought with friend and foe alike. His contribution to his country and to South Carolina was most important.

REFERENCES

N. Louise Bailey and Elizabeth Ivey Cooper (eds.), *Biographical Dictionary of the South Carolina House of Representatives* (Columbia: University of South Carolina Press, 1981), vol. 3; Robert D. Bass, *Gamecock, Life and Campaigns of Thomas Sumter* (New York: Holt, Rinehart, and Winston, 1961); Anne Gregorie, *Thomas Sumter* (Columbia: Publications of the South Carolina Historical Association, 1902, 1907). Sumter's papers are in the Library of Congress.

WILLIAM SYMMES, JR. *(?, 1760–January 14, 1807)* was born in Andover, Massachusetts. Decended from the first minister in Charlestown, he was raised in the famous home of Anne Bradstreet, the legendary poet and writer of Puritan New England. Symmes's uncle, Thomas Symmes, was an important leader of the American Revolution. Symmes's father was Reverend William Symmes, minister of the First Church in Andover, Massachusetts, descended from a long line of Puritan clergy. His mother was Anna (Gee), whose father was a minister in Boston. Afforded an excellent education at Phillips Andover Academy, where his father was a trustee, young William graduated from Harvard College in 1780. Too young to take part in the Revolution, he nevertheless supported and imbibed the principles of revolutionary republicanism.

Beginning his career as the war ended, the young man taught at the local grammar school and studied law at night. It was said that Symmes was the first lawyer licensed in Andover. Respected at an early age for his legal acumen, the state legislature selected him to draft a revised state constitution. In 1787 the Antifederalist Andoverians made him their representative at the Massachusetts ratification convention of 1788.

In November 1787, along with Peter Osgood, he published the "Sentiment" of Andover against the Constitution. He wrote in opposition to ratification mainly because of what he perceived as loose construction in the Constitution that ignored valued individual rights. But, as he turned to discuss the ideas of a bill of rights, Symmes began to show hesitation about his Antifederalist position. On February 6, 1788, he gave an important and, alas, unwieldy speech on why he had decided to support the Constitution. Symmes well knew the political consequences of his actions, especially since he had spoken about the importance of faithfully following his constituents' will. Sarah Bailey wrote that the townsmen of Andover, the "old and tried counsellors of the community," censored Symmes for his so-called betrayal (399). Referring to the legendary home of Anne Bradstreet, Bailey stated, "there was reared the first lawyer of Andover, William Symmes, son of the minister, who left his native town because of the censure of his townsmen for his conscientious change of convictions and action in advocating the adoption of the federal constitution" (331).

The odyssey of Symmes's move from Antifederalist to cautious Constitutionalist is worth recounting. At first Symmes alledged that Massachusetts had no power under the new Constitution. He resisted support for a standing army, fearing that the Constitution's support for military power would threaten republican government. In the Massachusetts convention, he spoke against the taxing power of the proposed central government (Storing, 66). But on February 6, 1788, Symmes explained his change of heart. He had been persuaded, he said, that Massachusetts had the power to thwart the federal government's taxing powers. Above all, the Federalist delegates in the convention promised to adopt a formal bill of rights, and that allayed most of his fears. (It is quite possible that Symmes had faith in the compromises Samuel Adams [q.v.] had made.) Besides, he declared, the Federalists, once other states had begin to ratify, had the upper hand and could pass the Constitution without help from the Antifederalists (Elliot, 70–75).

No longer welcome in Andover, Symmes moved to Portland, Maine. There he rose in the legal profession and became a trusted leader of his community. In what must have been a bittersweet action, in 1799 Symmes returned to Andover to speak in favor of a memorial to General George Washington. He died a disappointed man on January 14, 1807, in Portland, four months before his famous father.

REFERENCES

Sarah Bailey, *Historical Sketches of Andover, Massachusetts* (Boston: Houghton Mifflin, 1880); Elliot, *Debates*, vol. 2; Nathan Hazen, *Memorial of the Discourse on William Symmes* (Boston: Historical Collection of the Essex Institute, 1862); Storing, *Complete*, vol. 4.

T

ABSALOM (TATUM) TATOM *(?, 1742–December 20, 1802)* was born in Granville County, North Carolina. He became a surveyor, contractor, and tobacco agent in the Greenville area. In 1763 Tatom was in the Greenville militia. He served in the First North Carolina Continental Regiment as a lieutenant in 1775, a captain in 1776, and a major in 1777. Tatom resigned from active duty to become assistant quartermaster, and he ran the arsenal in Hillsborough, North Carolina, in 1778. In 1779 he served as clerk of Randolph County. That same year he became major of the North Carolina Light Horse cavalry. After being elected to the North Carolina State House in 1779, Tory unrest deprived Tatom of his seat. In August 1781, Tories captured him. Soon released, before the war's end, he became debt collector in Hillsborough. Tatom also became a member of the Masons.

In 1782 Tatom joined the committee to survey the western territory (later Tennessee). He next became private secretary to Governor Thomas Burke. Burke appointed Tatom surveyor of North Carolina in 1785. As surveyor he rose in political power and became a successful landowner in western North Carolina. A delegate to the state's first ratifying convention, Tatom represented Hillsborough, Orange County. He voted against ratification of the Constitution in 1788.

Elected as a Republican to the federal House of Representatives in 1795, Tatom resigned from that office in 1796, preferring state government service. Still, in his short time in national politics, Tatom made a reputation as an opponent of Federalist western land policies. He served in the North Carolina House of Representatives from 1797 until 1802. Tatom died in Raleigh, North Carolina, on December 20, 1802.

REFERENCES

John L. Cheney, Jr. (ed.), *North Carolina Government, 1585–1979* (Raleigh, N.C.: Dept. of Secretary of State, 1981); David J. Siemers, *Ratifying the Republic* (Stanford: Stanford University Press, 2002); Frederick G. Speidel, *North Carolina Masons in the American Revolution* (Oxford, N.C.: Press of Oxford Orphanage, 1975); Louise Irby

Trenholme, *The Ratification of the Federal Constitution in North Carolina* (New York: Columbia University Press, 1932).

JOHN TAYLOR *(c. 1734–April 27, 1794)* was probably born in the town of Townsend, Worcester County, Massachusetts. He later moved to nearby Douglass and then to Lunenburgh to practice medicine. But he seemed more interested in politics than in medicine. Taylor served as a selectman in Lunenburgh from 1771 until 1774. He then held office in the colonial house from 1772 until 1774. In 1774 Taylor represented Lunenburgh as a delegate to the second and third provisional legislature. From 1775 until 1778, he was a member of the state council to separate the Maine territory from Massachusetts. In 1774 he had bought land in Maine's Union County, with the intention of moving there. He did not, as his attempt at land speculation failed. For a time during the Revolution, he lived in Pomfret, Connecticut, but returned to Douglass, Massachusetts, by 1780. In 1784 he was imprisoned for debt.

Elected to the state legislature in 1787, Taylor supported the state's printing paper money to relieve farmer indebtedness. He became a delegate to the state ratifying convention from Worcester County in 1788. Considered a leading Antifederalist, Taylor spoke often at the convention and made a major speech on federal elections. Taylor believed that annual elections best safeguarded the people's liberties. He also wanted the right to recall elected officials. The membership numbers of the federal house were too small, he said, thus leaving many people unrepresented. Taylor, like many from Massachusetts, feared that the six-year term for the United States Senate meant office for life. Taylor also spoke on the amending process, as he worried over the Federalist demand to vote the Constitution up or down. Steven Boyd, a perceptive student of the ratification struggle, regards Taylor as a moderate who asked his fellow Antifederalists to accept the will of the majority and go along with the Constitution. Nevertheless, he voted against ratification, declaring he "had uniformly opposed the Constitution" (Jensen and Kaminski, vol. 7, 281).

Though he then said that he wanted "harmony and love among the people," after the vote Taylor traveled around the state drumming up support to elect Antifederalists to the new state legislature. He also plotted to get Elbridge Gerry (q.v.) elected governor in 1788. He served in the state house in 1788. Brilliant at debate but poor at finances, Taylor often sued and was sued for debts. Little else is known about this active Antifederalist's later life, save that he died of an overdose of laudanum in debtors' prison in Dudley, Worcester County, on April 27, 1794.

REFERENCES

Steven R. Boyd, *The Politics of Opposition* (Millwood, N.Y.: KTO Press, 1979); Elliot, *Debates*, vol. 2; Samuel B. Harding, *The Contest over the Ratification of the Federal*

Constitution in the State of Massachusetts (Cambridge: Harvard University Press, 1896); Duane Hamilton Hurd, *History of Worcester County, Massachusetts,* 2 vols. (Philadelphia: J.W. Lewis and Co., 1889); Jensen and Kaminski, *Documentary History,* vols. 7 and 9.

JOSEPH TAYLOR *(February 19, 1742–June 1815)* was born in Virginia. His father, John Taylor, and his mother, Catherine Pendleton, were from prominent Virginia families. Sometime before the American Revolution, the younger Taylor moved to Granville County, North Carolina. He became a lawyer, deemed honest if mediocre in his talents. Taylor largely devoted himself to planting, and he soon owned over 3,000 acres of fine tobacco land. He married Frances Anderson. During the Revolution, Taylor commanded as a colonel the Granville County Minutemen, and he also became a colonel in the state militia.

After the Revolution, Taylor became prominent in local politics, serving in the state senate in 1781. He was an Antifederalist delegate in 1788 to the first North Carolina ratifying convention for the Constitution. Taylor gave an important speech at the convention on July 30, 1788, in which he argued that Federalists wanted to impose a flawed Constitution on the people of North Carolina. Taylor saw danger in that part of the Constitution that allowed Congress to set the date and place for elections. He insisted that the states should control the time and place for all elections. Taylor also worried about the consolidation of the states, believing that individual states lost their identity, rights, and interests under the proposed Constitution. He claimed that the people of New England, so different than those of the south, "cannot with safety legislate for us." Most important to his opposition was his view that "a consolidated government can by no means suit the genuis of the people" (Elliot, 24). Taylor voted aginst ratification at the first state convention.

After the state finally ratified the Constitution and joined the union in 1790, Taylor became even more active in politics. He ran as a Republican for governor in 1800 but lost. He served in the state senate again in 1803. Taylor served as a presidential elector for Thomas Jefferson in 1800 and 1804, and for James Madison in 1808. But mainly, he retired from public life after 1803 to tend to his investments. Taylor died in June 1815.

REFERENCES

Samuel A. Ashe, *History of North Carolina* (Raleigh, N.C.: Edwards and Broughton Printing Co., 1925), vol. 2; Bailyn, *Debate,* vol. 2; Elliot, *Debates,* vol. 4; Louise Irby Trenholme, *The Ratification of the Federal Constitution in North Carolina* (New York: Columbia University Press, 1932).

SAMUEL THOMPSON *(March 22, 1735–?, 1797)* was probably born in the town of Topsham, in Lincoln County, Maine Territory of Massachusetts. He lived in Brunswick, Maine, at least until after the American Revolution. He was a lifelong member of the Universalist Church. Self-made, considered obstinate, Thompson rose rapidly in local politics. He was a selectman in Brunswick in 1768, 1770, and 1771. Voters in the territory elected him to the colonial Massachusetts legislature. In 1774 he became a lieutenant colonel of militia, and in 1776 he was promoted to brigadier general of the Cumberland County troops. He also headed the Committee of Safety for the district of Maine. In 1776 Thompson gained election to the state of Massachusetts General Court.

This well-to-do farmer and businessman rose in postwar state politics. Probably around 1783, he moved to Topsham and soon represented that district in the General Court. Thompson held office from 1784 to 1788. He figured prominently in debates over local issues concerning Maine in the legislature. Elected to the state senate in 1788, Thompson became an ally of William Widgery (q.v.) in the secessionist, or Maine statehood, movement.

Elected to the Massachusetts state ratifying convention from Maine in 1788, Thompson spoke often and effectively against the Constitution. He opposed biannual elections of federal congressmen on the grounds that the people had too little choice in who would serve them in public life. Elliot quotes him as saying: "Let these members know their dependence upon the people, and I say it will be a check on them" (16). Thompson also spoke against the danger of a standing army to the people's right of free speech. Everywhere he looked he saw conspiracy against and even threats of violence to free speech. He also opposed the Constitution on the rights of habeas corpus. But where Thompson made his most important mark was in the issue over slavery. As Samuel Harding pointed out, Thompson insisted that if the states would not give up slavery, he could not align with them. He even attacked General George Washington for owning slaves (71). Boisterous and gifted with the use of pungent speech, Thompson often apologized to his fellow delegates for his rough comments. In January 1788, Thompson moved to adjourn the state ratification convention without taking a vote, so that the delegates could wait to see what other states would do. When he lost that motion, the radical from Maine spoke out even more against the Constitution. He called for a bill of rights, annual elections, and attacked what he called excessive powers of Congress. Thompson voted against ratification.

Unlike many of his Antifederalist colleagues, even after ratification Thompson continued to argue against the Constitution. Some former friends suggested he spoke treason, but Thompson persevered. He called on the townspeople to speak out and demand their right to vote on the Constitution. Of course, he failed to arouse a Maine population now reconciled to the Constitution. He returned to state politics, and served in the General Court again from 1790 until 1794, and again in 1797. In 1797 he gained election to the state senate. There Thompson again called for Maine statehood. A man of wealth, he owned land assessed at $35,000. But Thompson also experienced a tragedy in his life. During his later years his wife went insane. He died in 1797 in Topsham, in the Maine Territory. George A. Wheeler, no friend to the Antifederalists, provided a fitting epitaph to this man of will: "At all events, the strength of his patriotism ought to overshadow many minor defects of character" (816).

REFERENCES

Elliot, *Debates*, vol. 2; William Goold, *Portland in the Past* (Portland: B. Thurston and Co., 1886); Van Beck Hall, *Politics Without Parties: Massachusetts, 1780–1791* (Pittsburgh: University of Pittsburgh Press, 1972); Samuel B. Harding, *The Contest over the Ratification of the Federal Constitution in the State of Massachusetts* (Cambridge: Harvard University Press, 1896); George A. Wheeler, *History of Brunswick, Topsham, Harpswell* (Boston: A. Mudge and Sons, 1878).

CHARLES TILLINGHAST *(c. 1748–1795),* born in New York City, was a distiller and merchant in the city. Also active in New York City social and political circles, Tillinghast made a fortunate marriage to the daughter of business and political leader John Lamb (q.v.). A patriot, Tillinghast joined the Sons of Liberty and became a Revolutionary War leader. As deputy quartermaster general of the Continental Army, he grew close to the radical Hugh Hughes (q.v.). Tillinghast also helped in the evacuation of Long Island in 1776.

Active in politics after the war, Tillinghast became an Antifederalist in the struggle over ratification of the federal Constitution in New York State. He was secretary of the Albany meeting that plotted against the Constitution. Although not a member of the state ratifying convention, Tillinghast became useful to the Antifederalist cause. In a letter to Hugh Hughes, Tillinghast said he had become so involved in writing about politics that he had no time for personal matters. Tillinghast helped his father-in-law distribute Antifederalist writings throughout the state. It was he who sent copies of "Centinel" to many New York Antifederalist leaders. Tillinghast aligned himself with the editor of the *New York Journal* and other papers, and this enabled the Antifederalist viewpoint to get printed in newspapers. He corresponded with many out-of-state Antifederalists, and shared their ideas with his radical Albany friends. Along with Hughes and Melancton Smith (q.v.), Tillinghast linked New York City's radicals with those in Albany.

In October 1788, Tillinghast became secretary of the New York Federal Republican Society. He joined members of that radical group in demanding a second state ratifying convention. He lost this bid, but the Antifederalist forces continued to agitate in the state under the auspices of the Federal Republicans. Tillinghast rose in local politics to become collector of the New York customs house. That was a post from which he could have launched even further his bid to lead the state's Antifederalists. But Tillinghast perished in the yellow fever epidemic of 1795 that swept through New York City.

REFERENCES

Bailyn, *Debate*, vol. 1; Steven R. Boyd, *The Politics of Opposition* (Millwood, N.Y.: KTO Press, 1979); Linda Grant DePauw, *The Eleventh Pillar* (Ithaca, N.Y.: Cornell University Press, 1966); Robert A. Rutland, *Ordeal of the Constitution* (Norman: University of Oklahoma Press, 1965); Eugene Wilder Spaulding, *New York in the Critical Period* (New York: Columbia University Press, 1932); Storing, *Complete*, vol. 2; Alfred Young, *Democratic Republicans of New York* (Chapel Hill: University of North Carolina Press, 1967).

JAMES TILTON *(June 1, 1745/46–May 14, 1822)* was born in Kent County, Delaware. His mother, a widow, sent him to Nottingham Academy in Maryland. Tilton then studied in Chester County, Pennsylvania, with Samuel Finley, later president of Dickinson College. He next apprenticed in medicine with Dr. Charles Ridgely (q.v.) in Dover, Delaware. A gifted and talented student, Tilton then went to the College of Philadelphia, where he received a bachelor of medicine in 1768 and an M.D. in 1771. He practiced medicine in Dover, Delaware.

A patriot, Tilton became a lieutenant of infantry in the Delaware line. He also served as a regimental surgeon. From 1777 until 1780, Tilton ran wartime hospitals in New Jersey and Maryland. In 1780 he was senior hospital physician and surgeon in Williamsburg, Virginia, and tended to the soldiers there. The editor of the *Historical and Biographical Encyclopedia of Delaware* said of Tilton's wartime career that "he was of inestimable service in correcting abuses and initiating reforms" (263). In 1781 Tilton became professor of medicine at the University of Pennsylvania, while remaining in the army. In 1782 he served on a medical committee of the Continental Congress and wrote a scathing report on conditions in military hospitals.

That report became his entree into political life, and in 1782 the legislature of Delaware elected him to the Continental Congress. He served there from 1783 until 1785. In that national body, he emerged as a strong defender of the rights of small states. For a short time, he also served as state treasurer. From 1785 until 1801, Tilton lived in Wilmington and held an important post as government commissioner of loans for Delaware. He had moved from Kent County to Wilmington because of ill health.

Tilton joined the few Antifederalists in Delaware. He wrote a bitter attack on the state's most powerful Federalist leader, George Read. Calling himself "Timoleum," Tilton claimed Read was a tyrant who had ties to ex-Tories. Perhaps because Read had removed Tilton as state treasurer, the famous physician attacked him. Tilton also accused Read of dealing in illegal debts. But the main thrust of his anti-Constitutionalist tirade against Read was in defense of Whig theory, the freedom of Presbyterians to practice their faith, and Irish immigrants whom he thought had become victims of the Federalists. Most later commentators have said that Tilton was one of the state's few outspoken Antifederalists. But the doctor knew himself that it was impossible to delay the state's ratification of the Constitution.

After the Constitutional crisis, Tilton became president of the Delaware Society of Cincinnati, a Federalist organization. He also continued as commissioner of loans until 1801. He belonged to the Delaware Society for Promoting the Abolition of Slavery. Tilton soon quit the practice of medicine to become a farmer. In 1812 President James Madison named him surgeon general of the United States. In that capacity, he journeyed to the northwestern frontier. In 1813 he published *Economic Observations on Military Hospitals*; and in 1814, *Regulations for the Medical Department*, an important medical manual. But in 1814 Tilton had an accident that cost him the loss of feeling in one leg, and in 1815 he had the leg amputated to the thigh. He died in Wilmington on May 14, 1822.

Tilton was an eccentric and a loner. He never married. He devoted himself to medical and political reforms. The editor of the *Historical and Biographical Encyclopedia of Delaware* said: "As a physician, a patriot, and a man, he was most eminent, and his whole life afforded an example of the effect of sound principles and moral rectitude, in both public and private life" (263). His "Timoleum" letter stands as the clearest statement of what little Antifederalism surfaced in Delaware in the Constitutional ratification debates there.

REFERENCES

Wilson L. Bevan (ed.), *History of Delaware Past and Present* (New York: Lewis Historical Publishing Co., 1929); Henry C. Conrad, *History of the State of Delaware*, 3 vols. (Wilmington: self-published, 1905); *Historical and Biographical Encyclopedia of Delaware* (Wilmington: Aldine Publishing and Engraving Co., 1882); John A. Munroe, *Federalist Delaware* (New Brunswick, N.J.: Rutgers University Press, 1954); William Thompson Read, *Life and Correspondence of George Read* (Philadelphia: J. B. Lippincott and Co., 1870); Francis T. Tilton, *History of the Tilton Family in America* (Clifton, N.J.: F. T. Tilton, 1979).

JOHN TIPTON *(August 15, 1730–August 1813)* was born in Baltimore County, Maryland, to Jonathan and Elizabeth Tipton. The younger Tipton was a lifelong Episcopalian. He was the brother of the powerful North Carolina political leader Joseph Tipton. Tipton moved from Maryland in 1750 to Frederick County, Virginia, to the Cedar Creek area. He later founded the town of Woodstock, Dunmore County, and became its sheriff. In the 1750s, he married Mary Butler and in 1779, Martha Moore. Altogether he had nine children. His son John would become a United States Senator from Indiana. Tipton served as vestryman of the Episcopal church and as justice of the peace in Beckford Parish. A staunch revolutionary, he fought against Lord Dunmore at the battle of Point Pleasant in 1774. Local constituents elected him to represent their revolutionary views on the Virginia Committee of Safety. From

1774 until 1781, Tipton served in the Virginia House of Delegates. He was also a member of the Virginia Constitutional Convention of 1776. During the war, Tipton served as colonel of revolutionary militia and as high sheriff of Shenandoah County. A wartime recruiting officer, he also saw much military action.

In 1783 this planter moved to fertile land in the Watauga settlement of North Carolina, following his successful older brother, Josseph. In 1785 Tipton gained election to the North Carolina Assembly from Washington County. He became an opponent of the powerful John Sevier and actually battled with him in 1788 near Jonesboro in what is now Tennessee. Tipton disagreed with Sevier over whether Tennessee settlers should remain as part of North Carolina. Tipton wanted to keep North Carolina connected to the fledgling settlements of eastern Tennessee. Tipton served in the North Carolina State Senate from 1786 until 1788.

A state's rights advocate, Tipton took an active part as an Antifederalist in the North Carolina ratifying convention at Hillsborough in 1788. Although he did not speak much, Tipton assumed leadership of the Tennessee territory Antifederalists. Again he opposed the Federalist Sevier. Tipton's political allegiances and localist beliefs came from his old connection to lower Virginia and to the rights of individual self-determination. He spoke against the Constitution's proposed effect on local government, maintaining that the Tennesseans wanted their own strong government to support their drive for a new state. Now a proponent of Tennessee statehood, Tipton voted against ratification of the Constitution in the first North Carolina convention.

When Tennessee was still a territory, Tipton became a large landowner there, possessing nearly 2,500 acres, which perhaps explains why he came around to support statehood. As a delegate to the territorial legislature from Washington County, he helped to draft the state constitution of Tennessee in 1796. Tipton served in the first Tennessee territorial assembly in 1793 and in the first state legislature in 1796. He also was in the state senate in 1796. He later retired to his farm. Tipton believed in the advancement of education, and he served as a trustee of the fledgling Washington College in east Tennessee from 1795 until 1813. He died at his home at Sinking Creek, near Johnson City, Tennessee, in August 1813. Ever the quester, ever the mover, this defender of local rights had at last settled in a place he could call his home. Grateful Tennesseans later named a county in his honor.

REFERENCES

Samuel A. Ashe, *History of North Carolina* (Raleigh, N.C.: Edwards and Broughton Printing Co., 1925), vol. 2; Charles B. Heinemann, *Tipton Family Records* (Washington, D.C.: C.B. Heinemann, 1950); Robert McBride and Dan M. Robison, *Biographical Dictionary of the Tennessee General Assembly* (Nashville: Tennessee State Library and Archives, 1975), vol. 1; Seldon Nelson, "The Tipton Family of Tennessee," *East Tennessee Historical Society Publications* (1929); Norman K. Risjord, *Chesapeake Politics* (New York: Columbia University Press, 1979).

THOMAS TREDWELL *(February 6, 1743–December 30, 1831)*

was born in Smithtown, New York. He had a decent preparatory education and graduated from the College of New Jersey (Princeton), where he had studied law, in 1764. He set up his office at Plattsburgh, New York. Tredwell then entered politics. He became a delegate to the provincial congress in 1774 and 1775. Tredwell attended the state constitutional convention in 1776 and 1777. He served in the state assembly from 1777 until 1783. In state government, Tredwell became a strong supporter of the revolutionary cause.

During the post-Revolutionary period, Tredwell moved to Suffolk County and served as a judge of the court of probate from Long Island, from 1778 until 1787. He also was in the state senate from 1786 until 1789. Tredwell, a rival of Melancton Smith (q.v.) in state politics, gained nomination to the 1787 Philadelphia Constitutional Convention but refused to serve. Smith supported Tredwell's action, as both of them worried about the legitimacy of that convention.

A delegate to the state ratification convention in 1788 from Long Island, Tredwell spoke often and opposed the Constitution. He may have assisted John Lansing (q.v.) with draft amendments to the proposed Constitution. Tredwell also joined Abraham Yates (q.v.) in writing the "Brutus" papers. Certainly he wrote the sections in praise of Governor George Clinton (q.v.), as Tredwell supported the governor and praised his negative opinions on the Constitution. At the convention itself, he spoke out against limitations on a free press, and for liberty of conscience. Robert Rutland quoted him as saying: "It is evidently to be wished that these and other invaluable rights of freemen had been as cautiously secured as some of the paltry interests of some of the individual states" (177–178). Tredwell separated from Smith over ratification, and recorded his emphatic dissent on all matters concerning the Constitution. He voted against ratification.

Tredwell's arguments against the way government was to function in the Constitution require further comment. He regarded "this government (as) founded in sin, and reared up in iniquity" (Elliot, 396). He maintained he could not be silent. Tredwell insisted that government existed for the "safety, peace, and welfare of the governed" (Elliot, 399). This proposed government, for him, did not look out for the people's best interests. In an attack on "Publius" the Federalist, he saw abuses, sloppy logic, and downright chicanery in the writer's intentions. The Constitution, he believed, made bad law, and he had no faith in the Federalists' claims that they had drafted a document that favored the states. "In this Constitution," he said, "we have departed widely from the principles and political faith of '76, when the spirit of liberty ran high" (Elliot, 403). The Consitution had "violated the public faith" (Elliot,

406). The people, he insisted, had been duped out of their liberties. To protect the memory of the Revolution, this document, he declared, had to be defeated.

After the convention, Tredwell continued as a judge and in state government. Elected to the second federal Congress, he took the side of the emerging Republican faction on all issues. He served in Congress from 1791 until 1795. Tredwell opposed the embargo of 1794, believing it would hurt New York commerce. All the while, he received the support of the small farmers. He ran again for Congress in 1794, but an opposing clique defeated him. Tredwell entered the state senate in 1803 and served there unil 1807. By that time, he had moved back to Plattsburgh to continue his law practice. He served as surrogate of Clinton County from 1807 until 1831. Tredwell died in Plattsburgh, Clinton County, New York, on December 30, 1831.

REFERENCES

Linda Grant De Pauw, *The Eleventh Pillar* (Ithaca, N.Y.: Cornell University Press, 1966); Elliot, *Debates*, vol. 2; Clarence E. Miner, *The Ratification of the Federal Constitution by the State of New York* (New York: AMS Press, 1968); Robert A. Rutland, *Birth of the Bill of Rights* (Chapel Hill: University of North Carolina Press, 1955); Alfred Young, *Democratic Republicans of New York* (Chapel Hill: University of North Carolina Press, 1967).

ABRAHAM TRIGG *(1750–1809)* was born on his father's plantation, Old Liberty, in Bedford County, Virginia. His father, also Abraham, had emigrated from Cornwall, England, around 1710. He had a private education and prepared for the law. Trigg practiced law in Montgomery County, Virginia. He also lived on his estate, Buchanan's Bottom, on the New River. He entered politics as a local town clerk and judge. During the Revolution, Trigg served as a lieutenant colonel and then a general of state militia. He saw military action in the western part of the state against the Indians.

As a delegate from Montgomery County to the Virginian Constitutional ratifying convention in 1788, Trigg opposed ratification. In 1792 he challenged the moderate Federalist Francis Preston for election to federal Congress. Trigg ran as an opponent of centralized government but lost that race for office. In 1797 he managed to get elected to Congress as a Republican, and he served in that capacity until 1809. Trigg always displayed in Congress an antipathy to the Federalists. He died on his family estate in Montgomery County, Virginia, sometime in 1809.

REFERENCES

Richard Beeman, *The Old Dominion and the New Nation* (Lexington: University Press of Kentucky, 1972); Charles W. Crush (comp.), *The Montgomery County Story* (Christianburg, Va.: Montgomery Museum, 2000); Elliot, *Debates,* vol. 3; David J. Siemers, *Ratifying the Republic* (Stanford: Stanford University Press, 2002).

JOHN JOHNS TRIGG *(?, 1748–May 17/June 28, 1804)* was born at Old Liberty, Bedford County, Virginia. He was the older brother of Abraham Trigg (q.v.), and one of five sons. His father, Abraham Trigg, was an immigrant from England. He received a private school education. Trigg farmed and planted, and eventually inherited his father's plantation. During the Revolution, he raised a militia company in Bedford County. He rose to become captain and then major of an artillery company. Trigg was with General George Washington at the siege and victory at Yorktown, Virginia, in 1781.

Elected to the Virginia House of Delegates in 1784, Trigg served until 1792. Like his brother, a committed small government leader, Trigg gained election to the Virginia ratifying convention of 1788. Although hardly a leader at the convention, he did vote against ratification. He served in the Virginia House of Delegates as an Antifederalist from 1788 until 1790. Trigg was also a lieutenant colonel of militia in 1791, and he was a justice of the peace in Bedford County. As a representative in the federal Congress from 1797 until 1804, Trigg ably served the interests of western Virginia farmers. He voted consistently with the Jeffersonian Republicans. Trigg also was a planter who owned fifteen slaves. He died at the plantation Old Liberty on May 17, 1804 (or June 28, 1804).

REFERENCES

Richard Beeman, *The Old Dominion and the New Nation* (Lexington: University Press of Kentucky, 1972); Elliot, *Debates*, vol. 3; Lula Eastman Parker, *History of Bedford County, Virginia* (Bedford, Va.: Hamilton's, 1988); Norman K. Risjord, *Chesapeake Politics* (New York: Columbia University Press, 1978); David J. Siemers, *Ratifying the Republic* (Stanford: Stanford University Press, 2002).

THOMAS TUDOR TUCKER *(June 6/25, 1745–May 2, 1828)* was born at Port Royal, Bermuda. He was the brother of the famous Virginia lawyer St. George Tucker, head of a long line of brilliant political theorists. Tucker was trained in England at a number of excellent schools, studied medicine at the University of Edinburgh, and took his degree in 1770. He settled in South Carolina and began a practice in Charleston, but failed in that first venture into medicine. A scandal surrounded his practice and private life in 1773. In 1774 he married Esther Evans. He moved to St. George, Dorchester Parish, in 1778, and resumed his medical practice.

During the American Revolution, Tucker served as a surgeon in a Continental Army hospital. For his contribution to the war effort, he received grants of land in Ninety-six District, and soon owned more than 8,000 acres of land and thirty-one slaves. Tucker also served in the South Carolina state legislature in 1776. The British took him prisoner during the war, and for a time after his release, Tucker stayed in Virginia close to family. Tucker again held office in the state legislature from 1782 to 1783, and in 1785, and he won a special election in 1787. Tucker was a member of the Continental Congress in 1787 and 1788.

Chosen to the South Carolina Constitutional ratification convention from Ninety-six District, Tucker joined the Antifederalists. He had previously fought a duel with the Federalist Ralph Izard and was unpopular among those low country Carolinians who favored a strong federal government. In 1784 Tucker had written an important pamphlet in support of localism entitled *Conciliatory Hints*, under the nom de plume "Philodensus," in which he claimed that all government received its authority directly from the people. He later said that the Constitution was faulty because it was not of the people. To his brother, St. George, Tucker had written that the proposed Constitution made for an unstable government. He feared that the powers given the president looked too much like the revival of a monarchy. As to the six-year term for federal senators, Tucker insisted that state legislatures lost power by giving leaders such long terms in office. In that letter to his brother, Tucker also commented on northern desire to abolish slavery and wondered whether ratification of the Constitution exacerbated that issue.

But Tucker also knew, as he told St. George, that South Carolina Antifederalists were in a distinct minority in the state. He had met earlier with William Grayson (q.v.), a Virginia Antifederalist, over that state's position on the Constitution. When he understood that Virginians had acquiesced in passage, Tucker felt he had no choice but to go along with the Federalist majority in his own state. Conservative and fearful, he knew he had to live and work in his adopted state.

Continuing his activities in medicine after the Constitutional crisis, Tucker helped to found the South Carolina Medical Association in 1789. But he also remained active in Antifederalist politics. He was elected to the federal Congress in 1789 and served until 1793. Tucker supported Republican policies but also made friends with some of South Carolina's Federalists. Nevertheless, Federalists succeeded in defeating him for Congress in 1792. He was a member of a committee to consider the Jay Treaty in 1794, and he opposed that treaty as detrimental to southern trade interests. President Thomas Jefferson named him United States Treasurer in 1801, and he held that office until 1828. Tucker died in Washington, D.C., on May 2, 1828. Never happy in this country, always a malcontent, Tucker considered himself a failure. Indeed, he was not. His fears of the results of the ratification of the Constitution for government and the people, in short his Antifederalist views, would come back to haunt the country in the future.

REFERENCES

Steven R. Boyd, *The Politics of Opposition* (Millwood, N.Y.: KTO Press, 1979); Diana Deer Dowdy, "A School for Stoicism: Thomas Tudor Tucker and the Republican

Age," *South Carolina Historical Magazine* 96 (April 1995): 102–118; Merrill Jensen, *The Documentary History of the First Federal Elections* (Madison: University of Wisconsin Press, 1976), vol. 2; Lewis Leary, "Literary Career of Nathaniel Tucker, 1780–1807" (PhD diss., Duke University, 1951); Joseph I. Waring, *South Carolina Medicine* (Charleston: South Carolina Medical Association, 1964).

The Tucker-Coleman papers at the College of William and Mary contain many letters from Tucker.

GEORGE LEE TURBERVILLE *(September 7, 1760–March 26, 1798)* was born in Westmoreland County, Virginia, to George and Martha (Lee) Turberville. He grew up on his wealthy family's plantation, Rechantone. Turberville received a primary education in England. He married Betty Tayloe Corbin, from another wealthy Virginia family. During the American Revolution, this young man became a captain of the Fifteenth Virginia regiment and later a major and aide to General Charles Lee. In 1781 he resigned from the army.

A planter and neighbor of George Washington, Turberville served in the Virginia House of Delegates from the Richmond district from 1785 until 1789. Defeated for election to the Virginia ratifying convention because he lived in a heavily Federalist part of the state, Turberville nevertheless contributed ably to the Antifederalist cause. Most importantly, he wrote a lengthy letter on December 11, 1787, to James Madison in which he discussed the Antifederalist case against the Constitution. The letter circulated throughout the state and influenced the Antifederalist argument for rejection of the Constitution. The letter, entitled "Some Puzzling Questions," began with a request for a bill of rights in order to protect private and individual rights. Turberville objected to the lack of a Council of State to assist the president, and in this he agreed with his hero, George Mason (q.v.). Turberville also asked why the federal government must have a national judiciary, and he speculated that the Constitution made state courts unimportant in the country. That the federal Congress had the power to fix the place and time for elections also worried Turberville, as he told Madison, and he feared for local political prerogatives. Rhetorically he asked, "why shou'd the Laws of the Union operate against and supersede the state Constitutions?" (Bailyn, 300). Surprisingly for a member of the landed wealth, Turberville wondered why the Constitution allowed the continued importation of slaves when the new country had enough slaves. Then he queried Madison over whether the government's right to set import duties meant the end of Virginia's power and wealth.

In that letter to Madison, Turberville most clearly expressed the worries the progressive Virginians had about their agrarian future in the new, large republic of the United States. After the controversy, Turberville retired to his plantation. All along he had feared he had offended other large landholders, and he did not like the radicalism of Patrick Henry (q.v.). But he stuck to the small government cause and became sheriff of Richmond County in 1798. His career—with all its potential for facing Virginia's future—sadly ended much too early, as he died at the plantation Epping in Richmond County, Virginia, on March 26, 1798.

REFERENCES

Bailyn, *Debate*, vol. 1; Jackson Turner Main, *The Antifederalists* (Chapel Hill: University of North Carolina Press, 1961); Thomas Roane Barnes Wright (comp.), *Westmoreland County Virginia* (Richmond: Whittet and Shepperson, 1912).

CHARLES TURNER *(September 3, 1732–August 10, 1818)* was born in Scituate, Plymouth County, Massachusetts. He was the son of Charles and Eunice (James) Turner. Young Turner graduated from Harvard College in 1752 and became the pastor of Truro Parish Church in Massachusetts. In 1753 he returned to Harvard. For a while he practiced law. Soon he took another church, this time in Duxbury. Turner was ordained to the Congregational ministry in 1755. Turner resigned his ministry at Duxbury in 1775. Considered a liberal Congregationalist, perhaps he was too progressive for his congregation. In 1757 he had married Mary Rand, and they had six children.

Early a revolutionary, Turner served on the Massachusetts Committee of Correspondence. He served in the colonial Massachusetts senate in 1773 and 1774. In 1775 he moved back to his old home in Scituate. He again held office in the state senate from 1780 until 1788. He became an ardent Antifederalist, and he represented Plymouth County at the Massachusetts state ratifying convention. In the convention, Turner spoke out about his desire for a bill of rights, as he claimed that liberty had been taken from the people. Turner wanted annual elections and deplored long-term service in government, fearing that lifetime tenure in public office meant aristocratic control of the government. Turner demanded that the Constitution be amended to achieve forced rotation in federal office. His principal concern seemed to be with the morals of public leaders. In January 17, 1788, he spoke out against paper money and privateering, because they "have produced a gradual decay of morals—introduced pride . . . ambition . . . envy . . . lust of power—produced a decay of patriotism." That meant for Turner that "as people become more luxurious, they become more incapacitated of governing themselves" (Storing, 219).

Just before the final vote was taken at the ratification convention, Turner decided to vote for the Constitution. Like Samuel Adams (q.v.), he believed that the Federalists accepted the need for the addition of a bill of rights to the Constitution. On February 5, 1788, claiming to be too old and tired to continue the struggle, he stated that he preferred the Constitution to the weak, old Confederation. He would vote, he said, for the Constitution with the proposed amendments. But Turner also added: "I hope it will be considered . . . that without the prevalence of Christian piety, and morals, the best republican Constitution can never save us from slavery and ruin" (Storing, 221). In this view his friend Nathaniel Barrell of Maine (q.v.) joined him.

For his apostasy, Turner's constituents from Scituate turned on him and refused him further office. He became a chaplain of prisons. In 1791 Turner moved to Maine, where he owned 23,000 acres of land. He also served well and long the local congregation there, no doubt having overcome his former liberal church leanings. Turner died on August 10, 1818, in the Turner District of Maine. Despite becoming pro-Constitution, Turner left a legacy of defense of personal liberty. His son Charles, Jr., continued that legacy in the federal Congress.

REFERENCES

Bailyn, *Debate*, vol. 1; Van Beck Hall, *Politics Without Parties: Massachusetts, 1780–1791* (Pittsburgh: University of Pittsburgh Press, 1972); Samuel B. Harding, *The Contest over the Ratification of the Federal Constitution in the State of Massachusetts* (Cambridge: Harvard University Press, 1896); Storing, *Complete*, vol. 4.

JOHN TYLER *(February 28, 1747–January 6, 1813)* was born in

York County, Virginia. His father was the wealthy planter John Tyler, whose family had been among Virginia's first settlers. His mother was Anne (Contesse). Like many other members of his class and family, Tyler received a classical education from private tutors and then went to the College of William and Mary. Tyler read law for five years under one of Virginia's most eminent lawyers, Robert Carter Nicholas. He practiced law in Charles City County and became close friends with Thomas Jefferson and Patrick Henry (q.v.). In 1776 he married Mary Ascot Armistead, also of a wealthy plantation family.

Like many of his class and standing in late colonial Virginia, Tyler embraced the Revolutionary cause. In 1774 the citizens of Charles City County appointed him to the Virginia Committee of Safety, a Revolutionary War propaganda and planning group. In 1775 he joined others to march against Royal Governor John Murray, Lord Dunmore's Williamsburg arsenal, precipitating war in Virginia. In 1776 Tyler became a judge of the High Court of Admiralty for the new state of Virginia. In 1777 the citizens elected him to the Virginia House of Delegates, where he ably supported the revolutionary cause. In 1780 the governor appointed him to the Council of State, and in 1781 Tyler became speaker of the House of Delegates.

As speaker during the Confederation period, Tyler called on the federal Congress to control imports from Great Britain and wanted an embargo on goods from abroad. He also opposed paying debts to England but wanted Virginia to pay off its financial obligation to the new federal government. Tyler at first became an ally of James Madison to seek a convention to discuss the adequacy of the Articles of Confederation for governing the new nation. In

1785 Tyler called for such a convention, and favored Virginia's meeting at Annapolis to work out an agreement with Maryland over navigation of the Potomac River.

As a conservative leader with ties to the national government, Tyler supported amending what he believed was a weak Articles of Confederation. But he turned against the proposal to hold a convention in Philadelphia during the summer of 1787. Elected to the Virginia state ratifying convention from Charles City County in 1788, he joined the Antifederalist camp and became a leading lieutenant of Patrick Henry (q.v.). Obviously he wanted the earlier constitution amended, but he did not like the powers given to the central government in the new proposed Constitution. In the state convention, Tyler moved to amend the Constitution before Virginia voted to ratify, and he offered Henry's and George Mason's (q.v.) amendments for a bill of rights as a formal motion for adoption. He stated, "we only wish to do away with the ambiguities, and to establish our rights on clear and explicit terms" (Elliot, vol. 2, 642). When his motion failed, Tyler, believing the Federalists had no plans to accept amendments, voted against ratification.

In the state convention, Tyler spoke of his reservations about the Constitution, which are well worth repeating. He attacked the slave trade provision, suggesting that the trade be abolished permanently. That Congress had powers to raise troops frightened him. He found the ten-mile zone for building the federal government offensive, believing such an enclave concentrated too much federal power in one place. Mostly, he talked about the lack of responsibility in the proposed government. "If we are to be consolidated," he said, "let it be on better grounds" (Elliot, vol. 3, 454). After all, "consolidation is contrary to our nature, and can only be supported by an arbitrary government" (Elliot, vol. 3, 639). Yes, Tyler said, he agreed with the Federalists that the Confederation needed revising, "but not at the expense of liberty" (Elliot, vol. 3, 641).

Disappointed over ratification, Tyler temporarily retired from public life and returned to planting. Still, he joined Thomas Jefferson to reform the court system of Virginia, and he supported the Republican cause. Elected governor in 1808, Tyler served in that office until 1811. As governor he became a leader in the development of public education in the state. He also supported President James Madison in resisting trade with England. In 1811 Tyler became a judge of the Federal Court of the District of Virginia. His judicial decisions always supported small government.

On January 6, 1813, Tyler died. He was buried at his Charles City County plantation, Greenway. Tyler left a legacy of local progressive reform and of suspicion of the federal government that his son John Tyler carried into his presidency of the United States (1841–1845). Tylers have remained active in public service, education, and the military through the end of the twentieth century. The great family patriarch certainly well served the Old Dominion.

REFERENCES

Elliot, *Debates*, vols. 2 and 3; Lyon G. Tyler (ed.), *Encyclopedia of Virginia Biography* (New York: Lewis Historical Publishing Co., 1915), vol. 2; Lyon G. Tyler, *Judge John Tyler, Senior and His Times* (Richmond, Va.: Richmond Press, Inc., Printers 1927); ——— (ed.), *The Letters and Times of the Tylers* (New York: Da Capo Press, 1970), vol. 1.

$\mathcal{V}$

JEREMIAH VAN RENSSELAER *(August 27, 1738–February 19, 1810)* was born in Albany, New York. He came from a family of wealthy merchant and landholding Dutch settlers. Forced to move up the Hudson River Valley after the British conquest in the seventeenth century, the Dutch families soon became great wealthy landowners. Van Rensselaer attended a preparatory school at Rensselaerwick and a private school in Albany. He graduated from the College of New Jersey (Princeton) in 1758. He became a field surveyor in the Albany region and managed to accumulate much land. But Van Rensselaer fell out with his wealthy family after he joined the radical George Clinton (q.v.) faction of upstate New York politics. Still, he married Judith Bayard, from a wealthy, conservative Albany merchant family and held on to his position in Dutch society. In 1772 he became inspector of Pot and Pearl Asher at Albany. Clinton next named him commissioner of forfeiture, a plum patronage position.

During the Revolution, Van Rensselaer joined the Albany Committee of Safety. He had previously been a member of the Sons of Liberty, a prorevolutionary organization. Van Rensselaer gained election to the New York State Assembly during the Constitutional ratification crisis of 1788. Unlike other members of his family and circle of former friends, he joined the Antifederalist forces. Van Rensselaer organized the Albany campaign against the Constitution. Abraham Yates (q.v.), a powerful Clinton ally and fellow Antifederalist, worked with the Dutch leader and helped him become chair of the local Antifederalist committee. Van Rensselaer obtained an editorial position for Thomas Greenleaf (q.v.), and together they also published and circulated a number of Antifederalist pamphlets and other publications in the upstate region. Those writings influenced the strong stand against the Constitution among the citizens of Albany. Van Rensselaer, certainly the most active Albany Antifederalist leader, thus worked behind the scenes to defeat ratification. In this endeavor he failed.

Elected in a flurry of Antifederalist political activity to the first United States Congress in 1789, the Federalists rallied in 1790 to defeat him for reelection.

Van Rensselaer had been elected to promote amendments to the Constitution, and before he left federal office he supported the Bill of Rights. He ran again for Congress in 1792, but his region had become Federalist, and he lost his bid. Van Rensselaer returned to his neglected business interests and joined the board of the Bank of Albany in 1792, where he served as president from 1798 until 1806. He also was a director of the Western Inland Navigation Company. In the mid-1790s, Van Rensselaer became a director of the Hamilton Manufacturing Company, a glassmaking business. A devout Christian, he helped found the Evangelical Lutheran Seminary in Albany in 1804. From 1801 untl 1804, he served as lieutenant govenor of New York. He belonged to the Jeffersonian Republican Party.

Van Rensselaer died in Albany, New York, on February 19, 1810. He is buried with many other famous leaders, a number of them Federalists, in the Dutch Reformed Cemetery there. Van Rensselaer's Antifederalist republicanism is an example of an upstate alliance against the powerful Federalist forces of New York City.

REFERENCES

Steven R. Boyd, *The Politics of Opposition* (Millwood, N.Y.: KTO Press, 1979); Linda Grant De Pauw, *The Eleventh Pillar* (Ithaca, N.Y.: Cornell University Press, 1966); Cynthia D. Kreiner, *Traders and Gentlefolk: The Livingstons of New York, 1765–1790* (Ithaca, N.Y.: Cornell University Press, 1992); Eugene Wilder Spaulding, *New York in the Critical Period* (New York: Columbia University Press, 1932).
There are Van Rensselaer papers in the New York State Library in Albany.

W

JAMES WADSWORTH *(July 8, 1730–September 17, 1817)* was born in Durham, Middlesex County, Connecticut. His family had originally come to Connecticut with Thomas Hooker in 1636. His father, James Wadsworth, was a farmer and public officeholder. His mother was Abigail (Benfield). Young Wadsworth's cousin, Jeremiah Wadsworth, became a general in the American Revolution and later the most powerful political leader in the state. Wadsworth attended local public schools and graduated from Yale College in 1748. He then studied law, gained admittance to the Connecticut bar, and developed a successful practice in the New Haven region. In 1753 he served as a lieutenant in the Connecticut militia. Wadsworth fought in the French and Indian War in 1758 and 1759, serving at Fort Ticonderoga. In 1757 Wadsworth married Katherine Guerney of Durham, Connecticut. They had two daughters.

Military service became Wadsworth's entree into political life. He served as Durham town clerk from 1756 until 1786. In 1759 he entered the colonial assembly. Named a justice of the peace in 1762, he rose to become a judge of the New Haven County Court in 1773. In 1778 Wadsworth gained election as presiding judge of that court, serving until 1789. In 1775 that ardent patriot became a member of the radical Connecticut Committee of Safety. That same year he was named colonel of the Tenth Regiment of Militia, and he went to the defense of Massachusetts after the battle of Lexington. As brigadier general of Connecticut troops in 1776, he assisted General George Washington in New York. In 1777 Wadsworth was named a major general in the Continental Army. In 1779 he resigned from the military. Throughout the war, he belonged to the Connecticut Council of Safety, and he also served in the state legislature. In 1780 Wadsworth became a delegate at the Hartford convention to discuss reforms in the Connecticut constitution.

Altogether, Wadsworth served in the lower house of the legislature from 1759 until 1785, holding the office of speaker of the state legislature in 1784 and 1785. He also gained election to the Continental Congress, holding office from 1784 to 1786. He joined the Governor's Council in 1785 and the state executive council from 1785 until 1789. From 1786 to 1788, Judge Wadsworth also was state comptroller. He served his state well during the so-called Critical Period and certainly helped it to adjust politically to the new United States government.

During the Constitutional ratification controversy in Connecticut, Wadsworth ably served the will of New Haven County's Antifederalist farmers as a member of the ratifying convention. As an ally of Judge Eliphalet Dyer, he worked to defeat the Constitution. Wadsworth at first tried to delay calling the state convention in hopes of building Antifederalist support. He had strong ties to New York's Antifederalist John Lamb (q.v.), and the two of them talked over how to defeat the Constitution. Wadsworth circulated Antifederalist pamphlets in Connecticut. At the state convention, Wadsworth spoke out against national government taxing powers, fearing penalties against small farmers because of excessive property taxes. As a former military commander and militia leader, Wadsworth knew what power an army could have. He feared a standing federal army and spoke against it at the convention. His more powerful cousin, Jeremiah, referred to him as "wrong-headed." Nevertheless, Wadsworth joined the minority in his state to vote against the Constitution.

After ratification, the Federalist majority took action against Wadsworth. Throughout the convention proceedings, he had been made the subject of brutal personal attacks, some thought even character assassination. In 1789 Federalists removed Wadsworth as state comptroller, as county judge, and then as state senator. Franklin Dexter, in his biographical sketches of Yale graduates, said that "not being able conscientiously to take the oath of fidelity to the new constitution, he retired thenceforth from public life" (193). Wadsworth returned to the practice of law in Durham County. A handsome, well-spoken man of enormous personal dignity, the stern Wadsworth was a strict moralist. He died at Durham, Connecticut, on September 17, 1817, and is interned at the Old Cemetary there. Members of his family later became major leaders in upstate New York politics.

REFERENCES

Franklin B. Dexter, *Yale Graduates* (New York: Henry Holt, 1896), vol. 2; Elliot, *Debates*, vol. 2; William C. Fowler, *History of Durham, Connecticut* (Durham, Conn.: Hartford Press, 1866); Henry P. Johnston, *Yale and Her Honor-Roll in the American Revolution, 1775–1783* (New York: G. P. Putnam, 1888); Horace A. Wadsworth, *Two Hundred Years of Wadsworths* (Lawrence, Mass: Eagle Steam Job Printing Rooms, 1883).

THOMAS BAKER WAIT *(1762–1830)*

THOMAS BAKER WAIT *(1762–1830)* was born in Lynn, Massachusetts. Wait apprenticed and became a printer and worked also as a writer on the Boston *Chronicle*. In 1784 he married Betsy Smith. In 1785 he established in Portland, Maine, the *Falmouth Gazette,* the first newspaper in that territory. That same year Wait also assisted in incorporating Portland in the

Maine territory. In 1786 he changed the name of the paper to the *Cumberland Gazette*. A man of ardent temperament who was outspoken and fiercely independent, he led the Antifederalist forces in that part of Massachusetts's territory. He was unpopular in part for his vigorous defense of free speech.

At first Wait favored a stronger Constitution. When he heard that Antifederalist members of the Pennsylvania ratifying convention seceded from the convention and then were forced under duress to return, Wait went into opposition. He reported on the writings and political efforts of the Antifederalists from a number of states and became a leading northern New England printer of Antifederalist works. In editorials Wait wrote about what he called the vague, poorly thought-out Constitution. He assailed the Constitution for giving the southern states power by counting slaves as part of the electorate. In support of his views favoring free speech, Wait called for the adoption of a bill of rights to guarantee personal liberties. Wait stated, "there is a certain darkness, duplicity and studied ambiguity of expression running thro the whole Constitution which renders a Bill of Rights necessary" (Bailyn, 731). He also traveled throughout Massachusetts and the Maine territory to speak out against ratification of the Constitution. Old friends and former colleagues assaulted Wait because he supported the Antifederalists. But he incurred the gratitude of the many Mainers who opposed the Constitution. His famous letter to the Federalist George Thatcher of January 8, 1788, in opposition to what he called a defective Constitution, was circulated in his newspaper and in pamphlet form. Thus, as editor, author, and in speeches, this newspaperman aided and abetted the Antifederalist forces.

The newspaperman-politician returned to Maine after the Massachusetts convention had ratified the Constitution. At one time thugs attacked him in the newspaper office. Losing subscribers, Wait's newspaper business began to fail. Wait moved to Boston, made friends with some former enemies, and received the contract to collect *The State Papers and Public Documents of the United States,* which he published in eight volumes in 1815. He had become an ally of the Federalist Rufus King and through him received many government contracts. It was rumored that for a time he lived in New York. But little is known about that difficult man's later life. Wait died in Boston, Massachusetts, in 1830.

REFERENCES

Bailyn, *Debate*, vol. 1; Steven Boyd, *The Politics of Opposition* (Millwood, N.Y.: KTO Press, 1979); William F. Goodwin, "The Thacher Papers," *The Historical Magazine* 6 (1869); Samuel B. Harding, *The Contest Over the Ratification of the Federal Constitution in the State of Massachusetts* (Cambridge: Harvard University Press, 1896); Jackson Turner Main, *The Antifederalists* (Chapel Hill: University of North Carolina Press, 1961); William Willis, *History of Portland from Its First Settlement* (Portland, Maine: Charles Day and Co., 1833), vol. 2; William Willis, *History of the Law Courts and Lawyers of Maine* (Portland, Maine: Bailey and Rogers, 1863).

MATTHEW WALTON *(?–January 18, 1819)* was probably born in Cumberland County, Virginia. He had a limited education and eventually moved to the Kentucky territory. He attended the conventions in Danville, Kentucky, of 1785 and 1787. Walton served in the Virginia legislature from Nelson County. Some of Walton's family moved to Georgia and rose in politics there. This man, with a lust for adventure and land, himself staked claims in Kentucky.

Although not a member of the Virginia Constitutional ratifying convention of 1788, Walton stood with those in the west who opposed the Constitution. James Madison, disturbed over lack of support from the Kentucky territory for the Constitution, blamed Walton for stirring up Antifederalist sentiment in Kentucky. Walton spoke to many of his neighbors there, both farmer and young politico alike, about the dangers of the new federal government to the new west. Although some of his allies believed in the use of a strong federal government to protect their advance westward, most of those who supported Walton had for years opposed federal resistance to their land speculation and treatment of the Indians.

After the ratification of the Constitution, Walton cast his lot with the west. He served as a member of the first Kentucky Constitutional Convention in 1792, and assisted in drafting that state document. In 1799 he helped to write the second Kentucky State Constitution. Walton served in the Kentucky house in 1792, 1795, and 1808. He was a Republican in the federal Congress from 1803 until 1807. In 1809 he voted as a presidential elector for James Madison. Walton died in Springfield, Kentucky, on January 18, 1819.

REFERENCES

Thomas D. Clark, *A History of Kentucky* (New York: Prentice-Hall, 1937); Lewis H. Collins, *History of Kentucky* (Covington, Ky.: Collins and Co., 1878); Jensen and Kaminski, *Documentary History*, vol. 10; David J. Siemers, *Ratifying the Republic* (Stanford: Stanford University Press, 2002).

JAMES WARREN *(September 28, 1726–November 28, 1808)* was born in Plymouth, Massachusetts, to James Warren, the sheriff of Plymouth County, and Penelope (Winslow). Young James was born in the family farmhouse and educated in local schools. He graduated from Harvard College in 1745, where he had become a close friend of James Otis. In 1754 Warren married Mercy Otis (q.v.), who would become one of the young country's most important historians. A close friend of the family was James Winthrop (q.v.), librarian of Harvard College. Those well-educated members of the greater Boston upper-middle class from high-status families soon made their presence felt in radical Massachusetts political life.

Following his family profession, Warren became a merchant and farmer in Plymouth. In 1757 he was made sheriff of his county. From 1766 to 1775, he served in the lower house of the colonial legislature. He joined Samuel Adams (q.v.) in 1773 to form the Massachusetts Committee of Safety. A friend of both John Adams and Elbridge Gerry (q.v.), Warren also befriended those who opposed the colonial trade policies of Great Britain toward Massachusetts. He served in the provisional revolutionary legislature that made Massachusetts a state in the new United States. When the mercurial Joseph Warren (his cousin and good friend) died, Warren became president of the provisional congress.

During the American Revolution, Warren had an active political life. In 1776 he was elected speaker of the house of the State General Court. Reelected in 1778, he lost his bid for state office in 1780. He also served for a time as major general of the provisional militia. Warren was a paymaster for the Continental Army. From 1776 to 1781, he served on the Naval Board, a policymaking agency of maritime trade. In 1780 Warren turned down the opportunity to become lieutenant governor under the popular John Hancock.

In the postwar Confederation period, Warren's politics became even more radical, as he feared the weak federal government's ablity to protect the maritime states from foreign aggression. He sympathized with Shays's rebels in 1786, believing that the state's western farmers had lost out in the bid to protect their land from excessive taxation. In 1787 Warren again became speaker of the Massachusetts House of Representatives.

Along with his radical friends from the Revolution, Warren served as a leader of the Antifederalist cause in Massachusetts's struggle over ratification of the new Constitution of 1787. At one time he had proposed a stronger federal government, but his support for state control over its own destiny was supreme in his political thought. Although neither he nor Gerry had been elected to the state convention, they made their opposition to ratification ably and forcefully. Warren called for a bill of rights before ratification. He argued that all of the precious rights gained from separation from Great Britain would be lost in a new government under a federal Constitution that as written made no effort to protect individual rights. Both the Warren and Gerry recommendations for amendments were adopted by the state convention that ratified the Constituton. Warren had written *A Republican Federalist*, a pamphlet much used in the struggles over ratification. His efforts would bear fruit in the congressional struggle of 1791 over a bill of rights.

Some scholars believe Warren wrote the celebrated Antifederalist document "Helvidius Prisacus," published in January and February 1788. In that work, he connected the Antifederalist cause to that of the American Revolution. Warren linked the character and freedoms of the Massachusetts people to the causes of the American Revolution, and he asked how those "who never participated in her sufferings" (Storing, 153) understood the nature of governance. Warren called out: "Let the old Patriots come forward" (Storing, 156) to resist this new oppression. He praised Pennsylvania Antifederalists John Smilie (q.v.) and William Findley (q.v.) for carrying the cause of the Revolution into the Constitutional period. Unlike the sophist Federalists, he said, the Antifederalsts behaved with "the modesty of benevolence and the boldness of truth . . . uncorrupted by the splendours of wealth"(Storing, 169).

Even more important to the Antifederalist cause than the "Helvidius" pamphlet was Warren's "Letters of a Republican Federalist," which he published in the *Massachusetts Sentinel*, from December 1787 to February 1788. Again, he attacked the Federalists' position on the Constitution. Warren began "Letters" with a survey of what the Philadelphia convention was supposed to have done and how the Federalists illegally rewrote the Articles of Confederation. Fearful of that proposed new Constitution, Warren claimed that the government of Massachusetts was in peril of dissolution. Unlimited power, he stated, was contrary to human nature. After all, those who represented the people were closest to the people's views, and most of the local political leaders opposed this new federal power. Why the state and the views of the people were in jeopardy, Warren claimed, was because the state stood to receive only a few federal legislators, unrepresentative and far below the state's population numbers. The Federalists also wanted to allow foreigners in the government, thus further eroding the prerogatives of the native people. That all elections came under the control of the national government, for Warren, further diminished state power. Warren strongly believed that state government depended on the will of the people while federal government did not. He concluded that aristocratic interest prevailed, "leaving out all the honest republicans" loyal to the citizenry (Storing, 187).

During the Confederation period, the Warrens had moved to Milton, Massachusetts, to farm and to be close to the political action. When he lost his bid for lieutenant governor in 1788, the gout- and debt-ridden leader returned to his family farm in Plymouth. Warren wrote to Gerry in a pitying tone about Federalist rough treatment of him politically. "No man," he said in July 1788, "was ever persecuted with such inveterate malice as I am" (Gardiner, 210). But he also wanted Gerry to return to public life, and he worked hard to help revive his and Gerry's reputation in the state. Warren and his followers became Jeffersonian Republicans. He ran and lost for the United States Congress. From 1792 to 1794, he again joined the Governor's Council. In 1804 Warren became a Republican presidential elector from Massachusetts. He died in Plymouth on November 28, 1808, leaving behind his able wife. Certainly, that coterie of upper middle-class radical revolutionaries deserves the name of Old Revolutionaries or old republicans given to them by Pauline Maier. As anti-Constitution defenders of the republican ideal, as they understood it, Warren and his friends were one group among the many types of Antifederalists.

REFERENCES

James T. Austin, *Life of Elbridge Gerry* (Boston: Wells and Lilly, 1829), vol. 2; Bailyn, *Debate*, vol. 1; C. Harvey Gardiner, *A Study In Dissent: The Warren-Gerry Correspondence* (Carbondale, Ill.: Southern Illinois University Press, 1968); Van Beck Hall, *Politics Without Parties: Massachusetts, 1780–1791* (Pittsburgh: University of Pittsburgh Press, 1972); D. Hamilton Hurd, *History of Plymouth County, Massachusetts* (Philadelphia: J.W. Lewis and Co., 1884); Pauline Maier, *The Old Revolutionaries*

(New York: Alfred Knopf, 1980); Storing, *Complete*, vol. 4; Charles Warren, "Elbridge Gerry, James Warren, Mercy Warren and the Ratification of the Federal Constitution in Massachusetts," *Massachusetts Historical Society Proceedings* 64 (October 1930–June 1932): 140–156; Warren-Adams Letters, *Massachusetts Historical Society, Collections* 64.

MERCY OTIS WARREN *(September 14, 1728–October 14, 1814)*

was born in Barnstable, Massachusetts, to James Otis and Mary (Allyne). Warren received an education, along with her brother James, from the Reverend Jonathan Russell, a famous teacher in colonial Massachusetts. She studied what amounted to a college preparatory curriculum. But her brother went on to Harvard College while she remained at home. It is said that Mercy Otis was a precocious student who read voraciously on her own and gained the equivalent of a college education in the confines of the family library. In 1754 she married James Warren (q.v.), a close friend of her brother. The Warrens settled in Plymouth, Massachusetts, and Mercy devoted herself to raising their children. She also began to write poetry and plays, often with a deeply religious and at times political view.

Along with a coterie of her husband's friends, including her brother, James, John and Abigail Adams, James Winthrop (q.v.), and Elbridge Gerry (q.v.), she joined the patriot cause. Her play of 1772, *The Adulator*, was a political satire of British oppression. Next followed *The Defeat* in 1773, and *The Groups* in 1775, all wickedly amusing and pointed attacks on British policies against Massachusetts trade and political privileges. Throughout the American Revolution, she supported the cause the only way she could, with her pen. In 1781 the family moved to Milton, Massachusetts, and Mercy became an aide to her husband's political career. The death of their son, James, in 1783—for years he had suffered from depression and at times appeared demented—made that family and their friends frightfully aware of the costs of their sacrifices for the cause of freedom and liberty. Mercy and James now believed they had no heir to carry on the fight for freedom and liberty and had to continue it themselves.

The Warrens and their friends became staunch defenders of the Articles of Confederation, believing that document the ideal representation of the Revolutionary cause. In 1786 Warren sympathized with the Shays's rebels, insisting the state had violated western farmers' rights. In 1787 she joined in the discussions with those who organized to defeat ratification in Massachusetts of the proposed federal Constitution. She wrote letters, lobbied friends, made some enemies, and generally did what a woman unable to hold political office could do.

The most important and lasting contribution Mercy Warren made to the Antifederalist cause was her 1788 *Observations on the New Constitution*, written under the name "A Columbian Patriot." Other Antifederalist leaders in states such as New York and Pennsylvania put that intellectual and political theoretical pamphlet to good use, even though it was not widely circulated at the time. A version of the pamphlet influenced the Massachusetts Antifederalist James Winthrop. Warren also struck up a correspondence with the British radical historian Rose Macaulay, and their letters across the Atlantic reveal Warren's opposition to the conservative ideas of Edmund Burke. Warren regarded that great English parliamentarian and political philosopher as a monarchist who opposed republican government. She used her antipathy to Burke to formulate her own views. Though Warren at times lamented her confinement to the home and use of her pen as the only means of attack, her pamphlet deserves further comment for its contribution to Antifederalist theory and to political action.

Observations on the New Constitution was suffused with the knowledge Warren derived from years of reading history and great political-philosophical thinkers. She wrote the pamphlet to influence a learned class of political thinkers on the nature of governance. In the work, Warren wrote of her fears that the new Constitution gave officeholders too much protection in office and provided too little accountability to the people. She recognized an absence of civic responsibility in postwar leaders and wanted a Constitution that promoted leadership responsibility. Also, Warren feared for a loss of the liberties so bravely fought for in the American Revolution. She wrote at length on how the new Constitution completely overlooked individual rights. It was as if the Federalist authors either did not care or believed a vague statement on rights would be sufficient to protect the people, she adroitly pointed out.

Listen to her rhetoric of opposition. Warren said, "I cannot silently witness this degradation." After all, men are born free, she claimed. "Man is not immediately corrupted, but power without limitation, or amenability, may endanger the brightest virtue." In response to those who called for amendments, which thus would compromise the future, she replied wth scorn: "The very suggestion, that we ought to trust to the precarious hope of amendments and redress, after we voluntarily fixed the shackles on our own necks should have awakened to a double degree of caution" (Storing, 284). Warren concluded her work with a note of circumspection because she feared that the Federalists had won and her side must accept defeat. But she also said, "the happiness of mankind depends much on the modes of government, and the virtues of the governors" (Storing, 301), thus also cautioning against blind acceptance in the supposed good will of the victors.

After the pro-Constitution forces had prevailed in Massachusetts, Mercy Warren felt that the victorious Federalists snubbed her socially and politically. But she remained feisty, writing in 1789 to Rose Macaulay that she disliked the new leaders and their legislative behavior. "It ill becomes," she said, "an infant government . . . to begin its career in the splendour of Royalty" (Brown, 271). She told Macaulay that she did not want to continue to worry about the dangers to liberty from the new federal government, but merely asked that it be honest and protective of personal rights and values. In the

1790s, the Warrens became pro-French and turned against President John Adams and his policies. Mercy became a staunch Jeffersonian Republican. Her exchange with President Adams over her historical writings led to a fissure between the two families. It appears that a number of the old revolutionary families had begun to split over the aftereffects of the Constitutional victory.

Eventually the Warrens returned to Plymouth, where James died in 1808. Mercy Otis Warren died on October 14, 1814. She was not yet through with her contributions to precious liberty, however. Warren left another republican legacy to confirm her Antifederalist views. Her monumental *History of the Rise, Progress, and Termination of the American Revolution*, published in three volumes in 1805, is the effort of a first-class historical mind. Her disagreements with John Adams over the interpretation of the events from 1776 to 1789 reveal in detail Warren's views of what the Revolution had meant to her circle of Massachusetts intellectual political leaders.

In volume three of the *History*, Warren discusses the struggle over ratification of the Constitution. Warren began by saying that the people were unprepared for such a new government, but "there yet remained a considerable class of these firm adherents to the principles of the revolution" to oppose ratification (311). For her, the "republican system" was "best adapted to the genius of Americans," and the Federalists were bent on setting republicanism aside (398). Warren surely meant to protect the principles of the Revolution with her historical account. Still, magnanimously, in hopes of accommodation with her opponents, Warren concluded her history: "though in her infantile state, the young Republic of America exhibits the happiest prospects" (434). Saddened by her personal and professional losses, disappointed by the plight of her gender in affairs of state, Mercy Otis Warren nevertheless ended her history of the times on a note of hope.

REFERENCES

Bailyn, *Debate*, vol. 2; Alice Brown, *Mercy Warren* (New York: Charles Scribner's Sons, 1903); Jean Fritz, *Cast for a Revolution: Some American Friends and Enemies* (Boston: Houghton Mifflin, 1972); C. Harvey Gardiner, *A Study in Dissent: Warren-Gerry Papers* (Carbondale, Ill.: Southern Illinois Universty Press, 1968); Samuel B. Harding, *The Contest Over the Ratification of the Federal Constitution in the State of Massachusetts* (Cambridge: Harvard University Press, 1896); Storing, *Complete*, vol. 4; Mercy Otis Warren, *History of the Rise, Progress, and Termination of the American Revolution* (Boston: Manning and Loring, 1805), vol. 3; Rosemarie Zagarri, *A Woman's Dilemma: Mercy Otis Warren and the American Revolution* (Chicago: Harlan Davidson, 1995).

ROBERT WEAKLEY *(July 20, 1764–February 4, 1845)* was born in Halifax County, Virginia. He attended the College of New Jersey (Princeton). It is said that he served in the American Revolution. Little else is known about his early life.

In 1783 Weakley's cousin, the Revolutionary War hero Griffith Rutherford (q.v.), sent him to explore the western Carolina territory known as Franklin.

In 1785 Weakley moved to that part of North Carolina that later became Tennessee. He farmed, owned a ferry, and acquired the rank of colonel in the militia. In 1789 Weakley joined the Antifederalist cause at the second North Carolina ratifying convention, where he voted against ratification of the Constitution. Although not active in debate, Weakley represented the future citizens of Tennessee with a ringing dissent from those who wanted to impose restrictions on their movements.

Elected to the first Tennessee State House in 1796, by 1799 he had become the state commissioner on finance. Weakley served as a Democratic-Republican in the federal Congress from 1809 to 1811, representing Davidson County, Tennessee. He supported the War of 1812. In 1815 he hoped to be elected governor of Tennessee but lost in his bid. He served in the state senate in 1823 and 1824 and presided over that body. Weakley also was a member of the state constitutional convention of 1834–1835 and helped to draft the revised state constitution. He belonged to the Methodist church. Weakley died in Nashville, Tennessee, at his estate, Lockland, on February 4, 1845. Because he had helped acquire Tennessee from the Chickasaw Indians, Weakley County was named for him in 1823. Weakley had belonged to the group of western Carolinians who supported the rights of states, and he remained loyal to the cause of Antifederalism throughout his life.

REFERENCES

Thomas P. Abernathy, *From Frontier to Plantation in Tennessee* (Chapel Hill: University of North Carolina Press, 1932); Robert E. Corlew, *Tennessee: A Short History* (Knoxville: University of Tennessee Press, 1981); John B. McFerrin, *History of Methodism in Tennessee* (Nashville: Publishing House of the Methodist Episcopal Church, South, 1886), vol. 1; W.W. Putnam, *History of Middle Tennessee* (Knoxville: University of Tennesse Press, 1971); David J. Siemers, *Ratifying the Republic* (Stanford: Stanford University Press, 2002); Ed Speer, *The Tennessee Handbook* (Jefferson, N.C.: McFarland and Co., 2002).

JOHN WHITEHILL *(December 11, 1729–September 16, 1815)*

was born in Salisbury Township, Lancaster County, Pennsylvania. He was the son of James and Rachel (Creswell) Whitehill, who had emigrated to the Pennsylvania frontier from Ireland in 1723. The elder Whitehill owned a farm and practiced as a blacksmith. Young Whitehill's brother, Robert Whitehill (q.v.), became a leading western Pennsylvania Antifederalist. A Presbyterian, he received a good primary education under Reverend Robert Smith at Pequea Academy. Whitehill studied law and practiced in Lancaster County. He became justice of the peace of the orphan's court in 1777. Whitehill entered the Pennsylvania state government to serve in the lower house in 1780, and he held office until 1782. A loyal defender of the state constitution, Whitehill also served on the council of Censors in 1783. He was a delegate to the Supreme Executive Council from 1784 until 1786.

As a member of the radical Constitutionalist Party, Whitehill believed that the proposed federal Constitution threatened the prerogatives of governance as set down in the state constitution. He was elected to the Pennsylvania ratifying convention from Lancaster County in 1787. In December of that year, he signed the document called "The Dissent of the Minority." Whitehill, like other Antifederalists, felt that the Federalists had forced the Constitution through the convention without proper consideration. He met at his brother Robert's farm to plan how to call another convention, but the forces were too small and could make little inroads in the state.

After the failure of the Antifederalists, Whitehill remained active in western politics. He gained election to the state constitutional convention in 1790. He also became associate judge in Lancaster County. Whitehill served as a Republican in the federal House of Representatives from 1803 to 1807. He supported President Thomas Jefferson. Whitehill died in Salisbury Township, Pennsylvania, on September 16, 1815.

REFERENCES

Bailyn, *Debate*, vol. 1; Steven R. Boyd, *The Politics of Opposition* (Millwood, N.Y.: KTO Press, 1979); Robert Grant Crist, *Robert Whitehill and the Struggle for Civil Rights* (Lemoyne, Pa.: Lemoyne Trust Co., 1958); Jackson Turner Main, *The Antifederalists* (Chapel Hill: University of North Carolina Press, 1961); John Bach McMaster (ed.), *Pennsylvania and the Federal Constitution* (New York: Da Capo Press, 1970); Alfred Nevin, *Men of Mark of the Cumberland Valley* (Philadelphia: Fulton Publishing Co., 1876); David J. Siemers, *Ratifying the Republic* (Stanford: Stanford University Press, 2002); Storing, *Complete*, vol. 3.

ROBERT WHITEHILL *(July 21, 1738–April 7, 1813)* was born

in the Pequea settlement in Lancaster County, Pennsylvania. His father, James, had come to Pennsylvania from northern Ireland in 1723 to farm with his mother, Rachel (Creswell). The elder Whitehill also owned a blacksmith shop and later served in the important post of county assessor. Young Whitehill received an excellent education, studying under the Presbyterian minister Reverend Francis Alison. He later farmed in Lancaster County and owned a few slaves before the system was abolished in Pennsylvania. Although Whitehill possessed a weak voice and spoke poorly, he soon rose in local politics to become a spokesman for the small farmers of western Pennsylvania. In 1765 he married Eleanor Reed, daughter of Colonel Adam Reed, a small landowner.

By 1770 Whitehill owned over 400 acres of land in Luther Manor near Harrisburg, in Cumberland County. He became county commissioner in 1774. Whitehill supported the revolutionary forces in Pennsylvania. Western farmers sent him to the 1776 Pennsylvania convention, where he assisted in drafting the first Pennsylvania State Constitution. There Whitehill became an ally of the radical Philadelphia political leader George Bryan (q.v.). Both leaders were proud of the state constitution's strong republican inclinations and especially its creation of a unicameral legislature. As a member of the Pennsylvania State Assembly from 1776 to 1778, Whitehill belonged to the Committee of Safety. From 1779 to 1781, he supported the revolutionary cause as a member of the State Executive Council. Whitehill served again as a member of the state assembly from 1784 to 1787.

While in the state legislature, Whitehill made common cause with and became close to another westerner, John Smilie (q.v.), and together they became staunch defenders of small government and the interests of the farmers. In March 1785, along with his brother, John Whitehill (q.v.) and Smilie Whitehill, he protested plans to recharter the Bank of North America, housed in Philadelphia. Whitehill distrusted the nationalist Philadelphians whom he thought favored merchant interests over those of the farming community. He insisted the bank had become so powerful that it controlled the activities of the state legislature, and he believed the British government directed the bank. Whitehill also demanded that the Pennsylvania assembly appropriate the funds itself rather than apply to the bank to reward the people for their investment in the revolutionary cause.

When the call came for Pennsylvania delegates to the 1787 convention to revive the Articles of Confederation, Whitehill moved that the legislature delay election of delegates to that national convention, but the legislature elected members anyway. Elected to the convention himself, Whitehll declined to attend. His wife had recently died, and Whitehill claimed he needed to work his farm. In reality he did not trust the convention members, fearing they meant to overhaul the federal government. In 1787 Whitehill wanted to join the state's Supreme Executive Council, but conservatives deprived him of that office.

Whitehill did accept membership in Pennsylvania's state ratifying convention, and, along with Smilie and William Findley (q.v.), he led the western Antifederalist delegation. His first tactic was to support delay in calling the convention. When that maneuver failed, he resolved to fight with words and deeds. Whitehill wrote often to his western allies about the convention's proceedings and criticized the urgency with which the state's eastern Federalists advocated ratification without any amendments. He assisted in writing the Stoney Ridge circular letter that called for a bill of rights to be added as a condition of ratification. Whitehill himself proposed amendments and, when his views were not heeded, voted against ratification. He then signed "The Dissent" circular at the convention, which condemned the actions of Federalist mobs that had threatened and disrupted meetings of Antifederalists.

In a major speech at the convention on November 30, 1787, "The Defect in the System Itself," in opposition to ratification, Whitehill addressed issues of freedom of speech. In that speech, he defended the right to free discourse and assembly. Whitehill called for printing articles of dissent from the majority. He accused Federalists of attempting to muzzle the press in order to deprive the people of the views of the Antifederalists. With that speech, Whitehill also became one of the convention's most outspoken defenders of a free press. He also spoke on December 3, 1787, against the slave trade. Whitehill believed that southerners planned to resist taxing the slave trade and instead propose taxing recent immigrants, which meant that Pennsylvania stood to lose many new citizens. His desire for a bill of rights, he said, was based on the necessity to protect the precious rights of free expression as well as free movement into and within the young country. On December 12, 1787, he spoke on "Amendments and the Final Vote" and offered a petition from his Cumberland County constituents insisting upon the addition of a bill of rights to the Constitution before the state convention ratified it (Bailyn, 811–815, 871–876).

Benjamin Workman (q.v.), the Philadelphia radical, praised Whitehill for his excellent representation of the localist values of the poor western farmers. Whitehill's biographer, Robert Grant Crist, quotes the westerner as insisting that "the people ought to be informed and ought to know in the clearest manner what is the nature and tendency of the government with which we have bound them. . . . Public favor," this leader said, "is of a transient and perishable nature," and therefore he would speak out for the rights of his constituents (22). Whitehill believed that the powers given to the states in the Articles of Confederation were adequate. For him, "an extravagant delegation of authority" meant a loss of personal liberty and local power (32). How to protect the ordinary people from being enslaved became his rhetorical taunt to the state's Federalists. Governors and other leaders must have severe and explicit restrictions on their authority. The taxing power as well as other excessive powers of Congress also worried him. When the states lost authority, Whitehill said, then other liberties of the people were lost. In his own low and indistinct voice, this leader had spoken eloquently on the relationship between local government and individual rights, and he would never deviate from his fears of excessive, centralized federal power.

Continuing in the struggle over government after defeat at the state convention, Whitehill became a leader of the 1789 Harrisburg convention called to ask for a second state constitutional convention to force a bill of rights on the new federal authorities. He assisted in drafting the address of those dissidents on the failings of the Constitution. In that document and in his future activities, Whitehill wrote about political and legal matters in Pennsylvania. Refusing to support the revised state constitution, because he believed it gave too much power to the Philadelphia merchants, Whitehill called for reinstating the original state constitution that he had assisted in drafting. In 1795 he joined the few western radical leaders who withheld praise for the Whiskey rebels and broke with his old ally, William Petrikin (q.v.). Though Whitehill continued to oppose the excise taxes that had aroused the Whiskey rebels, he did not condone the rebels' use of violence. His western constituents showed their support for his political integrity by sending him to the national Congress from 1805 to 1813. In Congress Whitehill strongly supported the policies of presidents Thomas Jefferson and James Madison on western expansion. He also earned a deserved reputation as a staunch opponent of Chief Justice John Marshall, fearing the justice had too much national judicial power. Active in resistance to oppressive government to the end, Whitehill died on April 7, 1813, at his farm, Luther Manor, in Cumberland County, Pennsylvania.

REFERENCES

Bailyn, *Debate*, vol. 1; Robert Grant Crist, *Robert Whitehill and the Struggle for Civil Rights* (Lemoyne, Pa.: Lemoyne Trust Co., 1958); William H. Egle, *Pennsylvania Geneaologics; Chiefly Scotch-Irish and Germans* (Harrisburg, Pa.: Harrisburg Publishers, 1896); Russell J. Ferguson, *Early Western Pennsylvania Politics* (Pittsburgh: University of Pittsburgh Press, 1938); Jensen and Kaminski, *Documentary History*, vol. 2; John Bach McMaster (ed.), *Pennsylvania and the Federal Constitution* (New York: Da Capo Press, 1970); Alfred Nevin, *Men of Mark of the Cumberland Valley* (Philadelphia: Fulton Publishing Co., 1876); I. Daniel Rupp, *Early History of Western Pennsylvania* (Loughntown, Pa.: Southwestern Pennsylvania Genealogical Services, 1989); I. Daniel Rupp, *History and Topography of Dauphin, Cumberland* (Lancaster, Pa.: G. Hills, 1846).
The Whitehill papers are in the Hamilton Library, at the Cumberland County Historical Society.

WILLIAM WIDGERY *(c. 1753–July 31, 1822)* was born in Devonshire, England. He emigrated to Philadelphia with his parents sometime before the American Revolution. The family was quite poor and Widgery received only a common school education. As a youth, Widgery worked in shipbuilding. During the Revolution, he served as a lieutenant on a privateer. He settled shortly after the Revolution in the Maine territory of Massachusetts, having acquired some property in New Gloucester. Widgery studied for the bar and set up a practice in Portland, Maine. He became active in politics, and joined those who wanted to separate Maine from Massachusetts. Widgery entered politics as a justice of the peace from Portland. He served in the Massachusetts state legislature from 1787 until 1794.

During the state controversy over the proposed federal Constitution, in the legislature Widgery spoke out against holding a state ratifying convention. He wondered why the Federalists seemed in such a rush to call a state convention. Widgery served as member of the committee of the state legislature that set up the rules for the state convention's procedures. The Antifederalist citizens of New Gloucester County elected Widgery to the Massachusetts ratification convention in 1788. At the convention, Widgery sponsored a bill to have the Constitution submitted to the people for a popular vote. Having failed in that political move, this Mainer asked that the convention vote immediately on the Constitution. Moderates such as Samuel Adams (q.v.) defeated his proposal and the convention set into a long debate. Widgery asked that the convention invite Elbridge Gerry (q.v.) to attend its sessions and was much disturbed when the Federalists insulted his hero and refused him permisson to speak.

Aside from his political maneuverings to forestall a vote on ratification, Widgery also spoke out against what he considered the flaws in the Constitution. He said he wanted to accept the convention's decision on the Constitution, but he reviled those moderates who wanted to vote for the Constitution with only the promise of a bill of rights. He believed that those compromisers really supported the Constitution and used the proposed Bill of Rights as protective cover for their actions. As for him, the Bill of Rights had to be added to the Constitution in order to protect the rights of the people, and there was no compromise in that position. Widgery also opposed the three-fifths clause, maintaining that the southern states had been given too much power in the new nation. He feared the Constitution gave excessive authority to national elected officials, especially in giving them control over the election process (Jensen and Kaminski, 572). Widgery said his final and main reason for rejecting the Constitution was because he believed it favored the commercial centers to the detriment of ordinary farmers. He voted against ratification and explained to his Portland constituents that the compromisers had sold out the people.

Having entered the state legislature in 1787, Widgery continued in state politics, serving continuously until 1794, and again from 1797 to 1798. He held office in the state senate from 1795 until 1796. Widgery also was a presidential elector in 1788. A delegate to the Massachusetts state constitutional convention in 1788, Widgery called for making Maine a separate state. His enemies there claimed that Widgery's opposition to the federal Constitution had been based on his thwarted desire for Maine statehood. Widgery was a town selectman in 1794 and 1795. He served on the executive committee in 1807 and 1808. In 1811 he gained election to the United States House of Representatives as a supporter of President James Madison. Widgery lost his bid for a second term. But this Republican made his mark in Congress as one of the few New Englanders who supported the War of 1812. He also worried about and spoke out against government taxes.

After his term in Congress, Widgery became a judge of the Court of Common Pleas. He remained active in the movement to make Maine a separate state, and he rejoiced when that happened in 1820. Widgery died in Portland, Maine, on July 31, 1822.

REFERENCES

Ronald F. Banks, *Maine Becomes a State* (Middletown, Conn.: Wesleyan University Press, 1970); Elliot, *Debates*, vol. 2; Van Beck Hall, *Politics Without Parties: Massachusetts, 1780–1791* (Pittsburgh: University of Pittsburgh Press, 1972); Samuel Harding, *The Ratification of the Federal Constitution in the State of Massachusetts* (Cambridge: Harvard University Press, 1896); Jensen and Kaminski, *Documentary History*, vol. 5; William Durkee Williamson, *History of the State of Maine* (Hallowell,

Maine: Glazier and Masters, 1832); William Willis, *The History of Portland* (Somerswerth, N.H.: New Hampshire Publication Co., 1972); William Willis, *Law Courts and Lawyers of Maine* (Portland: Bailey and Noyes, 1863).

BENJAMIN WILLIAMS *(January 1, 1751–July 14, 1814)* was
born in Smithfield, Johnston County (formerly Craven County), North Carolina. He was the son of Colonel John and Ferebee Savage (Pugh) Williams. Williams received a country school education and became a farmer. Williams served in the provincial congress in 1774 and 1775 from Johnston County. He belonged to the Committee of Safety in 1776. During the Revolution, he rose from second lieutenant to captain of the Second North Carolina Regiment, then resigned his commission in 1779. After the British invaded North Carolina, Williams returned to the state militia. He also was a colonel and hero at the battle of Guilford Court House in 1781.

This war hero also had a distinguished public career. Williams served in the North Carolina state legislature in 1779, 1785, and 1789. He was in the state senate in 1780, 1781, 1784, 1786, and from 1807 to 1809. At the first North Carolina ratification convention, Williams joined with the Antifederalists. Though he spoke little at the convention, he ably represented the small farmers of his region of North Carolina. In 1788 he voted against the Constitution.

Not only did Williams continue in state politics after the ratification convention, but in 1793 he went to the federal Congress. Norman Risjord referred to him as a Federalist there, but other evidence shows that he voted with the Antifederalist faction from his state (657). Williams also served as governor of North Carolina from 1799 until 1802, and in 1808. He called himself a Jeffersonian Republican and pursued policies as governor consistent with a small government political philosophy. In addition to his service in government, Williams continued to farm and to plant cotton. He served as president of the board of trustees of the fledgling University of North Carolina. Williams died in Moore County, North Carolina, at his home, "House in the Horseshoe," on July 14, 1814.

REFERENCES

W.J. Adams, *A Sketch of Governor Benjamin Williams* (Carthage, N.C.: News-Blade Job Print, 1920); Samuel A. Ashe, et al., *Biographical History of North Carolina* (Greensboro, N.C.: Charles L. Van Nappen, 1917), vols. 1 and 2; John L. Cheney, Jr., *North Carolina Government, 1585–1979* (Raleigh, N.C.: North Carolina Department of the Secretary of State, 1981); Norman K. Risjord, *Chesapeake Politics* (New York: Columbia University Press, 1978); David J. Siemers, *Ratifying the Republic* (Stanford: Stanford University Press, 2002); John H. Wheeler, *Historical Sketches of North Carolina* (Baltimore: Regional Publishing, Co., 1964), vols. 1 and 2.

JOHN WILLIAMS *(September ?, 1752–July 22, 1806)* was born in
Barnstable, England. He received a quality education there and studied med-

icine and surgery at the prestigious St. Thomas Hospital, London. Williams then served as a surgeon's mate on British ships. He came to the colonies in 1773 and settled at New Perth, Charlotte County, New York. There Williams practiced medicine and acquired a good deal of land. He married Seissmna Turner.

During the American Revolution, Williams served as a surgeon of New York troops in 1775, then as a colonel of the Charlotte County regiment in 1776. Williams also entered provincial and then state politics. He was in the provincial congress in 1775. He held office in the state house from 1776 until 1777, and again in 1781 and 1782. Williams also served in the state senate in 1777 and 1778, and from 1782 until 1785. However, his career in politics and the military was checkered. Expelled from the senate in 1777 for defrauding military pay, Williams later was proven innocent. His marriage into money and the fluidity of wartime opportunity allowed Williams to buy up much confiscated Tory land, and he became a county merchant and a wealthy landowner. He rose in status in his part of the state. Williams also was a regent of the fledgling New York University. In 1786 he served as a general of state militia.

As a member of the state senate in 1784, Williams showed anti–national government proclivities. He favored impost duties but worried about the federal government's excessive attention to New York trade activities. When the new federal Constitution was presented to the people of New York for ratification, Williams joined the opposition. He spoke often at the ratification convention. Williams wanted all of the people of the state to vote on ratification. He worried about the federal government's taxing powers. Like many other Antifederalists, he insisted the federal Congress was too small to represent the people adequately. He said, "if it be formed to contain principles that will lead to the subversion of liberty—if it tends to establish a despotism, or, what is worse, a tyrannical aristocracy,—let us insist upon the necessary alterations and amendments" (Elliot, 241). Williams spoke against federal powers in this way: "In forming a constitution for a free country like this, the greatest care should be taken to define its powers, and guard against abuse of authority" (Elliot, 242). Williams obviously had read widely in political philosophy, for he invoked Machiavelli and Philip Sidney to claim that annual elections were better than allowing federal officeholders multiple years in office. He claimed that "the great Montesquieu says that a poll tax upon the person is indicative of despotism" (Elliot, 340). In addition to his speeches at the convention, Williams probably contributed to Governor George Clinton's (q.v.) "Cato" letters.

At the convention, Williams had called for a temperate debate. But, in a final outburst kindled by frustration over his inability to sway the Federalists, as he rose to reject the Constitution, Williams declared that "to say that a bad government must be established for fear of anarchy, is, in reality, saying that we must kill ourselves for fear of dying" (Elliot, 242). That he refused to do, and he cast his vote against ratification.

After the debates had ended, Williams returned to state politics. He served on the state Council of Appointment in 1789. From 1795 until 1799, he was in the federal congress. Some say that this Antifederalist now sided with the Federalist Party. He had lost his bid for Congress in 1792 and perhaps thought he needed to join the new majority. Certainly he supported President John Adams's foreign policy. But Williams also opposed creating a federal navy, fearing the cost to the people in taxes. In his votes in Congress, he supported agricultural interests over those of commerce. Williams did not like Federalist policies on the federal debt, and he spoke out often against them. If he had become a Federalist, he was a peculiar one.

After his terms in Congress, Williams returned to Salem to his large farms, and he became a judge of the county court. He early advocated building the Erie Canal, and he became an organizer of the forces to build it. Williams died in Salem, New York, on July 22, 1806. If there is some confusion over his final loyalties, Williams's success with and devotion to state and local government mark him as a confirmed Antifederalist.

REFERENCES

Linda Grant De Pauw, *The Eleventh Pillar* (Ithaca, N.Y.: Cornell University Press, 1966); Elliot, *Debates*, vol. 2; Eugene Wilder Spaulding, *New York in the Critical Period* (New York: Columbia University Press, 1932); Alfred Young, *Democratic Republicans of New York* (Chapel Hill: University of North Carolina Press, 1967).
The John Williams papers are at the New York State Library.

JAMES WINTHROP *(March 28, 1752–September 26, 1821)* was born in Cambridge, Massachusetts. He was the son of John Winthrop, a descendent of the colony's founder and the famous Hollis Professor of Mathematics and Natural Philosophy at Harvard College. His mother was Rebecca (Townsend). After local preparatory school, the younger Winthrop had a distingushed student record at Harvard College. He expected to become a member of the Harvard faculty but instead became a librarian at the college. Winthrop wrote the catalogue of the Harvard Library in 1773. Elevated to head librarian in 1772, he held that position until 1787. Winthrop also was a gifted mathematician and astronomer. He published many important mathematics papers.

In 1775 Winthrop took the position of postmaster of Cambridge but resigned after six weeks to return to Harvard. At times he took an interest in the college's financial operations, but more often he concentrated on his books and papers. Winthrop became an ardent patriot during the American Revolution. Joining the forces in defense of Boston, he was wounded at the Battle of Bunker Hill. During the Revolution, he removed the Harvard library's holdings to Concord, thus preserving that valuable resource. Politically inept as well as eccentric, in 1780 he called upon the radical students to depose Harvard president Samuel Langdon. He had accused Langdon unjustly of lack of support for the Revolution. Fortunately, Winthrop's skills as a librarian made him indispensable.

During the Confederation period, Winthrop was elected to the prestigious American Academy of Arts and Sciences. He had an excellent reputation as a scholar and a bibliographer. Winthrop also served as register of probate in Cambridge and held that position until his death in 1821. He volunteered to assist in putting down the 1786 Shays's Rebellion. Winthrop believed the western farmers had a legitimate issue, but he feared the unrest might lead to a test of the republican government he loved. In 1787 he resigned as librarian of Harvard, claiming a Federalist plot to drive him out of office. Still well-regarded for his attainments in mathematics, Winthrop received an honorary M.A. from Dartmouth College in 1787.

In part, his resignation related to his political activities before and during the Constitutional ratification debates in Massachusetts. A radical revolutionary republican, Winthrop supported the Antifederalist cause during those debates. Although not a member of the state convention—Cambridge being a den of Federalism—Winthrop consulted with old friends and allies in his social circle, including James Warren (q.v.) and Elbridge Gerry (q.v.), on how to defeat the Constitution. He also wrote a series of Antifederalist letters to the *Massachusetts Gazette* between November 23, 1787, and February 5, 1788, collectively known as "Agrippa." Those letters surely influenced the debates in Massachusetts over the meaning of government in people's lives. Saul Cornell calls Winthrop "one of the most original and sophisticated Antifederalist writers," with a "distinctly libertarian outlook" (53).

Indeed, "Agrippa" reveals Winthrop's commitment to the freedom gained only through devotion to limited government. His support as a Bostonian for the protection of commercial interests combined with his revolutionary generation's experience of the workings of government influenced his efforts against the Constitution. Winthrop, unlike agrarian Antifederalists, spoke enthusiastically about the future of commercial success, but without government interference. The power of a central government to direct the flow of business became for him a direct threat to personal freedoms. Winthrop wrote also as a committed localist, fixated on economic opportunity for his community. Unlike those who believed in the virtues of abstinence, he called himself a student of human nature and its materialist drive. If seen as a bit impractical himself, Winthrop's anti–strong government, procommerce, and localist attitudes led him to conclude that common sense showed humans were competitive and materialist. The only means to stimulate growth, he said, was through competition. The state simply could not interfere with human nature.

"Agrippa" first appeared in the *Massachusetts Gazette* on November 30, 1787, and immediately influenced the debate over ratification in Massachusetts and in other states. Aside from his economic reasons for opposing ratification and his view of government and human nature, Winthrop argued against the excessive powers of the proposed federal government. He felt that the people of this young country were in peril of ridicule from abroad for putting so many of their rights in the hands of a flawed government. He called the new system of government overbearing and dangerous. For him, "no extensive empire can be governed on republican principles" (Bailyn, 448). As such, he took a decidedly sectionalist view of the proposed size of the new government. Winthrop said: "The inhabitants of warmer climates are more dissolute in their manners, and less industrious, than in colder countries" (Bailyn, 449). Further, "it is impossible for one code of laws to suit Georgia and Massachusetts" (Bailyn, 450). Congress, he believed, had the power to destroy state rivalries for what it said was the good of the whole. The result meant that Massachusetts's spirit of competition was lost to the control of outsiders (Storing, 68). Winthrop predicted that a distant federal government would be subject to corruption and favoritism. The new government and its support for the southern and middle states over New England meant a society with a "want of public" political responsibility (Bailyn, 769–773). Thus, Winthrop had predicted the inevitable clash of regions over material and political values and powers that heralded the future divisions in the country.

Some opponents and friends alike felt Winthrop lacked gravity in his pronouncements. After all, he made sport with what some considered precious values, and his personal and flippant behavior left people with a bad impression. Of course they had a point. Other leaders often misjudged his quickness of mind and his intolerance for those beneath him in intellect as signs of his indifference to serious issues. In reality, Winthrop's political activities were connected to his shrewd talent for business and his understanding of economic competition. Those who saw how he ran the Harvard library understood his abilities and his true seriousness.

In the post-Constitution period, he continued as register of probate, a lucrative job. Winthrop also became a promoter of and investor in bridges and canals to link various commercial centers in New England. He became an overseer to Allegheny College in Pennsylvania and left that small school his considerable personal library. Allegheny College rewarded him with an honorary doctor of laws in 1817. He also turned to writing works of religion. As a founder of the Massachusetts Historical Society, Winthrop assisted in the construction of a massive state archive. As such, he became quite useful as a research aide for his friend Mercy Otis Warren (q.v.) as she gathered evidence for her history. He read and critiqued much of her work, and she believed he helped her immeasurably. Certainly their conversations about revolutionary ideology and the flawed idea of one immense nation to govern appeared as a central argument in her important history of the creation of the new republic. Winthrop also kept active in post-Constitution political affairs, serving as judge of common pleas in Middlesex in 1791 and as a Republican presidential elector in 1804.

Winthrop died in Cambridge, Massachusetts, on September 26, 1821. He had never married. History has unjustifiably forgotten this important thinker. His libertarian views, unique in his own time and place, deserve careful study in order to flesh out the complex nature of Antifederalist values and biases.

REFERENCES

Bailyn, *Debate*, vol. 1; Saul Cornell, *The Other Founders* (Chapel Hill: University of North Carolina Press, 1999); Jean Fritz, *Cast for a Revolution* (Boston: Houghton Mifflin, 1972); Samuel B. Harding, *The Contest over the Ratification of the Federal Constitution in the State of Massachusetts* (Cambridge: Harvard University Press, 1896); Alfred C. Potter and Charles K. Bolton, *The Librarians of Harvard College, 1667–1877* (Cambridge: Library of Harvard, 1897); John L. Sibley and Clifford Shipton (eds.), *Biographical Sketches of the Graduates of Harvard University* (Boston: Massachusetts Historical Society, 1933); Storing, *Complete*, vol. 4.

ERASTUS WOLCOTT *(September 21, 1722–September 14, 1793)*

was probably born in Windsor, Connecticut. He was the son and twelfth child of Governor Roger Wolcott and Sarah (Drake). He received a local education and later an honorary degree from Yale College. Wolcott married Jerusha (?) in 1746. They had seven children. He practiced law in East Windsor.

This successful lawyer and member of an important family early became a political leader. Wolcott served in the colonial and state general assembly and eventually became speaker of the state legislature. Wolcott also was elected a justice of the peace and later a judge of the state supreme court. He was also a member of the Connecticut council. Wolcott had been general of Connecticut troops in the American Revolution. In 1776 he commanded troops under General George Washington in the fortification of New London, Connecticut. In 1777 he served at Peekskill, New York.

After the Revolution, Wolcott continued to remain active in Connecticut politics. He became close allies of James Wadsworth (q.v.) and Dr. Benjamin Gale (q.v.). Known as "Old Log Head," Wolcott led the state's Democratic-Republicans. In 1787 he was elected to the Philadelphia Constitutional Convention but refused to attend. He believed the convention members planned major changes in the Articles of Confederation, and he opposed them. As lieutenant governor of Connecticut in 1788, he took leadership of the minority Antifederalist forces. Wolcott opposed the Constitution. Perhaps less politically powerful than his Federalist brother, Oliver, Wolcott did much work in support of the futile cause of the Antifederalists. He died in Windsor, Connecticut, on September 14, 1793.

REFERENCES

William Richard Cutter, et al., *Genealogical and Family History of the State of Connecticut* (New York: Lewis Historical Publishing Co., 1911), vol. 4; Franklin B. Dexter, *Biographical Sketches of the Graduates of Yale University* (New York: Henry Holt, 1887), vol. 2; Jensen and Kaminski, *Documentary History*, vols. 1, 2, and 13; Leonard Woods Labaree (Comp.), *The Public Records of the State of Connecticut* (Hartford: Published by the state, 1945), vol. 6; Forrest Morgan (ed.), *Connecticut as a Colony and a State* (Hartford: The Publishing Company of Connecticut, 1904).

BENJAMIN WORKMAN *(?–c. 1799)* was a shadowy, radical figure in Pennsylvania politics during the Constitutional ratification controversy. It is said that at one time he was a professor in Dublin, Ireland. He probably came from Ireland to Pennsylvania in 1784. Workman served as a mathematics tutor at the young University of Pennsylvania from 1784 until 1788. Federalist faculty members attempted to get him fired, accusing Workman of writing for the Antifederalists. Provost John Ewing supported Workman in his Antifederalist position, but he later was fired from the university.

The importance of this mysterious man for Antifederalism was his article "Philadelphiensis." Widely reprinted and circulated throughout the states, the article influenced a number of Antifederalists. Samuel Bryan (q.v.), a friend and ally, had often spoken of his fears for a free press, and in the "Centinel" essays had defended the works of Workman against Federalist attacks bent on stifling his efforts. In his article, Workman vigorously attacked the aristocracy of Philadelphia. Building, he said, on the efforts of Robert Whitehill (q.v.), Workman wrote in defense of the freedom of publication. He claimed that newspapers were the only means by which the poorer folk could read about the issues of the times and, more importantly, find the ideas to express their own opinions. Combining his argument about free press with his understanding of the value of small republics, Workman insisted that each part of a state or local interest group should have its own independent press to represent its views. He also wrote against the existing libel laws, in the belief that the elite hid behind those laws to limit the authority of the opposition. In this way, Workman and other Antifederalists, in the view of Saul Cornell, linked fears of powerful central government to the ability to control public opinion.

Aside from his famous essay, Workman published a number of Antifederalist pieces in the *Freeman's Journal*, a newspaper he may have helped to edit. On December 19, 1787, he published "Diabolical Plot," an article in defense of personal liberties. In that article he praised the efforts of Robert Whitehill in the state ratifying convention. He claimed that the Antifederalists had been treated with contempt, and he wanted to set the record straight. The Federalists, Workman said, sounded like the British in 1776, making personal attacks on citizens without hearing their arguments. The despots, he claimed, had little regard for the ordinary people, while leaders like Whitehill regarded them as

true heirs of the revolution (Storing, 583–585). In like vein, Workman concluded his important "Philadelphiensis" with a ringing defense of the people:
"We will probably lose that small portion of national character which we now
enjoy. . . . We will sink into a state of insignificance and misery," as ordinary
people became the vassals under the control of an oppressive central government (Bailyn, 496–497).

During the Constitutional crisis, Workman also published *Father Tammany's Almanac*, somewhat similar to Benjamin Franklin's more famous Poor
Richard's Almanac, save that the Antifederalist's was more political. After 1787
Workman privately tutored young men. He continued in publishing as a supporter of the emerging Republican Party. As late as 1799, he lived and worked
in Philadelphia. His loss to history leaves a gap in knowledge of the urban
radicals who opposed the Constitution.

REFERENCES

Bailyn, *Debate*, vol. 1; Saul Cornell, *The Other Founders* (Chapel Hill: University of
North Carolina Press, 1999); Storing, *Complete*, vol. 5.

$\mathcal{Y}$

ABRAHAM YATES *(August?, 1724–June 30, 1796)* was born in Albany, New York, in August, 1724. His father was Christoffel Yates, a prosperous farmer. His mother was Callyntze (Winnie). Descended from the old Dutch settlers and still active in the Reformed Church, the family had high hopes for the children. Abraham was the ninth child, and the burdened parents apprenticed him to a shoemaker. (His political enemies would never let him forget his occupation as a young man. They labeled him a "crude cobbler.") Young Yates was ambitious. He became a surveyor, which allowed him to speculate in land. Yates also studied law and, through hard work and political contacts, developed a successful law practice. He married Antje De Ridder, a relation of the powerful John Lansing (q.v.) family of Albany. Yates soon entered politics as a radical electoral reformer and supporter of poorer farm interests. In 1754 he was elected sheriff of Albany, a post he held until 1759. Yates also served on the Albany Common Council from 1754 until 1773, where he became an ally of the populist leader George Clinton (q.v.). During the French and Indian War Yates outspokenly opposed quartering British troops in private homes.

As this Hudson River Valley leader forcefully opposed both British oppression and the wealthy landholders, he rose in public life. He made a reputation for attacking the upstate manor lords and defending the rights of renters and other small farmers. Yates joined the Revolutionary New York Provisional Congress in 1775, and served the new state there until 1777. He also chaired the radical Albany Committee of Safety. Yates led the prestigious committee that drafted the first state constitution. He held military rank under Governor George Clinton, but mainly assisted in a political capacity. In 1779 Governor Clinton named him Continental Loan Receiver for New York, a powerful patronage position. From 1777 until 1790 Yates served in the state senate where he rose to a position of prominence.

In the senate after the end of the Revolution, Yates led the rising agrarian democrats. Roundly despised by the young state's conservative merchants and landed interests, as author of the "Rough Hewer" article in 1783 he opposed their position on duties on imports. Yates gained the reputation of resisting all federal government powers to influence New York affairs. From his position in the state senate he spoke out against sending delegates to the Annapolis Convention of 1785, and later he voted against sending delegates to the 1787 convention in Philadelphia. In January 1787 the state legislature sent Yates to the Continental Congress. When the Constitutional convention met, Yates accused the members of conducting secret proceedings designed to overthrow the Articles of Confederation.

In 1787 Yates joined his nephew Robert Yates (q.v.), George Clinton, and John Lansing (q.v.) as leaders of the state's Antifederalists. Yates took it upon himself to reveal defects in the proposed Constitution. Once again he adopted the nom de plume "Rough Hewer" to write to ordinary people about the coercive powers contained in the new Constitution. Yates attempted to organize voters to postpone the calling of the state ratification convention. When he failed to stop the convention, Yates joined others to demand a Bill of Rights be appended to the Constitution. He also made plans to call a second convention to amend the proposed Constitution. Although he became ill and could not attend the state convention, Yates continued to agitate against ratification. Writing as "Sidney" (though some think his relative Robert was the author) in the *Albany Gazette*, in February 1788, and in the New York *Journal* in June 1788, Yates made his most strident attacks on the Constitution. He claimed that, "the new constitution will prove finally to dissolve all the power of the several state legislatures, and destroy the rights and liberties of the people" (Storing, vol. 6, 120). As the crisis came to its head, Yates began to write a history of the political proceedings surrounding the ratification debate. He never published his book, but the rough drafts are a useful source for New York's anti-Constitutional struggles.

During the state's political arguments with the new Federal government in 1789, Yates spoke out against his hated enemy Alexander Hamilton and opposed the schemes to fund the state debts. In 1790 he made a symbolic gesture of refusing to sign an oath in support of the new Constitution. He declined re-election to the state senate. But in that year, perhaps as a reward for services rendered, Governor Clinton named him mayor of Albany, a position he held until his death in 1796. As mayor Yates opposed giving the wealthy farmers land grants for building canals. In 1795 he attacked John Jay for his treaty in an attempt to embarrass New York's rising Federalist powers. Yates died on June 30, 1796 in Albany, New York.

Yates's biographer, Stefan Billinski, says that he had read widely in "Whig literature," and that he "feared above all the concentration of powers in the hands of an aloof, distant central government" (44). Yates also was a student of the history of revolutions and of the power structure of New York, and accordingly believed the ordinary people had become the victims of an aristocracy of landed wealth. He fought against those powers all of his life. Alfred

Young, in his book on New York Democratic Republicanism, has reprinted the epitaph on Yates's gravestone. It goes like this: "Beneath Lies Abraham Yates, Jr., who uniformly opposed the tyranny of Britain, and the corrupt, perfidious funding system; not for his own good but for the Public Good. He has directed this last testimonial of the sincerity of his apprehension that it will prove most injurious to the Equal Rights of Man and the essential interests of his country" (572).

REFERENCES

Stefan Bielinski, *Abraham Yates, Jr. and the New Political Order in New York* (Albany: New York State American Bicentennial Commission, 1975); Staughton Lynd, "Abraham Yates's History of the Movement for the United States Constitution," *William and Mary Quarterly* 30 (April 1963): 223–245; Joel Munsell, *The Annals of Albany* (Albany: J. Munsell, 1850–1859), vol. 4; Joel Munsell, *Collections on the History of Albany* (Albany: J. Munsell, 1865–1871), vol. 2; E. Wilder Spaulding, *New York in the Critical Period* (New York: Columbia University Press, 1932); Carol M. Spiegelberg, "Abraham Yates," M.A. Columbia Univ., 1960; Storing, *Complete*, vols. 2 and 6; Yates's papers are in the New York Public Library.

ROBERT YATES *(January 27, 1738–September 9, 1801)* was born in Schenectedy, New York, on January 27, 1738. His father was Joseph Yates, the elder brother of Abraham Yates (q.v.). His mother was Maria (Dunbar). Yates received his education in New York City and read law with the eminent jurist William Livingston. In 1760 he began the practice of law in Albany. In 1765 he married Jannetze Van Ness, daughter of a prosperous Dutch farmer. Yates entered local politics as an ally of his uncle, Abraham, and George Clinton (q.v.). He also had as a law pupil John Lansing (q.v.), who would become his political ally and fellow Antifederalist leader. From 1771 to 1775, Yates was a member of the Board of Aldermen of Albany.

A firm supporter of the American Revolution, Yates belonged to the Albany Committee of Safety. From 1775 until 1777, he represented Albany in the provisional and state legislature. Yates also assisted in the drafting of the first constitution of New York State in 1777, in which he worked with John Jay, a future enemy. He served on the staff of General Philip Schuyler in the attempt to keep the British navy out of the Hudson River. But Yates's major service during the revolutionary cause was as a justice of the new state supreme court. There he attempted to assist the state's Tories in retaining their lands and dealt with the ticklish 1780 border controversy between Massachusetts and New York. While a judge, Yates also joined other New York leaders, including Governor Clinton, in opposing impost duties. He served on the state supreme court altogether from 1777 until 1798, and as chief justice of that court from 1790 until 1798.

In 1786 he published *Political Papers Addressed to the Advocates for a Congressional Review*, in which he supported the government as constructed under the Articles of Confederation and opposed any revision of that constitution. Sent with his former law clerk John Lansing to the Philadelphia convention in 1787, Yates at once went into opposition to the proceedings. On July 10, 1787, he left the convention with Lansing, and thus New York did not have a vote in the decision on the shape of the proposed new Constitution. Yates insisted that he opposed all discussions that were designed to strengthen the new Constitution.

In late 1787 Yates joined the Antifederalist forces. His report of December 21, 1787, to Governor George Clinton became a major Antifederalist weapon to defeat ratification in New York. In that report, Yates claimed he rejected the proposed Constitution because it created a consolidated national government that weakened state and local government. He said that he had gone to Philadelphia only to revise the old constitution, and he would not be a party to such major changes. In his report, Yates also wrote of his fears for the civil rights of the people, as the Constitution made no clear declaration in favor of popular liberties. Yates served in the Poughkeepsie ratifying convention as an Antifederalist strategist. He may also have written part of his uncle Abraham's "Rough Hewer" essays. Yates chaired a special committee of the Antifederalists to correspond with and send pamphlets to Virginia's Antifederalists. His letter to Governor Clinton about the convention in Philadelphia was made use of by George Mason (q.v.) of Virginia, as well as others. Yates also presented amendments to the Constitution and wanted his state to call a second convention. When all his efforts to change the document had failed, Yates voted against ratification of the Constitution.

From October 1787 until April 1788, Yates published "Brutus," considered by Herbert J. Storing "as the most direct Anti-Federalist confrontation of the arguments of the Federalists" (Storing, vol. 2, 358). (There remains confusion over just what articles Yates actually wrote or merely had a hand in. Storing believes Yates to have been "Brutus.") In "Brutus" Yates advised the people to elect only experienced leaders to the convention because, he said, the very danger of reducing the country to "one great republic" existed. His view was that "if respect is to be paid to the opinion of the greatest and wisest men who have ever thought or wrote in the science of government, we shall be constrained to conclude, that a free republic cannot succeed over a country of such immense extent, containing such a number of inhabitants, and these increasing in such rapid progression as that of the whole United States" (Storing, vol. 1, 368). Yates went on in his discussion to find fault with the idea of representation where the leaders did not resemble their constituents. Yates also wrote of his worries of the powers given to the new federal government. If the federal government collected taxes, he said, then the states would wither and die. Remembering his role as a veteran, Yates attacked the powers of the federal government to have a standing army. "There is great hazard," he claimed, "that an army will subvert the forms of government, under whose authority, they are raised, and establish one according to the pleasure of their leader" (Storing, vol. 1, 413). Size, space, types of people, and most particularly power, given to the central government's leaders, thus worried men like Yates enough for them to oppose the formation of such a political system.

However, shortly after the Constitution was ratified in New York, the politically ambitious justice decided to support the convention's results. He claimed that only harm could come to New York if all its citizens did not find common cause. Furious Antifederalists withdrew their support for this able leader for the first United States Senate. In 1790 Yates ran as a Federalist against George Clinton for governor and lost. In 1792 he declined to run as a Federalist for governor. He had recently been made chief justice of the state supreme court. In 1795 Yates returned to the Antifederalist cause and became a Jeffersonian Republican. That year he lost his bid for governor to the Federalist John Jay. In 1800 he was made a commissioner to settle a land dispute in Onondaga County. Yates died in Albany on September 9, 1801.

That important localist left a major Antifederalist legacy. In 1821 his widow published his notes on the Philadelphia convention. Previously, in 1809, a few selections of his notes had been published to the embarrassment of some Federalists and even to President James Madison. Yates's *Secret Proceedings and Debates*, along with John Lansing's own notes, revealed the actual opinions on the nature of governance of the delegates at the convention. What Yates proved was that the Federalist explanation of how government was to function, *The Federalist Papers*, had been written to soften their real intent, which was to create a powerful central government with little check on its activities. Future students of that period have been grateful to Yates's eye-witness account of those proceedings.

REFERENCES

Christopher M. Duncan, *The Anti-Federalists and Early American Political Thought* (DeKalb Ill.: Northern Illinois University Press, 1995); John W. Francis, *Old New York* (New York: B. Blom, 1971); Joel Munsell, *The Annals of Albany* (Albany: J. Munsell, 1854), vol. 4; Storing, *Complete*, vols. 1 and 2; Robert Yates, *Secret Proceedings and Debates* (Washington, D.C.: United States Government Printing Office, 1909); Alfred Young, *Democratic Republicans of New York* (Chapel Hill: University of North Carolina Press, 1967).

APPENDIX: Biographical Information by State Ratification Date, Alphabetical within States

December 7, 1787 DELAWARE (30–0)

NAME	DATES	EDUCATION	CAREER	PRE/OFFICE	CONV	POST/OFFICE
Thomas Rodney	1744–1811	prep	farm	ContCong	speak	judge
James Tilton	c. 1745–1822	medical	physician	ContCong	author	SurgeonGen

December 12, 1787 PENNSYLVANIA (46–23)

NAME	DATES	EDUCATION	CAREER	PRE/OFFICE	CONV	POST/OFFICE
George Bryan	1731–1791	some	merchant	Stateleg	author	
Samuel Bryan	1759–1821	some	Govt clerk	Sec'y	author	StReg
William Findley	1741–1821	little	farm	Stateleg	del/author	USHouse
John A. Hanna	1761–1805	college	lawyer		del/speak	USHouse
James Hutchinson	1752–1793	medical	physician	ContCong	author/speak	
Blair McClenachan	?–1812	some	merchant		speak	USHouse
John Nicholson	1757–1800	some	merchant	Comptrol	speak/author	Comptrol
Eleazor Oswald	1755–1795	some	newspaper		publ/author	
William Petrikin	1761–1821	some	mechanic		author	Justice Peace
Charles Pettit	1736–1806	prep	law/merchant	ContCong	speak/author	
David Redick	?–1805	some	survey/law	Stateleg		
John Smilie	c. 1741–1812	prep	farm	Stateleg	del/speak	USHouse
Jonathan B. Smith	1742–1812	college	merchant	ContCong	speak	StAud
John Whitehill	1729–1815	prep	lawyer	Stateleg	del/speak	USHouse
Robert Whitehill	1738–1813	prep	farm	Stateleg	del/author	USHouse
Benjamin Workman	?–c. 1799	college	professor		author/editor	

December 8, 1787 NEW JERSEY (39–0)

NAME	DATES	EDUCATION	CAREER	PRE/OFFICE	CONV	POST/OFFICE
Abraham Clark	1726–1794	some	survey	ContCong	speak	USHouse

Appendix (continued)
December 29, 1787 GEORGIA (26–0)

NAME	DATES	EDUCATION	CAREER	PRE/OFFICE	CONV	POST/OFFICE
Lachlan McIntosh	1727–1806	some	planter	ContCong	author	

January 9, 1788 CONNECTICUT (128–40)

NAME	DATES	EDUCATION	CAREER	PRE/OFFICE	CONV	POST/OFFICE
Elisha Fitch	?	some	lawyer	Stateleg	speak	
Benjamin Gale	1715–1790	college	physician	Cololeg	author/speak	
Amos Granger	?		farm	Stateleg	speak	
Hugh Ledlie	c. 1720–c. 1798	some	shopkeeper	Stateleg	del/speak	
James Wadsworth	1730–1817	college	lawyer	ContCong	del/speak	
Erastus Wolcott	1722–1793	prep	lawyer	Stateleg	speak	LtGov

February 6, 1788 MASSACHUSETTS (187–168)

NAME	DATES	EDUCATION	CAREER	PRE/OFFICE	CONV	POST/OFFICE
Samuel Adams	1722–1803	college	lawyer	ContCong	del/author	Gov
Benjamin Austin	1752–1820	some	merchant	Statesen	author	Statesen
John Bacon	1738–1820	college	clergy/farm	judge	author	USHouse
Nathaniel Barrell	1732–1831	some	merchant	local	del/speak	Stateleg
Phaneul Bishop	1739–1812	some	innkeeper	Stateleg	del/speak	Stateleg
Nathan Dane	1752–1835	college	lawyer	ContCong	author	Statesen
Elbridge Gerry	1744–1814	college	merchant	ContCong	author/speak	VicePres
Jonathan Grout	1737–1807	some	lawyer	Statesen	del/author	USHouse
Daniel Ilsely	1740–1813	prep	shipper		del/speak	USHouse
Martin Kinsley	1754–1835	college	physician	Stateleg	del/speak	USHouse
Samuel Nasson	1744–1800	some	merchant	Stateleg	del/author	
Samuel Osgood	c. 1747–1813	college	merchant	ContCong	author	USPost
Amos Singletary	1721–1806	some	farmer	Statesen	del/speak	
William Symmes	1760–1807	college	lawyer		del/author	
John Taylor	c. 1734–1794	prep	physician	Stateleg	del/speak	Stateleg

Name	Years	Education	Occupation	Office 1	Office 2	Office 3
Samuel Thompson	1735–1797	some	farmer	Statesen	del/speak	Statesen
Charles Turner	1732–1818	college	clergy	Statesen	del/speak	
Thomas B. Wait	1762–1830	some	newspaper		publ/author	
James Warren	1726–1808	college	merchant	Stateleg	speak/author	GovCoun
Mercy O. Warren	1728–1814	prep	author		author	
William Widgery	c. 1753–1821	some	farm/law	Stateleg	del/speak	USHouse
James Winthrop	1752–1821	college	librarian		speak/author	judge

April 6, 1788 MARYLAND (63–11)

Name	Years	Education	Occupation	Office 1	Office 2	Office 3
Jeremiah Chase	1748–1828	prep	lawyer	ContCong	del/speak	judge
Samuel Chase	1741–1811	prep	lawyer	ContCong	del/author	USSupCt
Luther Martin	1744–1826	college	lawyer	ContCong	del/author	Stjudge
John F. Mercer	1759–1821	college	law/plant	ContCong	del/author	Gov
William Paca	1740–1799	college	lawyer	ContCong	del/speak	Disjudge
William Pinkney	1764–1822	prep	lawyer	Stateleg	del/speak	USSen
Charles Ridgely	1733–1790	some	merchant	Stateleg	del/speak	

May 23, 1788 SOUTH CAROLINA (149–73)

Name	Years	Education	Occupation	Office 1	Office 2	Office 3
Aedanus Burke	1743–1802	college	lawyer	Stateleg	del/author	USHouse
William Butler	1759–1821	some	planter	Stateleg	del/speak	USHouse
Joseph Calhoun	1750–1817	some	planter	Stateleg	del/speak	USHouse
Patrick Dollard	c. 1746–1800	some	planter	Stateleg	del/speak	judge
Peter Fayssoux	1745–1795	medschool	physician	Stateleg	del/speak	Stateleg
Wade Hampton	1754–1835	some	planter	Stateleg	del/speak	USHouse
James Lincoln	?–1791	some	farm	Stateleg	del/speak	Stateleg
Rawlins Lowndes	1721–1800	some	law/plant	Statesen	speak	
O'Brien Smith	1756–1811	some	planter		del/speak	USHouse
Thomas Sumter	1734–1832	some	planter	Stateleg	del/speak	USSen
Thomas T. Tucker	1745–1828	medschool	phys/plant	ContCong	del/speak	USTreas

Appendix (continued)
June 21, 1788 NEW HAMPSHIRE (57–47)

NAME	DATES	EDUCATION	CAREER	PRE/OFFICE	CONV	POST/OFFICE
Joshua Atherton	1737–1809	college	law/farm	JusticePeace	del/speak	StAttyG
Joseph Badger	1746–1809	some	farm	Stateleg	del/speak	Stateleg
Charles Barrett	1740–1808	some	farm	Stateleg	del/speak	Statesen
Nathaniel Peabody	1741–1823	prep	physician	ContCong	speak	Stateleg

June 25, 1788 VIRGINIA (89–79)

NAME	DATES	EDUCATION	CAREER	PRE/OFFICE	CONV	POST/OFFICE
Theodorick Bland	1742–1790	medschool	phys/plant	ContCong	del/speak	USHouse
Samuel J. Cabell	1756–1818	college	planter	Stateleg	del/speak	USHouse
William Cabell	1730–1798	college	planter	Statesen	del/speak	retire
Isaac Coles	1747–1813	college	planter	Stateleg	del/speak	USHouse
John Dawson	1762–1814	college	planter	ContCong	del/speak	USHouse
William Grayson	1736–1790	lawschool	law/plant	ContCong	del/speak	USSen
Benjamin Harrison	1726–1791	college	planter	ContCong/Gov	del/speak	Stateleg
Patrick Henry	1736–1799	prep	law/plant	Gov	del/speak	Stateleg
Samuel Hopkins	1753–1819	prep	lawyer	Stateleg	del/speak	USHouse
Joseph Jones	1727–1805	lawschool	lawyer	ContCong	del/speak	judge
Arthur Lee	1740–1792	medschool	leisure	ContCong	author	
Richard H. Lee	1732–1794	prep	planter	ContCong	author	USSen
George Mason	1725–1792	prep	planter	Stateleg	del/author	
Stevens T. Mason	1760–1803	college	law/plant	StateSen	del/speak	USSen
James Monroe	1758–1831	college	law/plant	ContCong	del/speak	PresUS
Thomas Nelson	1738–1789	college	planter	ContCong/Gov	speak	
Spencer Roane	1762–1822	college	lawyer	Stateleg	author	StJudge
Meriwether Smith	1730–c. 1794	prep	planter	ContCong	del/speak	
Abraham Trigg	1750–1809	prep	law/plant		del/speak	USHouse
John J. Trigg	1748–1804	prep	planter	Stateleg	del/speak	USHouse

Name	Dates	Education	Occupation		Activity	Office
George L. Turberville	1760–1798	prep	planter	Stateleg	author	sheriff
John Tyler	1747–1813	college	law/plant	Stateleg	del/speak	Gov
Matthew Walton	?–1819	some	farmer	Stateleg	speak	USHouse

July 26, 1788 NEW YORK (30–27)

Name	Dates	Education	Occupation		Activity	Office
DeWitt Clinton	1769–1828	college	lawyer	Stateleg	author	USSen/Gov
George Clinton	1739–1812	some	lawyer	Gov	del/author	VicePres
Thomas Greenleaf	1755–1798	some	newspaper		publish	
John Hathorn	1749–1825	prep	surveyor	ContCong	speak	USHouse
Hugh Hughes	1727–1802	prep	newspaper		author	
Samuel Jones	1734–1819	some	lawyer	Stateleg	del/author	Statesen
John Lamb	1735–1800	some	merchant	Stateleg	del/author	PortColl
John Lansing	1754–1829	prep	lawyer	ContCong	del/author	StJudge
Gilbert Livingston	1742–1806	some	lawyer	Stateleg	del/speak	Stateleg
Cornelius Schoonmaker	1745–1796	some	farmer	Stateleg	del/speak	USHouse
Melancton Smith	1744–1798	some	merchant/law	ContCong	del/author	
Charles Tillinghast	c. 1748–1795	some	merchant		speak	PortColl
Thomas Tredwell	1743–1831	college	lawyer	Statesen	del/author	USHouse
Jere Van Rensselaer	1738–1810	college	farmer	Stateleg	publish	USHouse
John Williams	1752–1806	medschool	phys/farm	Statesen	del/speak	USHouse
Abraham Yates	1724–1796	some	lawyer	ContCong	speak/author	mayor
Robert Yates	1738–1801	prep	lawyer	StJudge	del/author	StJudge

November 21, 1789 NORTH CAROLINA (194–77)

Name	Dates	Education	Occupation		Activity	Office
Samuel Ashe	1725–1813	prep	law/plant	judge	speaker	Gov
Elisha Battle	1723–1799	some	planter	Statesen	del/speak	Justice Peace
Timothy Bloodworth	1736–1814	some	farm	ContCong	del/speak	USSen
Lemuel Burkitt	1750–1807	some	clergy/farm		del/speak	

Appendix (continued)

NAME	DATES	EDUCATION	CAREER	PRE/OFFICE	CONV	POST/OFFICE
David Caldwell	1725–1824	college	clergy/teach		del/speak	
James Galloway	?–1798	some	planter	Stateleg	del/speak	
James Gillespie	1747–1805	prep	planter	Statesen	del/speak	USHouse
William Goudy	1745–1791	some	law/farm	Statesen	del/speak	Statesen
Willie Jones	1741–1801	prep	planter	ContCong	del/speak	
William Lenoir	1751–1839	some	survey/farm	Stateleg	del/speak	Statesen
Matthew Locke	1730–1801	some	planter	ContCong	del/speak	USHouse
Francois Martin	?–1846	prep	newspaper		del/publish	StJudge
Joseph McDowell	1756–1801	prep	law/farm	Stateleg	del/speak	USHouse
Duncan McFarlan	?–1816	some	farm		del/speak	USHouse
Alexander Mebane	1744–1795	some	planter	Stateleg	del/speak	USHouse
Thomas Person	1733–1800	some	survey/plant	Statesen	del/speak	Statesen
Griffith Rutherford	c. 1720–1805	some	planter	Statesen	del/speak	Stateleg
Samuel Spencer	1734–1793	college	law/plant	judge	del/speak	judge
William F. Strudwick	1770–1810	some	planter		del/speak	USHouse
Absalom Tatom	1742–1802	some	surveyor	Stateleg	del/speak	USHouse
Joseph Taylor	1742–1815	prep	law/plant	Statesen	del/speak	Statesen
John Tipton	1730–1813	some	planter	Statesen	del/speak	Statesen
Robert Weakley	1764–1845	college	farm		del/speak	USHouse
Benjamin Williams	1751–1814	some	farm	Statesen	del/speak	Gov

May 29, 1790 RHODE ISLAND (34–32)

NAME	DATES	EDUCATION	CAREER	PRE/OFFICE	CONV	POST/OFFICE
John Collins	1717–1795	prep	merchant	Gov	speak	Stateleg
Jonathan Hazard	1744–c. 1824	some	lawyer	ContCong	del/speak	Stateleg
David Howell	1747–1824	college	teach/law	ContCong	del/author	judge
Thomas Joslyn	?			Stateleg	del/speak	
Samuel J. Potter	1753–1804	prep	lawyer		del/speak	USSen
Joseph Stanton	1739–1807	prep	law/farm	Stateleg	del/speak	USSen

Essay on Essential Sources

The most recent, useful general study of the Antifederalists is Saul Cornell, *The Other Founders*. Cornell focuses mostly on Pennsylvania and adds three categories of Antifederalist leaders, including a common or working class contingent. Still useful and wise to consult are: Merrill Jensen, *Making the American Constitution* and *The New Nation*; Jackson Turner Main, *The Antifederalists*; Steven Boyd, *The Politics of Opposition*; Robert A. Rutland, *The Birth of the Bill of Rights* and *The Ordeal of the Constitution*; and John K. Alexander, *The Selling of the Constitution*. (Complete publishing information is included in the bibliography at the end of each entry.) For a perceptive view of the continued activities of the Antifederalists into the Federalist era, see David J. Siemers, *Ratifying the Republic: Antifederalists and Federalists in Constitutional Time*. Also see David C. Hendrickson, *Peace Pact: The Lost World of the American Founders*, a stunning attempt to reconfigure the diplomatic tensions in the state conventions. Most useful has been Michael A. Gillispie and Michael Lienesch (eds.), *Ratifying the Constitution*. In a class by itself for recent interpretation of the Antifederalists is Patrick T. Conley and John P. Kaminski (eds.), *The Constitution and the States*. That edited volume contains the most recent bibliography of works on the period.

Studies that place the Antifederalists in the early formation and growth of the republic have been very helpful. Singled out for their excellence and controversy are Jack P. Greene, *Peripheries and Center: Constitutional Development in the Extended Politics of the British Empire and the United States, 1607–1788*; Robert H. Wiebe, *The Opening of American Society*; John P. Diggins, *The Lost Soul of American Politics*; Yehoshua Areli, *Individualism and Nationalism in American Ideology*; Joyce Appleby, *Liberalism and Republicanism in American History*; Russell L. Hanson, *The Democratic Imagination in America*; Annabel Patterson, *Early Modern Liberalism*; Barry Alan Shain, *The Myth of American Individualism: The Protestant Origins of American Political Thought*; Christopher Grasso, *A Speaking Aristocracy: Transforming Public Discourse in Eighteenth Century Connecticut*; Gordon Wood, *The Radicalism of the Amercan Revolution*; Jack N. Rakove, *Original Meanings*; Roy

Porter, *The Creation of the Modern World*; Michael J. Sandel, *Democracy's Discontents*; and Thomas L. Pangle, *The Spirit of Modern Republicanism: The Moral Vision of the American Founders.*

Works on the political theory of the period and on those who influenced the Antifederalists include Pangle, Sandel, and Shain from the studies above. A number of recent books have taken the ideas of the Antifederalists seriously as political philosophy. See Michael Zuckert, *Natural Rights and Republicanism*, for a thoughtful critique of John Locke's influence on liberal thinking. Michael Lienesch, *New Order of the Ages* is an excellent reading of the Antifederalists' fears of the modern state. Unfortunately, Lienesch regards some of their worries as the mere rantings of older leaders still tied to the ideas of the American Revolutionary generation. Herbert J. Storing's first volume of his collection of the works of selected Antifederalists places those thinkers into the context of the political philosophy of their times. Storing's work is controversial and should be read alongside the other books on theory mentioned here. See also the older but still wise Whitney A. Griswold, *Farming and Democracy*, which shows the importance of an agricultural tradition on Antifederalist thinking. Jack N. Rakove, *Original Meanings*, mentioned earlier, also weighs fairly the thoughts of the Antifederalists. Quirky, but at times perceptive on Antifederalist political theory, is Christopher M. Duncan, *The Antifederalists and Early American Political Thought.* Less passionate but helpful for learning where the Antifederalists gained their political views is Bruce Ackerman, *We the People.*

There are only a few important biographies of the Antifederalists, and none of those leaders has had a recent quality analysis of their activities during the ratification process. Still, a number of biographies have proved useful. One way to look at those leaders is to see them in their collective activities. See Jean Fritz, *Cast for a Revolution*, on the Massachusetts cohort. Also important is Pauline Maier, *The Old Revolutionaries*, which ably shows the connection between Samuel Adams and Richard Henry Lee. See also John P. Kaminski, *George Clinton: Yeoman Politician of the New Republic*, on New York's most important Antifederalist. George A. Billias, *Elbridge Gerry*, is a model study of that mercurial Massachusetts leader. On Samuel Adams see Ralph V. Harlow, *Samuel Adams Promoter of American Revolution*, which grasps the connection between the pre-Revolution Adams and his role in the state ratification convention. Stefan Bielinski, *Abraham Yates, Jr. and the New Political Order of Revolutionary New York*, remains an important book on a neglected major figure. Joseph S. Foster, *In Pursuit of Equal Liberty: George Bryan and the Revolution in Pennsylvania*, recounts the life of that Pennsylvania radical and incidentally says something about his son Samuel. Helen Hill Miller, *George Mason, Constitutionalist*, is an older study. It is a disgrace that neither Henry, Mason, or the Lees has received recent treatment, given the importance of the Virginians to the debate over ratification. For useful biographical information one must return to the much older dictionaries of each state's leaders, and to state and county histories. (They are cited at the end of the individual biographical entries.)

State studies of ratification remain the most important sources for speeches, political maneuvers, and the friendships that bound the Antifederalists. Still the best on Massachusetts is Samuel B. Harding, *The Contest Over Ratification of the Federal Constitution in the State of Massachusetts*, first published in 1896. For New York, see Alfred F. Young, *The Democratic Republicans of New York*, which is more concerned with the Federalist era. Still useful is Clarence E. Miner, *Ratification of the Federal Constitution by the State of New York*. For a recent comparison of the background to Antifederalism in New York and Pennsylvania, see Alan Tully, *Forming American Politics*. Tully's detailed comparsion of early politics is a model that could be useful to study of the Antifederalist period. Irwin H. Polishook, *Rhode Island and the Union*, is a decent reading of the tensions in that state, which led to divisions over ratification. Jere R. Daniell, *Experiment in Republicanism*, sets New Hampshire's proximity to Massachusetts in context. Richard P. McCormick, *Experiment in Independence: New Jersey in the Critical Period*—still useful—has been added to by Mary R. Murrin, *To Save the State from Ruin: New Jersey and the Creation of the United States Constitution*. For the southern states, see Norman K. Risjord, *Chesapeake Politics, 1781–1800*. Still one of the best works on the controversy is Louise Irby Trenholme, *The Ratification of the Federal Constitution in North Carolina*. Trenholme's effort of 1932 has the benefit to the modern reader of short biographical sketches—as does Harding on Massachusetts—and allows the Antifederalist leaders in North Carolina to speak out.

The most useful primary works for this study have been the major collections of the writings and speeches of the Antifederalists. Jonathan Elliot (ed.), *The Debates on the Constitution* of the 1830s, set the standard for excellent collections of convention speeches. Unfortunately, Elliot did not have information on all of the states. He may be supplemented by the few collections of the debates of such states like Virginia. Morton Borden (ed.), *The Antifederalist Papers*, is a good collection of a few Antifederalist writers. Paul L. Ford (ed.), *Pamphlets on the Constitution of the United States*, includes a number of Antifederalists. Likewise, Ralph Ketchem (ed.), *Antifederalist Papers*, is helpful not the least because of the author's excellent commentary on their writings. The volume is also available in paperback. Some years ago, in a labor of love, the great medievalist Joseph Strayer edited *The Delegate from New York*, the notes of the Antifederalist John Lansing from the Constitutional convention. Unpublished during the ratification struggle, Lansing nevertheless used his notes to write a famous exposé of the Federalists that inflamed his fellow New York Antifederalists. Bernard Bailyn has recently compiled a two-volume collection, *Debates on the Constitution*, which includes a number of Antifederalists. Bailyn's work not only annotates the writings of the leaders but includes short sketches of a number of Antifederalists. Herbert J. Storing, in the *The Complete Anti-Federalists*, has collected and annotated in seven volumes many of the best pamphlets and speeches of those leaders. Storing has written the most important work to date on the Antifederalist pamphlets and speeches. Alas, Storing has a theory of just who the Antifederalists were and what they thought, and he has selected writings for his volumes to sustain his point of view. Far and away the most comprehensive collection of Antifederalist pamphlets and speeches is the monumental work begun by Merrill Jensen and continued by John Kaminski to the tune of eighteen volumes and counting, entitled *Documentary History of the Ratification of the Constitution*. Jensen and Kaminski also include biographical material and contextual notes. Anyone who wants to understand the thoughts and activities of the Antifederalists must begin with these volumes.

Index

Boldface characters are used to distinguish between the page numbers of the Biographies volume (**B**) and the Major Writings volume (**MW**). For example, page **B**xv is in the Biographies preface.

About the Author

JON L. WAKELYN is Professor of History at Kent State University. He is the author or editor of ten books, including *The Politics of a Literary Man*, *Southern Pamphlets on Secession*, *Leaders of th American Civil War*, *Southern and Unionist Pamphlets of the Civil War*, and *Confederates against the Confederacy*.